Work like a pro
with Word 6

WORD 6

Work like a pro with Word 6

For Windows

Mike Murach

Mike Murach & Associates

4697 West Jacquelyn Avenue, Fresno, California 93722-6427
(209) 275-3335

Editor:	Anne Prince
Graphics designer:	Steve Ehlers

Other books for Word users:	Word 6 for Windows: How to use the Mail Merge Feature
	The Essential Guide: Word 6.0 for Windows

Other books for Windows users:	Work Like a Pro with Excel 5 for Windows
	Excel 5: Lists, Pivot Tables & External Databases
	The Essential Guide: Excel 5.0 for Windows
	The Essential Guide: WordPerfect 6.0 for Windows
	The Essential Guide: 1-2-3 for Windows Release 4
	The Least You Need to Know about Windows 3.1

10 9 8 7 6 5 4 3 2 1

ISBN: 0-911625-90-9

Library of Congress Cataloging-in-Publication Data

Murach, Mike.
    Work like a pro with Word 6 for Windows / Mike Murach.
       p.   cm.
    Includes index.
    ISBN 0-911625-90-9 (pbk.)
    1. Microsoft Word for Windows. 2. Word processing. I. Title.
Z52.5.M523M875 1995
652.5'536--dc20
                                       95-32589
                                         CIP

Contents

Introduction

Ever notice how easy the best PC professionals make things look? Ask them to show you how to do something, and they do it so quickly and easily that you can't follow it. Ask them to slow down and do it again, and you wonder how they can remember all the details.

The good news is that it's surprisingly easy to become a skilled PC user. In just 253 pages, for example, this book shows you how to use Word the way the best professionals use it. It even includes exercises that help you get started the right way. All you have to add is some practice.

5 ways this book differs from other Word books

- Instead of showing you how to use all of the Word commands and techniques, this book shows you how to use the 20 to 30 percent that the best professionals use all the time. That's why this book is 253 pages long instead of 1200.

- Each Word function is presented in a single figure (illustration) that shows and summarizes everything you need to know to do that function. That's why we say that you can learn more just by paging through this book than by studying other books.

- The procedures in the figures can easily be applied to any situation you run into. In contrast, many books present procedures that apply only to specific situations. Those work fine until you want to do something a little more advanced or until Word displays a screen that's not shown in the procedure. That's when you'll appreciate the procedures in this book.

- Word often gives you several options for doing the same function. So besides showing you *how* to do each Word function, this book also shows you the fastest way to do it. You'll soon find yourself taking just 5 minutes to do jobs that take other Word users much longer.

- Each chapter includes practice exercises that get you started right. These exercises have you use the most efficient methods for doing each function; they encourage you to experiment with new functions; they require nothing but this book and your PC; and they are an essential part of the learning process.

Who this book is for

Because of the way the content is organized and presented, this book works for beginners as well as for experienced word processing users who are upgrading or converting to Word 6. From the start, you'll learn the skills of the best professionals, and that's what you need to learn whether Word 6 is your first word processing program or your fifth.

If you're a beginner, of course, it's going to take you longer to go through this book than if you have some experience. Not only will it take you longer to read the text and figures, but you should also make a point of doing all the exercises. As you will see, they often show you how easy it is to use a function or feature that may seem difficult when you first read about it.

In contrast, if you're an experienced word processing user, you should be able to go through this book quite rapidly. For most functions, you'll be able to get the information you need from the figures alone. You'll also be able to do the exercises more quickly. Please don't skip the exercises, though, because they force you to use some efficient new techniques that you might otherwise overlook.

What are the prerequisites for this book? The basic Windows skills that you probably have if you've used another Windows program or if you've taken a Windows course: opening, closing, and sizing windows; moving between windows; switching between applications; and working with menus, commands, dialog boxes, directories, and files. If you don't have these skills, or you're not sure that you have them, the prerequisites chapter that follows is a crash course in Windows that presents everything you need to know.

Let us know how this book works for you

It's clear by now that Windows is here to stay, and Word is here to stay too. In fact, with just some trivial changes, you can expect to use your Word 6 skills for years to come. Yes, there will be new and improved versions of Word, but they're going to work the way Word 6 does. As a result, you may want to learn some of the new features that become available, but you won't have to re-learn your Word 6 skills.

That's why it makes sense to master Word 6 now, and that's why this book does everything possible to help you master it. If this book helps you work just 20 percent faster and better than you would otherwise, you'll save dozens and even hundreds of hours during the next five years. But the best PC professionals work 100 or 150 percent faster than their peers, and this book teaches you everything you need to know to become one of the best.

If you have any comments about this book, we would enjoy hearing from you. That's why there's a postage-paid comment form at the back. In particular, we'd like to know whether the methods we've used to present the material help you learn faster than others you've used. As always, our goal is not only to help you get the most from your software, but to help you do that as quickly and easily as possible.

Anne Prince
Editor

Mike Murach
Author

Prerequisites

The essential Windows skills

This chapter presents the skills that are the same for all Windows programs. That includes working with windows, starting and ending programs, using menus and commands, and opening and saving files. So if you already have experience with one or more Windows programs, you can probably skip this chapter.

If you're new to PCs or to Windows, though, you need to study this chapter carefully and do all of its exercises. Once you master the skills of this chapter, you will have the background that you need for working with any Windows program. That will make it easier for you to master Word 6 as you learn about it in the other chapters of this book.

Throughout this book, all the examples are for Windows release 3.1. So if you're still using Windows 3.0, the screens will look somewhat different on your PC. Keep in mind, though, that the skills are the same for both releases.

If you eventually convert to the next Windows release (Windows 95), you'll see that Word 6 still works the same with some minor differences in appearance. You will, however, start programs like Word in a new way. These changes are summarized in the last two figures in this chapter.

An introduction to Windows 3.1 and its Program Manager

When you start your PC, Windows will probably start automatically. As it starts, a logo screen is displayed followed by an hour-glass that indicates that the start-up procedure is in progress. When this procedure is finished, a screen that looks something like the one in figure P-1 is displayed.

During the start-up procedure, Windows always starts at least one program called the *shell program*. On almost all Windows systems and in figure P-1, this shell program is the Program Manager. You use this program for starting your other Windows programs.

The first time you start Windows after you install it, the starting display looks like the one in figure P-1. But the starting display usually changes after that. As a result, the starting display on a PC in school or business may look quite different. On some PCs, for example, more than one program is started when you turn the PC on, so the starting display has several windows.

If Windows doesn't start automatically when you turn your PC on, you have to start it from DOS. To do that, just type *win* and press the Enter key as shown in figure P-1. Note, however, that the DOS prompt may not look exactly like the one in this figure.

If you're completely new to PCs, you may not know that DOS is the Disk Operating System that has been used to run most PCs since the early 1980s. Once you start Windows, though, you can forget about DOS.

How to start Windows from the DOS prompt

Type *win* and press the Enter key.

```
C:\>win
```

The starting Windows display right after installation

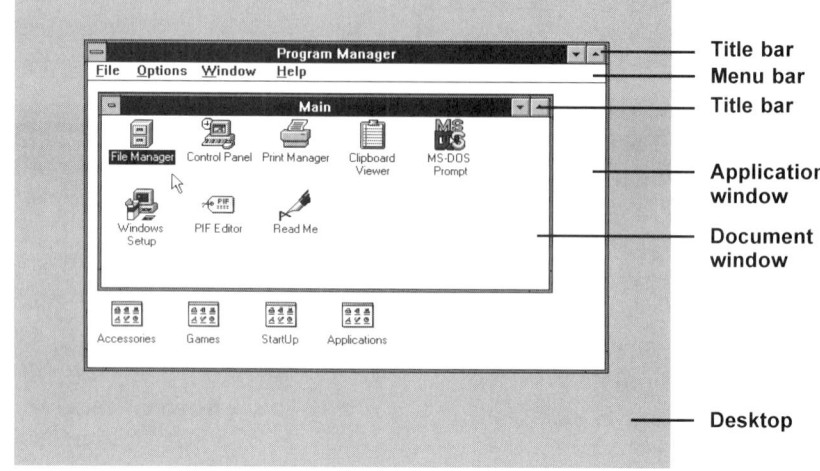

Concepts and terms

- On many PCs, Windows is started when you start the PC so you don't have to start it from the DOS prompt.

- A program runs in an *application window*. A *document window* provides a workspace for the program that's in the application window, and it's always within an application window.

- When you use the Program Manager, a document window is usually called a *group window* because it contains a group of programs.

- The *title bar* of an application window gives the program name. The title bar of a document window usually gives the document name.

- A *menu bar* appears only in an application window. It provides the menus that list the commands you can use with a program.

- The program that is running when you start Windows is called the *shell program*. This is usually the Program Manager as shown above.

Figure P-1   Windows concepts and terms

Application and document windows

In figure P-1, you can see three Windows components: the *desktop*, an *application window*, and a *document window*. The desktop is just the background that the windows are displayed on. An application window contains a program (in this case, the Program Manager). And a document window provides a workspace that's used by the program.

It's easy to tell the difference between an application window and a document window because a document window is always within an application window. In addition, application windows have menu bars, but document windows don't.

When you use the Program Manager, the document windows are generally referred to as *group windows* because they contain groups of programs. When you use other programs, the document windows may be referred to by other names. When you use Excel, for example, the document windows are known as *workbook windows*.

How to perform the four basic mouse actions

Windows was designed for use with a mouse. That's why you can perform many functions more quickly with a mouse than you can with the keyboard.

To use a mouse with Windows, you need to master the four mouse actions that are summarized in figure P-2. Although these actions may seem difficult if you haven't used a mouse before, you'll quickly become adept at using them.

Action	How to do it
Point	Move the mouse so the mouse pointer is positioned on the object that you're interested in.
Click	Without moving the mouse pointer off the object you're pointing to, press and release the left mouse button so it clicks.
Double-click	Without moving the mouse pointer off the object you're pointing to, press and release the left mouse button twice in succession. Do this quickly, in less than a second.
Drag	After you point to an object, press and hold down the left mouse button, move the mouse pointer to a new location, then release the left mouse button.

Notes

- You use the left mouse button for all of the actions above. In the other chapters of this book, you'll learn some uses for the right mouse button, but there are only a few.

- If you're left-handed, you can use one of the Windows programs to change the functions of the mouse buttons so you can click the right mouse button to perform the above actions. Because you won't learn how to do that in this book, you'll need to get technical help to make this change.

Figure P-2   The four basic mouse actions

How to minimize, maximize, or restore a window

Figure P-3 shows how to *minimize*, *maximize*, or *restore* either an application or a document window. To maximize the application window in figure P-1, for example, you just click on its maximize button. Then, the window covers the entire desktop as shown in the first part of figure P-3. When you use a program like Word, you'll work with a maximized application window most of the time. You'll also work with maximized document windows most of the time so you can see more of your work at one time.

From a maximized window, you can click on the restore button to return it to its previous size. Or, you can click on the minimize button to reduce the window to an *icon*. An icon for a minimized application window is displayed on the desktop as shown in the second part of figure P-3. In this example, four application programs have been minimized so four icons are shown on the desktop. In contrast, an icon for a minimized document window is displayed in the application window, but you'll probably never need to minimize a document window.

If you minimize a window by accident, it can be quite surprising, and novices often fear that they've lost their work when this happens. To restore the window to its previous state, however, you just need to double-click on its icon. Or, you can use the icon's *control menu* to restore or maximize the window.

The Windows display when the Program Manager is maximized and all group windows except the Main group are minimized

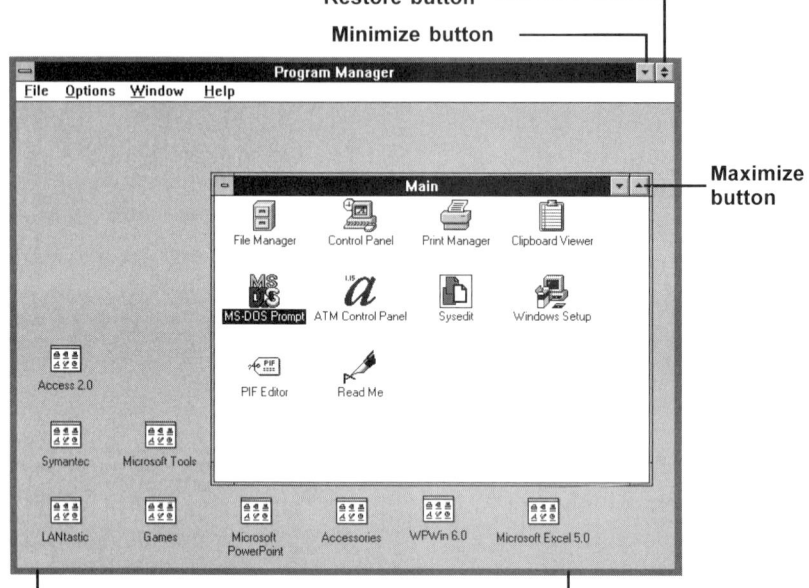

The icons that represent the minimized group windows

The Windows display when all application windows are minimized

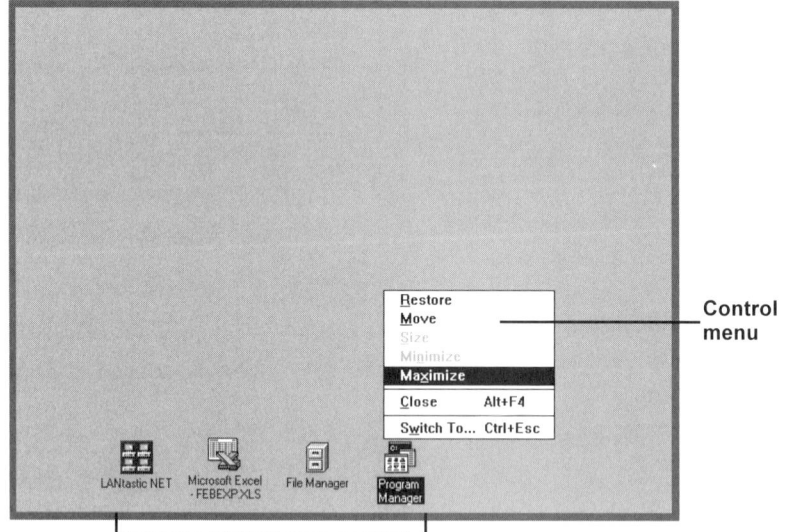

The icons that represent the minimized application windows

Operation

- Double-click on an icon to restore the size of a minimized window. Or, single-click on an icon to display its control menu. Then, click on Restore or Maximize in the menu.

- Click on the maximize button in a window to maximize it.

- Click on the restore button in a maximized window to return it to its previous size.

Figure P-3   How to minimize, maximize, or restore a window

How to move or size a window

When a window isn't maximized or minimized, you can move or size it as shown in figure P-4. To move a window, you just drag its title bar with the mouse. To size a window, you move the mouse pointer over a border or corner until its normal arrow shape changes to a double-headed arrow. Then, you drag the border or corner until the window is the size you want.

When will you want to move or size a window? Only for special circumstances. Sometimes, for example, you will want to move a window so you can see what's behind it. Sometimes, you will want to size and move windows so you can arrange two or more on the screen at the same time.

How to move a window

1. Place the mouse pointer over the window's title bar and drag it. As you drag, an outline appears to let you know where the window will be moved to:

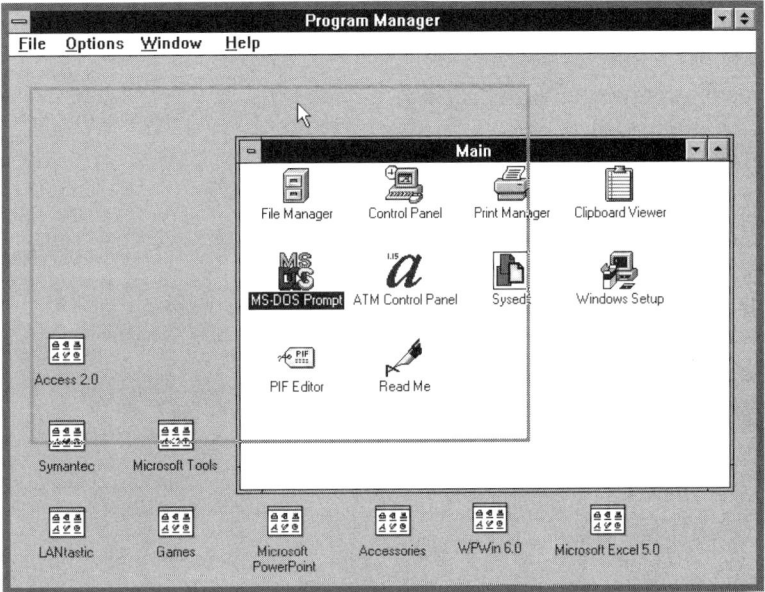

2. Release the mouse button and the window is moved to the new location.

How to size a window

1. Move the mouse pointer over the side or corner of a window until it changes to a double headed arrow. Then, drag the side or corner to increase or decrease the size of the window. As you drag, an outline appears to show you what the new size will be:

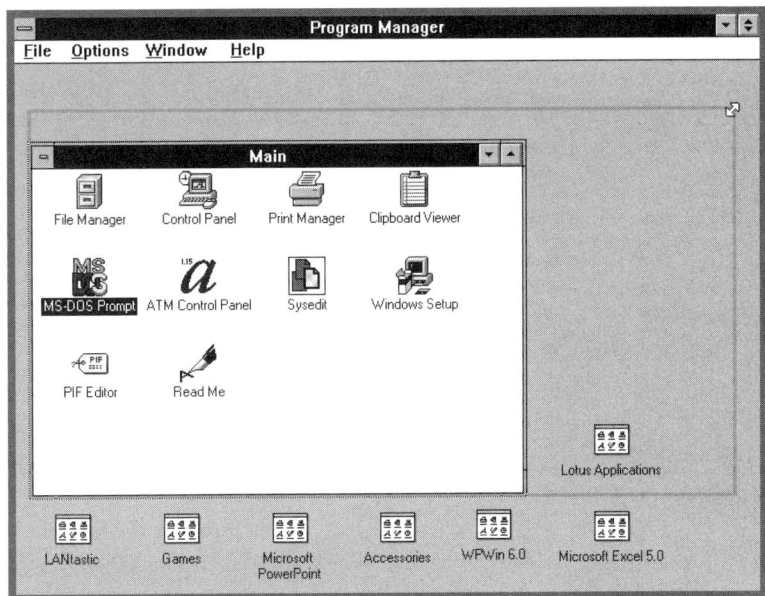

2. Release the mouse button and the window is changed to the new size.

Figure P-4   How to move or size a window

How to scroll through a window

If a window is too small to show all of its contents, *scroll bars* are automatically added to it. Then, you can use the mouse to scroll through the contents of the window as summarized in figure P-5. By clicking on the *scroll arrows* or scroll bar, you can scroll in small or large increments. By dragging the *scroll box* a distance that's relative to the entire scroll bar, you can scroll the contents of the window a proportional amount. If you experiment with these controls, you'll quickly see how easy they are to use.

A window with a vertical scroll bar

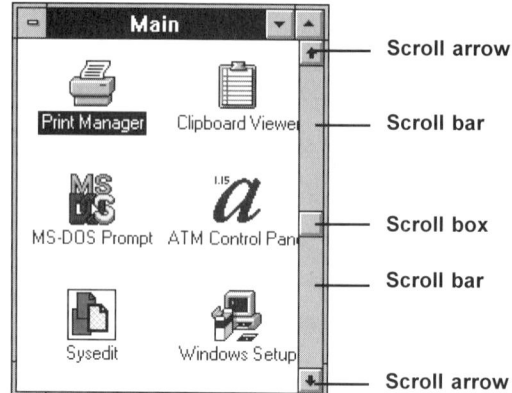

— Scroll arrow

— Scroll bar

— Scroll box

— Scroll bar

— Scroll arrow

How to use the vertical scroll bar

• Click on the up or down scroll arrow to scroll up or down in small increments. Press and hold the left mouse button on the up or down scroll arrow to scroll up or down continuously.

• Click on the scroll bar above or below the scroll box to scroll up or down in larger increments.

• Drag the scroll box up or down in the scroll bar to move to that relative position in the window's contents. If, for example, you drag the scroll box halfway down the scroll bar, the contents of the window are scrolled to their halfway point.

How to use a horizontal scroll bar

• When a horizontal scroll bar is displayed, you can scroll left or right to review the contents of a window. The horizontal scroll bar has the same components as the vertical scroll bar, and you use them the same way. The only difference is that the movement is left and right instead of up and down.

Figure P-5   How to scroll through a document window

How to exit from Windows

To exit from Windows and return to DOS, you can use the control menu for the Program Manager's window as shown in figure P-6. Since the Program Manager is the shell program, closing its window also closes the windows for all other programs. If any of your work hasn't been saved, however, Windows displays a dialog box that gives you a chance to save it.

Although you shouldn't really have to exit from Windows before you turn your PC off, it's still a recommended practice. That way, you can be sure that you've saved all your work. You can also be sure that Windows does whatever housekeeping it needs to do at the end of a work session.

The Program Manager with its control menu displayed

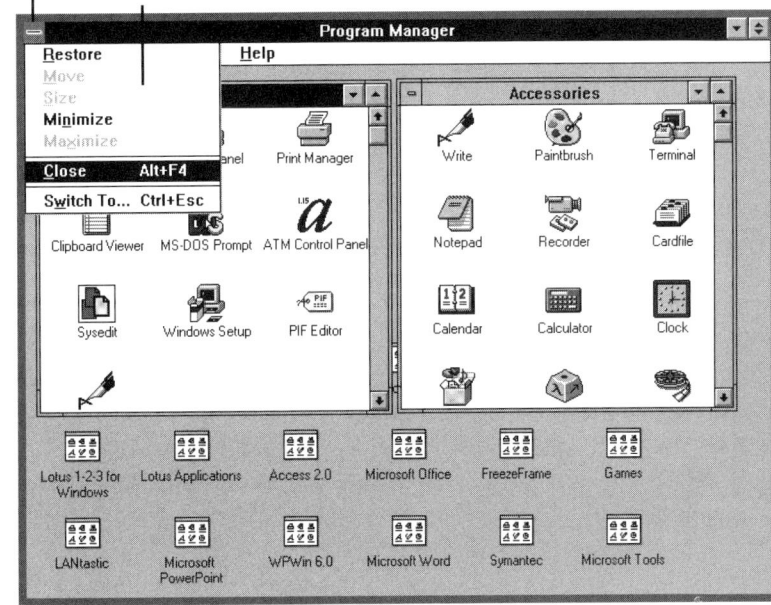

Two ways to exit from Windows

- Double-click on the control-menu box for the Program Manager's window.

- Single-click on the control-menu box for the Program Manager's window to display the control menu. Then, click on Close in the menu.

Notes

- Technically, a control menu applies to a window, not to the program or document in the window. When you close any application window, though, its program ends.

- When you close the application window for the Windows Program Manager, all programs are ended and you are returned to the DOS prompt. Before this happens, though, Windows displays a dialog box that gives you a chance to cancel the operation. Also, if you haven't saved all of the work that you did with other programs, dialog boxes are displayed that give you a chance to save the work.

- You can also use a control menu to restore, move, size, minimize, and maximize a window (see the options in the menu above). However, you can do these functions more quickly by using the mouse techniques that you've already learned.

Figure P-6   How to exit from Windows

Exercise set P-1

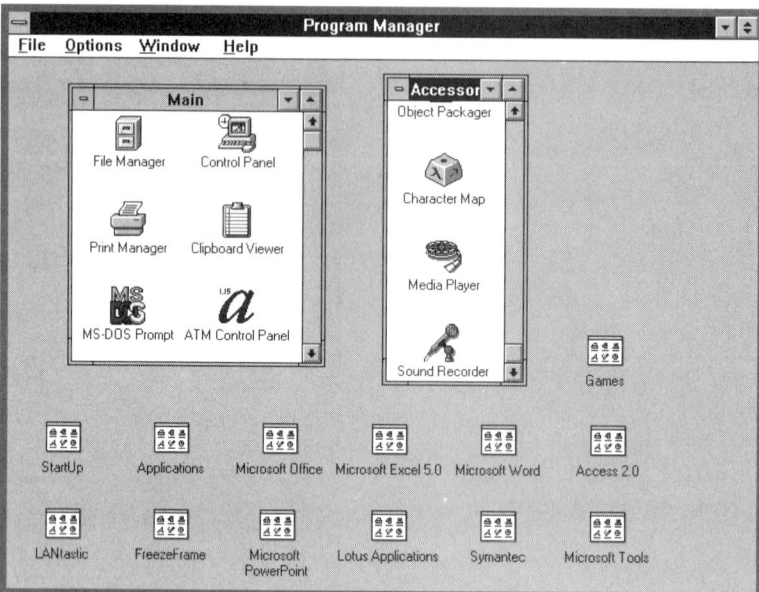

How the Program Manager window should look after exercise 5

The exercises that follow are designed to get you started with Windows and give you some practice with the four basic mouse actions.

1. Start your PC. Does Windows start automatically? If not, start Windows from DOS as shown in figure P-1. Is the Program Manager displayed when the start-up procedure finishes?

2. Minimize all of the application windows as shown in figure P-3. How many programs are running besides the Program Manager (if any)? Then, restore the window for the Program Manager, and maximize it if it isn't maximized already.

3. Minimize all of the group windows that are open (if any). Then, restore the Main group window, maximize it, and restore it again.

4. Move the Main group window to the upper left corner of the Program Manager window as shown in figure P-4. Next, enlarge it by dragging the lower right corner of the window. Then, decrease the width of the window to two icons by dragging its right edge, and decrease the height of the window to three icons by dragging its top or bottom. Last, maximize the window, and restore it again. Note that the window gets restored to its new size and location.

5. Open the Accessories window, size it so it's one icon wide and three deep, and move it so it doesn't overlap the Main group window. Then, use the scroll bar to scroll through it's contents: click on the down arrow until you reach the last icon in the window; drag the scroll box to the top of the scroll bar so the first icon is displayed; and click on the scroll bar until you reach the last icon again. At this point, your screen should look approximately like the one above.

6. Click on the control-menu box for the Accessories group window. Next, click on Close to close the window. This is the same as minimizing the window. Then, double-click on the Accessories icon to restore the window. Is it restored to the same size and location that it was last in?

7. Click on the control-menu box for the Program Manager's application window so the window's control menu is displayed. Note that the next to last command is Close. Don't issue that command now, or the Program Manager will end and you'll be returned to DOS. Instead, click outside the menu to remove it from the screen.

How to start, switch between, and end applications

One of the benefits that you get from using Windows is that you can run more than one program at the same time. This is referred to as *multitasking*. After you use the Program Manager to start the programs that you want to use, you can use Windows techniques to switch from one to the other.

How to start an application from the Program Manager

When you use Windows, your programs are referred to as *applications*. To start any Windows application, you can use the Program Manager as shown in figure P-7. In step 1, you double-click on a *program group icon* to open a group window. In step 2, you double-click on the *program icon* for the program you want to start.

When you use an application like Word, the program icon is likely to be in the *program group* for Microsoft Office as shown in figure P-7. If it's not there, it will probably be in a group that contains other programs that are related to it. Once you find the group icon, open its window, and double-click on the program icon, the application is started in a new application window and you are switched to that window.

The Program Manager with three group windows open

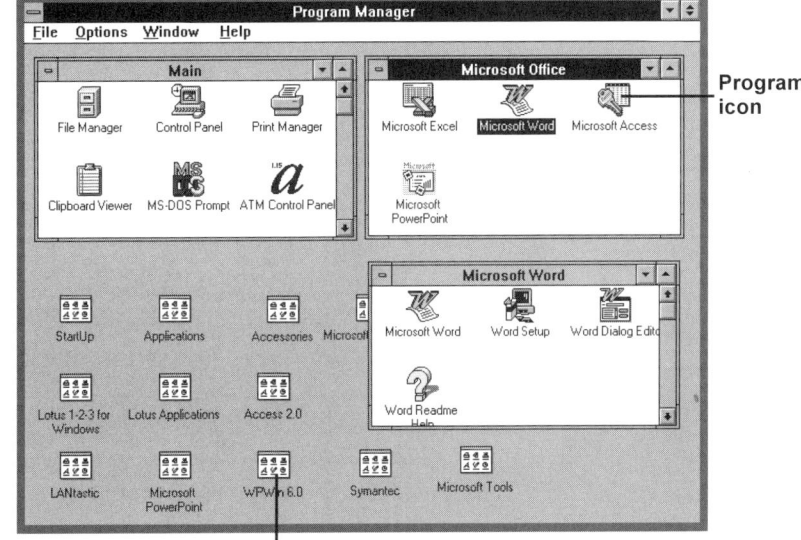

Program icon

Program group icon

Procedure

1. Double-click on the program group icon for the program group that contains the icon for the program you want to start. This opens a group window.

2. Double-click on the program icon for the program that you want to start. Or, click on the icon to highlight it, and press the Enter key.

Notes

- When you use Windows, a program is usually referred to as an *application*.

- When an application starts, an application window is opened for it, and you are switched to that window.

- It's possible that the icon for an application will be in two or more group windows. In the example above, the Microsoft Word program icon is in both the Microsoft Office and the Microsoft Word windows.

Figure P-7   How to start an application

How to switch from one application window to another

Although several applications can be running at one time when you use Windows, you can only work with one program at a time. That program is called the *active program*, and it runs in the *active application window*. If several application windows are displayed at the same time because the windows aren't maximized, the active window is always the one on top, and the title bar of the active program is always highlighted.

To switch from one application to another, you can use the techniques in figure P-8. Of these, Alt+Tab switching is probably easiest to use, so it's the technique that we recommend. If you're interested, though, you can experiment with the other techniques to see whether you prefer one of them.

How to exit from an application

One way to exit from an application is to close its window, just as you close the window for the Program Manager when you want to exit from Windows. To close a window, you can double-click on the control-menu box for the window or choose Close in the control menu itself. In the next topic, you'll learn another way to exit from an application.

How to use Alt+Tab switching

1. Hold down the Alt key and press the Tab key to display a panel that indicates the next application in sequence:

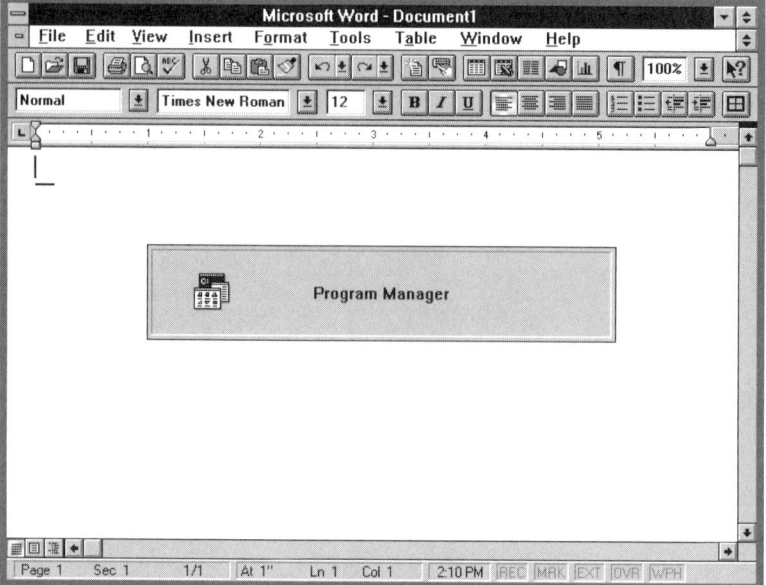

2. If that isn't the application that you want to switch to, press the Tab key again while you continue to hold down the Alt key. When the box displays the name of the application that you want to switch to, release the Alt key.

Four more ways to switch from one application to another

- If two or more application windows are displayed at the same time, click on any part of the window you want to switch to.

- Press Alt+Esc to move to the next application in sequence.

- Minimize all application windows. Then, double-click on the icon for the application that you want to switch to.

- Use the Switch To command in the control menu for the application window or press Ctrl+Esc to display a Task List. Then, double-click on the name of the program that you want to switch to.

Note

- It's possible (but unlikely) that someone has turned the option for Alt+Tab switching off on your PC. Then, you can use one of the other methods to switch from one program to another. Later, when you learn more about Windows, you can turn the option back on.

Figure P-8   How to switch from one application to another

Exercise set P-2

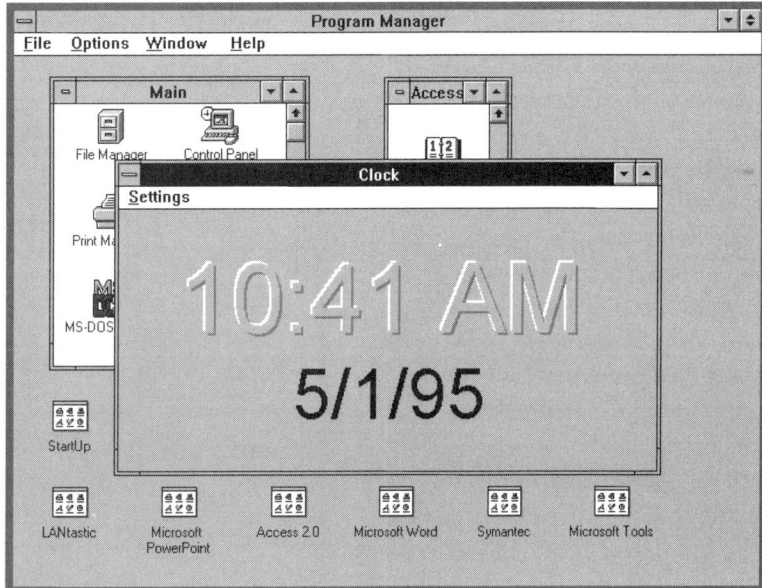

How your screen should look after you start the clock in exercise 4

This exercise set is designed to give you some experience with starting programs, switching between them, and ending them. For the time being, don't worry about what the programs do. Just concentrate on the starting, switching, and ending techniques.

1. If your PC is the way you left it at the end of the last exercise set, the Program Manager is the active application window and the Main and Accessories windows are open. If that's not the case, minimize all application windows, maximize the Program Manager window, minimize all group windows, and restore the Main and Accessories windows.

2. Use the technique shown in figure P-7 to start Word. If the Tip of the Day dialog box is displayed when it starts, click on the OK button. Then, maximize the application window if it's not already maximized. At least two applications are now running at the same time.

3. Use Alt+Tab switching to switch to the Program Manager as shown in figure P-8. Use it again to switch to Word. Then, use Alt+Esc to switch to the Program Manager.

4. Start the File Manager, which is one of the applications in the Main group. Switch back to the Program Manager, and start the Clock, which is one of the applications in the Accessories group. Next, use Alt+Tab switching to switch to Word, and use it again to switch to the File Manager. Then, use Alt+Esc to switch back to Word.

5. Minimize all of the application windows. Next, switch to Word by restoring its window. Then, minimize its application window, and switch to the Clock by restoring its window.

6. Exit from the Clock program by double-clicking on the control-menu box for its application window. Next, exit from the File Manager and Word by popping up their control menus from their minimized application windows and clicking on Close. Then, double-click on the Program Manager icon to restore it to its previous size.

How to work with menus and commands

Another benefit that you get from using Windows is that all Windows applications use a standard interface. In particular, the techniques that you use for accessing menus and issuing commands are the same in all Windows applications. So if you know how to use menus, commands, and dialog boxes in one Windows application, you know how to use them in all applications. These standard techniques are presented next.

How to issue a command

Figure P-9 shows how to issue a *command* from one of the *menus* that you can pull down from the menu bar for an application. These menus are sometimes called *program menus* or *application menus* to distinguish them from control menus, but that usually isn't necessary. As you can see, you can use either mouse or keyboard techniques to issue a command, and both are efficient. You can also combine mouse and keyboard techniques as you issue commands.

Two ways to issue a command with the mouse

• Click on the menu name in the menu bar to pull the menu down, then click on the command name:

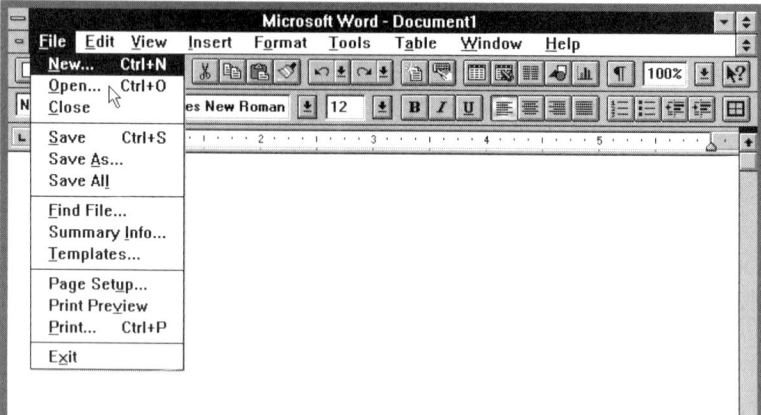

• Press and hold the mouse button on the menu name in the menu bar to pull the menu down. Then, drag the highlight from the menu name to the command you want to issue and release the mouse button.

Two ways to issue a command from the keyboard

• Press Alt to activate the menu bar; press the underlined letter in the menu that you want to pull down; and press the underlined letter in the command that you want to issue.

• Press Alt to activate the menu bar; press the right arrow key to highlight the menu you want and press the Enter key; press the down arrow key to highlight the command you want and press the Enter key.

How to close a menu without issuing a command

• With the mouse, click anywhere outside the menu, or drag the highlight off the menu. With the keyboard, press the Esc key twice.

Figure P-9   How to issue a command from a pull-down menu

How to work with a dialog box

If you look at the menu in figure P-9, you can see that some menu items are followed by three dots (...). This means that a *dialog box* is displayed by the command before the command is run. Then, to complete the command, you must fill in the dialog box.

Figure P-10 summarizes the basic techniques for working with dialog box controls. If you use a mouse, you'll find that it's easy to change controls like *option buttons*, *spin boxes*, and *check boxes*. You'll also find that it's easy to choose an item from a *list box*, to drop down a list from a *text box* and choose an item from the list, and to start the command that's represented by a *command button*. When you've got everything in a dialog box set the way you want it, you can start the command by clicking on the OK button. The dialog box in figure P-10 illustrates all of these controls except for a list box. You'll see a list box later in this chapter when you learn how to use the Open command.

Often, a dialog box is set the way you want it when it's first displayed. For instance, the Print dialog box in figure P-10 is ready for use if you want to print all the pages in a Word document. Then, if the OK button has a dark outline as it does in this example, you can start the command by pressing the Enter key.

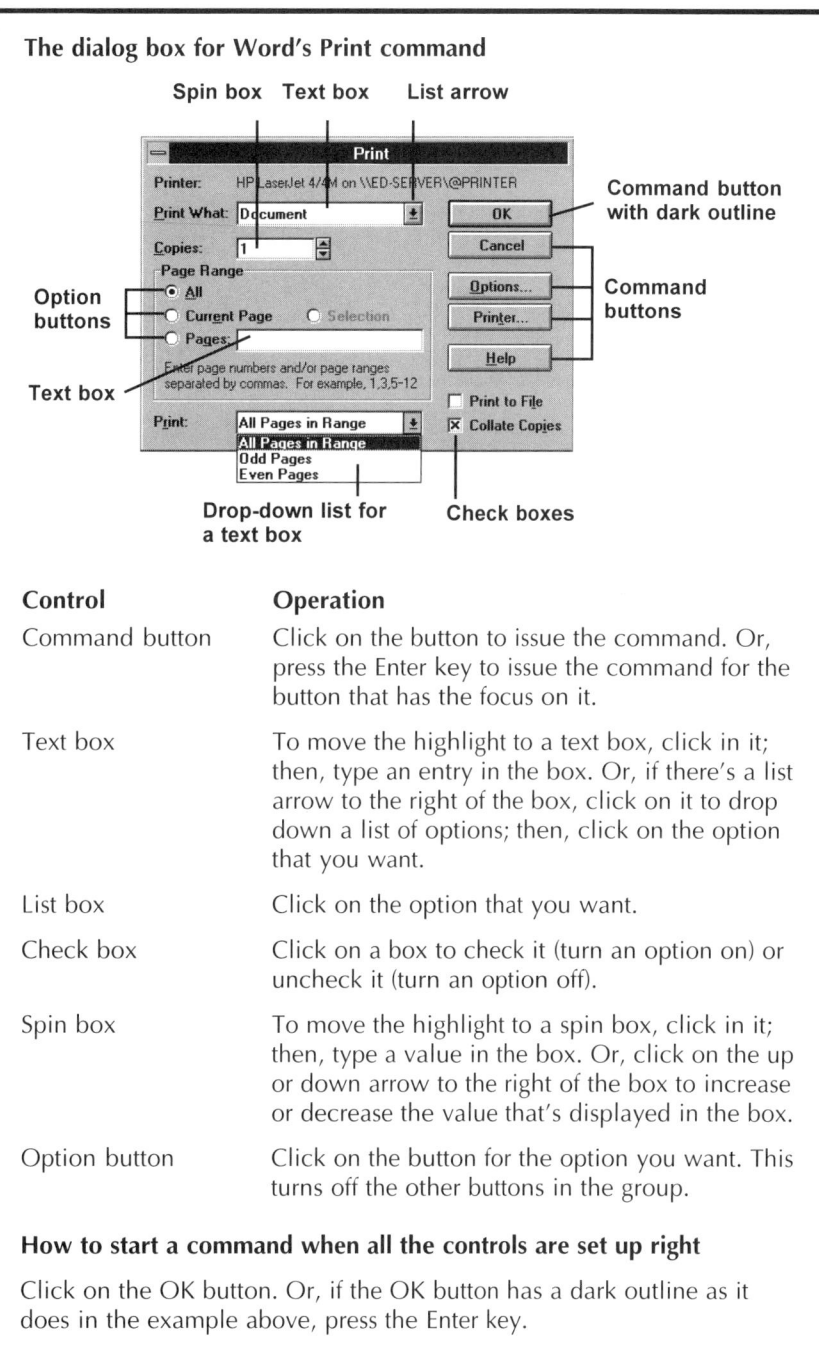

The dialog box for Word's Print command

Control	Operation
Command button	Click on the button to issue the command. Or, press the Enter key to issue the command for the button that has the focus on it.
Text box	To move the highlight to a text box, click in it; then, type an entry in the box. Or, if there's a list arrow to the right of the box, click on it to drop down a list of options; then, click on the option that you want.
List box	Click on the option that you want.
Check box	Click on a box to check it (turn an option on) or uncheck it (turn an option off).
Spin box	To move the highlight to a spin box, click in it; then, type a value in the box. Or, click on the up or down arrow to the right of the box to increase or decrease the value that's displayed in the box.
Option button	Click on the button for the option you want. This turns off the other buttons in the group.

How to start a command when all the controls are set up right

Click on the OK button. Or, if the OK button has a dark outline as it does in the example above, press the Enter key.

How to cancel a command and remove the dialog box from the screen

Press the Esc key or click on the Cancel button.

Figure P-10   How to work with a dialog box

Keyboard techniques for working with dialog boxes

For most people, using the mouse is the most efficient way to work with dialog boxes. If you prefer to use the keyboard, though, you can use the techniques presented in figure P-11.

Before you can use the keyboard to change a control setting, you have to move the *focus* to it. To do that, you can use the techniques shown at the start of figure P-11. Then, you can use the remaining techniques to change the setting.

Sometimes, it's difficult to tell which control has the focus on it so you have to look closely for it. If, for example, an option button or check box has the focus, that's indicated by a light dotted line around the option or box name. In contrast, the focus on a text box is indicated by the insertion point or highlighting, and the focus on a command button is indicated by a dark outline.

The Print dialog box with the focus on a check box

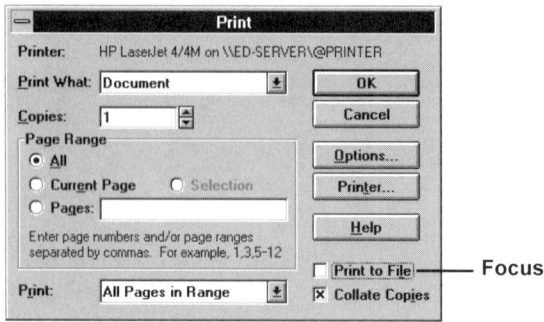

Keys for moving the focus

Key	Function
Tab	Moves the focus forward from one control to the next.
Shift+Tab	Moves the focus backward from one control to the next.
Alt+Underlined-letter	Moves the focus to the control with the underlined letter in its name. If the control is a command button, this also activates the button. If the control is a text box that has a list arrow to its right, this also drops down the list.

Keyboard techniques for working with controls

Control	Operation
Command button	Press the Enter key to activate the button.
Text box	Type the new value. Or, if the text box has a list arrow to its right, press Alt+Down-arrow to drop down the list; then, use the Down-arrow or Up-arrow key to highlight the option that you want.
List box	Use the Down-arrow or Up-arrow key to highlight the option that you want.
Check box	Press the Spacebar to turn the option on or off.
Option button	Press the arrow keys to move to another option in the group and turn it on.
Spin box	Type the new value. Or press the Up-arrow or Down-arrow key to increase or decrease the value.

Figure P-11   Keyboard techniques for working with a dialog box

How to work with a dialog box that contains tabs

When you use Word, some of the dialog boxes have *tabs* as shown in figure P-12. These tabs are often used to organize a series of options. To switch from one tab to another, just click on the tab. When you complete the command, any changes that you've made to any of the tabs are put into effect.

How to use the Exit command

To exit from a program, you can use the Exit command in the File menu. This has the same effect as double-clicking on the control-menu box for the application window.

A dialog box that contains 12 tabs with the Edit tab displayed

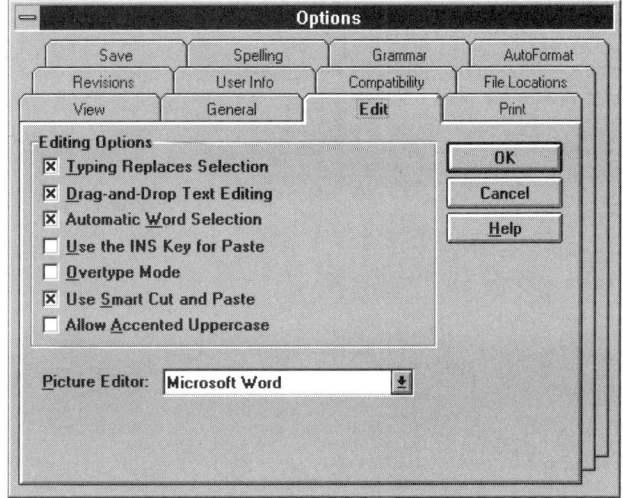

The same dialog box with the Save tab displayed

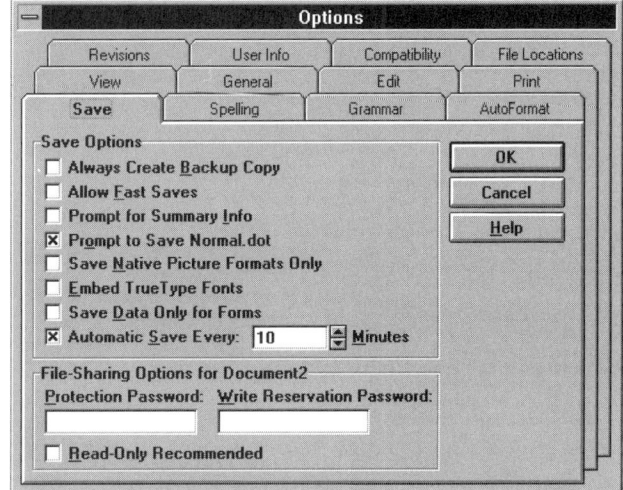

Operation

• To switch from one tab to another, click on a tab name. You can also press Ctrl+Tab to switch to the next tab or Shift+Ctrl+Tab to switch to the previous tab.

• When you click on the OK button in a tab to close the dialog box, all changes that you made to any of the tabs go into effect.

Figure P-12   How to work with dialog boxes that contain tabs

Exercise set P-3

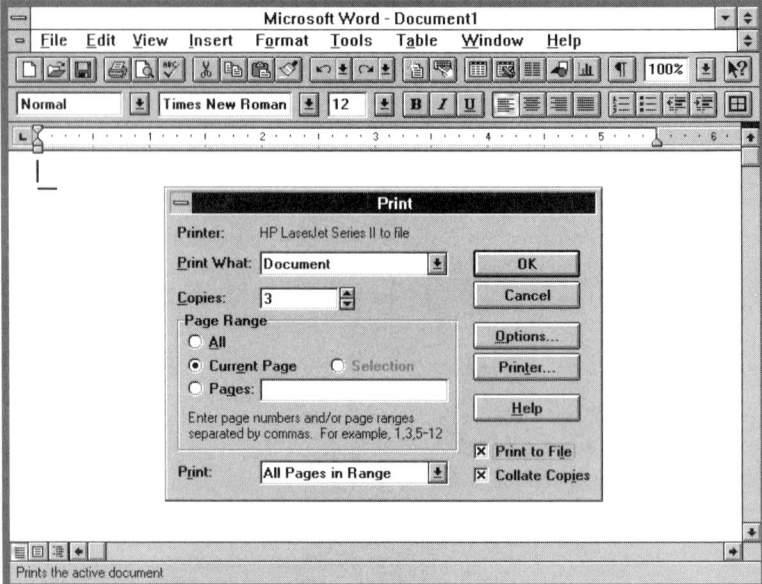

How the Print dialog box should look after you change the controls as described in exercise 3

1. Activate the Program Manager if it's not already the active program, and open the Main and Accessories group windows if they're not already open. Next, use the first mouse method in figure P-9 to issue the Tile command from the Window menu. Then, use the second mouse method to issue the Cascade command from the Window menu. Note that neither command requires a dialog box.

2. Use the first keyboard method in figure P-9 to issue the Tile command again. Note that you can access any command with just three keystrokes. Then, use the second method to issue the Cascade command again. This isn't as efficient, but it lets you review the menus and commands at a leisurely pace.

3. Start Word, click on the OK button if the Tip of the Day is displayed, and issue the Print command from the File menu. In the dialog box that's displayed, use the mouse techniques of figure P-10 to drop the list for the Print What and Print boxes, to change the Page Range option from All to Current Page, to change the Copies count to 3, and to check the Print to File box. At this point, the Print dialog box should look like the one shown above. Click on the Cancel button to cancel the command.

4. Issue Word's Print command again. This time, use the keyboard techniques of figure P-11 to increase the Copies count to 3, change the Page Range option to Current Page, drop the list for the Print box, and check the Print to File box. Then, press the Esc key to cancel the command.

5. Issue the Options command from the Tools menu, and switch to the General tab in the resulting dialog box. Next, change the value in the Recently Used File List box to 5 if it isn't that value already. Then, switch to the View tab. Are the Horizontal and Vertical Scroll Bar boxes checked? Then, click on the Cancel button to cancel the command, and issue the Exit command to end Word.

How to work with directories and files

When you use any PC program, you save your work in *files* that are stored on *disk drives.* To help keep these files organized, they are kept in *directories.* If you've been using DOS programs, you may have had trouble working with directories and files because some of the required notation was so difficult.

When you use Windows programs, though, standard dialog boxes let you select the directories and files that you want to work with. In addition, Windows provides a program called the File Manager that makes it easier to create directories, copy and move files, and so on. As a result, you shouldn't have any trouble with files and directories, but you need to get started right.

Figure P-13 presents the concepts and terms that you need for working with directories and files. It also illustrates the application window for the File Manager. By experimenting with this program, you can better understand the directories and files that are part of a Windows system.

When you use the File Manager, its document window is normally referred to as a *directory window.* Within this window, the *tree pane* shows the structure of the directories that are stored on a disk. The *directory pane* shows the files that are stored in the directory that's highlighted in the tree pane.

In figure P-13, the highlighted directory is the WINWORD directory that's set up when you install Word 6. If you study the directory pane in this figure, you can see that this directory contains

The application and directory window for the File Manager

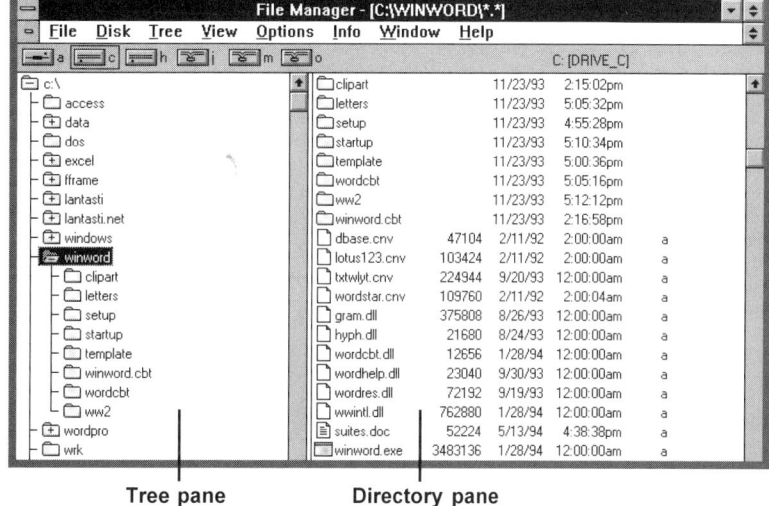

Tree pane   Directory pane

General

- When you use any Windows program, you save your work in *files* that are stored on *hard disks* or *diskettes.* The devices that save files on a disk or retrieve files from a disk are called *disk drives.*

- A file is always stored in a *directory.* A hard disk is likely to contain dozens of directories, but a diskette is likely to contain only one.

- The File Manager is a Windows program that's found in the Main program group. It can help you manage the files and directories on your disk drives. Its document windows are usually called *directory windows,* and each one contains two *panes* by default.

Disk drives

- The icons below the menu bar of the File Manager represent the available disk drives. Drives A and B are the *diskette drives* on your PC (if you have two of them). Drive C is the primary *hard disk drive* on your PC, but there may be others like drive H in the example above. Note the different icons for diskette and hard disk drives.

- If your PC is attached to a network, a third type of disk icon represents a hard disk drive on the network. In the example above, drives J, M, and O are *network disk drives.*

Directories and files

- The File Manager's *tree pane* shows the structure of the directories on a disk. This structure starts at the top with the *root directory.* On a hard disk, the root directory always contains other directories, which can be called *subdirectories.* These directories in turn can contain other directories, so this structure is usually several levels deep.

- The File Manager's *directory pane* lists the directories, programs, and files that are stored in the directory that's highlighted in the tree pane. The icons before the entries indicate the type of entry.

Figure P-13   Concepts and terms for working with files

eight subdirectories (see the directory icon in front of the first eight entries), at least one program file (see the program icon in front of the last entry in this figure), and many data files (note the icons for the files between the directories and the program file). If you check the directories for Word 6 and for other programs on your PC, you'll see that what we often think of as one program is actually one or more directories that contain dozens of program and data files.

Paths, file names, and wildcard specifications

Figure P-14 presents other information that you need for working with files and directories. This time, the directory pane of the File Manager shows the files that are stored in a data directory for Word 6 documents.

In the title bar for the application window, you can see the *path* of the highlighted directory. With DOS programs, you often had to type paths like that. With Windows programs, you never need to type them, but you occasionally need to interpret them.

When you create a new file, you need to know how to create valid *file names* so figure P-14 gives the rules for forming them. Most of the time, you can omit the *extension* of the file because the application you're working with will add it automatically.

Last, figure P-14 presents what you need to know about *wildcard specifications*. You need to know what these specifications mean because they are used by the File Manager and by applications like Word. You'll see an example in just a moment.

A File Manager window for another directory on the C drive

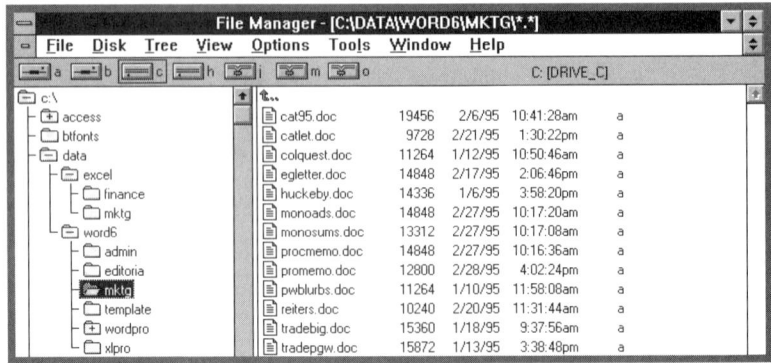

Paths

- In the title bar of the application window shown above, you can see the notation for the directory that's highlighted in the tree pane:

    `C:\DATA\WORD6\MKTG\*.*`

- The letter and colon at the start of this notation indicate the disk drive that the directory is on. After that, you can see the *path* of the directory. Starting with the root directory, the path gives the sequence of directories that you have to go through to reach the highlighted directory. The directory names in the path are separated by backslashes.

File names

- A *file name* consists of a name that is 1 to 8 characters long, a dot (or period), and an *extension* that is from 1 to 3 characters long. If the extension is omitted, the dot can be omitted too.

- A file name must start with a letter or number. After that, the characters in the name or the extension can be letters (either uppercase or lowercase), numbers, or any of these special characters: ! @ # $ % ^ & ( ) _ + - { } < > ' ~

Wildcard specifications

- After the path in the title bar above, you can see this *wildcard specification*: *.*

- Since the * *wildcard* means "any characters," this specification means that file names with any characters before the dot and any characters after the dot should be listed in the directory pane (all files). In contrast, a specification like *.DOC means that only files with DOC as the extension should be listed.

Figure P-14   Paths, file names, and wildcard specifications

An introduction to the functions of the File Manager

When you use a Windows application like Word, you use the Windows File Manager to manage the directories and files that you use. To give you some idea of how easy the File Manager is to use, figure P-15 summarizes some of its basic functions.

Note that you can even start an application from the File Manager. To do that, you just double-click on a file name that has an icon like the ones in figure P-14 or P-15 before it. This icon indicates that the file is associated with a program. If, for example, you double-click on a file that has DOC as the extension, Word is started. When the application starts, it also retrieves the data file that you double-clicked on.

This summary, however, doesn't begin to indicate the power of the File Manager. To move or copy several files at a time, for example, you can highlight the files before you drag them to a new directory. And to move or copy files from one disk drive to another, you can open two directory windows at the same time and drag the files from one window to another. In short, if you frequently need to reorganize your files and directories, you should make a point of learning more about the File Manager.

A File Manager window for a diskette drive

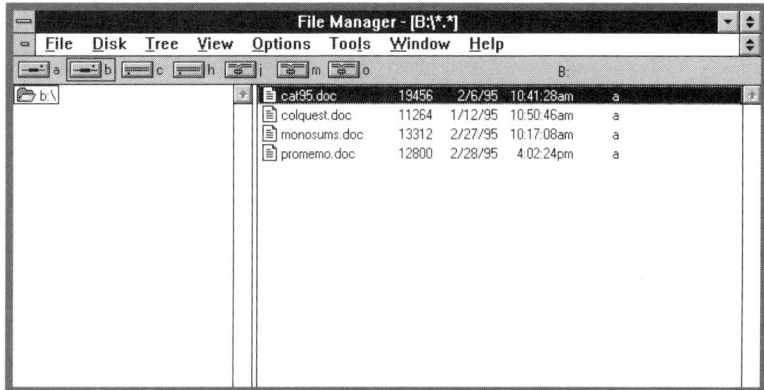

How to change the display in the tree and directory panes

- To change the drive that's displayed, click on one of the drive icons at the top of the window.

- To display the files for another directory in the directory pane, click on a directory in the tree pane.

- To hide subdirectories in the tree pane, double-click on the icon for the directory that they're subordinate to. To display the subdirectories for a directory that has an icon with a plus sign on it, double-click on the icon.

How to create a new directory

- Click on the directory in the tree pane that you want to create a subordinate directory for. Then, issue the Create Directory command from the File menu.

How to start an application that's associated with a file

- The icons before the files in the directory pane above indicate that the files are associated with an application. To start that program, just double-click on the file name. After the program starts, it retrieves that file.

- A file name is associated with an application through its extension. By default, DOC is associated with Word.

How to delete or rename a file or directory

- To delete a file or directory, highlight it, press the Delete key, and respond to the dialog boxes that follow.

- To rename a file or directory, highlight it, issue the Rename command from the File menu, and respond to the dialog box that follows.

How to move or copy a file on the same disk

- To move the highlighted file, drag the file name to a directory in the tree pane and release the mouse button.

- To copy the highlighted file, hold down the Ctrl key while you drag the file name to the directory.

Figure P-15   An introduction to the functions of the File Manager

How to use the standard Open command

The Open command in any Windows application retrieves a file from disk, opens a document window for it, and displays the contents of the file in the window. To use this command, you need to know what disk drive the file is stored on, what directory the file is in, and what the name of the file is. This is true for all Windows applications, and the dialog box for the Open command works the same in all Windows applications.

Figure P-16 presents the dialog box that's displayed when you issue the Open command in Word 6. Because identifying the drive, directory, and file can be confusing if you haven't used a dialog box like this before, you'll learn how to do that in the next two figures. Once you learn the techniques in those figures, you'll be able to identify files in other dialog boxes as well.

The Word dialog box for the Open command

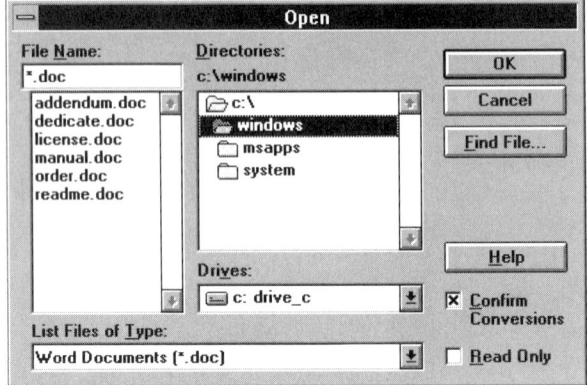

What the Open command does

- Retrieves a file from disk, opens a document window for it, and displays the file in the document window.
- The file can be stored on a diskette, a hard disk on your own PC, or a hard disk on the network.

What you have to know to use the Open command

- What disk drive the file is stored on
- What directory the file is stored in
- What the name of the file is

Figure P-16   An introduction to the standard Open command

How to select a drive and directory in a dialog box

To identify the drive that contains the file you want to open, you select it from the list that drops down from the Drives box in the Open dialog box. This list is shown at the top of figure P-17. After you identify the drive, Word displays the directory structure for that drive in the Directories list box. When this dialog box is first displayed as shown in figure P-16, only one directory at each level but the last is displayed, and the indentation shows the levels of directories.

To change to a different directory, you have to first find the directory using the techniques in figure P-17. These techniques are similar to the ones you use in the tree pane of the File Manager. To start, you usually scroll to the root directory at the top of the *directory tree*. When you double-click on the root directory, all the directories at the next level are displayed. You can then continue down the levels of directories until you find the one you want to use.

When you complete the procedure in figure P-17, the path of the directory that you selected is shown above the directory tree. Then, you can check to make sure that this is the directory that contains the file you want to retrieve. If you didn't double-click properly on the last directory in the path, the directory tree may appear to be correct, but the notation won't be.

How to select a disk drive

1. Click on the arrow to the right of the Drives box to drop down the drives list:

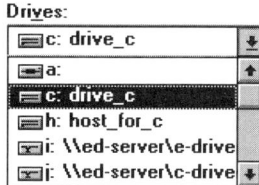

2. Click on the letter of the drive you want to use.

How to select a directory

1. Double-click on the root directory at the top of the directory tree. This displays the first level of directories on the drive:

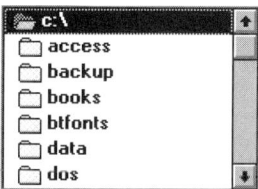

2. If necessary, scroll to the directory that you want to use at the next level. Then, double-click on it to display the next level of directories:

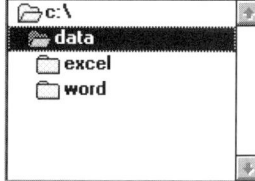

3. Continue down the tree in this way until you double-click on the directory that you want. At this point, the path for the directory should be displayed above the Directories box:

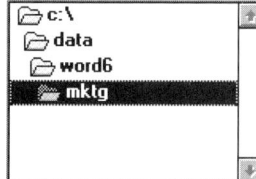

Figure P-17 How to select a drive and directory

How to select a file in a dialog box

Figure P-18 shows how the Open dialog box looks after you identify the drive and directory for a file. Since this is the Open dialog box for Word 6, the wildcard specification in the File Name box is for files that have DOC as the extension. As a result, only files with a matching extension are listed in the File Name list box.

To open one of the files that are listed in the box, you can double-click on its file name. Or, you can move the highlight to the file name before choosing the OK button to start the command.

If all the file names in the directory don't fit in the list box, you can use the scroll bars to scroll through the list. Or, you can type one or more characters in the File Name text box to jump the highlight to the file name that begins with those characters.

Finally, if you want to open a file that doesn't have the extension given by the wildcard specification, you can select a different wildcard specification from the List Files of Type list. Or, you can type your own wildcard specification into the File Name text box. Although most Word 6 files have DOC as the extension, that's not a requirement.

The Open dialog box after the drive and directory have been selected

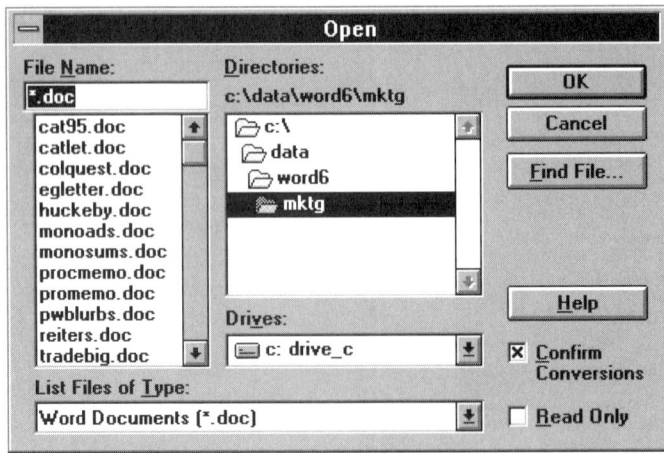

Two ways to select a file in the list box and start the command

- Double-click on the file name in the File Name list box.

- Move the highlight to the file name by using mouse or keyboard techniques. This moves the file name into the File Name text box. Then, choose the OK button by clicking on it or by pressing the Enter key (since the OK button has a dark outline).

How to change the types of files that are displayed

- By default, an application displays only those file names that have the extension that is related to it. For instance, Word 6 displays only files with the DOC extension.

- To display files with another extension, drop down the list from the List Files of Type box and choose the file type. To display all files regardless of the extension, choose All Files.

- If you want to display files in the File Name list box that have an extension that isn't in the List Files of Type box, you can type your own wildcard specification in the File Name text box.

Note

- If the file you want doesn't appear in the File Name list, you can use the scroll bars or the Down-arrow key to scroll through the list. Or, you can type one or more characters into the File Name text box to move the highlight to the first file name that starts with those characters.

Figure P-18   How to select a file

How to use the standard Save As command

Figure P-19 shows how to use the standard Save As command. This is the command that you use when you save your work on a diskette or hard disk. After you select the disk drive and directory that you want to store the file in, you type a valid file name in the File Name text box and complete the command.

The Word 6 dialog box for the Save As command

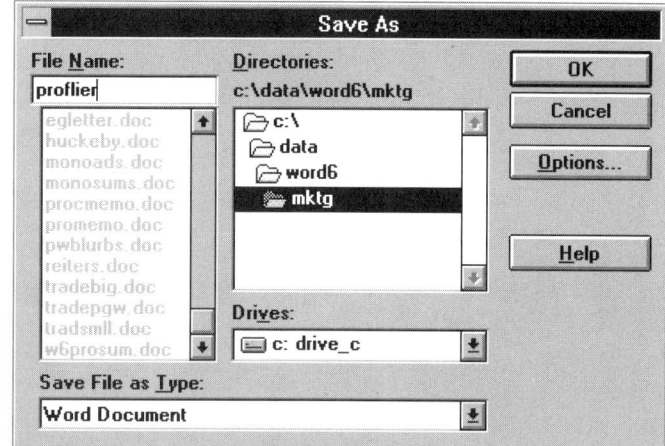

What the command does

• Copies your work from the document window to a diskette, hard disk on your PC, or hard disk on the network.

• When you save a file, it remains in the document window.

The importance of this command

• If you don't save your work on a diskette or hard disk, it is lost when you turn off the PC.

How to use this command

• Select the drive and directory that you want to save the file in just as you do for an Open command.

• Enter a valid file name in the File Name text box and click on the OK button. If you omit the extension, the application program usually adds the extension that is related to it. For instance, Word adds DOC as the extension.

• To replace a file name in the File Name text box with a new name, just start typing when the name is highlighted. To highlight the name, you can drag the mouse across it, double-click on it, or press Alt+N (the keyboard method for moving the insertion point to the File Name box). These are standard Windows techniques for working with the text in text boxes.

Notes

• Before you start saving files on a PC at school or in business, you need to find out what disk drive and what directory your files should be saved in.

• Before you start saving files on your own PC, you should use the File Manager to create one or more directories for them.

Figure P-19   An introduction to the standard Save As command

Exercise set P-4

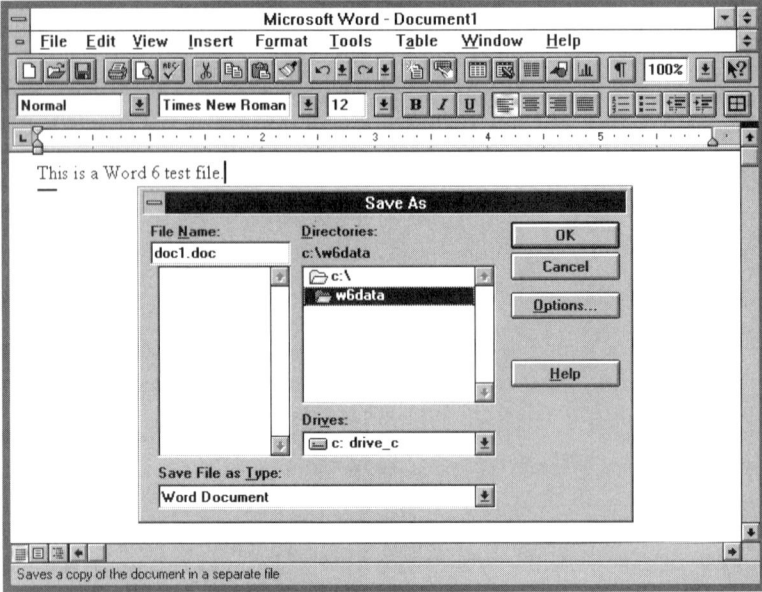

How the Save As dialog box should look after you change the directory in exercise 5

1. Start the File Manager from the Main group of the Program Manager. If the application and directory window aren't maximized, maximize them. Then, study the disk drive icons at the top of the directory window. What diskette drives are available to your PC? What hard drives? What network drives?

2. If necessary, click on the icon for drive C so the hard disk on your PC is displayed in the directory window. Then, scroll down to the Windows directory in the tree pane and double-click on it to display its subdirectories in the tree pane and its files in the directory pane. How many subdirectories does this directory contain? These are the first entries in the directory pane. How many files altogether are there in this directory? You can see a summary at the bottom of the directory window.

3. Highlight the root directory on the C drive. Then, access the Create Directory command in the File menu and create a directory named W6DATA. When that's done, scroll down the directory tree until you find this directory.

4. Switch to the Program Manager and start Word. Then, type "This is a Word 6 test file." in the blank document window.

5. Issue the Save As command from the File menu. What is the starting drive and directory? If necessary, use the first technique in figure P-17 to change the drive to the C drive. Next, use the second technique in that figure to change the directory in the Directories box to the one you created in exercise 3. At this point, the Save As dialog box should look like the one above. Then, highlight the default file name (doc1.doc) by dragging the mouse across it, double-clicking on it, or pressing Alt+N, and replace the default name by typing TESTFILE as the file name. Don't include an extension, though, because Word will add DOC automatically. To complete the command, click on the OK button or press the Enter key. Last, issue the Close command from the File menu to close the document window.

6. Issue the Open command from the File menu, and open the file that you just saved. To do that, double-click on TESTFILE in the File Name list box. This should display the file that you created in its own window. Then, issue the Exit command from the File menu to end Word.

7. Switch to the File Manager. Then, highlight the TESTFILE file in the Directory pane, press the Delete key, and respond to the dialog boxes that follow until the file is deleted. Next, highlight the W6DATA directory in the tree pane, press the Delete key, and respond to the dialog boxes that follow until the directory is deleted.

8. Exit from Windows. This closes all applications and returns control of the PC to DOS.

How to use Windows 95 with your applications

Windows 95 is the name of the next release of Windows. If you're interested in how that release will affect the skills that are presented in this book, please read on. Otherwise, you can skip to the Perspective heading near the end of this chapter.

The good news is that Windows 95 will have little or no effect on applications like Word 6, although there will be minor differences in the appearance of the application windows. Even the File Manager will work the same as it does with Windows 3.1. On the other hand, the Program Manager has been dropped from Windows 95 so you will have to use different techniques for starting your applications.

Of course, Windows 95 will come with many new functions and features that aren't available in Windows 3.1. I just want you to know that these functions and features will have little effect on what you learn in this book.

How to start an application

Figure P-20 shows how to start an application from Windows 95. Instead of using group windows and icons, you use menus with simplified mouse actions. To move from menu to menu, you just move the mouse pointer (no clicking). To start a program from a menu, you single click (no double-clicking).

The starting Windows 95 screen with menus displayed

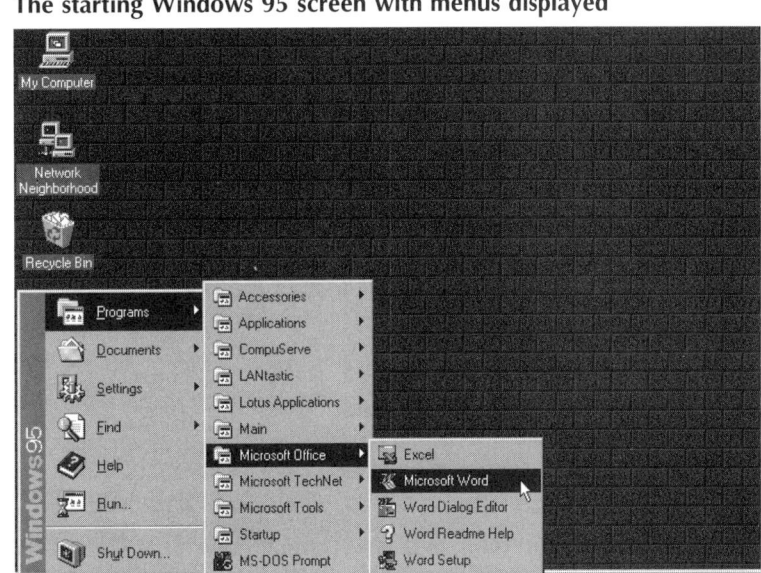

Procedure

1. Click on the Start button in the lower left corner to display the first menu on the left of the screen.

2. Move (don't drag) the mouse pointer to Programs in the first menu. That displays the next menu to the right.

3. Move the mouse pointer to the type of program you want to start. That displays the next menu to the right.

4. Click (don't double-click) on the name of the program that you want to start.

Figure P-20   How to start an application in Windows 95

Differences in the application window

Figure P-21 summarizes the differences you can expect in the application window for Word 6. As you can see, the appearance of the bars above the document window has been changed slightly, and all of the window buttons are on the right side of the title bar.

At the bottom of the application window is a row of buttons that represent the applications that are running. To switch to one of these applications, you can just click on its button. However, you can still use Alt+Tab switching and most of the other switching methods that work with Windows 3.1.

Everything else in your applications should work the same way it works in Windows 3.1. With some minor operational changes, that should also be true when upgraded versions of your applications become available for use with Windows 95. As a result, the skills that you learn in this book should serve you well for many years to come.

The Word 6 window when displayed by Windows 95

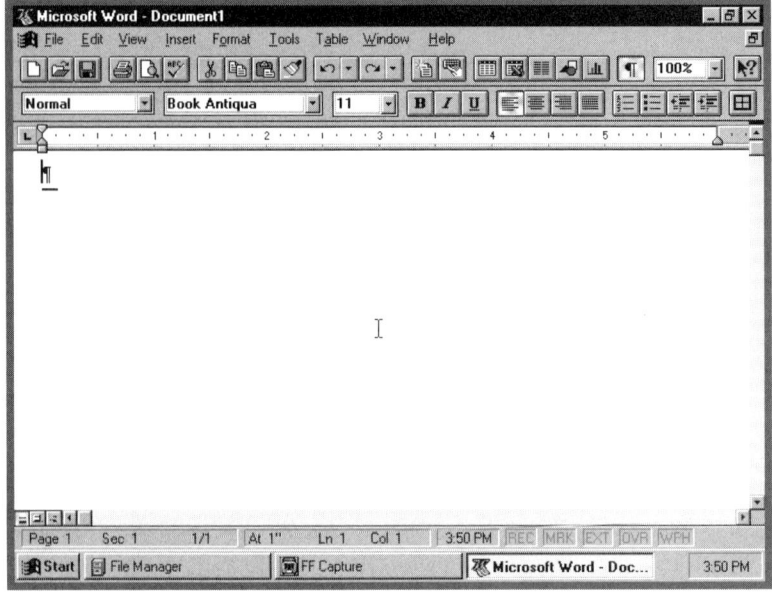

Primary differences in appearance

- The title bar has three buttons, all on the right side. The first is the minimize button; the second is the restore or maximize button; the third is the button for closing the window and exiting from the program. Just one click on any of these buttons starts the action.

- Below the status bar is a row of buttons that represent the programs that are in operation.

How to switch from one program to another

- Click on one of the buttons at the bottom of the window.

- You can also use Alt+Tab switching just as you can with Windows 3.1.

Figure P-21   Differences in the application window for Windows 95

Perspective   You can think of this chapter as a crash course in Windows. It has presented the minimum set of skills that every Windows user should have. Because this chapter has presented so much information, though, you may be slightly overwhelmed by it. That's even more likely if you're new to PCs or Windows.

In practice, though, the skills that are presented in this chapter shouldn't give you much trouble. After a few trials, starting a program from the Program Manager becomes a trivial task, and switching from one program to another does too. Later, when you start using Word, you'll find that issuing commands from menus and working with dialog boxes also becomes routine.

In fact, the only skills that continue to give people trouble are those for working with directories and files. So if you're at all uneasy about those skills, you may want to go through exercise set P-4 again. In particular, you should make sure that you know how to select a directory as you open or save a file. Once you're confident that you can do that, you're ready for Word.

Summary

- When Windows starts, its *shell program* is started too. This program is usually the Program Manager. That's the program that you use to start your *applications*.

- When you start an application, an *application window* is opened for it. Within this application window, a program creates its own workspaces called *document windows*.

- To use the mouse, you need to know the four basic mouse actions: *point*, *click*, *double-click*, and *drag*.

- You can *maximize*, *restore*, or *minimize* an application or document window by clicking on its maximize, restore, or minimize button. When a window is minimized, it takes the form of an *icon* that you can restore or maximize with the mouse. You can also move or size a window with the mouse if it's not maximized.

- When a window is too small to show all of its contents, *scroll bars* are added to it. Then, you can use the mouse to scroll through the window by clicking on the scroll bar or *scroll arrows* or by dragging the *scroll box*.

- To close a window, you can double-click on the *control-menu box* or use the *control menu* for the window. If the window is an application window, this also ends the application. If the window contains the Program Manager, this ends all programs and returns you to DOS.

- The Program Manager organizes your applications in *program groups*. To open a *group window*, you double-click on a *program group icon*. To start a program, you double-click on its *program icon*.

- Windows provides several methods for switching from one application to another. One of the best is Alt+Tab switching.

- You can use either mouse or keyboard techniques to access *menus* from the *menu bar* and to issue *commands* from the menus. These techniques work the same in all Windows programs.

- When you issue some commands, a *dialog box* is displayed. To change the settings or supply the information that's required by the dialog box, you can use the mouse or the keyboard. Some of the common dialog box controls are *command buttons, option buttons, spin boxes, check boxes, tabs, list boxes,* and *text boxes*.

- When you use any Windows program, you save your work on a *hard disk* or *diskette* in *files* that are organized in *directories*. A *path* shows how to get to a directory from the *root directory*. A *file name* consists of a name and an optional *extension* that are separated by a dot (or period).

- The File Manager is a Windows program that helps you manage directories and files. The *tree pane* in one of its *directory windows* shows the directory structure for a disk drive; the *directory pane* shows the files that are in the highlighted directory in the tree pane.

- The Open command is the standard Windows command for opening a file. The Save As command is the standard Windows command for saving a file on a diskette or hard disk. To use these commands, you don't need to enter *path* specifications. Instead, you select the drive and directory that you want to use.

- Although Windows 95 will offer some important new functions and features, it should have only a trivial effect on how you start and use applications like Word 6.

Section 1

The essential word processing skills

The first three chapters in this section show you how to create, edit, and format a Word document. You need to master those skills for any document you create. Then, the fourth chapter presents the extra commands and features that you need when you work with documents of two or more pages.

Whether you're a word processing novice or a person who's upgrading or converting to Word 6, you should read all four chapters in sequence. From the start, you'll be learning the most useful and productive ways to work with Word 6. When you complete this section, you will be able to use Word 6 to create, edit, and format documents the way the best professionals do.

Chapter 1

How to create, print, and save a document

Word 6 is a complex program that provides dozens of commands and features. To learn all of them would take many hours. To create, print, and save short documents like letters or memos, though, you only need to master a few of those commands and features. You can learn them in just an hour or two, and that's what this chapter is designed to teach you.

This chapter will get you started with Word 6 whether you're a complete beginner or a person who is upgrading or converting to Word 6 from another word processing program. The intent is to teach you Word 6 the way the best professionals use it right from the start. How much experience you have will of course determine how long it takes you to complete this chapter. But when you're done, you'll be well on your way to Word 6 competence.

If you haven't used a word processing program before, it's especially important to do the exercises that are presented throughout this chapter. They are a critical part of the learning process because they force you to use the skills that are described in the text. As you will often see, a skill that seems difficult when you read about it is quite manageable when you actually try it.

An introduction to Word 6

If you've used other Windows programs and you know how to use the Program Manager to start them, you shouldn't have any trouble starting Word 6. Otherwise, you need to read the prerequisites chapter at the start of this book. It presents the essential skills that you need for working with any Windows program. It also shows you how to start Word 6.

How to work with the Tip of the Day

When Word 6 starts, an empty document window is displayed. Unless the Tip of the Day option has been turned off, the Tip of the Day dialog box is displayed in this window as shown in figure 1-1. To remove this dialog box from the screen, you can just click on the OK button. You can then enter a document into the empty window.

The starting Word screen when the Tip of the Day option is on

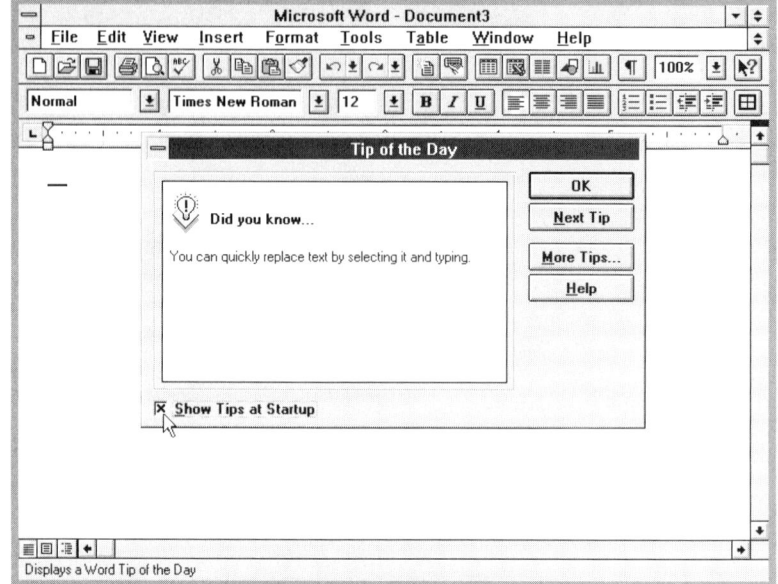

How to turn off the Tip of the Day

- To turn it off for the day, click the mouse on the OK button.

- To turn it off so it isn't displayed automatically when you start Word, click on the Show Tips at Startup check box in the lower left corner of this dialog box. Then, click on the OK button.

How to display the Tip of the Day other than at startup

- Choose the Tip of the Day command from the Help menu. This displays a dialog box like the one above. If necessary, you can then click on the Show Tips at Startup check box to restart the Tip of the Day.

How to display additional tips

- To display the next tip, click on the Next Tip button.

- To display a list of all of the tips that are available, click on the More Tips button.

Figure 1-1   How to work with the Tip of the Day

The components of the Word window

After you enter a document, the Word window will look something like the one in figure 1-2. As you can see, a *document* is displayed in the *document window* within the Word *application window*.

Above the document window are four bars: the *title bar*, the *menu bar*, and two *toolbars*. All four of these bars are normally displayed as you enter and edit documents. You'll learn how to use these bars in this chapter and throughout this book.

Below the bars is the *horizontal ruler*. You can use this ruler to set tabs, align paragraphs, change margins, and tell the horizontal location of the parts of the document. You can also display a vertical ruler that helps you tell the vertical location of the parts of a document and lets you change the top and bottom margins.

Within the document window, there can be both an *insertion point* and an *I-beam*. The insertion point shows where the next action is going to take place. The I-beam is the form that the *mouse pointer* takes when it's within the document area.

At the bottom of the application window is the *status bar*. It gives the location of the insertion point within the document (like page 1, section 1). It also gives the location of the insertion point within the current page.

You can also see the vertical and horizontal scroll bars in figure 1-2. If you've read the prerequisites chapter, though, you should already be familiar with them.

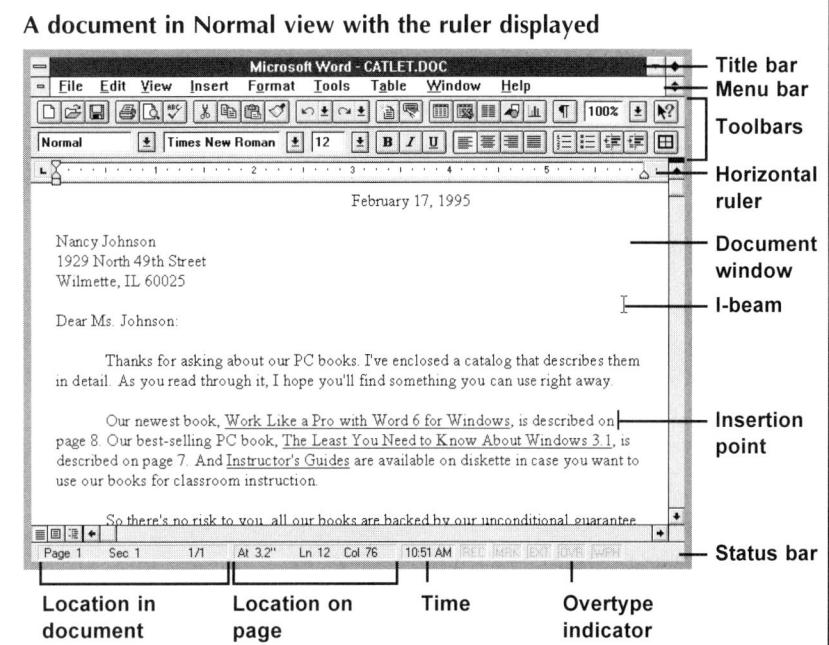

A document in Normal view with the ruler displayed

- Title bar
- Menu bar
- Toolbars
- Horizontal ruler
- Document window
- I-beam
- Insertion point
- Status bar

Location in document   Location on page   Time   Overtype indicator

Concepts

- The name of the *document* in the *document window* is displayed in the *title bar* at the top of the Word window, unless the document window isn't maximized. In that case, the name is displayed in the title bar of the document window.

- The *insertion point* is a blinking line that indicates where the next character that you type will be entered into the document. The location of the insertion point within the document and within the current page is shown in the left side of the *status bar* at the bottom of the window.

- The *I-beam* is the form that the mouse pointer takes when it's within the document. When you move the mouse pointer outside the document, it changes to an arrowhead.

- The *menu bar* near the top of the Word window contains the menus you can use to issue commands. The *toolbars* contain buttons and drop-down lists that let you perform predefined functions. And the *horizontal ruler* lets you set tabs, align paragraphs, and change margins.

- You can work in either of two *views* as you enter and edit a document: Normal view and Page Layout view (see figure 1-4).

- The status bar includes five indicators. In the example above, all five indicators are dimmed, which means they're off. The most important of these is the Overtype indicator, which is indicated by the letters OVR. You'll learn more about the Overtype indicator in figure 1-5.

Figure 1-2   The Word application window after a document has been entered in its document window

How to use toolbar buttons and lists

Figure 1-3 shows how to use the toolbar buttons and lists. When you click on one of the buttons with the mouse, a command or function is started. When you click on a down arrow, a list is displayed like the Zoom Control list shown in this figure. Then, you can click on any item in the list. If, for example, you click on 75% in the Zoom list, the document is displayed at 75 percent of its actual size.

If you can't tell what a toolbar button or control does, you can hold the mouse pointer on it for a moment. Then, Word displays a brief description in the status bar. If the ToolTip option is on (as it is by default), Word also displays a ToolTip in a small box next to the mouse pointer.

The toolbars shown in figure 1-3 are called the Standard and Formatting toolbars. They're the ones you'll use most of the time, and they're displayed by default. In later chapters, you'll learn how to use some of the six other toolbars that come with Word 6.

How to change the view

To a large extent, you can customize the appearance of Word's application window so it suits your working style. For instance, you can change to a different *view*, you can display or hide the ruler, and you can change the display size of the characters on the screen. Figure 1-4 shows how to do that.

A document with the non-printing characters displayed

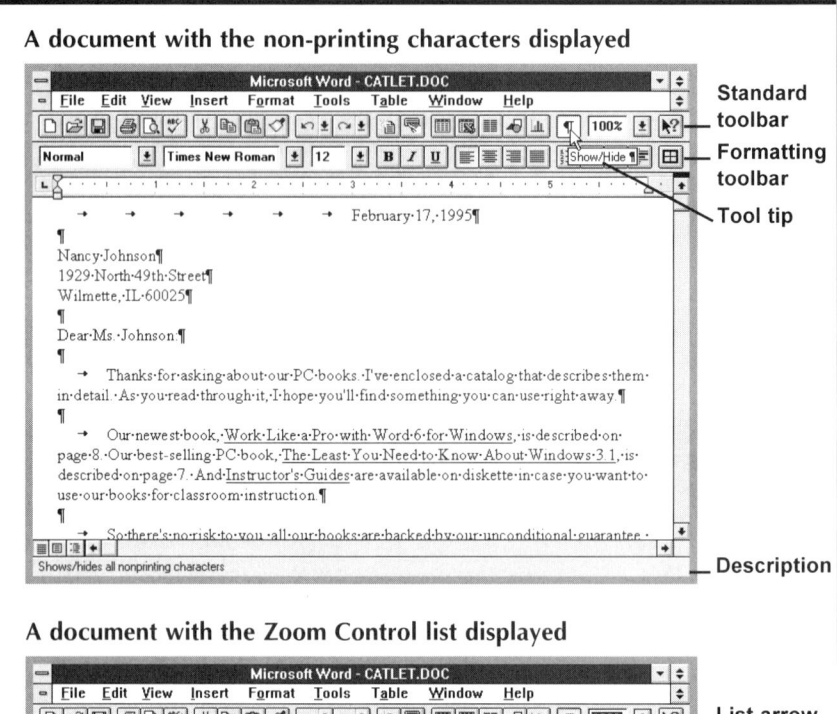

A document with the Zoom Control list displayed

Operation

- When you point to a toolbar button or control, its name is displayed in the ToolTip and its function is displayed in the status bar.

- When you click on a button, its function is started.

- If you click on a down arrow to the right of a text box, a list is displayed. Then, you can choose an option from the list.

Note

- If the ToolTip isn't displayed when you point to a toolbar button or control, it means that the ToolTip option has been turned off. To turn it on, choose the Toolbars command from the View menu. Then, check the Show ToolTips box.

Figure 1-3   How to use the toolbar buttons and lists

One way to change the view is by using the View menu. To do that, just pull down the menu and choose the appropriate command. To hide or display the ruler, for example, you choose the Ruler command.

The first four items in the View menu represent the different views that you can use when working with a document. Of these, Normal view shown in figure 1-3 and Page Layout view shown in figure 1-4 are the ones you'll use most often, so you can ignore the other two for now. You can also change to Normal or Page Layout view by clicking on the appropriate button near the bottom left corner of the window.

In Page Layout view, you can see the top and bottom margins. If the vertical ruler is displayed, you can use it to change these margins. If the document contains a header or footer, you can see and edit it in Page Layout view. You'll also want to use Page Layout view if you're working with frames or graphic objects.

Most of the time, you'll work with your documents displayed at 100% so the characters on the screen are the size they will be when they're printed. If you want to change the display size for a document, however, you can use the Zoom command in the View menu. This command displays a dialog box that lets you choose from several options. Since most of these options are also available from the list that drops down from the Zoom Control box in the Standard toolbar, you may never need to use the Zoom command.

A document in Page Layout view with the View menu displayed

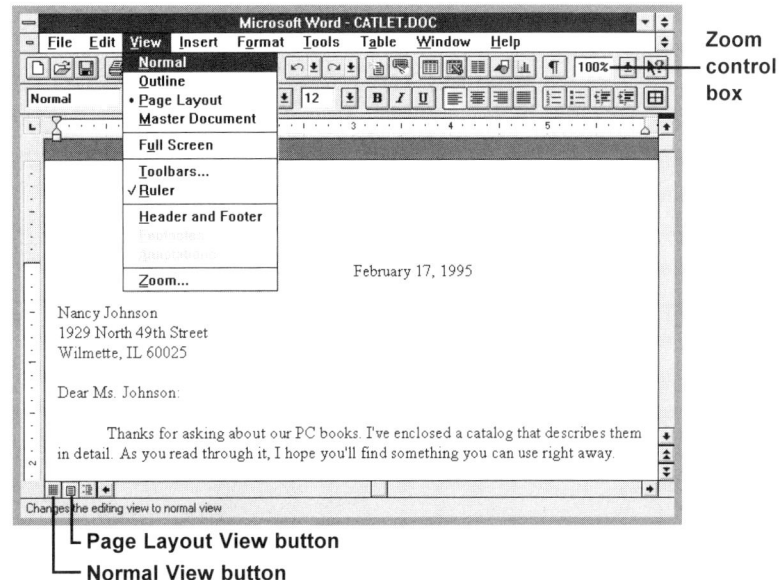

Zoom control box

└ **Page Layout View button**
└ **Normal View button**

The commands in the View menu you'll use most often

Command	Description
Normal	Displays the document in Normal view. This is the view you'll use most often as you create a document.
Page Layout	Displays the document as it will be printed, including headers and footers.
Ruler	Displays or hides the horizontal ruler. In Page Layout view, also displays or hides the vertical ruler if the Vertical Ruler option is on.
Zoom	Displays a dialog box that lets you change the magnification of the window. Affects only the current view.

How to change the view using the mouse

- To change to Normal view, click on the Normal View button. To change to Page Layout view, click on the Page Layout View button.

- To change the magnification of the window, click on the arrow to the right of the Zoom Control box in the Standard toolbar and choose a magnification option from the list that's displayed (see figure 1-3). Affects only the current view.

Note

- By default, the vertical ruler is not displayed. To display it in Page Layout view, choose the Options command from the Tools menu, click on the View tab, and check the Vertical Ruler option.

Figure 1-4   How to change the view

Exercise set 1-1

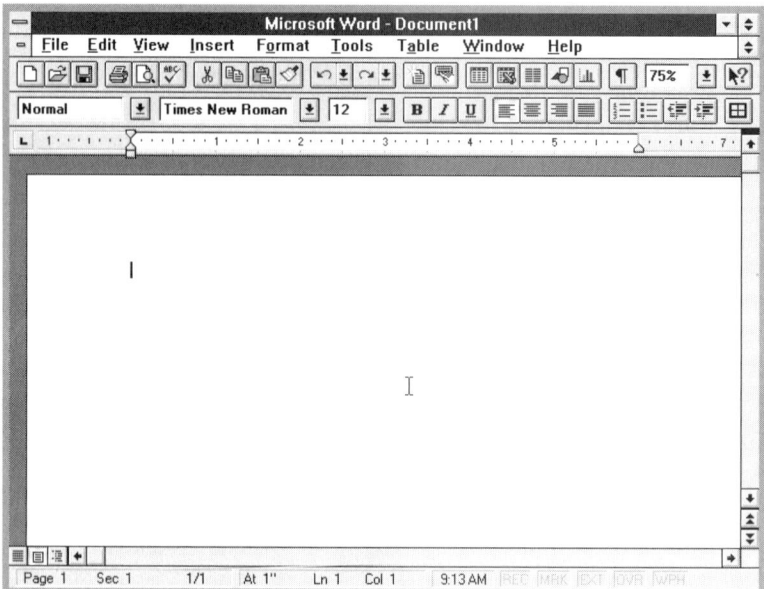

How the Word window should look after exercise 5

1. Start Word 6 for Windows. Is the Tip of the Day dialog box displayed as shown in figure 1-1? If not, choose the Tip of the Day command from the Help menu to display this dialog box. Does the Tip of the Day make sense to you at this stage of your Word 6 training? Click on the Next Tip button and ask yourself that question again. If the Tip of the Day was displayed automatically, turn it off by clicking on the Show Tips at Startup check box. Then, click on the OK button to close the dialog box.

2. What components are displayed in the Word application window on your PC? To test your terminology, name each of the components. If necessary, refer to figure 1-2. What is the current location of the insertion point? Is Overtype mode on? Move the mouse pointer inside the text area so it's displayed as an I-beam. Then, move it outside the text area to see how it changes to an arrowhead.

3. Place the mouse pointer over any of the buttons or boxes in the Standard or Formatting toolbar. Note the description of the button's function in the status bar. Is the ToolTip displayed near the button? If not, choose the Toolbars command from the View menu, check the Show ToolTips box, and click on the OK button to complete the command.

4. Click on the Show/Hide button in the Standard toolbar to display the nonprinting characters. Because you haven't entered any text, only a paragraph mark is displayed. Click on this button again to hide the paragraph mark.

5. Use the View menu as summarized in figure 1-4 to change the view in the Word application window. First, switch between Normal and Page Layout view, ending in Page Layout view. Second, turn the ruler on and off, ending with the ruler on. Third, access the Zoom dialog box and set the option to 75%. Then, click on the OK button to return to the document. Your application window should now look like the one above.

6. Use the Zoom Control list to change the display back to 100%. Then, click on the Normal View button near the bottom left of the window to return to Normal view.

Basic skills for creating a document

When you create a document with Word, you can use either the keyboard or the mouse to access commands and functions. As you enter a document, it usually makes sense to use keyboard techniques so you don't have to switch your hands between the keyboard and the mouse. Once the first draft of a document has been entered, though, it's often more efficient to use the mouse. You'll learn how to use both keyboard and mouse techniques in this topic.

How to enter text

Figure 1-5 presents the keys and keystroke combinations that you'll use most often as you enter a document. If you don't have word processing experience, you need to know that you don't have to tell Word when to start a new line. Instead, the *word wrap* feature of Word causes the text that you enter to flow automatically from the end of one line to the next line.

When you want to start a new paragraph, you press the Enter key. To start a new line without starting a new paragraph, press Shift+Enter. This notation means that you hold down the Shift key while you press the Enter key.

To start a new page at any point in a document, press Ctrl+Enter. Otherwise, a new page is automatically started when you reach the end of the previous page.

The Tab key moves the text that follows to the next *tab stop*. By default, Word has tab stops every half inch. You'll learn how to change the tab stops in chapter 3.

Keys you can use as you enter text

Key	Description
Enter	Starts a new paragraph.
Shift+Enter	Starts a new line without ending the current paragraph.
Ctrl+Enter	Starts a new page.
Tab	Tabs to the next tab stop. By default, tab stops are every half inch.

Keys that change the keyboard mode

Key	Description
Insert	Switches between Overtype and Insert mode. In Overtype mode, the characters you type replace any characters at the insertion point. In Insert mode, the characters you type are inserted into the document at the insertion point. You normally work in Insert mode. The OVR indicator in the status bar is highlighted when Overtype mode is on. You can also turn Overtype mode on or off by double-clicking on this indicator.
Caps Lock	Turns Caps Lock on or off. When it's on, the letter keys enter all capital letters. When it's off, they enter lowercase letters. The Caps Lock light on the keyboard is lit when Caps Lock is on.
Num Lock	Turns Num Lock on or off. When it's on, you can use the numeric keypad to enter numbers. When it's off, you can use the numeric keypad to move the insertion point. The Num Lock light on the keyboard is lit when Num Lock is on.

Figure 1-5   Keys for entering text and changing keyboard modes

Figure 1-5 also presents three keys that affect the operation modes of the keyboard. Most of the time, you want Overtype mode off. That way, the characters that you type are inserted into the document at the insertion point; they don't type over (or replace) the existing characters. When this mode is off, the OVR indicator in the status bar is dimmed.

You also want Caps Lock mode off unless you're entering a series of capital letters. And if your keyboard has a numeric keypad, you want Num Lock mode on so you can use the ten-key pad to enter numbers into a document.

How to move the insertion point

Figure 1-6 presents the keys you can use to move the insertion point. To start, you just need to know that the arrow keys move the insertion point one character right or left or one line up or down. As you get more experience, though, you'll find the need for faster movement of the insertion point. Then, you can experiment with the other keys that are listed.

Key	Moves the insertion point
Right arrow	Right one character
Left arrow	Left one character
Up arrow	Up one line
Down arrow	Down one line
Ctrl+Right-arrow	Right one word
Ctrl+Left-arrow	Left one word
Ctrl+Up-arrow	Up one paragraph
Ctrl+Down-arrow	Down one paragraph
Home	To the beginning of the line
End	To the end of the line
Ctrl+Home	To the start of the document
Ctrl+End	To the end of the document
Page-up	Up one screen
Page-down	Down one screen
Ctrl+Page-up	To the top of the current screen
Ctrl+Page-down	To the bottom of the current screen
Ctrl+Alt+Page-up	To the top of the previous page
Ctrl+Alt+Page-down	To the top of the next page

Figure 1-6   Keys that move the insertion point

You can also use the mouse to move the insertion point as described in figure 1-7. If the location you want to move the insertion point to is already displayed in the document window, you just click the mouse in the document.

If the location you want to move the insertion point to isn't displayed in the document window, you'll need to scroll the document to that location before you can click in the document. To scroll a document, you can use the horizontal and vertical scrolls bars. Or, if you're working in Page Layout view, you can use the Page Back and Page Forward buttons below the vertical scroll bar to scroll a full page.

It's important to note that the insertion point doesn't move when you scroll. So if you forget to click the mouse before you start typing, Word jumps back to the original insertion point.

A document in Page Layout view

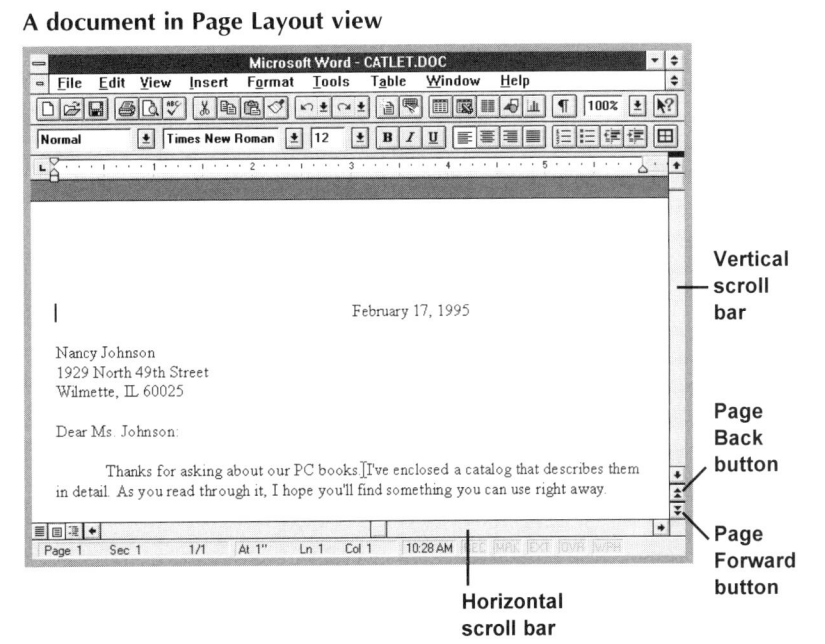

How to move the insertion point with the mouse

• Click in the document to move the insertion point to that location. If the part of the document you want to move the insertion point to isn't visible, use one of the techniques below to scroll the document window so that part of the document is visible.

How to scroll through a document

• To scroll up and down, click on the vertical scroll bar or its arrows or drag its scroll box.

• Click on the Page Back or Page Forward buttons to move one full page up or down in Page Layout view.

• To scroll left and right, click on the horizontal scroll bar or its arrows or drag its scroll box.

Figure 1-7   How to use the mouse to move the insertion point

How to select text

When you *select text* in Word, you highlight a portion of text so you can perform another operation on it, like deleting it or applying italics to it. You can use either the keyboard or the mouse to select text.

Figure 1-8 presents the skills for selecting text with the keyboard. As that figure shows, you just hold down the Shift key and use the keys that move the insertion point to select text. When you release the Shift key, the highlight remains in place until you move the insertion point. If you want to reduce or extend a selection, you can press the Shift key again and change the ending point for the selection.

A document with selected text

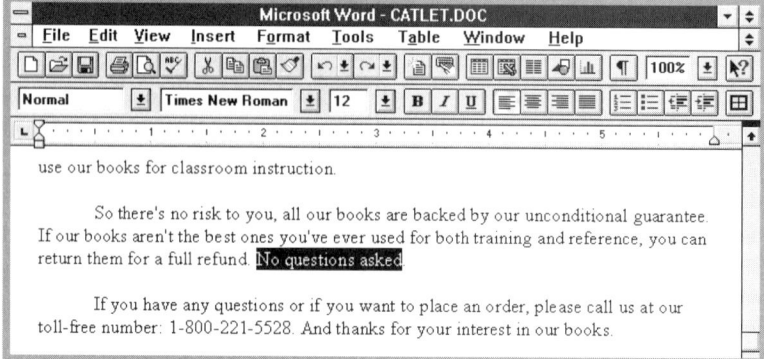

How to select text

1. Move the insertion point to the start of the text that you want to select.

2. Hold down the Shift key and use the keys in figure 1-6 to highlight the text that you want to select.

3. Release the Shift key, and the highlight remains.

How to reduce or extend a selection

• Hold down the Shift key while you move the highlight to a new ending point. Then, release the Shift key.

How to select the entire document

• Press Ctrl+A.

How to cancel the selection

• Move the insertion point.

Figure 1-8   How to select text with the keyboard

Figure 1-9 shows how to select text with the mouse. One of the easiest ways to select lines and paragraphs is to use the *selection bar* to the left of the document. When the mouse pointer reaches this area, it changes from an I-beam to an arrow that's pointing slightly to the right. Then, you can use the techniques in this figure to select lines, paragraphs, or the entire document.

When you drag the mouse to select text, you often select too much or too little text. To correct this, you can just hold down the Shift key and click on the desired ending point. This reduces or extends the selection.

If you select entire words, sentences, or paragraphs and then want to reduce or extend the selection, the selection is extended by complete words, sentences, or paragraphs. If, for example, you select a paragraph by double-clicking in the selection bar, you can extend the selection by another full paragraph just by clicking anywhere in the next paragraph while you hold down the Shift key.

A document with text selected from the selection bar

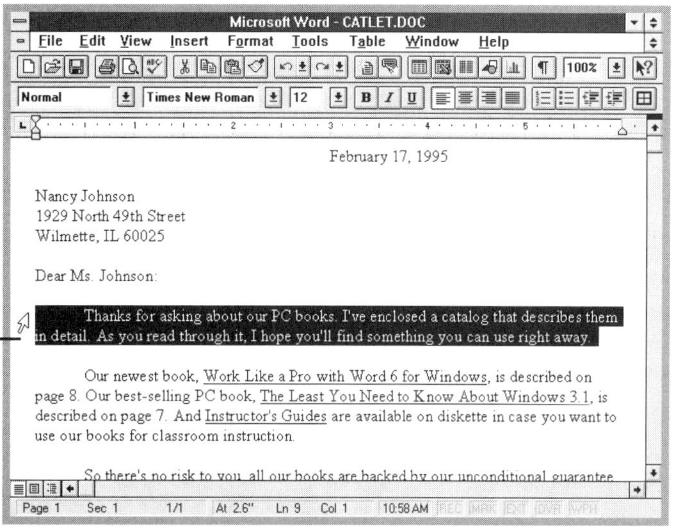

How to use the selection bar to select text

- Move the mouse pointer into the *selection bar* in the left margin of the document. When the mouse pointer is in the correct position, it changes to an arrow that points to the right.

- Click to the left of a line to select it, double-click to the left of a paragraph to select it, or triple-click anywhere in the selection bar to select the entire document.

- Drag the mouse to select more than one line. To select more than one paragraph, double-click and hold the mouse button on the second click, then drag the mouse.

Other ways to select text with the mouse

Action	What it selects
Drag	Text that it highlights
Ctrl+Click	One sentence
Double-click	One word
Triple-click	One paragraph

How to reduce or extend a selection

- Hold down the Shift key, then click at a different ending point for the selection. If you used the selection bar or multiple clicks to select text, this method reduces or extends the selection by the unit that you originally selected (word, line, sentence, or paragraph).

Note

- By default, if you begin a selection in the middle of a word and drag to include part of the next word, Word automatically selects both words and continues to select whole words as you drag. To turn this option off, choose the Options command from the Tools menu, click on the Edit tab, and click on the Automatic Word Selection option.

Figure 1-9   How to select text with the mouse

How to replace or delete text

Figure 1-10 presents the techniques for replacing and deleting text. To replace text, you select it, then type any character. If the selected text isn't replaced with the character you typed, it means that the related editing option isn't set that way on your PC. To change it, you can use the Options command in the Tools menu as described in the figure.

To delete text, you use the keys listed in figure 1-10. Note that these keys work differently depending on whether any text is selected when you use them. If, for example, you select text and press the Delete key, all of the selected text is deleted. If you press the Delete key when no text is selected, the character to the right of the insertion point is deleted.

The paragraph selected in figure 1-9 after a tab character was entered

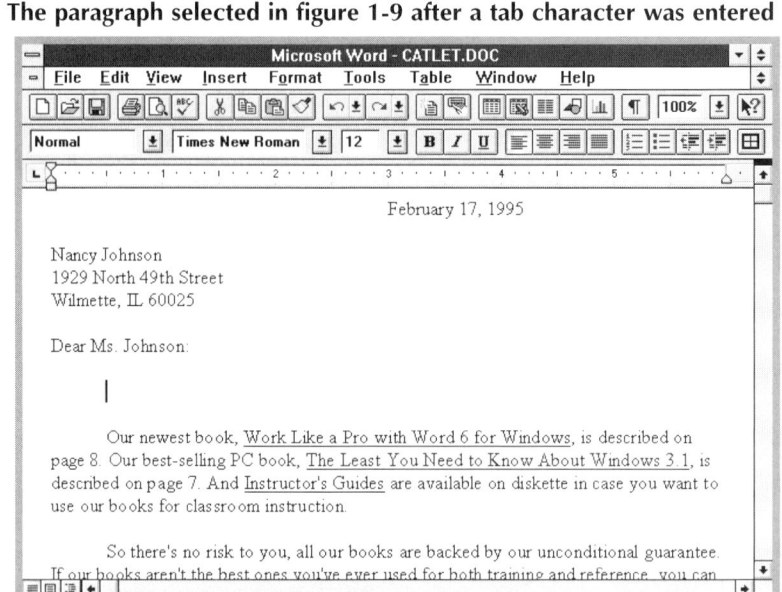

How to replace text

*   Select the text you want to replace, then type the first character of the replacement text. This deletes the selected text and replaces it with the character that you typed (unless the editing option isn't set that way).

How to delete text

Key	Deletes
Backspace	The character to the left of the insertion point or the selected text
Delete	The character to the right of the insertion point or the selected text
Ctrl+Backspace	The word to the left of the insertion point or selected text
Ctrl+Delete	The word to the right of the insertion point or the first word in the selected text

Notes

*   If the selected text isn't replaced by the next character you type as described above, it's because this editing option isn't turned on. To turn it on, choose the Options command from the Tools menu, click on the Edit tab, and click on the Typing Replaces Selection option.

*   You can also delete selected text using the Clear command in the Edit menu.

Figure 1-10   How to replace or delete text

How to apply bold, italics, and underlining to text

As you enter a document, you need to underline or italicize items like book titles and foreign words. You also need to use bold type for headings and subheadings. In Word, this type of formatting is called *character formatting*. Figure 1-11 presents two ways to apply this type of formatting.

If you've already entered the words that you want to format, you can select the words using the techniques in figure 1-8 or 1-9. Then, you can click on the appropriate button in the Formatting toolbar or press the appropriate *shortcut key* to apply bold, italics, or underlining. If necessary, you can apply more than one type of formatting to the selected text such as bold and italics.

If you want to apply character formatting as you enter the words, you can click on the appropriate toolbar buttons or press the appropriate shortcut keys to start the formatting. Then, the formatting is applied as you type the words. When you're done, click on the toolbar buttons or press the shortcut keys again to end the formatting. This can improve your efficiency because you don't have to select and format as a separate step.

If you want to remove character formatting from selected text, you can either click on the same toolbar button or press the same shortcut key you used to apply the formatting. Or, you can press Ctrl+Spacebar to remove all character formatting that has been applied to the selected text.

A document that contains underlined words

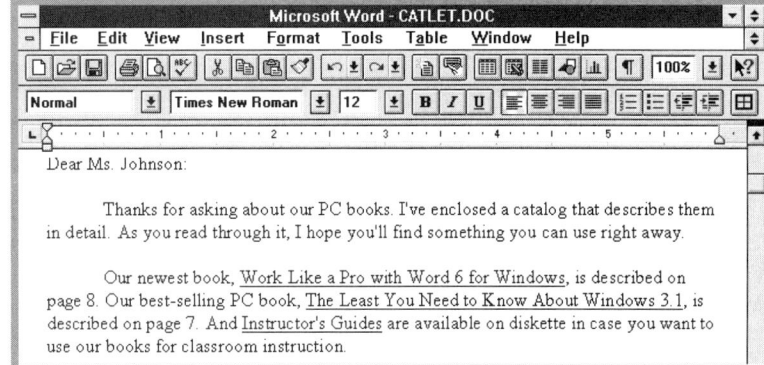

The toolbar buttons and shortcut keys for formatting characters

Button	Key	Description
B	Ctrl+B	Bold
I	Ctrl+I	Italics
U	Ctrl+U	Underlining

How to format characters after you enter them

1. Select the text that you want to format. If you want to format a single word, just move the insertion point into the word; you don't have to select the entire word.

2. Click on the toolbar button or press the shortcut key for the type of formatting that you want to apply to the selected characters.

How to format characters as you enter them

1. Click on the toolbar button or press the shortcut key for the type of formatting that you want to apply.

2. Type the characters that you want to apply the formatting to. As you type, you can see the formatting that's applied.

3. Click or. the toolbar button or press the shortcut key that started the formatting again. This ends the formatting.

How to remove character formatting

1. Select the characters that have the formatting applied to them.

2. Click on the toolbar button or press the shortcut key for the type of formatting you want to remove. Or, press Ctrl+Spacebar to remove all character formatting.

Figure 1-11   How to apply bold, italics, and underlining to text

How to insert the current date

All letters, memos, and reports should include the date. The professional way to enter the current date into a document is to use the command that's summarized in figure 1-12. To access this command, you choose the Date and Time command from the Insert menu as indicated by the notation at the top of the figure.

If you check the Insert as Field box in the Date and Time dialog box, the current date is inserted as a *field* that is brought up-to-date each time you print a document. Then, if you create a document one day and print it two days letter, the printed document has the current date. In contrast, if you insert a date as *text*, the date doesn't change unless you edit it.

You can also use the first shortcut key in figure 1-12 to enter the date. When you use this shortcut key, the date is inserted into the document as a field. If that's not what you want, you can use the second shortcut key shown in this figure to convert the date from a field to text. But first, you have to move the insertion point into the date field.

In figure 1-12, you can see that many formats are available for the date. Some of these include the current time. These formats are useful when you are printing several drafts of a document on the same day. Then, the times help you keep track of the different versions.

Access

Menu   Insert ➡ Date and Time

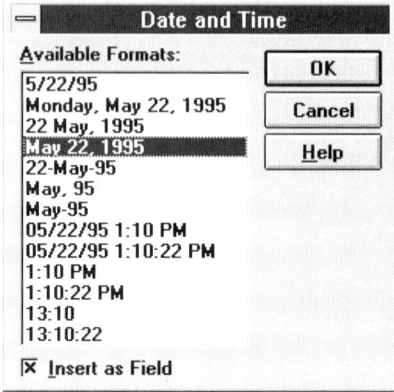

Operation

- Double-click on the format you want to use for the current date to insert the date and return to your document. Or click on the format, then click on the OK button.

- If the Insert as Field box is checked, the date is inserted into your document as a *field* so it's automatically updated to reflect the current date. If this box isn't checked, the date is inserted as text just as if you entered it from the keyboard. To turn this option on or off, just click on the check box.

Keys for inserting the date

Key	Description
Alt+Shift+D	Inserts the current date as a field in the default date format or in the date format that you last used.
Ctrl+Shift+F9	Converts the selected date from an automatically updated field to text. To select the date, move the insertion point into the field. (By default, the field will be shaded when the insertion point is in it.)

Notes

- By default, Word fields are displayed as *field results*. In the case of a date field, the field results are a date in the format you choose. Word fields can also be displayed as *field codes*, which are cryptic instructions enclosed in brackets that tell Word how to produce the results.

- If you insert a field and it's displayed as a field code, press Alt+F9 to display the field results.

- By default, fields are updated automatically when you print a document. If you print a document and the fields aren't updated, choose the Options command from the Tools menu, click on the Print tab, and check the Update Fields option.

Figure 1-12   How to insert the current date into a document

Exercise set 1-2

June 17, 1995

Nancy Johnson
1929 North 49th Street
Wilmette, IL 60025

Dear Ms. Johnson:

      Thanks for asking about our PC books. I've enclosed a catalog that describes them in detail. As you read through it, I hope you'll find something you can use right away.

      Our newest book, <u>Work Like a Pro with Word 6 for Windows</u>, is described on page 8. Our best-selling PC book, <u>The Least You Need to Know About Windows 3.1</u>, is described on page 7. And <u>Instructor's Guides</u> are available on diskette in case you want to use our books for classroom instruction.

      So there's no risk to you, all our books are backed by our unconditional guarantee. If our books aren't the best ones you've ever used for both training and reference, you can return them for a full refund. <u>No questions asked</u>.

      If you have any questions or if you want to place an order, please call us at our toll-free number: 1-800-221-5528. And thanks for your interest in our books.

      Sincerely,

      Your Name

The document you'll enter in this exercise set

This exercise set has you enter the letter above into an empty document window. If you understand everything so far and feel confident that you can enter this document without any help, go to it. Otherwise, you can get some guidance as you enter the document by going through the steps that follow.

1. Press the Insert key and note how the OVR indicator in the status bar changes each time you press it. When it is off (dimmed), continue.

2. Press the Tab key six times to tab in three inches from the left margin of the document. Next, insert the current date as a field using one of the techniques presented in figure 1-12. Then, press the Enter key twice to drop down two lines.

3. Type the name and address. To end each line, press the Enter key once. After the last line, press the Enter key a second time to skip a line between the name and address and the greeting.

4. Type the greeting (Dear Ms. Johnson:), and press the Enter key twice to skip a line before the first paragraph in the body of the letter.

5. Type the first paragraph in the body of the letter. To indent the paragraph, press the Tab key once. Then, as you type, notice the automatic word wrap at the end of each line. But don't expect your lines to end at the same points as those in the letter above because your page margins, font, and font size may be different. If you make a mistake as you're typing, use the techniques in figure 1-10 to replace or delete the text. To end the paragraph and skip one line, press the Enter key twice.

6. Use the same techniques to type the next three paragraphs in the body of the letter. To underline the book titles and the last sentence in the third paragraph, click on the Underline button in the Formatting toolbar or press Ctrl+U before you begin typing them. Click on the Underline button or press Ctrl+U when you're done so the text that follows isn't underlined.

7. To type the signature block, press the Tab key six times to tab in three inches from the left margin, type the word *Sincerely*, and press the Enter key four times. Then, tab six times, and type your name.

Exercise set 1-3

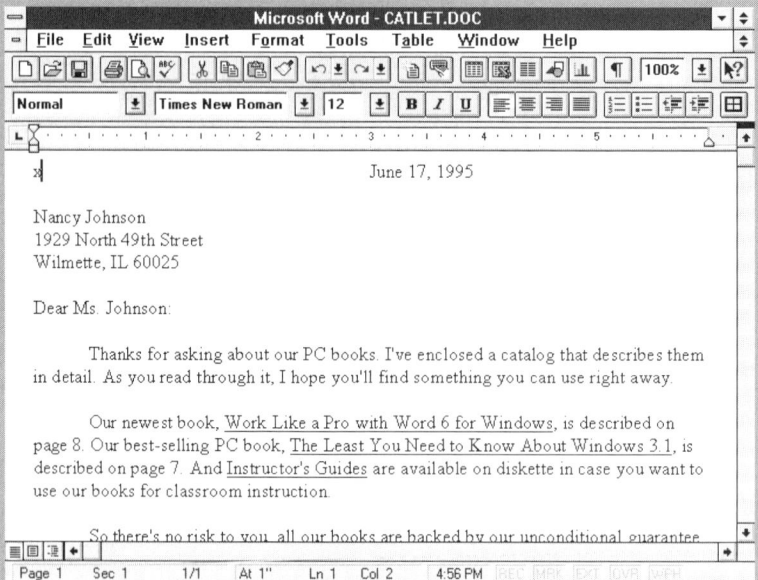

How the document should look after you enter the letter *X* in exercise 1

With the letter that you created for exercise set 1-2 still on the screen, perform the following exercises.

1. Press Ctrl+Home to move the insertion point to the top of the document. Next, use the mouse to scroll to the bottom of the document, but don't click in the document. Then, type the letter *X*. Where is this letter inserted into the document? Press the backspace key to delete it.

2. Move the insertion point to the beginning of the first paragraph in the body of the letter before the tab character. Then, hold down the Shift key and press Ctrl+Down-arrow to select the entire paragraph. Move the insertion point to cancel the selection. Now, double-click in the selection bar to the left of the first paragraph to select it. Click outside the paragraph to cancel the selection. Then, triple-click on the first paragraph to select it. Which of these three techniques do you prefer? Click outside the selected paragraph to cancel the selection.

3. Use the selection bar as described in figure 1-9 to select all four paragraphs in the body of the letter. Next, click somewhere else in the document to cancel the selection. Then, triple-click on the first paragraph in the letter to select it; hold down the Shift key and click in the last paragraph to extend the selection to all four paragraphs; and click anywhere in the document to cancel the selection.

4. Select the last sentence of the third paragraph by holding down the Ctrl key and clicking the mouse in the sentence. Then, click on the Underline button in the toolbar or press Ctrl+U to remove the underline; click on the Italic button or press Ctrl+I to apply italics; and click elsewhere in the document to remove the highlighting so you can see the result.

5. Select the first book title in the second paragraph of the letter. This title should be underlined. Then, use the toolbar buttons or shortcut keys to remove the underline and apply italics. Repeat this procedure for the other italicized titles.

How to use the commands in the File menu

Figure 1-13 summarizes the commands in the File menu that you should know how to use. If you've used other Windows programs, you may already be familiar with many of these commands. In this chapter, you'll learn how to use all of the commands in this summary except for Templates, Page Setup, and Print Preview, which are presented in later chapters. The Find File command isn't presented in this book because it doesn't perform a basic Word function.

The File menu

New...	Ctrl+N
Open...	Ctrl+O
Close	
Save	Ctrl+S
Save As...	
Save All	
Find File...	
Summary Info...	
Templates...	
Page Setup...	
Print Preview	
Print...	Ctrl+P
1 RWMANUAL.DOC	
2 STAFFMTG.DOC	
Exit	

Command	Description
New	Starts a new document in a new window and lets you choose the template to be used for the new document.
Open	Retrieves an existing document into a new document window.
Close	Closes the active document window and document.
Save	Saves the active document on disk. If the document hasn't been saved before, this works like the Save As command.
Save As	Saves the active document on disk after you choose a drive and directory and provide a file name.
Save All	Saves all the open documents on disk.
Summary Info	Displays the Summary Info dialog box (see figure 1-15).
Templates	Lets you work with templates (see chapter 5).
Page Setup	Lets you change the page setup for the active document (see chapter 3).
Print Preview	Displays the active document as it will appear when printed (see chapter 3).
Print	Prints the active document.
filename	Opens the file that's named.
Exit	Exits from Word. If necessary, gives you a chance to save the open documents.

Figure 1-13   The commands in the File menu

How to print a document

Figure 1-14 summarizes the use of the Print command. The notation at the top of this figure shows three ways to start this command. First, you can choose the Print command from the File menu. Second, you can click on the Print button in the Standard toolbar. Third, you can press Ctrl+P. This notation is used throughout this book to show at a glance the various ways that a command can be accessed.

When the Print dialog box is displayed, you specify the number of copies you want printed. If the document consists of more than one page, you can also specify the pages you want printed. If you want to print one copy of all the pages in a document, though, you can just click on the OK button.

If your PC is on a network so more than one printer is available to you, you can click on the Printer button to display another dialog box. Then, you can choose the printer that you want to use.

Access

Menu   File ➡ Print

Standard toolbar   🖨 (no dialog box is displayed)

Shortcut key   Ctrl+P

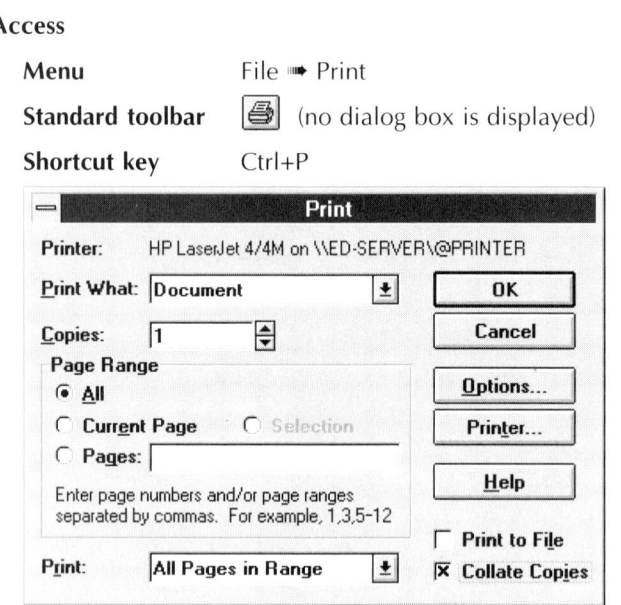

How to use the Print dialog box

- To print one copy of the document on the default printer, just click on the OK button. To print more than one copy, enter a number in the Copies box before you click on the OK button.

- A description of the printer that's going to be used is given at the top of the Print dialog box. If you want to change to another printer, click on the Printer button in the Print dialog box. Then, in the Print Setup dialog box that's displayed, double-click on the printer that you want to change to.

- To print the summary information for a document (see figure 1-15), choose the Summary Info option from the Print What list. This list also includes options for printing other information related to the document.

How to use the Print toolbar button

- The Print button in the Standard toolbar prints one copy of the document with the print settings that you last used. No dialog box is displayed when you start the Print command this way.

Figure 1-14   How to print a document

How to save a document

If you've used PCs before, you know that a document on the screen is lost when you turn the PC off. So if you want to be able to use the document again, you need to save it on disk. To do that, you use the Save or Save As command as described in figure 1-15.

When you issue the Save or Save As command for a new document, Word displays the Save As dialog box. This dialog box lets you choose the drive and directory for the file and supply a file name for it. If you don't supply a file name, Word creates one for you like DOC1.DOC, but you usually don't want that.

When you finish the Save As dialog box, the Summary Info dialog box may be displayed before the file is saved. This dialog box lets you enter information that can help you identify the contents of the file. If necessary, you can change that information later by using the Summary Info command in the File menu.

Once a document has been saved, the Save command doesn't display the Save As dialog box. Instead, Word automatically saves the updated file in its previous location. So if you want to save the updated version of the document in a new file with a new name, you have to use the Save As command.

Additional information

✓ You can use the Save tab of the Options command in the Tools menu to turn the Prompt for Summary Info option on or off. You can also access this tab by clicking on the Options button in the Save As dialog box.

Access

Menu   File ➡ Save (for a new file)
                File ➡ Save As (for an old file)

Standard toolbar   🖫 (for a new file)

Shortcut key   Ctrl+S (for a new file)

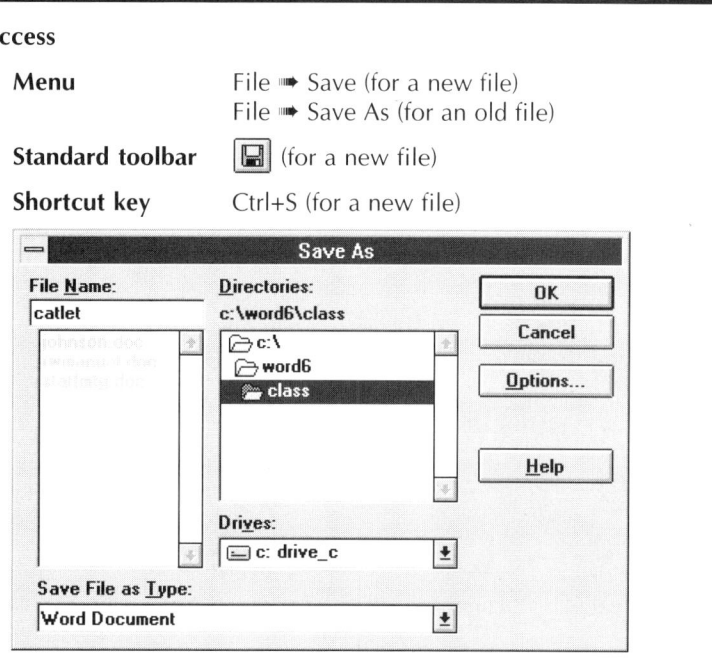

Procedure

1. Access the Save As dialog box, and identify the drive and directory for the file in the Drives and Directories boxes.

2. Replace the default name in the File Name box by typing a valid file name when the default name is highlighted. If the default name isn't highlighted, you can double-click on it or press Alt+N to highlight it. If you omit the extension, DOC is used.

3. Click on the OK button. If the Summary Info option is on, this dialog box appears:

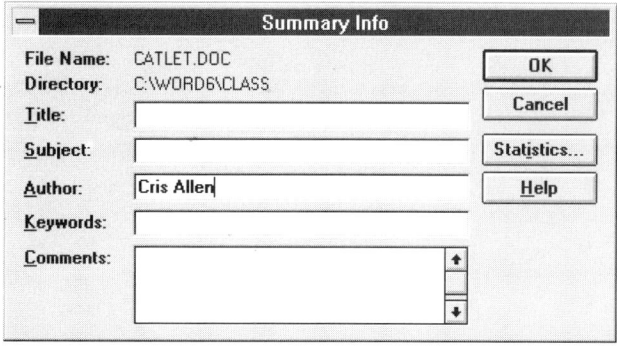

4. Type the required information into this dialog box, and click on the OK button to complete the command. Or, click on the Cancel button to save the document without summary information.

Notes

• The first time you access the Save command for a new document, the Save As dialog box is displayed. After that, the document is saved with no intervening dialog box, thus replacing the previous version of the file.

• If you have any trouble identifying the drive or directory in step 1, please refer to figure P-17 in the prerequisites chapter.

Figure 1-15   How to save a document

When you use Word, you should know that you can open more than one document at the same time. Then, you can use the Save All command to save all the open documents with a single command. If a document hasn't been saved before, the Save As dialog box is displayed for it. Otherwise, the document is saved with no intervening dialog box.

How to close a document

When you close a document, you close its document window. To do that, you can use the Close command as summarized in figure 1-16. If you haven't made any changes to the document since you last saved it, the active document window is closed immediately. Otherwise, a dialog box like the one in this figure is displayed. Then, you can save your last changes or close the document without saving the changes.

Procedure

1. Choose the Close command from the File menu. If the document hasn't been saved, this dialog box appears:

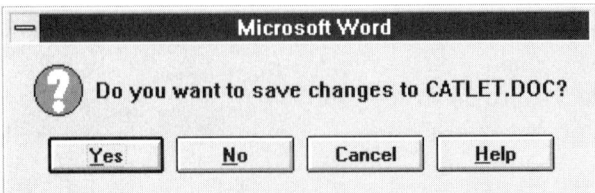

2. Click on the Yes button if you want to save the changes; click on the No button if you don't want to save the changes; and click on the Cancel button if you want to cancel the operation and return to the document.

Notes

- If you're closing a new document and you click on the Yes button to save the changes, Word displays the Save As and Summary Info dialog boxes shown in figure 1-15. When you complete these dialog boxes, the file is saved and closed.

- If you're saving an old document and you click on the Yes button, the file is saved and closed without any intervening dialog boxes.

- When a file is closed, its document window is closed too.

Figure 1-16   How to close a document

How to open a document

Figure 1-17 summarizes the use of the Open command. This is the command you use when you want to retrieve a file that you saved previously. When you open a file, it is retrieved from disk and displayed in a new document window.

In the Open dialog box, you identify the drive and directory that the file is stored in. When the correct path is shown at the top of the Directories box, all files in that directory with the DOC extension are listed in the File Name list. Then, you can double-click on the file name that you want to open.

By default, Word lists the last four files you opened at the bottom of the File menu, just before the Exit command. To open any one of these files, just pull down the File menu and click on the file name or press the number before the file name. This is the fastest way to open the files that you've worked on most recently.

Additional information

✓ If you use one directory for all or most of your files, you can establish that directory as the default by using the Options command in the Tools menu. To do that, click on the File Locations tab and change the Documents directory. Then, when the Open or Save As dialog box is displayed for the first time in each Word session, the default directory is assumed.

✓ You can also change the number of file names that are displayed at the bottom of the File menu by using the Options command in the Tools menu. To do that, click on the General tab and enter a number for the Recently Used File List option.

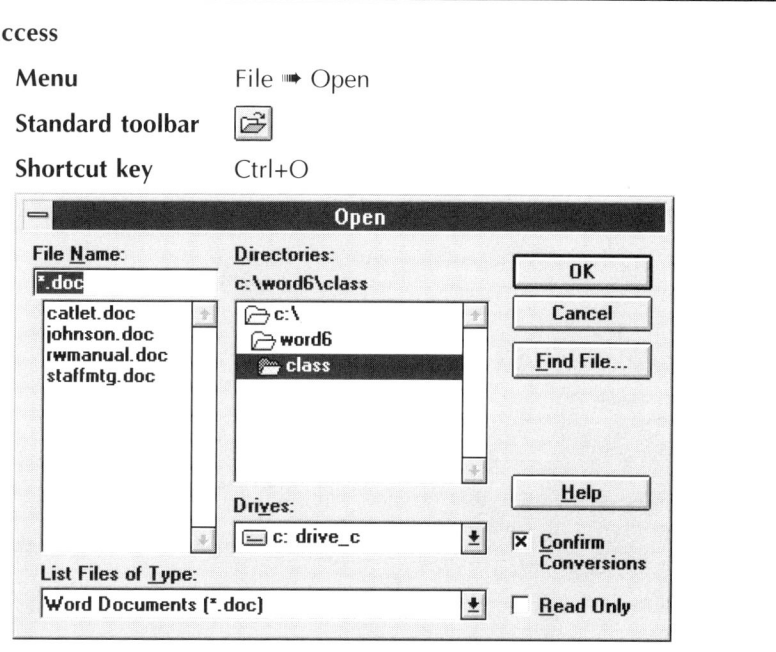

Access

Menu	File ➡ Open
Standard toolbar	🖿
Shortcut key	Ctrl+O

Procedure

1. Access the Open dialog box.

2. Identify the drive and directory that contains the document using the Drives and Directories lists. Then, the files in that directory are displayed in the File Name list box.

3. Double-click on the name of the file you want to open, or highlight the name and click on the OK button.

Notes

• A file that has the DOC extension is automatically associated with Word. However, a Word file doesn't have to have that extension.

• If you want to open a file that doesn't have the DOC extension, you can use the List Files of Type list to display files with other extensions. To display all the documents in a directory, choose All Files from this list.

• If you have any trouble identifying the drive or directory in step 2, please refer to figure P-17 in the prerequisites chapter.

• If the file you want to open is one of the last four files you worked on, you can open the file by choosing the file name from the bottom of the File menu.

Figure 1-17   How to open a document

How to start a new document

If you want to start a new document when you're working on another open document, you can use the New command that's summarized in figure 1-18. This command opens another document window so you can enter a new document.

If you use the toolbar button or Ctrl+N to start the New command, no dialog box is displayed; the document window is opened right away. If you start the New command from the File menu, though, the New dialog box is displayed. This box lets you choose a *template* or *wizard* that the new document should be started from.

In chapter 5, you'll learn how templates and wizards can help you work more professionally and productively. For now, though, you just need to know that all Word documents are based on a template. If none is specifically selected, the Normal template is used, and this template is satisfactory for simple documents. When the New dialog box is displayed, the Normal template is shown by default so you can just click on the OK button to start a new document based on that template.

How to exit from Word

When you issue the Exit command, Word ends. If you haven't saved the changes that you made to one or more open documents, a dialog box is displayed for each one. Then, you can save or ignore the last changes that you made to that document. To avoid confusion when several documents are open, though, it's often best to close one file at a time before you exit from Word.

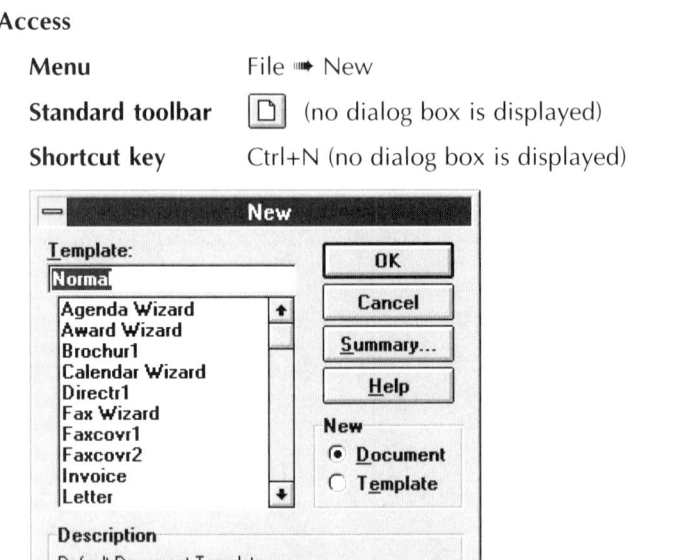

Access

Menu	File ➡ New
Standard toolbar	🗋 (no dialog box is displayed)
Shortcut key	Ctrl+N (no dialog box is displayed)

Operation

- If you use the toolbar button or Ctrl+N to start a new document, the new document is based on the Normal template.

- To start a document from the Normal template when the New dialog box is displayed, click on the OK button.

- To start a document from another template or a wizard when the New dialog box is displayed, double-click on the template or wizard name. Or, click on the name, then click on the OK button.

Notes

- All Word documents are based on a template. The template can provide page formatting, styles, and text.

- The default template is the Normal template. For now, you can start all documents from that template. Then, you can learn how to use other templates in chapter 5.

Figure 1-18   How to start a new document

Exercise set 1-4

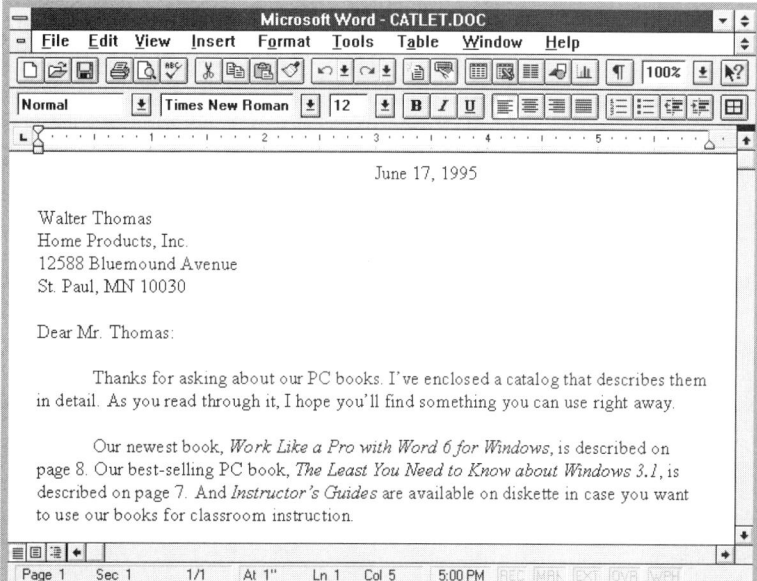

**How the document should look
after exercise 7**

1. Use the Print command or Print button as described in figure 1-14 to print one copy of the letter that you developed in exercise sets 1-2 and 1-3.

2. Click on the Save button in the Standard toolbar so the Save As dialog box is displayed. Next, choose the drive and directory that you want to save the letter on, and type CATLET in the File Name box without an extension. Then, click on the OK button.

3. Is the Summary Info dialog box displayed when you complete the Save As dialog box? If so, enter Catalog Letter as the title, enter Marketing as the subject, enter your name as Author, and click on the OK button to complete the Save command.

4. Use the Save command to save the file again. Start this command from the File menu, with the Save toolbar button, or by pressing Ctrl+S. Note that no dialog box is displayed.

5. Delete the last sentence in the second paragraph by selecting it and pressing the Delete key. Then, use the Close command to close the file. In the Close dialog box, choose No so this last change isn't saved on disk.

6. Use the Open command in the File menu to open the CATLET file. Then, use the Save As command to save it in a new file with the name JOHNSON. While the Save As dialog box is displayed, click on the Options button. If the Prompt for Summary Info option is on, click on it to turn it off. Then, click on the OK button to return to the Save As dialog box, and click on the OK button to save the file. Note that the file name in the title bar of the document window has changed. Then, close the file.

7. Use the file name at the bottom of the File menu to open the CATLET file again. Then, change the inside address and greeting as indicated in the document shown above and print the file.

8. Press Ctrl+N or click on the New button in the Standard toolbar to open a new document window. Note that two document windows are now open. Type your name in the new document window.

9. Close the new document window without saving the changes. Close the CATLET file, but save the changes. And exit from Word.

Perspective

If you've done the exercises for this chapter, you have now entered, printed, and saved two documents. You've done this using the same commands and techniques that the best professionals use. And you're ready to learn the editing and formatting skills that are presented in the next two chapters.

Summary

- When you use Word, a *document* is entered into a *document window* that's within the Word *application window*. Within a document window, the *insertion point* indicates where the next action will take place. When the mouse pointer is within a document, it takes the form of an *I-beam*.

- The Standard and Formatting toolbars contain *toolbar buttons* that let you perform pre-defined functions and drop-down lists that let you choose from a variety of options.

- You can change the appearance of the Word window by hiding or displaying the rulers, by displaying a document in Normal or Page Layout view, or by changing the display size.

- To efficiently enter a document, you need to know the functions of special keys and keystroke combinations. You also need to know how to *select text*, how to delete or replace text, and how to apply bold, italics, and underlining to the characters you enter. You can perform most of these functions with either the keyboard or the mouse.

- You can insert the current date into a document as a *field* or as *text*. By default, a date field is automatically updated whenever the document is printed.

- You can use commands in the File menu to print, save, close, and open a document, start a new document, or exit from Word. When you save or open a file, you need to specify the drive and directory for the file. You can also use buttons in the Standard toolbar and shortcut keys to start some of these commands.

Chapter 2

How to edit a document

When you *edit* a document, you make changes to it. That includes functions that you've already learned like adding text to and deleting text from a document. It also includes functions like correcting misspellings, rearranging the sentences in a paragraph, and rearranging the paragraphs in a document.

In this chapter, you'll learn the Word 6 features that make editing so easy. If you like to use the keyboard to perform these editing functions, you can do that. If you prefer to use the mouse for most editing functions, you can do that too. With Word 6, you can use the editing techniques that work best for you.

An introduction to the editing functions

When you use Word 6, you can start most commands and functions in two or more ways, and that's particularly true for editing functions. In this introduction, you'll learn how to start editing functions with menu commands, with toolbar buttons, with shortcut keys, and with shortcut menus. Then, you'll learn how to undo or repeat an editing action.

The editing commands that every Word user should know

Figure 2-1 summarizes the editing commands that every Word user should know how to use. All of these commands except the last three are in the Edit menu. The last three commands are in the Tools menu.

Note that most of the commands in figure 2-1 have shortcut keys listed to their right. If you use a command frequently, it's worth taking the time to memorize its shortcut key. Then, you can perform the function from the keyboard without using the menu.

The Edit menu

Undo Clear	Ctrl+Z
Repeat Clear	Ctrl+Y
Cut	Ctrl+X
Copy	Ctrl+C
Paste	Ctrl+V
Paste Special...	
Clear	Delete
Select All	Ctrl+A
Find...	Ctrl+F
Replace...	Ctrl+H
Go To...	Ctrl+G
AutoText...	
Bookmark...	

The Tools menu

Spelling...	F7
Grammar...	
Thesaurus...	Shift+F7
Hyphenation...	
Language...	
Word Count...	
AutoCorrect...	
Mail Merge...	
Envelopes and Labels...	
Protect Document...	
Revisions...	
Macro...	
Customize...	
Options...	

Command	Shortcut	Function
Undo	Ctrl+Z	Reverses the last action.
Repeat	Ctrl+Y or F4	Repeats the last action. This command changes to Redo if the last action was an Undo operation.
Cut	Ctrl+X	Deletes the selected text and copies it to the clipboard.
Copy	Ctrl+C	Copies the selected text to the clipboard.
Paste	Ctrl+V	Inserts the contents of the clipboard into the document at the insertion point.
Clear	Delete	Deletes the selected text.
Select All	Ctrl+A	Selects the entire document.
Find	Ctrl+F	Lets you search for text, formatting, and special characters.
Replace	Ctrl+H	Lets you search for and replace text, formatting, and special characters.
AutoText		Lets you create abbreviations and their replacements so you can use the abbreviations as a quick way to enter text into a document.
Spelling	F7	Starts a spelling check.
Thesaurus	Shift+F7	Starts the thesaurus.
AutoCorrect		Automatically replaces abbreviations with the replacements you specify. You can also use this feature to automatically correct entry errors you specify.

Figure 2-1   Editing commands that every Word user should know

The toolbar buttons for editing

Figure 2-2 presents the buttons in the Standard toolbar that you can use for editing. If you compare these toolbar buttons to the commands in figure 2-1, you'll see that the toolbar buttons provide another way to access some of these commands. So if you like working with a mouse, you'll want to take advantage of these buttons.

Button	Name	Function
	Spelling	Starts a spelling check.
	Cut	Deletes the selected text and copies it to the clipboard.
	Copy	Copies the selected text to the clipboard.
	Paste	Inserts the contents of the clipboard into the document at the insertion point.
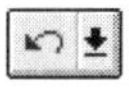	Undo	Reverses the last action. If you click on the arrow to the right of this button, a list is displayed that lets you reverse more than one of the last actions.
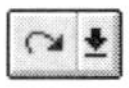	Redo	Reverses the last Undo action. If you click on the arrow to the right of this button, a list is displayed that lets you reverse more than one of the last Undo actions.
	AutoText	Lets you add an abbreviation to the AutoText list for the selected text or replace an abbreviation with its AutoText entry. The name of the button changes from Insert AutoText when no text is selected to Edit AutoText when text is selected.

Figure 2-2 **Editing buttons in the Standard toolbar**

How to use shortcut menus

Yet another way to start some of the editing functions is to use *shortcut menus* as summarized in figure 2-3. To display a shortcut menu, you just point the mouse at one of the areas listed in the figure and click on the right mouse button.

The shortcut menus are *context sensitive*. In other words, they include the commands that are appropriate for the area that you pointed to. In figure 2-3, for example, the mouse pointer was pointing at selected text, so the menu includes three editing commands and three formatting commands that can be used with a selection.

In contrast, if you point the mouse at a toolbar and click the right mouse button, the menu includes the names of seven of the available toolbars. Then, to hide or display a toolbar, you can just click on its name.

The shortcut menu for selected text

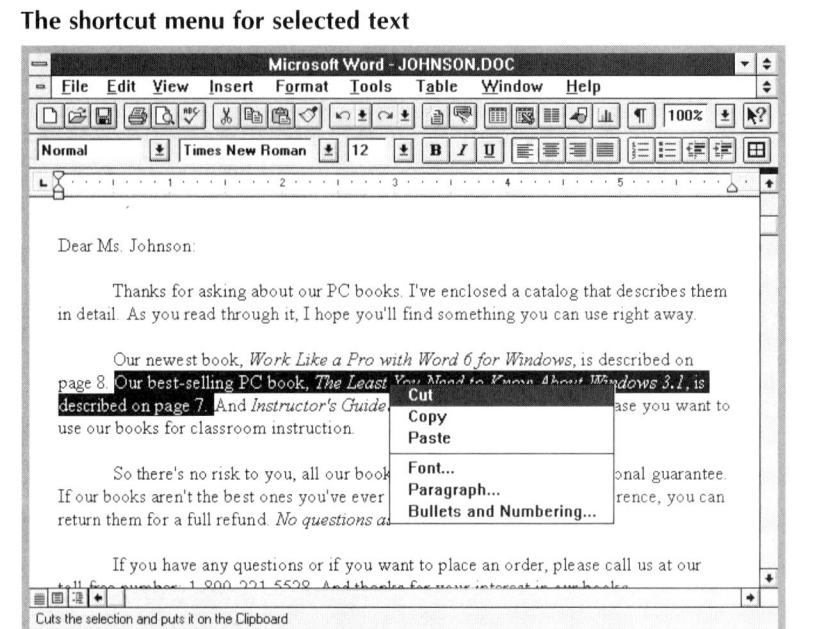

How to display a shortcut menu

- Press the right mouse button when the mouse pointer is in an area that provides a shortcut menu.

Areas that provide shortcut menus

- Text area
- Selected text
- Selection bar
- Toolbars

How to choose a command from a shortcut menu

- Press and hold the right mouse button down to display the shortcut menu; drag the highlight to the command you want; and release the right mouse button.

- Click and release the right mouse button to display the shortcut menu. Then, point to the command you want and click the left mouse button.

Figure 2-3   How to use shortcut menus

How to undo or redo an action

Occasionally, you'll accidentally delete text or perform an editing action that didn't work the way you expected. Then, you'll wish you could undo the action...and you can. Just use the techniques that are summarized in figure 2-4.

From the keyboard, just press Ctrl+Z. With the mouse, just click on the Undo button in the Standard toolbar.

Change your mind and want to reverse what you've undone? Just press Ctrl+Y or click on the Redo button.

If want to undo or redo more than one action, you can press or click repeatedly. You can also use the Undo and Redo lists that drop down from the Standard toolbar. Unless you're going to undo or redo many actions, though, there's little or no benefit to using the lists.

How to repeat an action

The second command in the Edit menu is the Repeat command. The word following the command changes based on your last action, and it becomes the Redo command if you've just used the Undo command. Although the Redo command can be useful, you rarely need the Repeat command and it doesn't always work the way you expect it to.

An Undo list that has been dropped down from the Standard toolbar

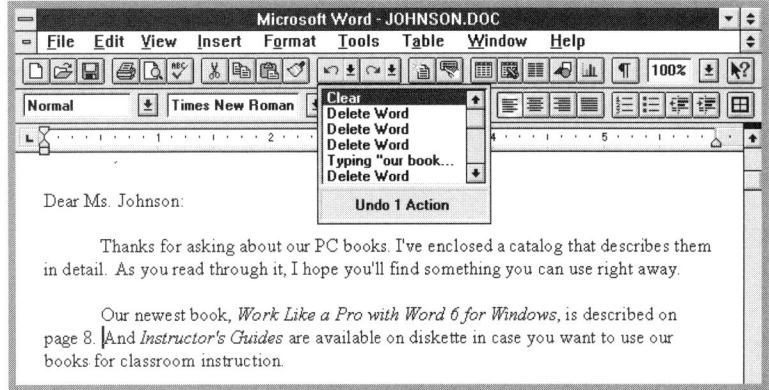

How to start the Undo and Redo commands

	Undo	Redo
Edit menu	Undo	Redo
Standard toolbar	↺ ±	↻ ±
Shortcut key	Ctrl+Z	Ctrl+Y or F4

How to undo the last editing actions

• Start the Undo command using one of the methods shown above. To undo more than one action, issue the command repeatedly. As you issue the command, you can see the actions undone.

How to redo the last actions that were undone

• Start the Redo command using one of the methods shown above. Issue the command repeatedly to redo more than one action. As you issue the command, you can see the undone actions redone.

How to use the Undo or Redo lists

• Click on the arrow to the right of the Undo button to display a list of the last editing actions as shown above. Then, click on the deepest item in the list that you want to undo to undo all of the last actions up to and including the one you click on.

• The Redo list works like the Undo list, but it only lists items if the last action was an Undo operation. If it wasn't, no list is displayed.

Note

• You can't undo all word processing actions. For instance, you can't undo actions like saving or printing a file. You can, however, undo most editing actions.

Figure 2-4   How to undo and redo editing actions

60

Exercise set 2-1

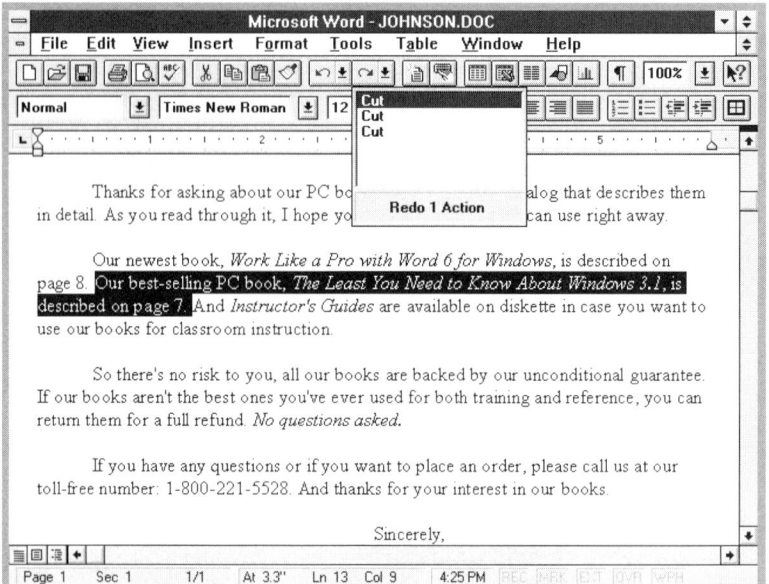

How the Redo list should look when you pull it down in exercise 6

1. Start Word and open the file named JOHNSON that you created for chapter 1. Move the mouse pointer anywhere in the document, and click the right mouse button to display the shortcut menu. Note the commands that are displayed. Then, click the left mouse button outside the menu to close it.

2. Select the second paragraph in the body of the letter, click the right mouse button on the selection to display the shortcut menu, and choose the Cut command to delete the paragraph. To undo that deletion, press Ctrl+Z.

3. Move the mouse pointer over one of the toolbars, click the right mouse button, and choose the Borders command so that toolbar is displayed along with the others. Press Ctrl+Z to see if that action can be undone. If it can't be undone, display the shortcut menu for toolbars again, and choose the Borders command again to hide that toolbar.

4. Delete the second sentence in both the second and third paragraphs of the letter, and delete the entire fourth paragraph. To undo all three deletions, click on the Undo button three times in a row. To redo the deletions, click on the Redo button three times in a row.

5. Click on the arrow to the right of the Undo button to see the list of actions that can be undone, and click on the second action in the list to redo the last two actions. Note that the fourth paragraph and the second sentence in the third paragraph are restored, but the second sentence in the second paragraph is still deleted. Then, use the Undo button or list to restore the second sentence in the second paragraph.

6. Click on the arrow to the right of the Redo button to see that you can still redo any of the last three Undo actions. Click outside the list to close it. Then, close the file without saving the changes.

How to move and copy selected text

When you edit a document, you often move words, sentences, or paragraphs from one place in the document to another. You may also want to copy text from one place to another. With Word 6, you can perform either of these functions in two ways.

With the Cut, Copy, and Paste commands

The standard way to move and copy text with any Windows program is to use the Cut, Copy, and Paste commands. This is illustrated in figure 2-5. Note that you can access these commands from the Edit or shortcut menu or with shortcut keys or toolbar buttons.

To start a move or copy operation, select the text that you want to move or copy. Then, use the Cut or Copy command to place the selection on the *clipboard*. This is a temporary storage area that you don't see. To copy the text from the clipboard into the document, use the Paste command. If you want to repeat the Paste command, you can because the contents of the clipboard remain there until replaced by the next Cut or Copy command.

How to start the Cut, Copy, and Paste commands

	Cut	**Copy**	**Paste**
Edit or shortcut menu	Cut	Copy	Paste
Standard toolbar	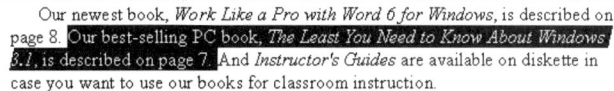		
Shortcut key	Ctrl+X	Ctrl+C	Ctrl+V

How to move text

1. Select the text you want to move:

   > Our newest book, *Work Like a Pro with Word 6 for Windows*, is described on page 8. Our best-selling PC book, *The Least You Need to Know About Windows 3.1*, is described on page 7. And *Instructor's Guides* are available on diskette in case you want to use our books for classroom instruction.

2. Issue the Cut command using one of the methods shown above. The text is deleted from the document and placed on the clipboard:

   > Our newest book, *Work Like a Pro with Word 6 for Windows*, is described on page 8. And *Instructor's Guides* are available on diskette in case you want to use our books for classroom instruction.

3. Move the insertion point where you want to insert the text:

   > Our newest book, *Work Like a Pro with Word 6 for Windows*, is described on page 8. And *Instructor's Guides* are available on diskette in case you want to use our books for classroom instruction.

4. Issue the Paste command using one of the methods shown above, and the clipboard text is inserted into the document:

   > Our best-selling PC book, *The Least You Need to Know About Windows 3.1*, is described on page 7. Our newest book, *Work Like a Pro with Word 6 for Windows*, is described on page 8. And *Instructor's Guides* are available on diskette in case you want to use our books for classroom instruction.

How to copy text

- Use the same procedure as for moving text, but issue the Copy command in step 2 using one of the methods shown above.

Notes

- The text on the clipboard remains there after a Paste operation so you can paste it in more than one location. It isn't replaced until the next Cut or Copy operation.

- To help remember the shortcut keys for the Cut, Copy, and Paste commands, think of the X in Ctrl+X as a scissors; think of the C in Ctrl+C as the first letter in copy; and think of the V in Ctrl+V as a pointer showing where something should be inserted. Note also that the letters X, C, and V are in succession in the bottom row of the keyboard, and they are preceded by the letter Z, which is used for the Undo command (Ctrl+Z).

Figure 2-5   How to move or copy text with the Cut, Copy, and Paste commands

With drag-and-drop editing

Figure 2-6 presents another technique for moving and copying text called *drag-and-drop editing*. If you're good with a mouse, this is a technique you may enjoy using. Otherwise, you can prob-ably work more efficiently by using the Cut, Copy, and Paste commands.

If you experiment with drag-and-drop editing, you'll see that it works best when you move or copy text short distances. If you have to move or copy text across several pages, you may decide that the Cut, Copy, and Paste tech-niques are easier to use.

How to move text

1. Select the text you want to move:

   > Our newest book, *Work Like a Pro with Word 6 for Windows*, is described on page 8. Our best-selling PC book, *The Least You Need to Know About Windows 3.1*, is described on page 7. And *Instructor's Guides* are available on diskette in case you want to use our books for classroom instruction.

2. Move the I-beam pointer over the selected text until it turns into the arrow pointer:

   > Our newest book, *Work Like a Pro with Word 6 for Windows*, is described on page 8. Our best-selling PC book, *The Least You Need to Know About Windows 3.1*, is described on page 7. And *Instructor's Guides* are available on diskette in case you want to use our books for classroom instruction.

3. Drag the selected text to its new location. Notice that the arrow pointer turns into a *drag-and-drop pointer* that consists of a rectangle, an arrow, and an insertion point:

   > Our newest book, *Work Like a Pro with Word 6 for Windows*, is described on page 8. Our best-selling PC book, *The Least You Need to Know About Windows 3.1*, is described on page 7. And *Instructor's Guides* are available on diskette in case you want to use our books for classroom instruction.

4. Release the mouse button and Word drops the selection into the new location:

   > Our best-selling PC book, *The Least You Need to Know About Windows 3.1*, is described on page 7. Our newest book, *Work Like a Pro with Word 6 for Windows*, is described on page 8. And *Instructor's Guides* are available on diskette in case you want to use our books for classroom instruction.

How to copy text

- Use the same procedure as for moving text, but hold down the Ctrl key as you drag in step 3. When you do, a small plus sign is displayed as part of the drag-and-drop pointer to indicate a copy operation.

Notes

- Drag-and-drop editing is active by default. If it isn't active on your PC, choose the Options command from the Tools menu, click on the Edit tab, and click on the Drag-and-Drop Text Editing option.

- Drag-and-drop editing is most useful when you need to copy or move small selections short distances. Otherwise, you're better off with the cut, copy, and paste technique.

Figure 2-6   How to move or copy text with drag-and-drop editing

Exercise set 2-2

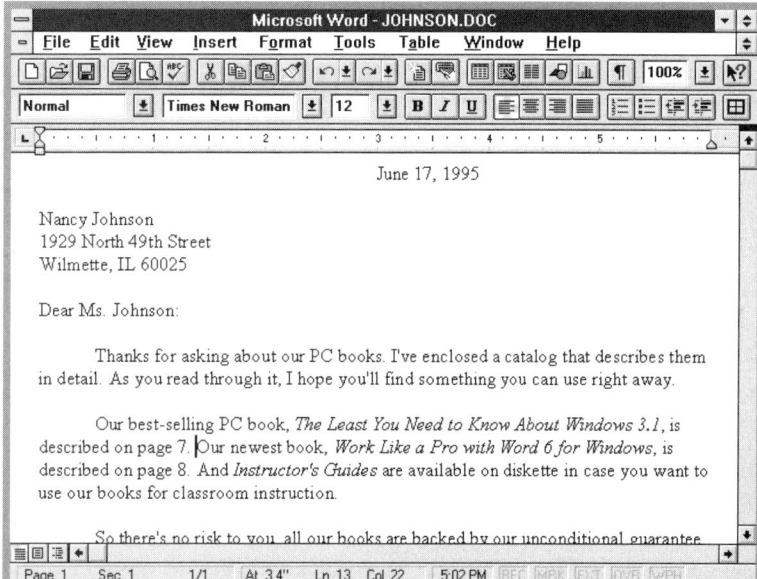

How the document should look after you perform the move operation in exercise 1

1. Open the JOHNSON file. With figure 2-5 as a guide, use the shortcut keys to move the second sentence in the second paragraph in the body of the letter so it becomes the first sentence in the second paragraph. Then, press Ctrl+Z until this sentence is back where it started.

2. Perform the same operation as in exercise 1, but this time use the toolbar buttons to cut and paste the text and to return the text to its original location.

3. With figure 2-6 as a guide, drag and drop the second sentence in the second paragraph so it becomes the first sentence in that paragraph. Then, undo the operation so you can see that it's considered one action in contrast to the Cut and Paste commands.

4. Just for practice, copy the second paragraph in the body of the letter and paste it after the third paragraph. The second and the fourth paragraphs should now be the same. If so, delete the fourth paragraph and repeat the copy function using drag-and-drop editing.

5. Close the file without saving the changes.

How to work with two or more open documents

When you use Word 6, you can open more than one document at the same time. Then, you can switch from one document to another. You can also display all the open documents at the same time. And you can move and copy text from one document to another.

How to switch from one document to another

When a document is open, its name is listed at the bottom of the Window menu as shown in figure 2-7. In this example, three documents are open. Two have already been saved, so their file names are listed in the Window menu: CATLET and STAFFMTG. The other document hasn't been saved, so a document number is listed for it.

To switch from one open document to another, you can choose the document from the Window menu. Or, you can use the shortcut keys that are given in figure 2-7. If all the open documents are displayed at the same time, you can also switch to any of those documents by clicking in its document window.

The Window menu with three open documents

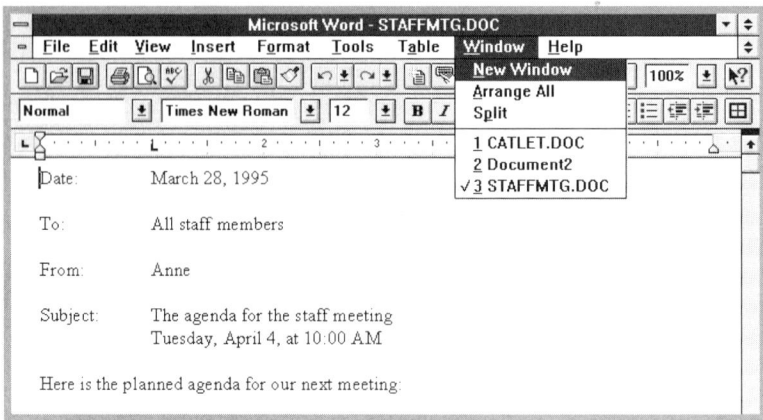

How to use the Window menu to switch to another document

Pull down the Window menu, then choose the name of the document you want to switch to or enter the number in front of the document name. If a file has been saved, its file name is listed. Otherwise, it is listed as Document followed by a number like Document2 shown above.

Shortcut keys for switching to another document

Key	Function
Ctrl+F6	Switches to the next window.
Ctrl+Shift+F6	Switches to the previous window.

How to switch to another document when all the open documents are displayed

Click on the document window that contains the document you want to switch to. See figure 2-8 for details on how to display all the open documents.

Figure 2-7   How to switch from one document to another

How to display all open documents at the same time

If you want to display all the open documents at the same time, you can choose the Arrange All command from the Window menu. Then, the documents are arranged on the screen as shown in figure 2-8. Note that each document window has its own scroll bars and ruler.

In this example, only two documents are open so both document windows are large enough for editing work. If several documents are open, though, the windows become so small that they're hard to use. To return all the windows to their maximized size, just click on the maximize button in the upper right corner of the active document window.

How to move or copy text from one document to another

To move or copy text from one document to another, you can always use the Cut, Copy, and Paste commands. After you select and cut or copy text in one document, you just switch to the other document and paste the contents of the clipboard. You can do this when only one document window at a time is displayed or when two or more document windows are displayed. Often, though, you can work more efficiently if you display both documents at the same time.

You can also use drag-and-drop editing to move or copy text from one document to another. To use this technique, though, both of the documents that you're working with have to be displayed at the same time.

Two documents that were arranged using the Arrange All command

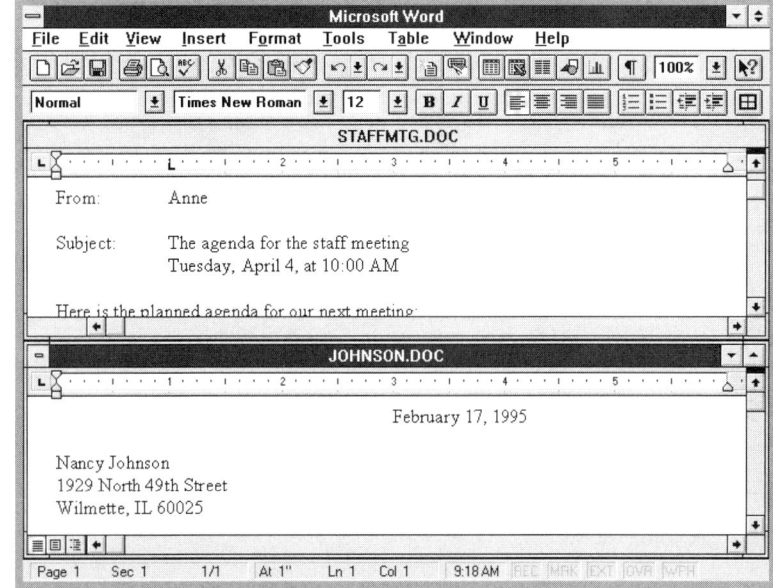

How to display all of the open documents

- Choose the Arrange All command from the Window menu.

Two ways to move or copy text from one document to another

- Switch to the window that contains the text you want to move or copy. Select the text, then issue the Cut or Copy command to cut or copy the text to the clipboard. Switch to the window where you want to move or copy the text, position the insertion point, and issue the Paste command.

- Switch to the window that contains the text you want to move or copy and select the text. Drag the text to a location in another document to move the text to that document. To copy the text, hold down the Ctrl key as you drag. Both documents must be displayed as shown above to use this technique.

How to return all the document windows to their maximized size

- Click on the maximize button in the active window.

Figure 2-8   How to work with two or more open documents

Exercise set 2-3

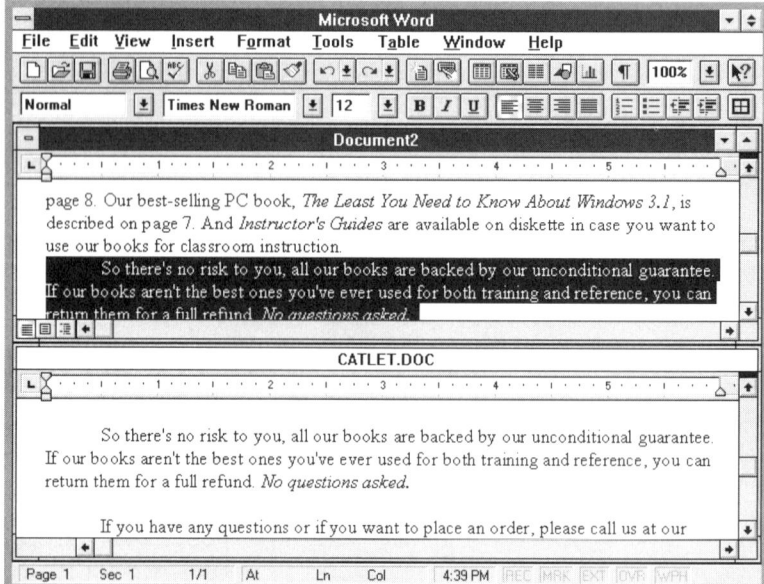

How the Word window should look after exercise 4

1. Open the JOHNSON and CATLET files in that order so CATLET becomes the active document. Then, use the Window menu to switch back to the JOHNSON document.

2. Press Ctrl+N to start a new document and open a window for it. Next, pull down the Window menu to see how the new document window is identified, and click outside the menu to close it. Then, press Ctrl+F6 to switch to the next window, and press it again to see which window it switches to. Then, press Ctrl+Shift+F6 twice to see which windows it switches to.

3. Use the Window menu to switch to the JOHNSON document if you're not already there. Then, use the Copy and Paste commands to copy the first two paragraphs in the body of the letter to the new document.

4. Switch back to the JOHNSON document and close it. Next, use the Arrange All command in the Window menu to display both open documents at the same time. Then, use drag-and-drop editing to copy the third paragraph in the CATLET letter to the end of the new document. Was that more difficult than using Copy and Paste?

5. Click on the maximize button in the active window to maximize both document windows. Next, switch from one window to the other to see that they are maximized. Then, close the new document and the CATLET document without saving them.

How to check the spelling and use the thesaurus

Word's spelling checker is so quick and easy to use that you should use it to check the spelling in every document that is going to be read by someone else. There's just no excuse for a simple misspelling any more. Word's thesaurus is also quick and easy to use, so it comes in handy whenever you're trying to think of a synonym or antonym for a word.

The Spelling command

Figure 2-9 shows how to use the Spelling command in the Tools menu. Although the Spelling dialog box has many buttons and this figure has extensive explanation, the normal use of the Spelling command is quite simple. You just start the command and respond to the dialog boxes that are displayed as the spelling in the document is checked.

To check the spelling, Word looks up each word in its *main dictionary*. By default, Word also checks the *custom dictionary* if the word isn't found in the main dictionary. The first time you use the Spelling command, the custom dictionary is empty. You'll learn how to add words to this dictionary in just a moment.

If a word isn't found in the main or custom dictionary, Word assumes it is misspelled. Otherwise, Word assumes the spelling is correct. That means that some misspellings won't be identified. If, for example, you type *though* when you meant to type *through*, the error won't be caught.

Access

Menu	Tools ➡ Spelling
Standard toolbar	
Shortcut key	F7

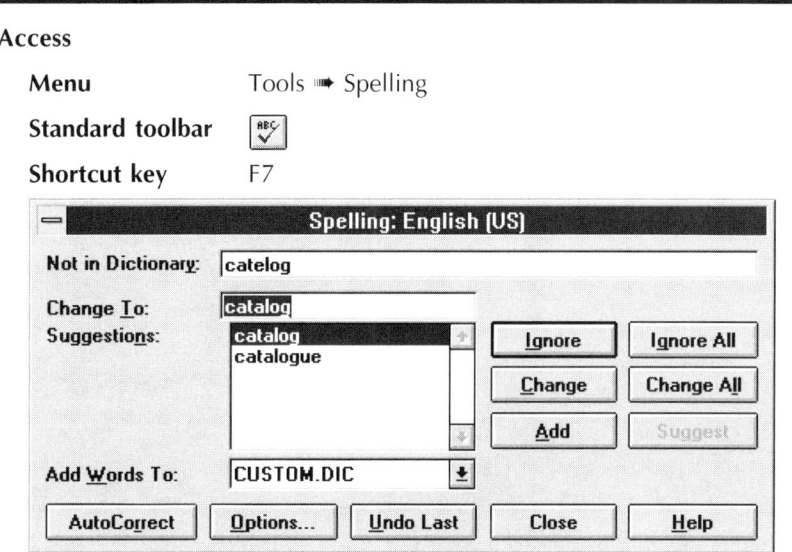

Operation

- To check the spelling in the entire document starting from the insertion point, start the spelling check. To check just a portion of a document, select that text before you start the spelling check.

- Word looks for words that aren't in its dictionary, for words that are repeated (like *the the*) and for irregular capitalization (like *THere*). When it finds an error, it displays the Spelling dialog box. To continue the spelling check, click on the appropriate button in the dialog box.

Button	Meaning or function
Ignore	Ignore the word that's identified.
Ignore All	Ignore the word for the rest of the spelling check.
Change	Replace the current occurrence of the word with the word in the Change To box. To move a word into this box from the Suggestions list, click on it. If no suggestion is correct, you can type a word into the Change To box.
Change All	Replace all remaining occurrences of the word automatically.
Delete	For word repetitions, the Change button becomes the Delete button. It deletes the second word.
Add	Add the word to the custom dictionary. Then, the word is considered correct in all subsequent spelling checks.
Suggest	Suggest likely corrections. (You don't need this if the Always Suggest option in the Spelling tab of the Options dialog box is on.)
AutoCorrect	Add the word to the AutoCorrect list (see figure 2-12).
Options	Display a dialog box that lets you set the spelling options.
Undo Last	Undo and return to the last correction made.

Figure 2-9 **How to check the spelling in a document**

Similarly, since the main dictionary doesn't include every word or technical term, some correct words are assumed to be errors. Then, you can click on the Ignore button to skip the word one time or you can click on the Ignore All button to skip the word for the rest of the document. Another alternative is to click on the Add button so the word is added to the custom dictionary. Then, that word will be considered correct in all future spelling checks.

For most of us, the main and custom dictionaries are the only ones we'll ever need. If necessary, though, you can add other dictionaries like a medical or technical dictionary to the spelling check and you can create your own dictionaries. To perform these functions, you use the Add and New buttons in the Spelling tab of the Options dialog box.

Additional information

✓ If you accidentally add a word to the custom dictionary and want to delete it, you can edit the dictionary in Word. To do that, choose the Options command from the Tools menu and click on the Spelling tab. Then, click on the Edit button while the custom dictionary is highlighted to open it as a Word document. Delete the word, then save and close the file.

The Thesaurus command

Figure 2-10 shows how to use the Word thesaurus. If you experiment with it, you'll see that it's easy to use, but it's no substitute for a dictionary. You still need to be able to choose the word that has just the right meaning for your purpose.

Access

Menu   Tools ➡ Thesaurus

Shortcut key   Shift+F7

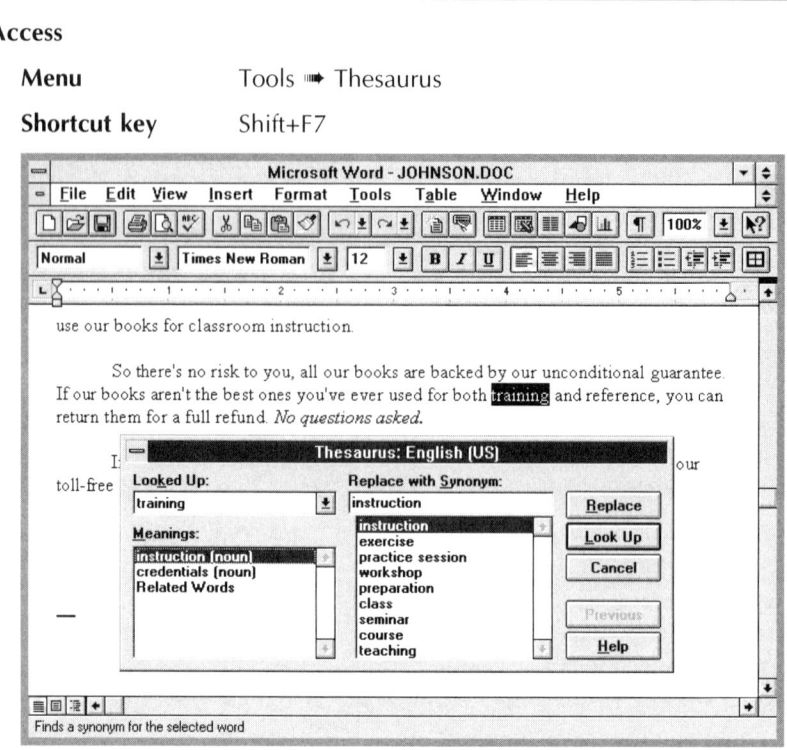

Operation

- Move the insertion point into the word you want to look up, and access the Thesaurus dialog box. Different meanings for the word are displayed in the Meanings list, and the synonyms for the first word in the list are displayed in the Replace with Synonym list.

- To display the synonyms for another word in the Meanings list, click on the word.

- To replace the original word in the document with a word in the Replace with Synonym list, highlight the word and click on the Replace button.

- To look up a word in the Meanings or Replace with Synonym list, double-click on it.

- To look up a word that isn't shown in the dialog box, type it in the Replace with Synonym box and click on the Look Up button.

- To display the synonym list for a previous word, click on the Previous button. Or, choose a word from the list that drops down from the Looked Up box.

Note

- The Meanings list identifies the parts of speech (noun, verb, and so on), antonyms (words with opposite meanings), and related words (words based on the same root).

Figure 2-10   How to use the thesaurus

Exercise set 2-4

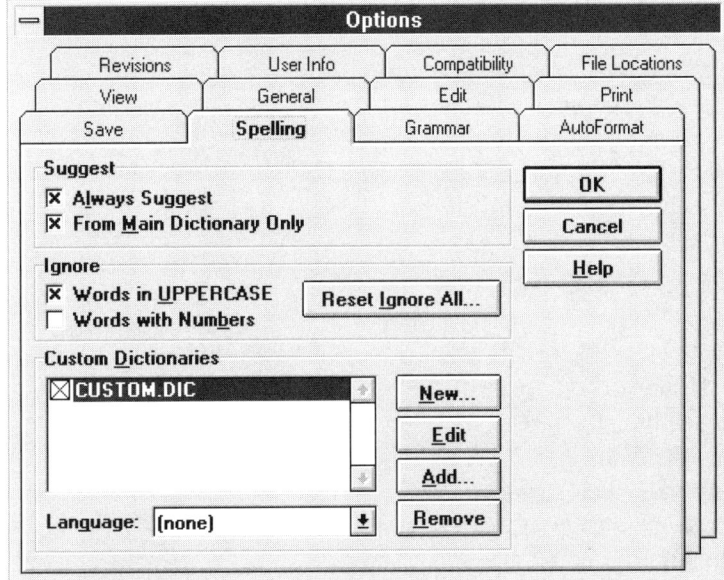

The dialog box that you display in exercise 3

1. Open the JOHNSON file. Then, check the spelling in the document, but use the Ignore button to ignore any word that the spelling check stops for. What words were identified as possible errors? Were all of them errors?

2. Change the first sentence in the letter so it contains the three errors that follow (the errors are in italics): "Thanks for *for* a*ks*ing about our *Pc* books." Run the spelling check for the entire document to see how these errors are handled. This time, use the Ignore All button for any correct words that are identified as possible errors, but correct all errors. Then, run the spelling check again. It should run to completion without stopping.

3. Choose the Options command from the Tools menu, and click on the Spelling tab. By default, the two options in the Suggest group should be checked. If the first one isn't checked, you won't be getting suggested corrections when you run the spelling check, so you should check it now. Next, click on the Reset Ignore All button, click on the Yes button in the next dialog box, click on the OK button to return to the JOHNSON document, and run the spelling check again. Note that the words you ignored in exercise 2 are no longer ignored. Save the document, but don't close it.

4. Move the insertion point into the word *book* near the beginning of the second paragraph and access the thesaurus. Click on the word *text* in the Replace with Synonym list to move it to the Replace box, and click on the Replace button to make the replacement in the letter.

5. Move the insertion point into the word *text*, and access the thesaurus. Next, double-click on *printed matter* in the Replace with Synonym list to look up its synonyms, then double-click on *brochure* to look up its synonyms. Then, drop the list from the Looked Up box and select *text* so its synonyms are displayed again. Click on *course book* in the Meanings list to look up its synonyms. Last, type *book* into the Replace with Synonym box and click on the Replace button. Close the file without saving the changes.

How to use the AutoText and AutoCorrect features

The AutoText and AutoCorrect features let you type abbreviations for longer portions of text, then replace the abbreviations with the text. This helps you increase your entry speed. The AutoCorrect feature also provides other functions that help you increase your entry accuracy and speed.

The AutoText feature

Figure 2-11 shows how to use the AutoText feature. To start, you build a list that consists of abbreviations and their replacements. These replacements can be text strings that are formatted or unformatted. For instance, you can use your initials as the abbreviation for an AutoText item and your name as the replacement. In the dialog box in figure 2-11, the abbreviation is *w6w* and the replacement is the title of this book with italic formatting.

After you add an item to the AutoText list, you can use the abbreviation to enter the replacement into the document. To do that, you type the abbreviation and press F3 or click on the Insert AutoText button in the Standard toolbar.

When you add an item to the AutoText list, it's usually added to the Normal template so it's available to all other documents too. Then, when you exit from Word at the end of a session, Word asks whether you want to save the changes in that template. If you do, click on the Yes button.

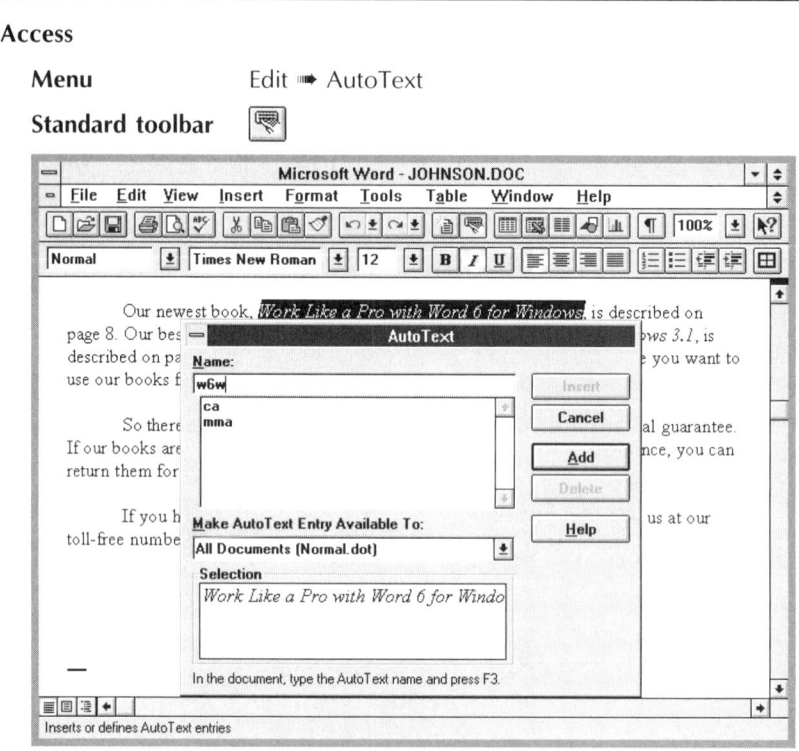

Access

Menu   Edit ➡ AutoText

Standard toolbar

How to add an item to the AutoText list

1. Enter, format, and select the text that you want to create an abbreviation for. In the example above, a book title in italics has been selected.

2. Access the AutoText dialog box; enter an appropriate abbreviation in the Name box; and click on the Add button to add it to the list.

How to expand an AutoText abbreviation in the document

- Type the abbreviation for the item in the document and press the F3 key or click on the AutoText button in the Standard toolbar. The abbreviation is then replaced by the formatted text.

- If you can't remember the abbreviation or you want to insert a formatted item without its formatting, access the AutoText dialog box from the Edit menu with no text selected. This box is slightly different from the one shown above. Then, you can click on the abbreviation that you want to insert into the text; click on the Plain Text option if you want the item unformatted; and click on the Insert button to insert the expanded item into the document.

Note

- The AutoText items are saved in the template that's shown in the Make AutoText Entry Available To box. By default, these items are saved in the Normal template, which is usually what you want. To learn more about templates, please read chapter 5.

Figure 2-11   How to use the AutoText feature

The AutoCorrect feature

One function of the AutoCorrect feature is similar to the AutoText feature. It lets you replace the abbreviations that you enter into a document with formatted or unformatted text. However, the AutoCorrect abbreviations are replaced automatically when you enter the space or punctuation mark that follows the abbreviation. You can also use this feature to correct some of your frequent typing errors.

Figure 2-12 shows how to use the AutoCorrect feature. The five check boxes at the top of its dialog box are for the five types of corrections that this feature can make automatically. For automatic replacement of abbreviations or correction of typing errors, you need to check the fifth box.

If you access the AutoCorrect dialog box right after you install Word 6, you'll see that some items are already in the AutoCorrect list. One of these items automatically corrects a common typing error (*adn* when you mean to type *and*). When you use the spelling checker, you can add your own typing errors to the list by clicking on the AutoCorrect button.

Access

Menu   Tools ➡ AutoCorrect

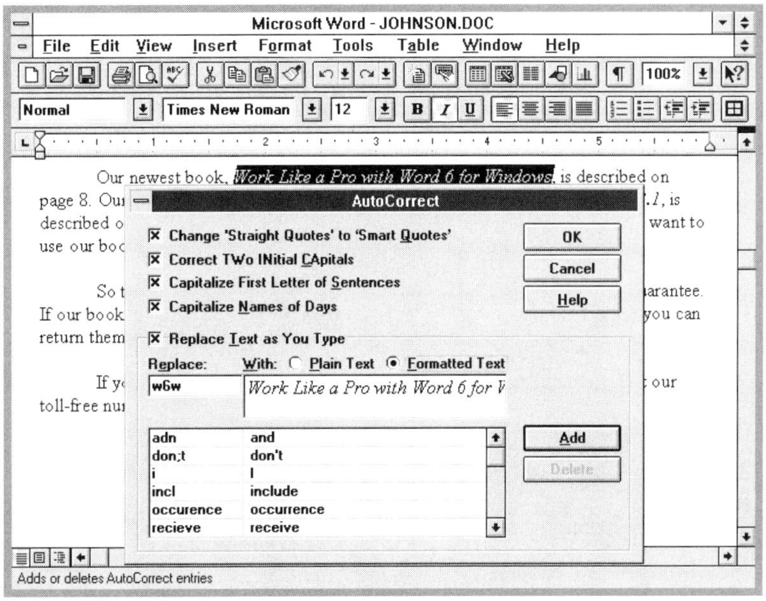

How to add an item to the AutoCorrect list

- To add an unformatted item, access the AutoCorrect dialog box; enter an appropriate abbreviation in the Replace box; enter the replacement text in the With box; and click on the Add button.

- To add a formatted item, enter, format, and select the text that you want to add. Then, access the AutoCorrect dialog box; enter an appropriate abbreviation in the Replace box; click on the Formatted Text option; and click on the Add button.

How to expand an AutoCorrect abbreviation in the document

- Type the abbreviation for the item in the document, and type the space or punctuation mark that follows it. The item is automatically expanded as you type, provided that the Replace Text as You Type box is checked in the AutoCorrrect dialog box.

Notes

- Some AutoCorrect items come with Word. For instance, Word automatically replaces "adn" with "and."

- If you don't like the way some of the five AutoCorrect options work, you can turn them off by clicking on them.

- You can also add items to the AutoCorrect list by clicking on the AutoCorrect button during a spelling check (see figure 2-9).

Figure 2-12   How to use the AutoCorrect feature

Exercise set 2-5

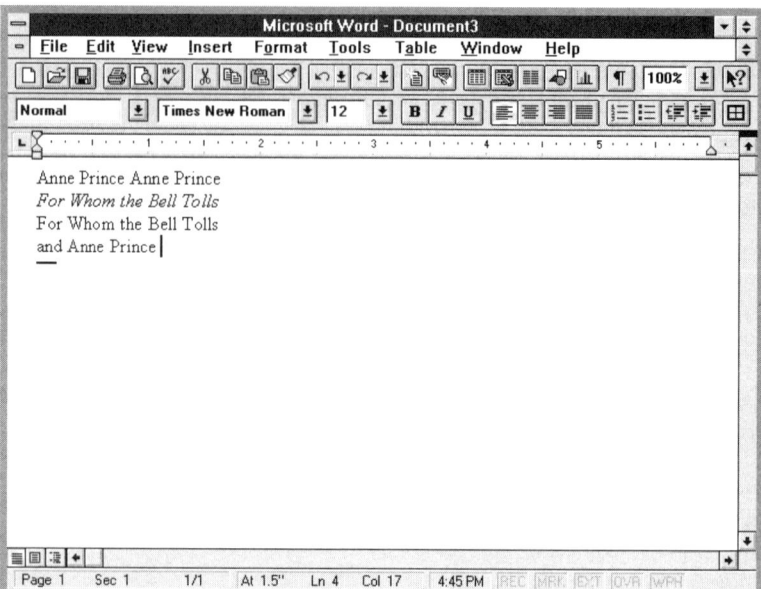

How the document should look after exercise 5

1. Click on the New button in the Standard toolbar to open a new document. Type your name into the document, then select it. (Be sure not to include the paragraph mark at the end of your name.) Click on the Edit AutoText button in the toolbar. In the resulting dialog box, you'll see your name in both the Name and Selection boxes. Type your initials into the Name box, and press the Enter key to add the name to the AutoText list and return to the document. Then, delete your name, type your initials, and click on the Insert AutoText button in the toolbar. Watch how your initials are replaced by your name. Type a space, type your initials again, and replace them again by pressing F3. That's how easy it is to use the AutoText feature.

2. Type *For Whom the Bell Tolls* in italics on a new line and add it to the AutoText list with the abbreviation *wbt*. Then, return to the document, delete the book title, type its abbreviation, and replace it.

3. Press the Enter key to start a new line. Then, choose the AutoText command from the Edit menu. This displays the AutoText dialog box in a slightly different form. Choose the *wbt* abbreviation, click on the Plain Text option, and click on the Insert button. Note that the book title is inserted into the document without italics.

4. Access the AutoCorrect dialog box as shown in figure 2-12. Is the Replace Text as You Type option checked? If not, check it. Is one of the first Replace items in the AutoCorrect list, *adn*, and is its replacement *and*? If it isn't, add this item to the list. Then, click on the OK button to return to the document and type *adn* followed by a space on a new line. It should be automatically corrected.

5. Add another item to the AutoCorrect list that consists of your initials and your full name. Then, return to the document, type your initials followed by a space, and watch them get replaced by your full name.

6. Add *For Whom the Bell Tolls* in italics to the AutoCorrect list with the abbreviation *wbt*. Then, return to the document, type the abbreviation followed by a space, and watch the automatic expansion. Do you like working this way better than using the AutoText feature?

7. Close the file without saving the changes.

How to use the Find and Replace commands

The Find and Replace commands are powerful editing commands because they let you find and replace text, formatting, and nonprinting characters. With these commands, for example, you can search for all uses of the word *which* and replace selected uses with *that*; you can search for all underlined words and replace them with italicized words; and you can search for and indent all non-indented paragraphs. In short, these commands can help you edit more efficiently.

The Find command

Figure 2-13 shows how to use the Find command for a simple search. If, for example, you frequently type *your* when you mean to type *you're*, you can search for and examine all occurrences of *your* to make sure they're correct. To do that, just type the word *your* into the Find What box. This entry can be referred to as the *find value*. Then, check the Find Whole Words Only option. If the Match Case option isn't checked, the search will find the word whether or not it is capitalized.

If you experiment with the Find command, you'll see how easy it is to use for simple searches. Then, if you find something in the document that you want to change, you can click in the document window to activate it and make the change. To return to the dialog box and continue the search, just click on the Find Next button.

Access

Menu	Edit ➡ Find
Shortcut key	Ctrl+F

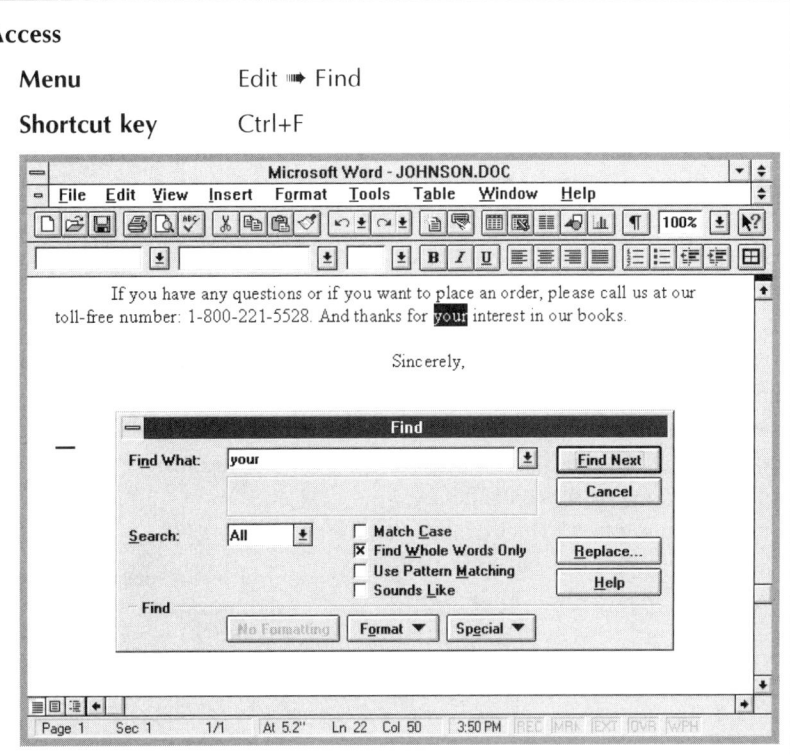

How to find unformatted text

1. Type the text that you want to find in the Find What box.

2. If you want to search only for whole words, check the Find Whole Words Only option.

3. If you want to find only text that has the same capitalization that you've used, check the Match Case option.

4. Click on the Find Next button to start the search operation.

Notes

• When Word finds an occurrence of the text that you've specified, it stops with that occurrence highlighted as shown above. Then, you can click on the Find Next button to find the next occurrence.

• You can make a change to the document without closing the Find dialog box. To do that, just click in the document window to activate it and make the change. If you need to, you can move the Find dialog box by dragging it by its title bar. To return to the Find dialog box, just click in it.

• If you close the Find dialog box, you can find the next match without displaying the dialog box again by pressing Shift+F4.

• To look for one of the last four text strings that you used in a find operation, choose an item from the Find What list.

Figure 2-13   How to use the Find command for a simple search

For more complicated searches, you can use the techniques, options, and buttons that are summarized in figure 2-14. If, for example, you want to look for find values that are formatted with bold, italic, or underlining, you can use shortcut keys or toolbar buttons to apply the formatting just as you apply it in a document.

For other formatting, you can use the menu that drops down from the Format button in the Find dialog box. And if you want to search for nonprinting characters, you can click on the Special button and choose one or more of the available characters. Most of the time, though, you only need to use simple searches with a minimum of formatting.

A Find dialog box that searches for formatted text

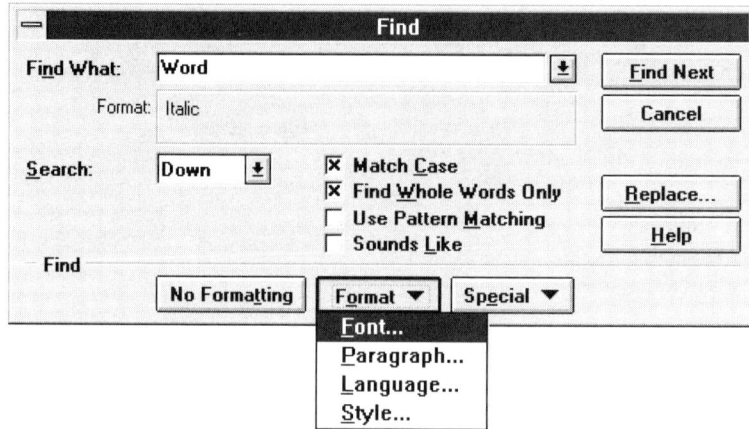

How to find formatted text

- To specify bold, italic, or underlined text in the Find What box, you can use the shortcut keys or the toolbar buttons. If you use the keys or buttons a second time, you can specify that the text be not bold, italic, or underlined. If you use the keys or buttons a third time, no formatting is specified. The formatting is displayed in the Format box below the Find What box.

- To apply other types of formatting, you can use the menu that's displayed when you click on the Format button.

- To remove all formatting from a text string, click on the No Formatting button.

How to find nonprinting characters

- To look for special characters like Tab characters or paragraph marks, you can choose an item from the list that's displayed when you click on the Special button.

How to use the other controls in the Find dialog box

- The three options in the drop-down Search list are Down for a forward search, Up for a backward search, and All for a search of the entire document. If you use Down or Up, Word asks if you want to continue with the rest of the document when it reaches the bottom or the top of the document. If you use All, Word searches down the document and automatically continues at the top when it reaches the bottom.

- The Replace button lets you change from a Find command to a Replace command.

- You probably won't ever need the third and fourth search options. The Pattern Matching option lets you use wildcards and other search operations to create complex find values. The Sounds Like option lets you find words that sound alike but are spelled differently, and it doesn't always work the way you expect.

Figure 2-14   Other uses of the Find command

The Replace command

When you use the Replace command, you set up both a *find value* and a *replace value*. Then, you can replace any or all occurrences of the find value with the replace value.

As you can see in figure 2-15, the Replace dialog box is similar to the Find dialog box. In fact, you use the same techniques to enter the replace value that you use to enter the find value. Then, to start the replace operation, you click on the Find Next button.

When Word finds the first occurrence of the find value, you have three options. If you don't want to replace it, click on the Find Next button. If you want to replace it and go on to the next occurrence, click on the Replace button. And if you want to replace it and all other occurrences of the find value without any further stops, click on the Replace All button. If you can't see an occurrence in the document because the Replace dialog box is over it, you can move the box by dragging its title bar.

If you experiment with the Replace command, you'll see that it's quick and easy to use for simple replacements. For more complex replacements in lengthy documents, you may have to experiment a while, but you should be able to get the result you're after.

Access

Menu	Edit ➡ Replace
Shortcut key	Ctrl+H
Find dialog box	Replace button

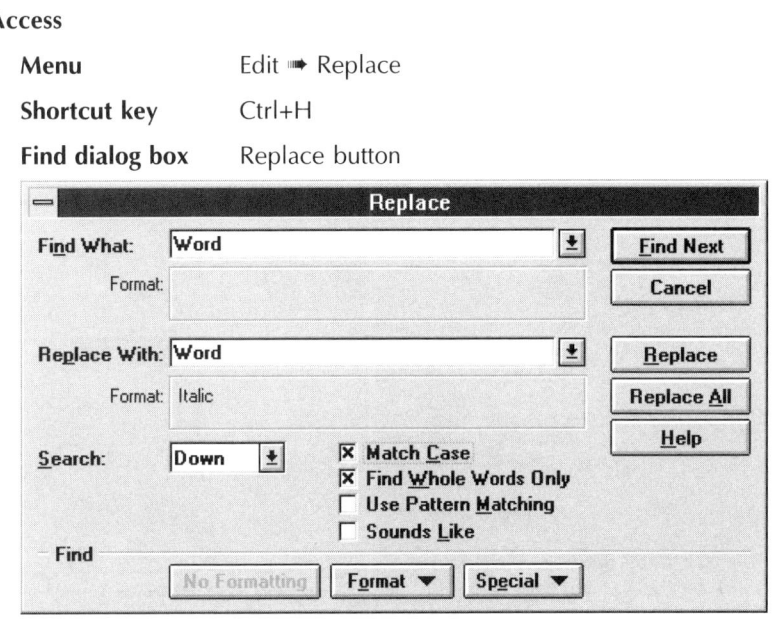

Operation

- The Find What and Replace With boxes work the same way that the Find What box works in the Find dialog box. You can apply bold, italics, or underlining to the text in either box by using the shortcut keys or the toolbar buttons. To apply other types of formatting, you can use the list that's displayed when you click on the Format button. And to insert special characters, you can use the list that's displayed when you click on the Special button.

- When Word finds an occurrence of the Find What text that you've specified, it stops with that occurrence highlighted. Then, you can click on the Find Next button to find the next occurrence; click on the Replace button to replace that occurrence with the Replace With text; or click on the Replace All button to replace all occurrences with the Replace With text.

Notes

- In the example above, an unformatted word is replaced with the same word, but with italic formatting.

- If you leave the Replace With box empty, the Find What text is deleted from the document (it's replaced with nothing).

- You can also replace formatting options without specifying any text. For instance, you can replace all underlining with italics. Just leave the Find What and Replace With boxes empty and apply the formatting that you want to find and replace to those boxes.

- You can use the Undo command to undo a replace operation.

Figure 2-15   How to use the Replace command

Exercise set 2-6

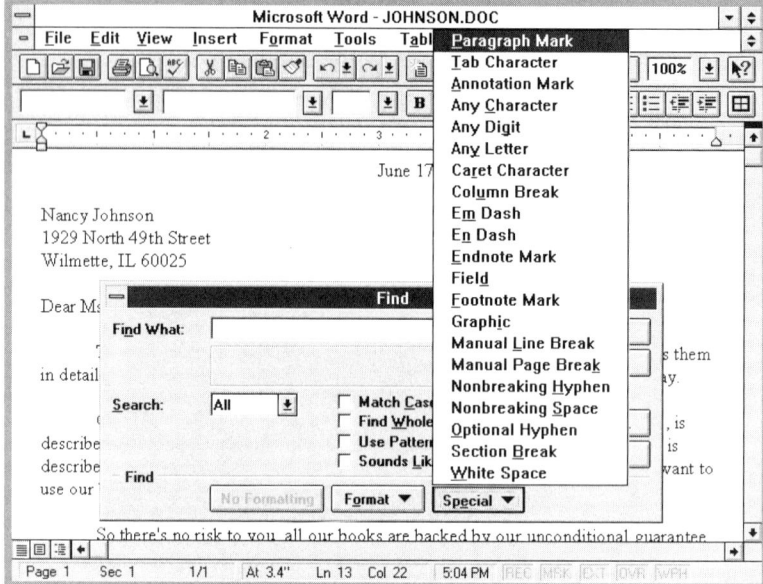

The list that's displayed when you click on the Special button in exercise 5

1. Open the JOHNSON file. Then, use the Find command to search for the letters *he* with none of the options checked. Note that these letters are found within words like *the* and *them*. Now, run the find operation again with the Find Whole Words Only option on. Note that the word *he* isn't found in the document.

2. Use the Find command to search for *windows*. The characters should be entered in all lower-case letters, and none of the options should be checked. Note that two occurrences are found. Next, check the Match Case option and search the document again. Note that no occurrences are found.

3. Use the Find command to search for the word *to* but only when it's in italics. How many occurrences are found?

4. Use the Find command to search for the use of italics. To do that, the Find What box should be empty but should have italic formatting. (Be sure to remove the check mark from the Find Whole Words Only option or Word will find each italicized word separately.) How many occurrences are found?

5. Use the Find command to search for a Tab character. To do that, remove the italic formatting, click on the Special button, and choose Tab Character. Then, use the Find command to search for one paragraph mark followed by a Tab character.

6. Click on the Replace button in the Find dialog box to change to a Replace command. Then, to practice your use of this command, do four replacements. First, replace all uses of the word *book* with the word *product*. Second, replace all uses of italics with underlines. Third, delete the Tab character at the start of each paragraph in the body of the letter by searching for a paragraph mark followed by a Tab character and replacing them with just a paragraph mark. (Be sure to remove the formatting from both the Find What and Replace With boxes.) Fourth, replace all occurrences of two spaces with a single space (you can type the spaces into the find and replace values, but they won't be visible). If you can do all four of these replacements, you shouldn't have any trouble with the Replace command. When you're done, close the file without saving it.

7. Exit from Word. If you did exercise set 2-5, Word will display a dialog box that asks whether you want to save the AutoText entries that you made in the Normal template. Click on the No button so these entries aren't saved.

Perspective

If you've done all the exercises for this chapter, you should now realize how quickly and easily you can edit a document. In fact, it's the editing features that are most likely to help you increase your productivity when you use a modern word processing program. As you will see in the next chapter, most of the other features help you improve the appearance of a document.

Summary

- You can start editing commands and functions with shortcut keys, *shortcut menus*, toolbar buttons, and menu commands.

- The Undo command lets you undo one or more editing actions. The Redo command lets you redo one or more of the editing actions that you've just undone.

- To move and copy text selections within a document, you can use the Cut, Copy, and Paste commands or *drag-and-drop editing*. These techniques can also be used to move or copy text from one open document to another.

- To switch from one open document to another, you can use the Window menu or shortcut keys. You can also use the Window menu to display all the open documents at the same time. When all the open documents are displayed at the same time, you can switch to a document by clicking on it.

- To check the spelling in a document, Word normally uses a *main dictionary* and a *custom dictionary*. It also checks for words that are repeated twice in succession and for irregular capitalization.

- The AutoText and AutoCorrect features let you replace abbreviations with full text. The AutoCorrect feature can also be used to automatically correct certain types of entry errors.

- The Find and Replace commands let you search for and replace formatted and unformatted text strings. They also let you find and replace formatting by itself and nonprinting characters.

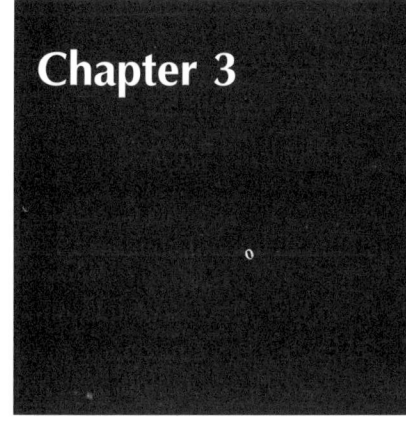

Chapter 3

How to format characters, paragraphs, and pages

When you use Word, it's easy to change the formatting of the characters, paragraphs, and pages in the document. Then, since the character and paragraph formatting is shown immediately in the document window, you can tell at a glance whether you've got the formatting the way you want it. To check the page formatting that's applied to a document, you can preview the document before you print it. In this chapter, you'll learn the skills that help you format quickly and confidently.

An introduction to the formatting functions

In chapter 2, you learned that you can perform most editing functions from the keyboard or with the mouse. That's also true for formatting functions.

In this introduction, you'll learn about the character and paragraph formatting that you can apply from the Format menu, from the Formatting toolbar, and with shortcut keys. Later in this chapter, you'll learn that you can also use the shortcut menus, the ruler, and the Borders toolbar to apply some character and paragraph formatting. You'll also learn about the Page Setup command in the File menu, which you can use to apply most page formatting.

When you format characters and paragraphs with Word, one of the basic principles is to select the characters or paragraphs first, then format. If you want to apply formatting to just one word or paragraph, though, you don't have to select all the characters in the word or paragraph. The insertion point just has to be in the word or paragraph.

The commands in the Format menu

Figure 3-1 shows the Format menu and summarizes the commands that are presented in this book. These are the commands that you should at least be aware of. By the time you complete this chapter, though, you'll realize that you can perform most of these commands without accessing the Format menu.

The Format menu

| Font... |
| Paragraph... |
| Tabs... |
| Borders and Shading... |
| Columns... |
| Change Case... |
| |
| Bullets and Numbering... |
| Heading Numbering... |
| AutoFormat... |
| Style Gallery... |
| Style... |
| |
| Drawing Object... |

Command	Function
Font	Lets you apply character formatting to the selected text.
Paragraph	Lets you apply paragraph formatting to the selected paragraphs.
Tabs	Lets you set tab stops for the selected paragraphs.
Borders and Shading	Lets you apply borders and shading to the selected paragraphs.
Columns	Lets you divide a section of a document into two or more columns (see chapter 10).
Change Case	Lets you change the capitalization in the selected text.
Bullets and Numbering	Lets you apply bullets and numbers to the selected paragraphs.
Style Gallery	Lets you change the styles that have been used for a document (see chapter 6).
Style	Lets you apply, modify, or create styles (see chapter 6).

Figure 3-1   The commands in the Format menu that are presented in this book

The buttons and lists in the Formatting toolbar

Figure 3-2 presents the buttons and lists in the Formatting toolbar that is normally displayed in the Word window. The first list is used to apply styles. You'll learn more about it in the next chapter. The next two lists and three buttons let you apply formatting to the selected characters. And the next eight buttons let you apply formatting to the selected paragraphs. The last button displays or hides the Borders toolbar, which you can use to apply borders and shading to selected paragraphs.

If you experiment with these lists and buttons, you'll see that they're easy to use. And once you see what each one does, you'll be better able to identify them by their icons. Otherwise, you can always find out what a toolbar control does by pointing at it with the mouse. Then, a functional description is given in the status bar and a short description is given in the ToolTip.

The Standard toolbar also has a couple of buttons that apply to formatting. The most important one is the Undo button because you can undo most formatting functions, just as you can undo most editing functions. The other button is the Format Painter button that's presented near the end of this chapter.

Button or list	Name	Function
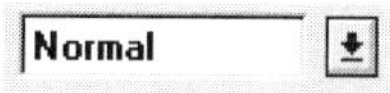 Normal	Style	Applies the style you choose to the selected paragraphs.
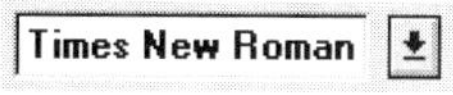 Times New Roman	Font	Applies the font you choose to the selected text.
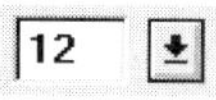 12	Font Size	Applies the font size you choose to the selected text.
B	Bold	Applies or removes boldfacing from the selected text.
I	Italic	Applies or removes italics from the selected text.
U	Underline	Applies or removes underlining from the selected text.
(align left icon)	Align Left	Left aligns the selected paragraphs.
(center icon)	Center	Centers the selected paragraphs.
(align right icon)	Align Right	Right aligns the selected paragraphs.
(justify icon)	Justify	Justifies the selected paragraphs so their text is aligned on both the left and right.
(numbering icon)	Numbering	Numbers the selected paragraphs.
(bullets icon)	Bullets	Bullets the selected paragraphs.
(decrease indent icon)	Decrease Indent	Moves the indentation for the selected paragraphs one tab stop to the left.
(increase indent icon)	Increase Indent	Moves the indentation for the selected paragraphs one tab stop to the right.
(borders icon)	Borders	Displays or hides the Borders toolbar.

Figure 3-2   The buttons and lists in the Formatting toolbar

The shortcut keys for formatting

Figure 3-3 presents the shortcut keys for formatting that you're most likely to need. Two keys that every Word user should know are the last one in the group for formatting characters and the last one in the group for formatting paragraphs. Ctrl+Spacebar removes any formatting that has been applied to the selected characters. Ctrl+Q removes any formatting that has been applied to the selected paragraphs. Remember too that Ctrl+Z will undo most formatting right after you apply it.

If you like to use shortcut keys for formatting characters and wish there was one for some other type of formatting, it's likely that there is. To find out, you can choose the Contents command from the Help menu; click on Reference Information; click on Keyboard Guide; and click on Using Shortcut Keys to Format Characters. Or, you can refer to appendix B. In contrast, the list of keys for formatting paragraphs is complete in figure 3-3.

Shortcut keys for formatting characters

Key	Function
Ctrl+B	Applies or removes boldfacing from the selected text.
Ctrl+I	Applies or removes italics from the selected text.
Ctrl+U	Applies or removes underlining from the selected text.
Ctrl+Spacebar or Ctrl+Shift+Z	Removes all character formatting from the selected text.

Shortcut keys for formatting paragraphs

Key	Function
Ctrl+L	Left aligns the selected paragraphs.
Ctrl+E	Centers the selected paragraphs.
Ctrl+R	Right aligns the selected paragraphs.
Ctrl+J	Justifies the selected paragraphs.
Ctrl+M	Increases the indentation for the selected paragraphs by one tab stop.
Ctrl+Shift+M	Decreases the indentation for the selected paragraphs by one tab stop.
Ctrl+T	Increases the hanging indent for the selected paragraphs by one tab stop.
Ctrl+Shift+T	Decreases the hanging indent for the selected paragraphs by one tab stop.
Ctrl+1	Single spaces the lines in the selected paragraphs.
Ctrl+2	Double spaces the lines in the selected paragraphs.
Ctrl+5	Spaces the lines in the selected paragraphs by 1.5 lines.
Ctrl+0 (zero)	Adds or removes one line of space before the selected paragraphs.
Ctrl+Q	Removes all paragraph formatting from the selected paragraphs.

Figure 3-3   The shortcut keys for formatting

Exercise set 3-1

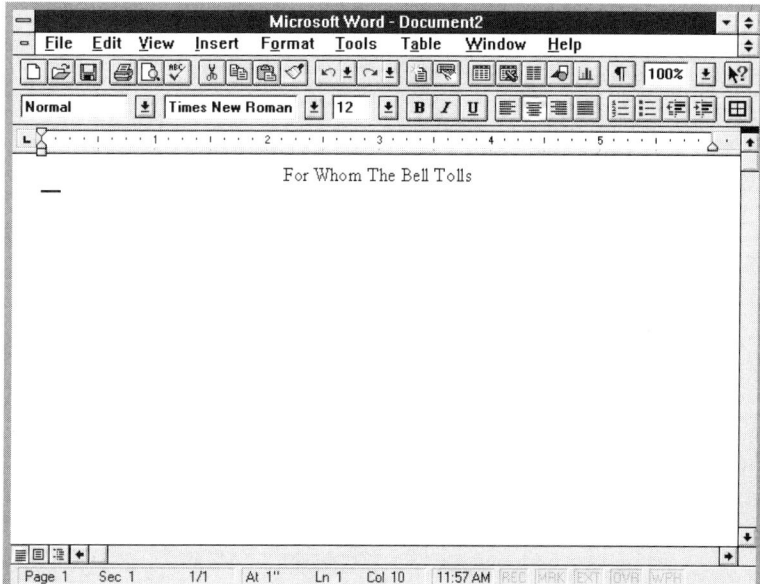

How the book title should look after you center it in exercise 2

1. Start a new document, and type this book title: *For Whom the Bell Tolls.* Then, select all the text in the title, access the Change Case command, and apply the lowercase option. Repeat this two more times, once with the UPPERCASE option and once with the Title Case option. When you finish, the first letter in each word of the title should be capitalized with the rest of each word in lowercase letters.

2. With the insertion point anywhere in the book title and no text selected, click on the Center button in the Formatting toolbar. What happens? Then, click on the Align Right button to see what it does, followed by the Align Left button to return the paragraph to the left margin.

3. With the insertion point anywhere in the book title, click on the Numbering button in the Formatting toolbar to see how that works, followed by the Bullets button, and the Bullets button again to remove the bullet in front of the paragraph. Then, click on the Increase Indent button in the Formatting toolbar two times to see how that works, and press Ctrl+Q to remove the formatting and return the paragraph to the left margin.

4. With the insertion point anywhere in the book title, experiment with the first six shortcut keys for paragraph formatting in figure 3-3. Note that these keys perform the same functions as the toolbar buttons. Now, close the document without saving it.

5. Open the JOHNSON file, and delete the Tab character at the start of the first paragraph in the body of the letter. Next, with the insertion point in this paragraph, experiment with the other shortcut keys for paragraph formatting in figure 3-3. When you're through, press Ctrl+Q to remove the paragraph formatting. Then, close the file without saving it.

How to format characters

In chapter 1, you learned how to apply bold, italics, and underlining to selected characters. In addition to that type of formatting, you can change the appearance and size of the characters. And, you can add special effects to the characters. After you learn some basic character formatting concepts, you'll learn how to apply the various character formatting.

Character formatting concepts

Figure 3-4 presents the character formatting concepts that Word users need to know. At this point, you should already be familiar with most of these concepts. In particular, you should already know how to format characters as you enter them and after you enter them.

When you create Word documents, you can choose from a variety of *fonts*. A font is a set of characters including letters, numbers, signs, and symbols. Each font is available in a variety of sizes, expressed in *points*. At the top of figure 3-4, you can see examples of three different fonts and font sizes as well as some other character formatting.

Character formatting examples

This is an example of Times New Roman in 9.5 point size.

This is an example of Arial in 9.5 point size.

This is an example of Courier New in 9.5 point size.

This is an example of Times New Roman in 18 point size with boldfacing.

This is an example of Arial in 12 point size with each word underlined separately.

THIS IS AN EXAMPLE OF COURIER NEW IN 12 POINT SIZE WITH SMALL CAPS.

The types of formatting that can be applied to characters

- Bold, italics, underlining, and color
- Font and font size
- Special effects, including strikethrough, superscript, subscript, hidden, small caps, and all caps

Fonts and font sizes

- Windows comes with a variety of character sets, or *fonts*, that are available from Word. Two of the most commonly used fonts are Times New Roman and Arial, which are shown above.
- Font size is expressed in *points*, with 72 points to the vertical inch.

How to format characters after you enter them

- Select the text that you want to format. If you want to format a single word, just move the insertion point into the word. Then, apply the formatting.

How to format characters as you enter them

- With no text selected, apply the formatting. Without moving the insertion point, type the characters and the formatting is applied. When you're done, remove the formatting so it's not applied to any additional characters you type.

How to return characters to the default formatting

- Select the characters, then press Ctrl+Spacebar or Ctrl+Shift+Z.

Figure 3-4   Character formatting concepts

How to change the font

Figure 3-5 shows the best method for changing the font. Just select the text and choose a font from the Font list that drops down from the Formatting toolbar.

If you have typographical training, you should be able to choose a font that's appropriate for the text that you've selected. Otherwise, you can't go wrong if you use Times New Roman (the default font) for the body text in all your documents and Arial for the titles, headings, and subheadings.

Arial is a *sans serif* type, which means it doesn't have horizontal lines on the bottoms or tops of the vertical lines in characters like *l*, *m*, or *p*. In contrast, Times New Roman does have serifs, which makes it easier to read in blocks of type like the body paragraphs of a document. Since both fonts come with *Windows*, they should be available on your PC. In addition, both are TrueType fonts so they're going to look the same on your screen as they'll look when printed.

The Font list that drops down from the Formatting toolbar

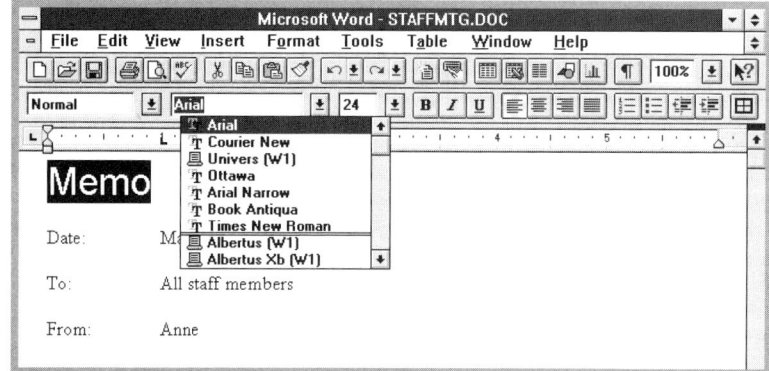

How to change the font of selected text

1. Click on the arrow to the right of the Font box to display a list of the available fonts.

2. Choose a font from the list. The ones above the double line are the ones you've used most recently; the ones after that are in alphabetical order. If necessary, scroll down the list to find the font you want.

Notes

- The small icons to the left of the font names indicate the font types. The double T icon indicates a TrueType font; the printer icon indicates a printer font. For most documents, you'll want to use TrueType fonts because they are displayed on the screen the way they'll look when they're printed. In contrast, printer fonts are designed for printing speed, and they don't always look the same on the screen as they look when printed.

- For reading ease, you should use a font that has serifs like Times New Roman. For titles, headings, and subheadings, you can use a type with serifs or a sans serif type like Arial. For special purposes, you may require a monospaced font like Courier New.

Figure 3-5   How to change the font

How to change the font size

Figure 3-6 shows how to change the *font size*. In most cases, you simply choose a size from the Font Size list that drops down from the Formatting toolbar. If you're working with a scaleable font like a TrueType font, however, you can use a font size other than those in the Font Size list. To do that, just type the size you want to use in the Font Size box.

The Font Size list that drops down from the Formatting toolbar

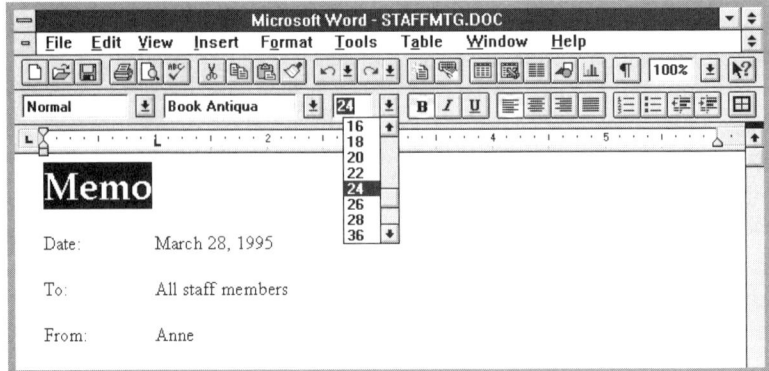

Two ways to change the font size

- Click on the arrow to the right of the Font Size box to display a list of the available font sizes. Then, choose a font size from the list.

- Click in the Font Size box. Then, type the font size that you want to use and press the Enter key.

Notes

- For reading ease, a font size of 10 to 12 points is recommended. Then, you can use larger sizes for titles, headings, and subheadings, and smaller sizes for less important text like footnotes.

- If you're using a TrueType font or another scaleable font, you can type any number into the Font Size box, even a fraction like 11.5.

Figure 3-6   **How to change the font size**

How to use the Font command to apply other formatting

Figure 3-7 shows how to use the Font command. However, you only need this command when you want to use special font effects, when you want to use a special type of underlining, when you want to use color, or when you want to change the default font. Otherwise, you can work more efficiently by using the Formatting toolbar.

How to set the default font

After you choose a font and font size from the Font dialog box, you can click on the Default button to make that your default font. When you change the default font, it is changed in the template that the active document is based on. Then, that font will be used in all new documents that are based on that template. At this point, you should be using the Normal template for all your documents, so the default font will be changed in that template. When in doubt, you can't go wrong by using Times New Roman in 12 point size as the default font.

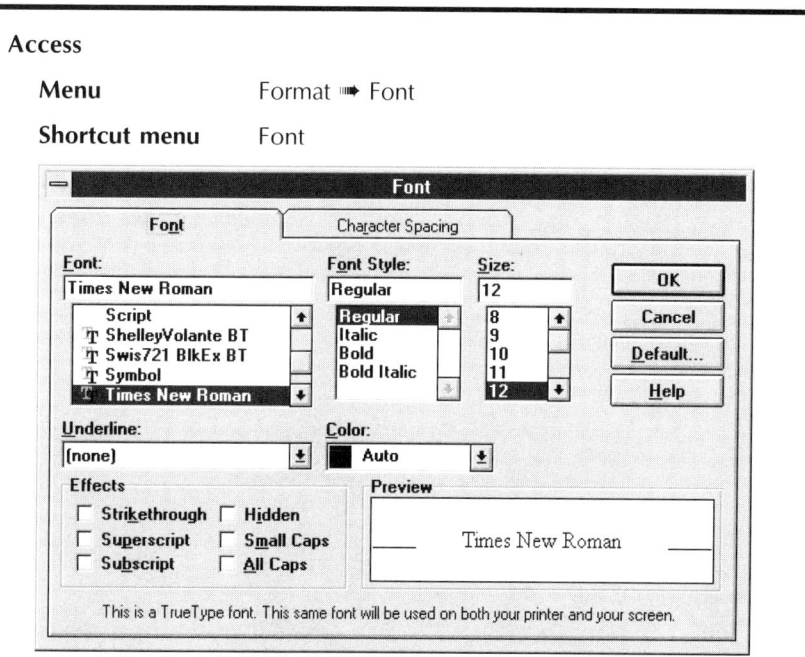

Access

Menu   Format ⟹ Font

Shortcut menu   Font

Operation

- To choose a font, font style, or font size, use the Font, Font Style, and Size boxes and lists. However, it's easier to do this kind of formatting from the Formatting toolbar.

- To specify the type of underlining you want to apply, choose an option from the Underline list. The choices are Single, Words Only, Double, or Dotted.

- To specify the color to be used, choose from one of 16 predefined colors in the Color list.

- For special font effects, check one or more of the boxes in the Effects group.

- Look at the Preview box to see how your choices and effects are going to look in the document before clicking on the OK button to complete the command.

How to change the default font for the template you're using

- After you choose the font and font size, click on the Default button. Word then displays a dialog box that asks whether you want to change the default font for the template that you're using. If you reply Yes, the default font is changed in the current document and in the template it's based on.

- The default font in the Normal template is Times New Roman in 12 point size. This font works well for the text in most documents.

Figure 3-7   How to use the Font command

Exercise set 3-2

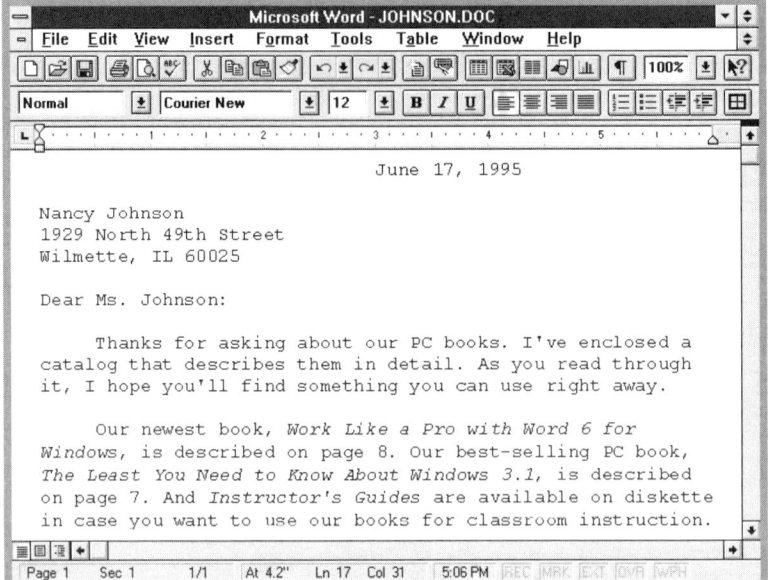

How the JOHNSON document should look after the font is changed to Courier New in exercise 2

1. Open the JOHNSON file, look at the Formatting toolbar, and note the font and font size. Then, press Ctrl+A to select the entire document, change the font to Arial, and click in the document to remove the selection. Note that Arial is a sans serif font. Is the text easier or harder to read than it was before?

2. Select the entire document again, change the font to Courier New, and click in the document to remove the selection. This is a monospaced font with serifs. Is it easier or harder to read than Arial?

3. Select the entire document again, change the font to Times New Roman, and click in the document to remove the selection. Note that this font has serifs. Is it easy to read? Next, select the entire document again and reduce the font size by two points. Is this font still easy to read? Now, select the entire document and press Ctrl+Spacebar to return to the default font and font size.

4. Access the Font dialog box as shown in figure 3-7. If necessary, change the font to Times New Roman and change the point size to 12. Next, click on the Default button to see the dialog box that's displayed when you change the default font. If you want to change the default, click on the Yes button; otherwise, click on the No button. Then, close the file without saving the changes. If you've changed the default font, a dialog box will be displayed when you exit from Word so you can confirm the change.

5. Start a new document and type the word *Memorandum.* With the insertion point anywhere in the word, click on the Bold button in the Formatting toolbar or press Ctrl+B. Next, use the toolbar to change the font to Arial and the font size to 36. Then, change the font size to 50.5. Last, press Ctrl+Spacebar to remove all character formatting, and close the document without saving it.

How to format paragraphs

You can usually format paragraphs faster than characters because you can select paragraphs faster than you can select characters. To select a single paragraph, just move the insertion point into it. To select two or more paragraphs, select any part of each paragraph. You don't have to carefully select all the characters in the paragraphs.

On the other hand, paragraph formatting gives many Word users trouble, and it tends to be especially troublesome to WordPerfect users who are converting to Word. The problem is that Word and WordPerfect are based on different concepts.

Paragraph formatting concepts

Figure 3-8 presents the paragraph formatting concepts that you need to understand when you're working with Word. The most important concept is that the formatting for a paragraph is stored in the *paragraph mark* at the end of the paragraph. So if you delete a paragraph mark, its formatting is lost and the paragraph takes on the formatting of the paragraph that follows it. This means that the formatting for a paragraph can change instantly if you accidentally delete a paragraph...but you can get it right back by pressing Ctrl+Z to undo the deletion of the paragraph mark.

After you use Word for a while, you'll find that the use of paragraph marks has certain benefits. In particular, you can carry formatting from one paragraph to the next by pressing the Enter key. When you first start using Word, though, you may want

---

A paragraph with default formatting followed by a numbered paragraph

Here·is·the·planned·agenda·for·our·next·meeting¶

1.   A·review·of·our·five·primary·goals·for·the·first·quarter¶

The paragraphs above after the first paragraph mark has been deleted

1.   Here·is·the·planned·agenda·for·our·next·meeting:·A·review· of·our·five·primary·goals·for·the·first·quarter¶

The types of formatting that can be applied to a paragraph

- Left, center, right, or justified alignment relative to the margins

- Bullets or numbers at the start of each paragraph with indentation after the bullet or number

- Indentation from left and right margins

- Tab stops for left, right, centered, or decimal alignment

- Spacing before, after, or within the paragraph

- Text flow options like keeping the following paragraph on the same page with the formatted paragraph

The significance of the paragraph mark at the end of each paragraph

- The formatting for a paragraph is stored in its paragraph mark (¶). If the nonprinting characters aren't displayed, you won't see the paragraph marks. To display the nonprinting characters, click on the Show/Hide button in the Standard toolbar.

- If you press the Enter key when the insertion point is at the end of a paragraph, that paragraph's formatting is carried forward into the new paragraph.

- If you delete a paragraph mark, that paragraph's formatting is lost and its text takes on the formatting of the paragraph that follows.

How to format paragraphs after they've been entered into a document

- Select any portion of the paragraphs that you want to format. You don't have to select entire paragraphs. If you want to format just one paragraph, move the insertion point into that paragraph. Then, apply the formatting.

How to return paragraphs to the default formatting

- Select the paragraphs, then press Ctrl+Q.

Figure 3-8   Paragraph formatting concepts

to display the nonprinting characters so the paragraph marks are visible. To do that, you can just click on the Show/Hide button in the Standard toolbar.

How to set tab stops

Figure 3-9 shows how to set the tab stops for one or more paragraphs using the ruler. As you can see, Word provides four different types of tab stops. Three can be used to align text to the left, center, or right of a tab stop. The fourth can be used to align numbers on their decimal points.

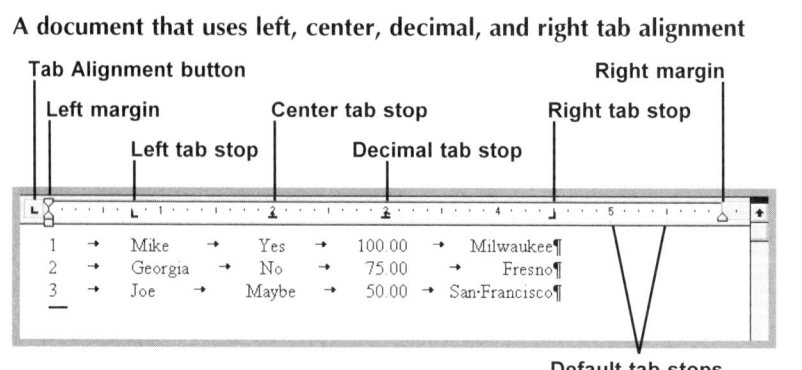

A document that uses left, center, decimal, and right tab alignment

How to set a tab stop in the selected paragraphs

- If necessary, click on the Tab Alignment button until the type of tab stop you want to use is displayed on the button: Left, Center, Right, or Decimal.

- Click the mouse in the lower half of the ruler where you want to set the tab stop. This sets a tab stop that becomes part of the formatting for the selected paragraphs. This also removes the default tab stops to the left of the new tab stop.

How to move a tab stop

- Drag the tab stop to a new position.

How to remove a tab stop

- Drag the tab stop off the ruler.

How to clear all the tab stops

- Double-click on a tab stop in the ruler to display the Tabs dialog box. Click on the Clear All button, then click on the OK button. The tab stops are then returned to their defaults.

Notes

- When you press the Tab key to move to a tab stop, the alignment that follows depends upon the type of tab stop you've used.

- The default tab stops appear as small marks along the bottom of the ruler. These tab stops remain in effect to the right of the last tab stop that you set.

- You can also set and clear tab stops using the Tabs dialog box. To display this dialog box, choose the Tabs command from the Format menu or double-click on a tab stop. The Tabs dialog box also lets you specify a leader (a dotted, dashed, or solid line) that's used to fill the empty space to the left of a tab stop.

Figure 3-9   How to set tab stops

How to indent paragraphs

You can also use the ruler to indent paragraphs as shown in figure 3-10. If, for example, you want to indent a paragraph from both the left and the right margins as in the second example, you just drag the left and right indent markers. Notice that when you drag the box at the bottom of the left indent marker, the first-line indent marker moves with it. To indent all of the lines in a paragraph except the first line, drag the triangle at the top of the left indent marker. The result is a hanging indent as shown in the third example in figure 3-10.

A paragraph with its first line indented

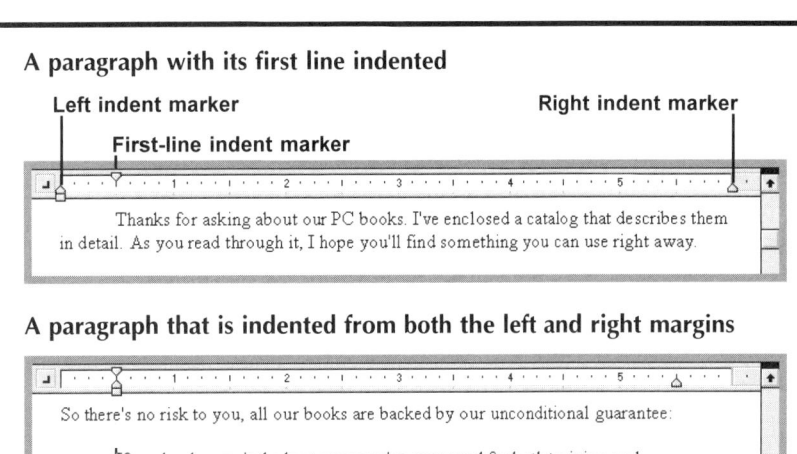

A paragraph that is indented from both the left and right margins

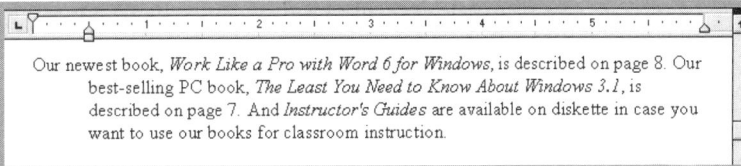

A paragraph with a hanging indent

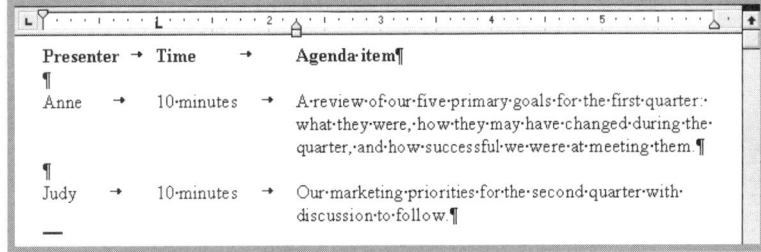

Three paragraphs that use one tab stop followed by a hanging indent

How to indent the selected paragraphs

- To indent the first lines, drag the first-line indent marker.

- To indent all lines, drag the bottom box of the left indent marker. This moves the first-line indent marker with it.

- To indent all lines but the first line, drag the top triangle of the left indent marker. This doesn't move the first-line indent marker with it.

- To indent from the right margin, drag the right indent marker.

Note

- You can also indent paragraphs using the Indents and Spacing tab of the Paragraph dialog box that's shown in figure 3-12.

Figure 3-10   How to indent paragraphs

How to bullet and number paragraphs

Figure 3-11 shows how easy it is to bullet and number paragraphs. Just select them and click on the correct button in the toolbar. This is particularly efficient for numbered lists, because the paragraphs are automatically numbered if you delete or rearrange them.

Remember, though, that the bullet or number formatting is stored in the paragraph marks. So if you press the Enter key with the insertion point at the end of a bulleted or numbered paragraph, a bullet or number is applied to the new paragraph. That means that if you want to leave space between two bulleted or numbered paragraphs, you can't just press the Enter key. Instead, you have to use one of the techniques described in figure 3-11.

A document that uses a numbered list

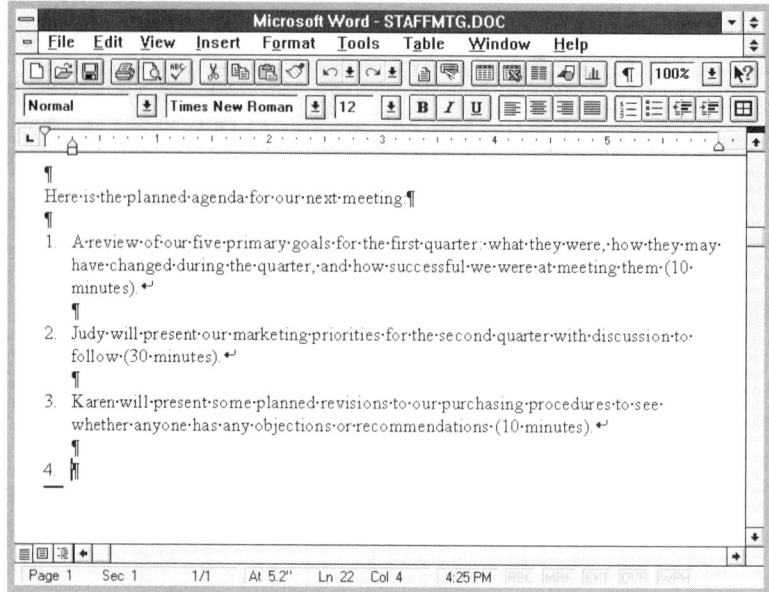

How to bullet the selected paragraphs

• Click on the Bullets button in the Formatting toolbar.

How to number the selected paragraphs

• Click on the Numbering button in the Formatting toolbar.

Two ways to add space between bulleted or numbered paragraphs

• Press Shift+Enter at the end of a paragraph. This starts a new line without starting a new paragraph that's automatically bulleted or numbered. In the example above, you can see the new line character in the paragraphs numbered 1 through 3.

• Leave a blank paragraph between each item in the list. When you're done entering the list, remove the numbers or bullets from the blank paragraphs. If the list is numbered, the remaining paragraphs are renumbered accordingly.

Two ways to remove bullets or numbers from selected paragraphs

• Click on the Bullets or Numbering button.

• Press Ctrl+Q to return to the default paragraph formatting.

Notes

• If you delete or move one of the numbered paragraphs in a numbered list, the paragraphs are renumbered automatically.

• Notice how the indent markers in the ruler indicate the indentation that is automatically applied to a numbered or bulleted paragraph.

• You can also apply bullets and numbers to paragraphs using the Bullets and Numbering command in the Format menu. See figure 3-13 for details.

Figure 3-11   How to apply bullets and numbers to paragraphs

Exercise set 3-3

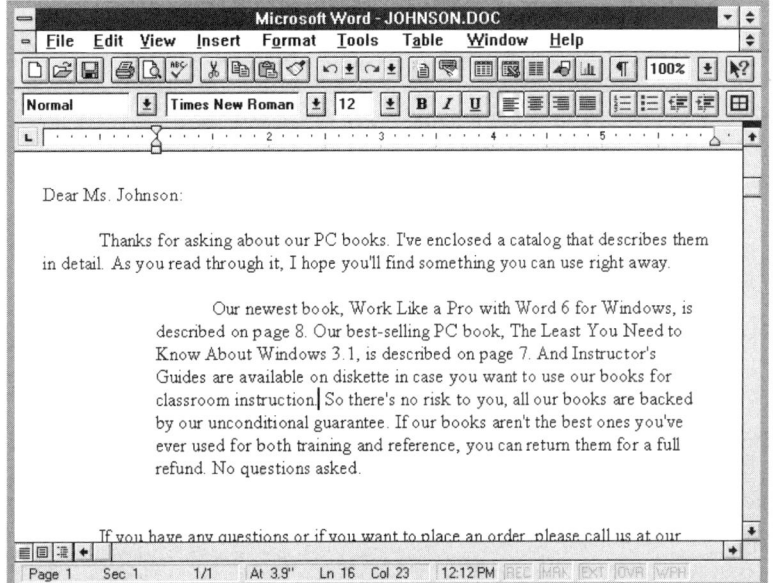

How the JOHNSON document should look after exercise 1

1. Open the JOHNSON document, and use the toolbar or shortcut key to indent the third paragraph in the body of the letter two tab stops (see figures 3-2 and 3-3). Next, move the insertion point to the end of this paragraph and press the Enter key. Note that the new paragraph mark is also indented two tab stops. In other words, the paragraph formatting is continued in the new paragraph. Then, move the insertion point to the end of the second paragraph and press the Delete key twice to delete the paragraph marks between the second and third paragraphs. Note that the formatting of the indented paragraph is applied to the second paragraph. Now, close the document, but don't save the changes.

2. Start a new document, display the ruler, and type the first line shown in figure 3-9 with Tab characters separating the five items in the line. Next, with the insertion point in this paragraph, set the four types of tab stops that are illustrated. These tab stops become part of the formatting for the first paragraph. Then, with the insertion point at the end of the first paragraph, press the Enter key to start a new paragraph that has the same tab stops and type the second line in this figure. Repeat this for the third line. Last, close the document without saving it.

3. Open the JOHNSON document, and delete the Tab character at the start of each of the paragraphs in the body of the letter. Next, use the ruler as shown in figure 3-10 to apply the first three types of indentation to the second paragraph in the body of the letter. Then, press Ctrl+Q to remove the formatting, press Ctrl+T to apply a hanging indent to the paragraph, and press Ctrl+Shift+T to remove the hanging indent.

4. Select a portion of all four paragraphs in the body of the letter. Next, use the ruler to indent the first lines in these paragraphs by one-half inch.

5. Start a new document, and type the text shown in figure 3-11. When you reach the paragraph that should be numbered 1, click on the Numbering button in the toolbar. Then, type the remaining paragraphs, pressing Shift+Enter at the end of each one to add extra space. When you reach the last paragraph and the number 4 is automatically applied to it, press Ctrl+Q to remove this formatting.

6. Move paragraph 3 up so it becomes paragraph 2 and note that the paragraphs are automatically renumbered. Then, select all of the numbered paragraphs and click on the Bullets button in the toolbar to change the numbers to bullets. Last, click on the Bullets button again to remove the bullets.

7. Close the open files without saving them.

More paragraph formatting

If you just did exercise set 3-3, I hope you already feel comfortable with paragraph formatting in Word. If so, you're ready to learn some additional formatting skills.

How to set the paragraph spacing before, after, and within paragraphs

An accomplished Word user doesn't press the Enter key twice to skip a line between paragraphs. Instead, the spacing before and after paragraphs is part of the formatting that's applied to each paragraph.

To apply spacing before or after a paragraph, you have to use the Indents and Spacing tab of the Paragraph dialog box that's summarized in figure 3-12. If, for example, the default font size is 12 points, you can set the Spacing After value to 12 points if you want to skip one line after a paragraph.

You can also use the Indents and Spacing tab to change the spacing within paragraphs. Remember, though, that you can use shortcut keys to change to single, double, and one and a half line spacing. So you'll only need to use this dialog box to change the line spacing if you want to use one of the custom options.

The Indents and Spacing tab also lets you align and change the indentation for selected paragraphs. Since that can usually be done more easily with the ruler, the Formatting toolbar, or shortcut keys, you probably won't use this dialog box to apply those types of formatting.

Access

Menu	Format ➡ Paragraph
Shortcut menu	Paragraph
Ruler	Double-click on an indent marker

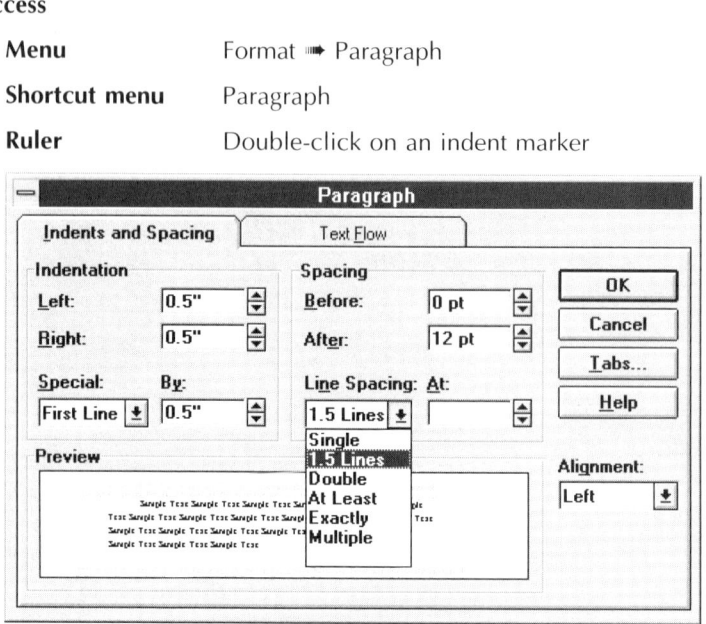

How to set the spacing before or after the selected paragraphs

- The Before and After boxes in the Spacing group let you set the spacing to be used before or after the selected paragraphs. If, for example, you set the After value to 12 points, one line is skipped after each paragraph. That way, you don't have to press the Enter key twice at the end of each paragraph to skip a line.

How to set the spacing within selected paragraphs

- The Line Spacing list lets you choose single, 1.5, or double spacing within the selected paragraphs. You can also use shortcut keys to set those line spacings. The At Least, Exactly, and Multiple options in the Line Spacing list let you specify custom line spacings. If you choose one of these options, you can specify the line spacing you want in the At box.

Other formatting that you can apply from the Paragraph dialog box

- The Left and Right boxes in the Indentation group let you set the indents from the margins, and the Special and By boxes let you set the first line or hanging indent. You can also set paragraph indents using the ruler, the Formatting toolbar, and shortcut keys.

- The Alignment list lets you choose the alignment for the selected paragraphs. You can also align paragraphs using buttons in the Formatting toolbar.

- The Tab button displays a dialog box that lets you set tab stops. You can also set tab stops using the ruler as described in figure 3-9.

- The Text Flow tab lets you specify advanced paragraph formatting, such as keeping the following paragraph on the same page as the selected paragraph. See chapter 4 for details.

Figure 3-12   How to set the spacing before, after, or within paragraphs

How to use the Bullets and Numbering command

For standard numbering and bulleting of paragraphs, it's easiest to use the buttons on the Formatting toolbar. But if you want to customize the bullets or numbers that are used, you need to use the Bullets and Numbering command that's summarized in figure 3-13.

Suppose, for example, that you want to use check marks as the bullets for the paragraphs in a list. To do that, you access the Bullets and Numbering command and click on the Bulleted tab shown at the top of figure 3-13. Because the check mark is not one of the default bullet options, you have to modify one of the options by clicking on it and then clicking on the Modify button. Then, the second dialog box shown in the figure is displayed. From this dialog box, you click on the Bullet button. This displays the Symbol dialog box, which you'll learn how to use in figure 3-21. There, you can choose the check mark symbol.

Although the Numbered tab of the Bullets and Numbering dialog box isn't shown, it provides six basic numbering options. If you don't want to use one of these, you can click on its Modify button to access another dialog box. There, you can change the starting number for the selected paragraphs, add text before or after the numbers, change the font and font size for the numbers, and so on. If you experiment, you should be able to get the result you want without much trouble. Unless you have strong reasons for customizing the numbers, though, you're probably better off using the default formats.

Access

Menu	Format ➜ Bullets and Numbering
Shortcut menu	Bullets and Numbering

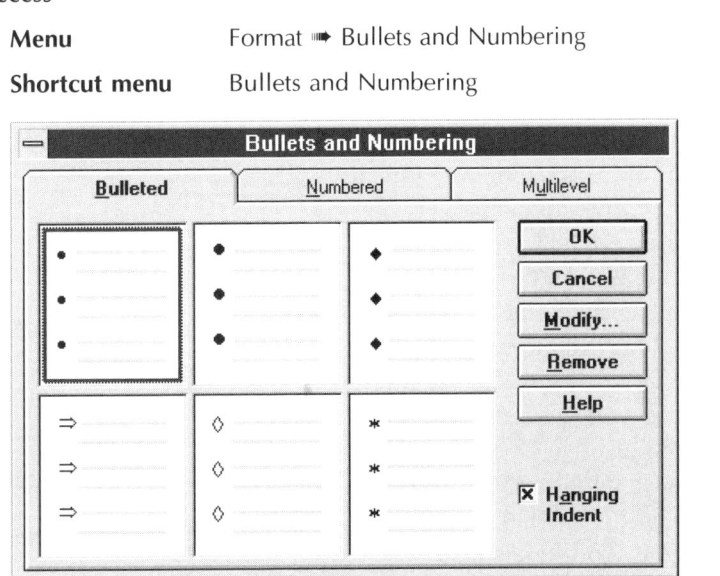

How to apply bullets to the selected paragraphs

- If necessary, click on the Bulleted tab to display that tab. Then, choose one of the six examples of bullets. Or, click on the Modify button to display this dialog box:

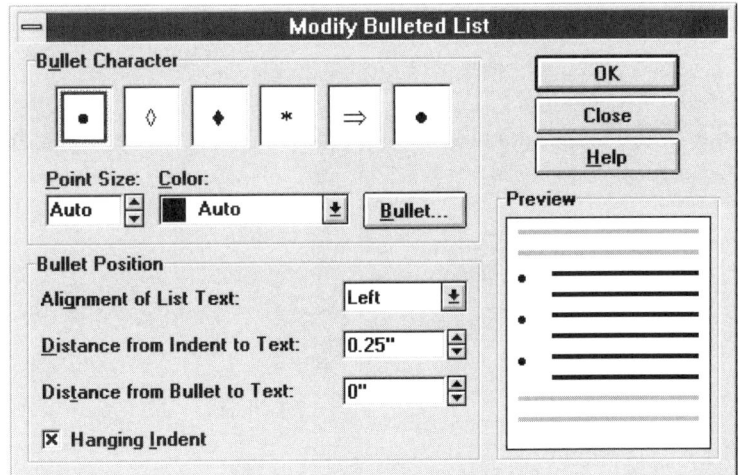

To choose a different bullet character, click on the Bullet button and choose the character from the Symbol dialog box that's displayed (see figure 3-21). You can also change the size, color, and position of the bullet character using the other options in the Modify Bulleted List dialog box.

How to apply numbers to the selected paragraphs

- If necessary, click on the Numbered tab to display that tab. Then, choose one of the six examples of numbering. Or, click on the Modify button to display a dialog box that gives you complete control over the number formatting, including the starting number in the series.

Figure 3-13   How to use the Bullets and Numbering command

How to apply borders and shading

With Word, you can apply borders to the selected paragraphs with just a few clicks of the mouse. Just click on the Borders button on the right end of the Formatting toolbar to display the Borders toolbar. Then, click on the button that represents the type of border you want to apply. This is summarized in figure 3-14. If you experiment with this, you'll see how easy it is.

Although you can also apply shading with just two clicks of the mouse, you should limit your use of shading because it makes text harder to read. You should also limit your use of borders because overuse makes them more distracting than useful.

Here again, you can use one of the commands in the Format menu if you need more control over the borders and shading that you apply. From a practical point of view, though, you should rarely need the Borders and Shading command.

The Borders toolbar and a paragraph with a bottom border

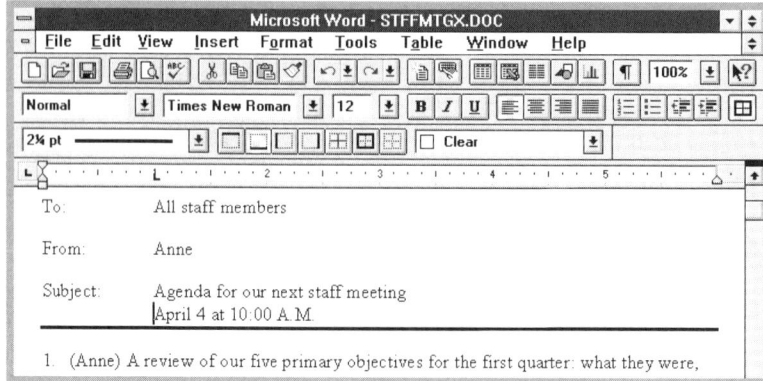

How to display the Borders toolbar

- Click on the Borders button in the Formatting toolbar.

How to apply a border to the selected paragraphs

1. If necessary, choose a line style from the Line Style list that drops down on the left side of the Borders toolbar.

2. Click on the Top, Bottom, Left, Right, or Outside Border buttons. This applies the border to the selected paragraphs, and makes the button look like it is pushed in.

How to remove a border from the selected paragraphs

- Click on the Top, Bottom, Left, Right, or Outside Border button that applied the border. Or, click on the No Border button.

How to apply and remove shading

- To apply shading to the selected paragraphs, choose a shading style from the Shading list that drops down on the right side of the Borders toolbar.

- To remove shading from the selected paragraphs, choose the Clear option in the Shading list.

Notes

- Borders on the top or bottom of a paragraph extend from the left indent to the right indent.

- The fifth button on the Borders toolbar adds borders between the cells in a table. It can also be used to add a border between the selected paragraphs.

- Since shading makes the text in a paragraph more difficult to read, it should be used with discretion.

- You can also use the Borders and Shading command in the Format menu to apply borders and shading. This command lets you apply a shadow box border and color, which you can't do from the Borders toolbar. And it lets you set the distance between the text and the border.

Figure 3-14   How to apply borders and shading to paragraphs

Exercise set 3-4

Memo¶

Date: →   March·28,·1995¶

To: →   All·staff·members¶

From: →   Anne¶

Subject: →   Agenda·for·our·next·staff·meeting↵
    →   April·4·at·10:00·A.M.¶

1. (Anne)·A·review·of·our·five·primary·objectives·for·the·first·quarter:·what·they·were,·
    how·they·may·have·changed·during·the·quarter,·and·how·successful·we·were·at·
    meeting·them.¶

2. (Judy)·Our·marketing·priorities·and·plans·for·the·second·quarter.¶

3. (Karen)·A·recommendation·for·price·increases·due·to·the·rapid·rise·in·paper·costs·
    during·the·last·nine·months.¶

If·you·want·to·add·something·to·the·agenda,·please·contact·me·by·Friday.¶

—

The document you'll create in this exercise set

This exercise set has you enter and format a memo like the one shown above. The nonprinting characters are shown in this document so you can better tell how the paragraphs are formatted. In particular, please note (1) that the paragraphs are formatted with 12 points of spacing after each so you only press the Enter key once at the end of each paragraph; (2) that top and bottom borders are applied to the first and last paragraphs in the memo heading; and (3) that a tab stop is set at one inch from the left margin for the paragraphs in the heading so it takes only one Tab character to align the text in these paragraphs. The exercises that follow guide you through the development of a memo like this.

1. Start a new document, and use the Paragraph command in the Format menu to format the first paragraph with 12 points of spacing after it. This spacing will be continued in the paragraphs that follow unless you remove the formatting.

2. Type the word *Memo* and press the Enter key. Then, select the word and boldface it, center it, and change the font size to 24 points.

3. Type the Date paragraph, entering the date as a field, and set a left tab stop at one-inch. This tab stop will be continued in the paragraphs that follow unless you remove the formatting. Next, type the To, From, and Subject paragraphs, entering a date that is one week from the current date in the Subject paragraph. (Note in the Subject paragraph that you have to use Shift+Enter to start the second line of the paragraph without starting a new paragraph.) Press the Enter key one more time

to start the next paragraph. Then, use the Borders toolbar to apply a 2-1/4 point top border to the Date paragraph and a 2-1/4 point bottom border to the Subject paragraph.

4. Type paragraph 1 in the body of the memo, and click on the Numbering button to number it. Then, type the rest of the memo. To remove the number 4 from the last paragraph, click on the Numbering button again.

5. Check the spelling in the memo. Then, save it with the name STFFMEMO and print it.

6. Use the Bullets and Numbering command in the Format menu to change the numbered paragraphs to paragraphs that are bulleted with an asterisk (*). Then, print the memo, and close the file without saving it.

7. This exercise shows how you can use the AutoText feature that you learned about in chapter 2 to start a memo. First, open the STFFMEMO file. Next, delete everything below the border for the Subject paragraph; delete the entries after To and Subject in those paragraphs; and replace the name Anne with your own name. Then, select the entire document (Ctrl+A), click on the Edit AutoText button in the Standard toolbar, and enter *memo* as the abbreviation for this AutoText entry. To test this entry, start a new document, type *memo*, and press F3. This gives you some idea of how useful this feature can be. In chapter 5, though, you'll learn a better way to start documents. To complete this exercise, close all files without saving them.

How to format pages

The most common page formatting function is setting the margins for all the pages in the entire document. As you will see, that can be done with a few clicks of the mouse. For more advanced page formatting, though, you need to understand the page formatting concepts.

Page formatting concepts

Figure 3-15 presents the page formatting concepts that Word users need to know. Here again, the concepts differ from the ones that WordPerfect users are accustomed to so it's worth taking the time to review them.

Perhaps most important is the notion that the page formatting usually applies to the *section* that the insertion point is in, not to the remainder of the document. Since most documents consist of only one section, that means you can format all the pages no matter where the insertion point is in the document. This is quite different from the way WordPerfect works.

If you do divide a document into two or more sections, the formatting of a section is stored in the *section break*. This is comparable to the notion that the formatting for a paragraph is stored in the paragraph mark. Then, if you delete the section break, you also reformat the section with the formatting of the section that followed it.

A document in Normal view that contains two sections

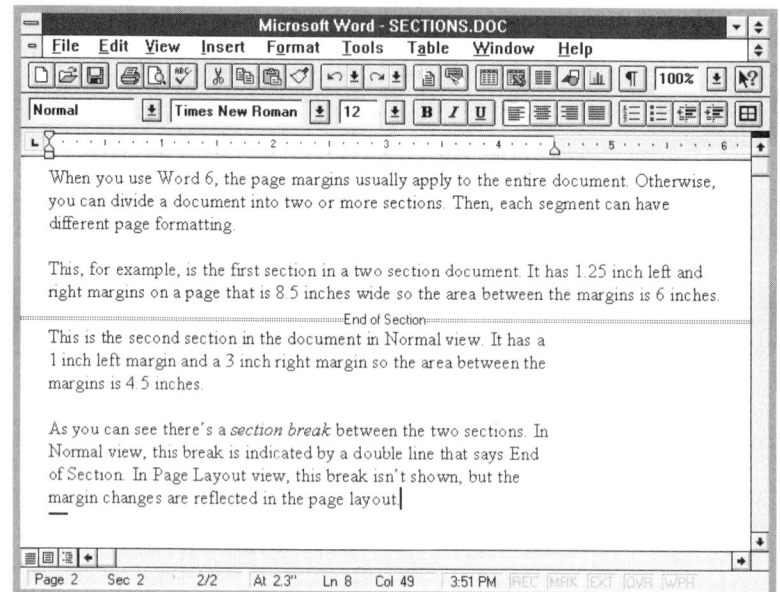

The types of page formatting that can be applied to a section

- Top, bottom, left, and right margins
- Paper size
- Vertical or horizontal orientation
- Vertical alignment (top, center, or justified)
- Line numbering
- Paper source

The significance of the section break at the end of a section

- The formatting for a section is stored in the section break at the end of the section.
- If you delete a section break, that section's formatting is lost and it takes on the formatting of the section that follows it.

Notes

- Most documents consist of only one section.
- If you want to use different page formats for two different portions of a document, you need to divide the document into sections. To do that, you can use the Page Setup command.

Figure 3-15   Page formatting concepts

How to set margins

Figure 3-16 shows how easy it is to change the margins for a document that contains only one section. Just access the Margins tab of the Page Setup dialog box, change the margin values, and make sure that the Apply To option is Whole Document.

The other Apply To option for a document that consists of one section is This Point Forward. If you choose this option, a new section is started at the insertion point and the page formatting is applied to that section only. For most documents, though, you don't need to do that.

When you set the left and right margins for a document, you should relate them to the font and font size that you're using. As a general rule, the margins should be set so the line length isn't longer than 65 or 70 characters. Beyond that, the text becomes increasingly difficult to read.

That means that the default margins of 1.25 inches are about right for 12-point Times New Roman. That way, the area between the margins is six inches, which accommodates about 70 characters per line. Then, if you reduce the font size to 10 points, you should increase the left and right margins to 1.75 so the area between them is only five inches. Failing to do this is a common problem in modern business documents.

Access

 Menu   File ➡ Page Setup

 Ruler   Double-click in gray area

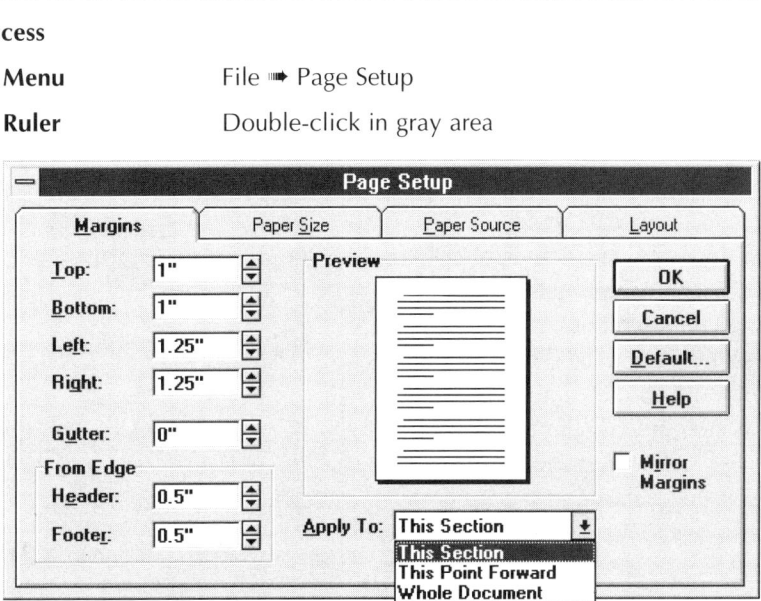

How to set the margins for the entire document

- If necessary, click on the Margins tab. Then, change any of the values in the Top, Bottom, Left, or Right boxes, and choose the Whole Document option from the Apply To list.

How to start a new section that the margin settings apply to

- Choose the This Point Forward option from the Apply To list.

Notes

- This Section isn't one of the options in the Apply To list until the document contains two or more sections. If you choose This Section, the page formatting is applied to the section that the insertion point is in.

- In Page Layout view, you can also change the margins by dragging the Left or Right margin of the horizontal ruler or the Top or Bottom margin of the vertical ruler. The changes are then applied to the section that the insertion point is in.

- The Header and Footer values give the location of the headers and footers. See chapter 4 to learn more about them.

- The Mirror Margins check box can be used when printing on both sides of the paper. If checked, the even numbered pages have the same margins as the odd numbered pages, but reversed (or mirrored).

- To save the page setup in the template that the document is based on, click on the Default button.

Figure 3-16   How to set the page margins

How to set layout options

Figure 3-17 shows the Layout tab of the Page Setup dialog box. This tab is useful for letters because the Vertical Alignment list lets you vertically center the text on a page. Because this can significantly improve the appearance of a letter, it's worth using for most letters.

The Layout tab in figure 3-17 also illustrates the This Point Forward option. In this example, this option will start a new section on a new page as indicated by the New Page option in the Section Start box. That's normally the way you want a new section started.

The Layout tab of the Page Setup dialog box

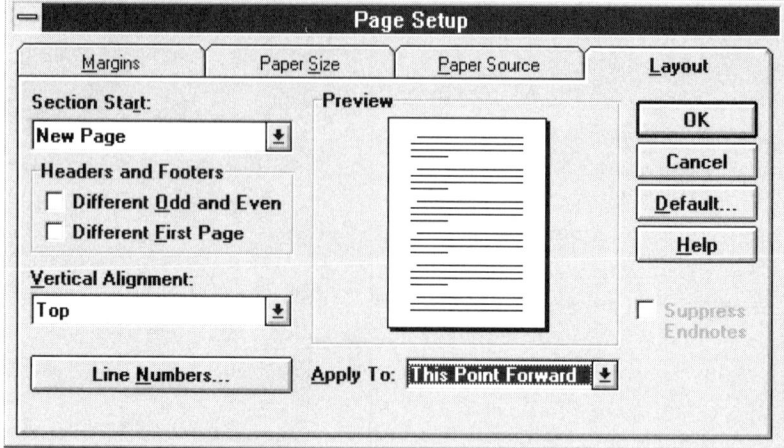

How to vertically center pages between the top and bottom margins

- Choose the Center option from the Vertical Alignment list. This is a useful option for letters.

How to start a new section that the layout settings apply to

- Choose the This Point Forward option from the Apply To list. Then, choose an option from the Section Start list to indicate where the new section should start: right after the insertion point (Continuous), on the next page (New Page), on the next even page (Even Page), or on the next odd page (Odd Page). The default is New Page, which is usually what you want.

Other options in the Layout tab

- The check boxes in the Headers and Footers group let you specify whether you want different headers and footers on odd and even pages or a different header on the first page. You'll learn more about these options in the next chapter.

- If you want to number the lines in a document, you can click on the Line Numbers button. This displays a dialog box that lets you give the line numbering specifications. Then, when you print the document or display it in Page Layout view, you can see the line numbers to the left of the text.

Figure 3-17   How to use the Layout tab of the Page Setup command

How to set the options for paper size, orientation, and source

Figure 3-18 illustrates the other two tabs for the Page Setup command. If you want to print on non-standard paper sizes or if you want to print sideways on the paper, you need to use the Paper Size tab. If you want to print one portion of a document on the paper from one feed of a printer and another portion of a document on paper from another feed, you need to use the Paper Source tab.

The Paper Size tab of the Page Setup dialog box

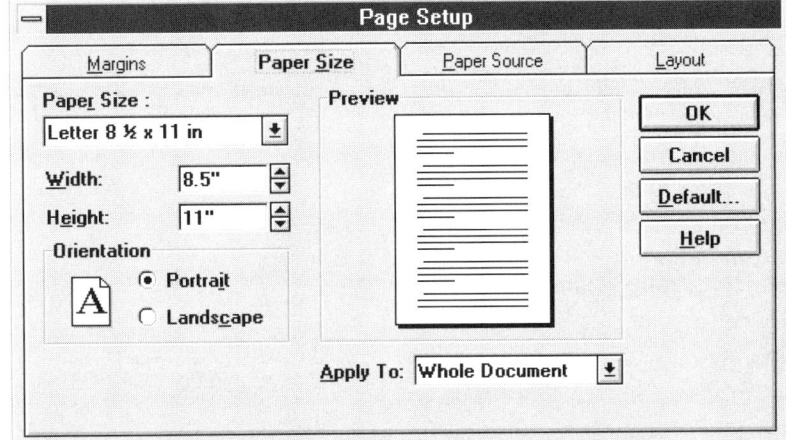

Operation

• To change the paper size, choose a size from the Paper Size list. Or, to create a custom size, set the Width and Height values.

• To print the document horizontally instead of vertically on the page, click on the Landscape option.

The Paper Source tab of the Page Setup dialog box

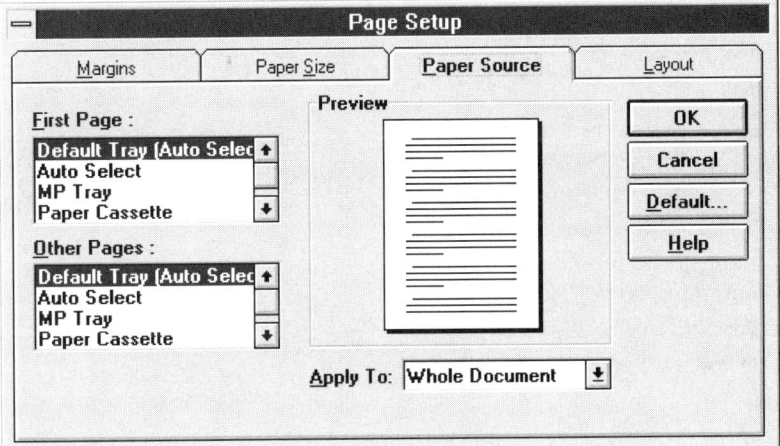

Operation

• If you want to print the first page of a document on the paper from one feed of the printer and the other pages on paper from another feed, choose the feeds in the First Page and Other Pages boxes.

Notes

• You don't need to use the Paper Source tab if you want to print the entire document on a special feed of the printer you're using. To do that, click on the Options button in the Print dialog box and choose the feed from the Default Tray list.

• You can use the Apply To list in either tab to indicate the part of the document you want the options applied to.

Figure 3-18   The Paper Size and Paper Source tabs of the Page Setup command

How to preview a document before you print it

When you first start using Word, it's a good idea to preview your documents before you print them to be sure that they'll print the way you want them to. To do that, you use the techniques presented in figure 3-19. In the example at the top of the figure, you can see the JOHNSON letter in preview mode after it's been centered vertically on the page.

After you've used Word for a while, you probably won't need to preview short documents like the one in figure 3-19. However, you will want to preview larger documents that contain additional features such as headers or footers. That way, you can save yourself the time and cost of reprinting long documents. You'll learn about the features for preparing multi-page documents in the next chapter.

Notice in figure 3-19 that you can also edit a document and change its margins in preview mode. Normally, though, you're better off editing in Normal or Page Layout view, and you're better off using the Page Setup command to change the margins.

Access

Menu	File ➡ Print Preview
Standard toolbar	🔍

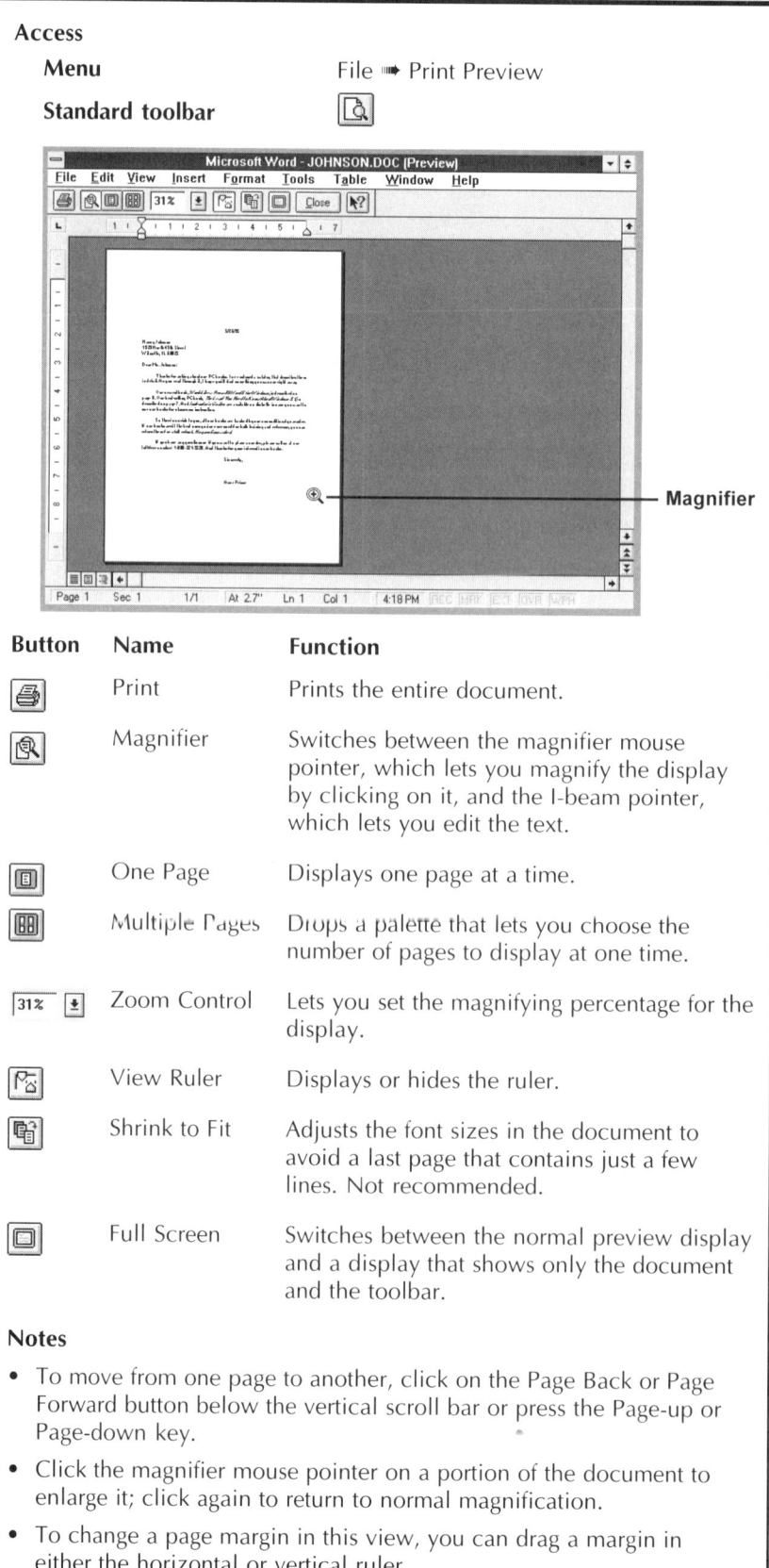

Button	Name	Function
🖨	Print	Prints the entire document.
🔍	Magnifier	Switches between the magnifier mouse pointer, which lets you magnify the display by clicking on it, and the I-beam pointer, which lets you edit the text.
▦	One Page	Displays one page at a time.
▦	Multiple Pages	Drops a palette that lets you choose the number of pages to display at one time.
31% ▼	Zoom Control	Lets you set the magnifying percentage for the display.
▦	View Ruler	Displays or hides the ruler.
▦	Shrink to Fit	Adjusts the font sizes in the document to avoid a last page that contains just a few lines. Not recommended.
▦	Full Screen	Switches between the normal preview display and a display that shows only the document and the toolbar.

Notes

- To move from one page to another, click on the Page Back or Page Forward button below the vertical scroll bar or press the Page-up or Page-down key.

- Click the magnifier mouse pointer on a portion of the document to enlarge it; click again to return to normal magnification.

- To change a page margin in this view, you can drag a margin in either the horizontal or vertical ruler.

Figure 3-19   How to preview a document

Exercise set 3-5

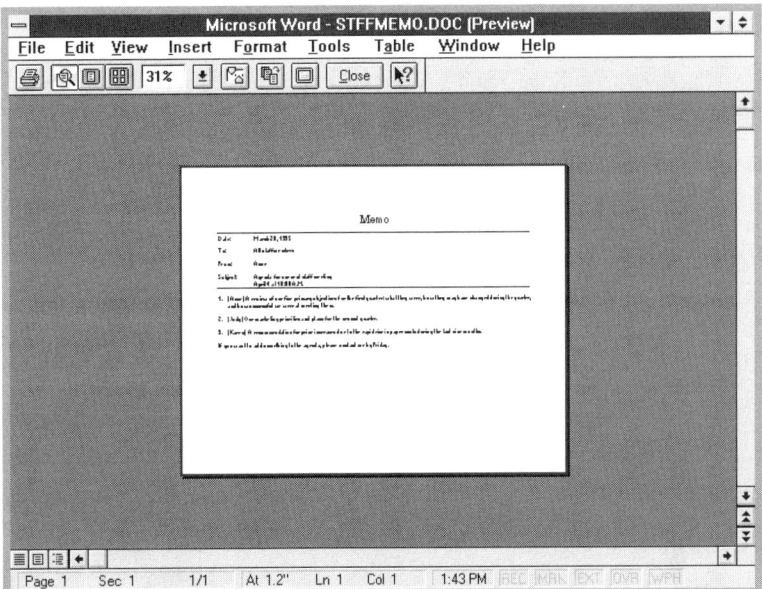

How the STFFMEMO document should look when you preview it in exercise 2

1. Open the JOHNSON document. Assuming that this letter is going to be printed on paper with a two inch letterhead, access the Page Setup command and change the top margin to 2 inches. Also, access the Layout tab and choose the Center option from the Vertical Alignment list. (Both changes should of course apply to the whole document.) Then, click on the OK button to complete the command, and click on the Print Preview button in the Standard toolbar to see how these formatting changes will affect the layout of the letter. Print the document using the Print button in the Print Preview toolbar; save the document; and close it.

2. Open the STFFMEMO document. Next, use the Page Setup command to change the orientation of this document from Portrait to Landscape. Then, preview the document to see how this formatting change affects the appearance of the memo. Close the document without saving it.

Three skills for special purposes

To complete this chapter, you'll learn how to use two more commands and the Format Painter button. The first command makes it easy to prepare an envelope from a letter in the special format that's required for an envelope. The second command lets you insert special characters and symbols into a document. And the Format Painter button is occasionally useful for quick formatting.

How to create and print an envelope

Figure 3-20 shows how to use the Envelopes and Labels command to print an envelope. If the options are set right, you just access the dialog box and click on the Print or Add to Document button. Everything else is automatic. This is an excellent feature that makes letter writing easier than ever.

If you're not familiar with POSTNET bar codes, they are supposed to improve the speed and accuracy of postal delivery. As a result, it's usually worth setting this option so they are automatically printed.

Access

Menu   Tools ➡ Envelopes and Labels

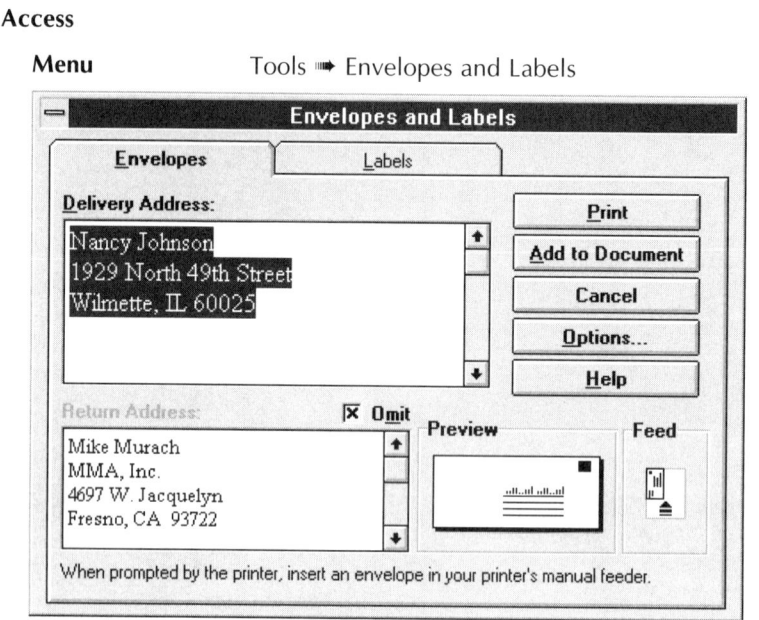

Operation

- When you access this command from a document that starts with a letter, Word automatically picks up the delivery address from the document.

- To print the envelope, click on the Print button. To add the envelope at the start of the document in its own section, click on the Add to Document button.

- If you're going to print on a standard size 10 business envelope, the options are probably set the way you want them. Otherwise, you can click on the Options button and adjust the options.

- If you are going to print on envelopes with preprinted return addresses, make sure that the Omit box above the return address is checked.

- When you print the envelope, feed it into the printer as shown in the Feed box. Note, however, that this doesn't work correctly for every printer so you may have to experiment with it.

Notes

- One of the options that you can set by clicking on the Options button is the Delivery Point Bar Code. When this option is on, a POSTNET bar code is printed above the mailing address on the envelope. This can increase the speed and accuracy of mail delivery.

- The return address is taken from the User Info tab of the Options dialog box that you access from the Tools menu.

Figure 3-20   How to print an envelope for a letter

How to insert symbols into a document

If you occasionally need to use symbols that aren't part of the font you're using, you can use the Symbol command to access them. Figure 3-21 shows how. Although Word comes with a variety of fonts that contain symbols, the two fonts that are most useful are Symbol and Wingdings. The Symbol font is most useful when you're developing a document with mathematical or scientific formulas. The Wingdings font has symbols that can be used for a wider range of purposes.

Access

Menu   Insert ➡ Symbol

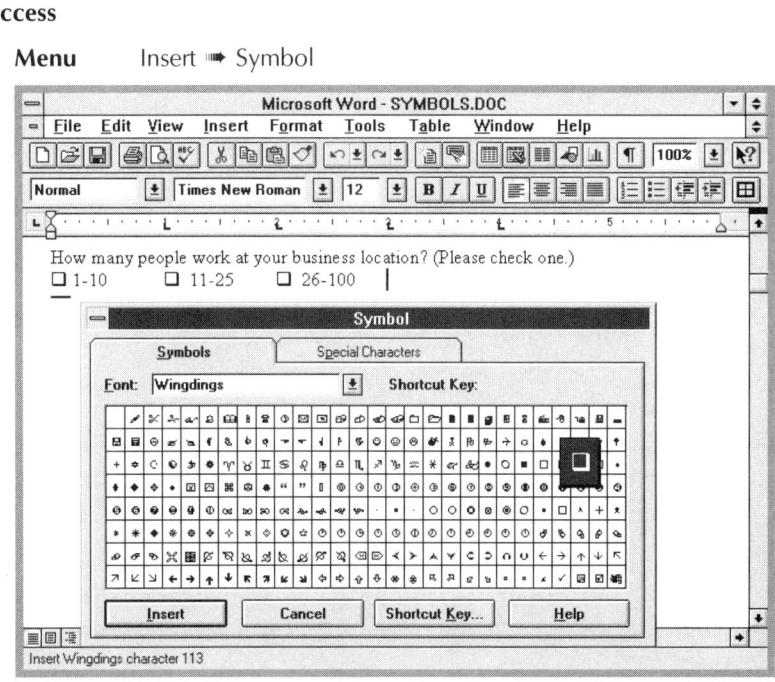

Operation

- Use the Font list to choose a font. The Symbol and Wingdings fonts are two of the most useful, and they come with Windows so they should be available on your system.

- To look more closely at a symbol, click on it. Then, it is enlarged as shown above.

- To insert the highlighted symbol into the document, click on the Insert button. Or double-click on any symbol to insert it.

- To edit a document while the Symbol dialog box is still on your screen, click in the document.

- To enlarge a symbol in the document, select it and change the font size.

- If a symbol has a shortcut key that you can use for inserting it into a document, it is displayed in the upper right corner of the Symbols tab when that symbol is highlighted. To assign your own shortcut key to the highlighted symbol, click on the Shortcut Key button.

Notes

- All fonts have some special characters that there's no key on the keyboard for. To see what other characters or symbols are available for the default font, choose normal text from the top of the Font list.

- The Special Characters tab of the Symbol dialog box lets you insert additional characters into a document. Most of these characters are used for typesetting documents, so you'll probably never need them.

Figure 3-21   How to insert symbols into a document

How to copy formats with the Format Painter

To the right of the Paste button in the Standard toolbar, you'll find the Format Painter button. You can use it to format both characters and paragraphs as shown in figure 3-22.

This skill is presented last because you don't need it if you format a document as you create and edit it. In general, the Format Painter button is most useful when you're reformatting characters in a completed document.

A document that shows the paintbrush mouse pointer

Format Painter button

Paintbrush pointer

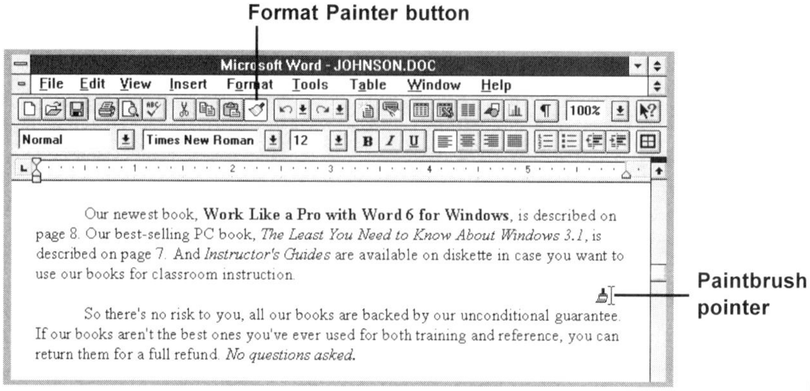

How to reformat several text selections

1. Move the insertion point into a word that has the character formatting that you want to apply to other text selections.

2. Double-click on the Format Painter button in the Standard toolbar. This changes the mouse pointer to the paintbrush and I-beam pointer shown above.

3. Drag the paintbrush mouse pointer over the text that you want to reformat. When you release the mouse button, the new formatting replaces the old. You can repeat this operation until you've painted all the selections.

4. To end the reformatting, click on the Format Painter button again or press the Esc key.

How to reformat just one text selection

- Instead of double-clicking on the Format Painter button in step 2, single-click. Then, the function automatically ends after you drag over one selection so you don't need to do step 4. You probably don't need the Format Painter, though, if you're only going to reformat one selection.

How to reformat paragraphs

- If you include a paragraph mark in step 1, both character and paragraph formatting are applied as you paint selections.

Figure 3-22   How to use the Format Painter to copy formatting

Exercise set 3-6

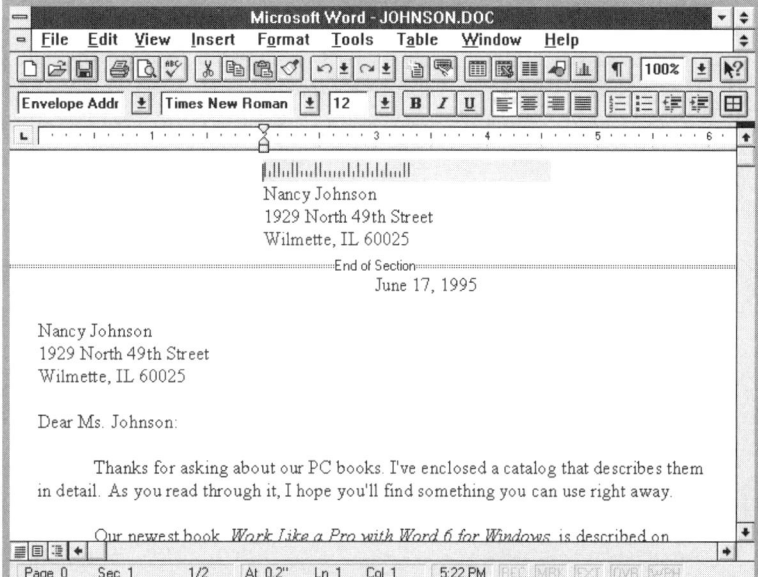

How the JOHNSON document should look after you add an envelope in exercise 1

1. Open the JOHNSON document, and access the Envelopes tab of the Envelopes and Labels dialog box as shown in figure 3-20. If a bar code isn't shown above the mailing address in the Preview box, click on the Options button; click on the Delivery Point Bar Code option; and click on the OK button to return to the Envelopes and Labels dialog box. Assuming that the mailing address is going to be printed on an envelope with a preprinted return address, make sure that the Omit option for the return address is checked. Then, click on the Add to Document button to insert the envelope into the document. In the document, you can see that the envelope is in one section of the document and the letter is in another. Last, click on the Print Preview button in the Standard toolbar to see how the envelope and letter are going to look when printed. When you're satisfied that this feature works the way you want it to, close the file without saving it.

2. Start a new document, and use the Symbol command to insert one of the symbols in the Wingdings font into the document. Then, increase the font size of the symbol to 30 points. That's how easy it is to insert a symbol into a document. Now, close the document without saving it.

3. Open the JOHNSON document, and change the formatting for the word *Work* in the second paragraph from italic to bold. Next, with the insertion point in this bold word, double-click on the Format Painter button so the mouse pointer becomes a paint brush for applying bold formatting. Then, paint the rest of the italic characters in the letter so they are changed to bold. When you're through, click on the Format Painter button again to end the painting function, and close the document without saving it. Could you do this reformatting of the document more quickly another way? How?

4. Exit from Word. If you changed the default font in exercise set 3-2, a dialog box is displayed that asks you if you want to save the changes to the Normal template. Click on the Yes button if you want to save the changes.

Perspective

If you've done all the exercises for this chapter, you should start to see how quickly and easily you can format the characters, paragraphs, and pages in a Word document. You should also be able to format simple documents so they look just the way you want them to.

To work as an accomplished professional, though, you need to master the use of styles and templates. So in the next chapter, you'll be introduced to styles. In chapter 5, you'll learn how to use templates. And in chapter 6, you'll master the use of styles.

Summary

- You can start formatting commands and functions with shortcut keys, shortcut menus, the ruler, the Formatting toolbar, the Borders toolbar, and the Format menu. You can apply formatting to characters, paragraphs, and pages.

- To change the *font* or font size for selected text, you can use the Formatting toolbar. To remove the character formatting from selected text, you can press Ctrl+Spacebar.

- The formatting for a paragraph is stored in its *paragraph mark*. If you press the Enter key at the end of a paragraph, its paragraph formatting is carried forward into the new paragraph.

- The quickest way to set tabs and indents for selected paragraphs is to use the ruler. The quickest way to align, bullet, or number paragraphs is to use the Formatting toolbar. And the quickest way to apply borders and shading to paragraphs is to use the Borders toolbar.

- To set the spacing before, after, or within a paragraph, you need to use the Paragraph command in the Format menu.

- To format the pages in an entire document, you use the Page Setup command in the File menu. If you want to use different page formatting for different parts of a document, you need to divide the document into *sections*. Then, the formatting for each section is stored in its *section break*.

- Before you print a document, you can preview it. That way, you can be sure that the document is formatted the way you want it before you print it.

- The Envelopes and Labels command in the Tools menu provides a quick way to prepare an envelope for a letter. The Symbol command in the Insert menu lets you insert special characters and symbols into a document. And the Format Painter button in the Standard toolbar is occasionally useful for reformatting a document.

Chapter 4

Commands and features for preparing multi-page documents

In this chapter, you'll learn the skills that you need for preparing multi-page documents like reports and proposals. Most importantly, you'll learn how to use styles to quickly and easily format the headings and subheadings that are used in a document. And you'll learn how to use headers and footers to date and number the pages in a document.

How to use styles to format headings and subheadings

In business, any document of two or more pages should include headings and subheadings that identify the topics within the document. To make it easy to format these headings and sub-headings, Word provides heading *styles*. Each style provides all the formatting that you need for a heading or subheading paragraph including both character and paragraph formatting, and you can apply each style with just one shortcut key or two clicks of the mouse.

When you start a new document, it is always based on a *template* that includes a variety of styles. If you don't apply any of these styles to a document, Word automatically uses the Normal style for each paragraph you enter. That's true whether the document is based on the Normal template, which is the default, or any other template. No matter what template you use though, the heading styles are always available and they're easy to apply so you should use them in any document that contains headings.

How to apply a heading style to a paragraph

Figure 4-1 shows how easy it is to apply a heading style to a paragraph. Just select the paragraph and choose the heading style you want from the Style list. Or, use the shortcut keys shown in the figure. You can use the same techniques to apply other styles to paragraphs, but the heading styles are the ones you'll apply the most.

The Style list that drops down from the Formatting toolbar

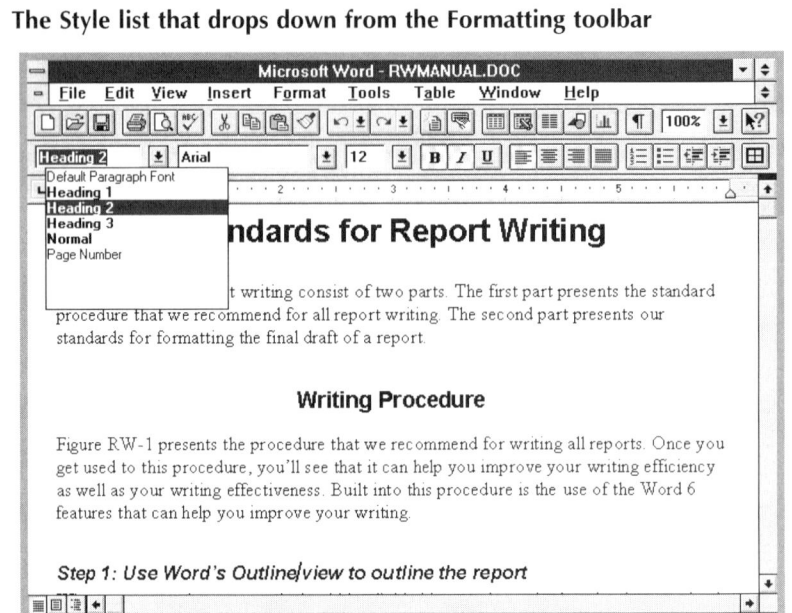

How to use the toolbar to apply a style to a paragraph

1. Move the insertion point into the paragraph.

2. Click on the arrow to the right of the Style box to display the Style list.

3. Click on style you want to apply.

The shortcut keys for applying the styles in the Normal template

Key	Style
Ctrl+Shift+N	Normal
Ctrl+Alt+1	Heading 1
Ctrl+Alt+2	Heading 2
Ctrl+Alt+3	Heading 3

Note

- The Normal template contains styles in addition to those shown above. Some of these styles are applied automatically when you use certain features of Word. Later in this chapter, for example, you'll learn that the Header and Footer styles are automatically applied to the headers and footers in a document. Once these styles are applied, they appear in the Style list along with the other styles.

Figure 4-1   How to apply a style to a paragraph

How styles and direct formatting work together

When you use styles to format the paragraphs in a document, the formatting is applied *indirectly*: You apply the styles, and the styles apply the formatting. In contrast, when you use the skills presented in chapter 3 to format the characters and paragraphs in a document, you apply the formatting *directly*. What happens when you mix indirect and direct formatting? Figure 4-2 explains.

When you apply a style to a paragraph that has been directly formatted, the style overrides the direct formatting. Similarly, if you apply direct formatting to a paragraph that has a style applied to it, the direct formatting overrides the style formatting.

In practice, that means that you should apply styles to the paragraphs in a document before you apply any direct formatting. Then, if you want to adjust the formatting of the style for just a paragraph or two, you can apply direct formatting to those paragraphs. If, for example, you want to increase or decrease the space before or after a heading style, you can use the Paragraph command to change just the spacing while leaving all the other style formatting intact.

In figure 4-2, direct formatting has been applied to the title paragraph in the document, which has the Normal style applied to it. If you look in the formatting information that's displayed for this paragraph, you can see that direct formatting has been used to center the paragraph, to change the spacing after, and to change the font.

The formatting information that can be displayed for a paragraph

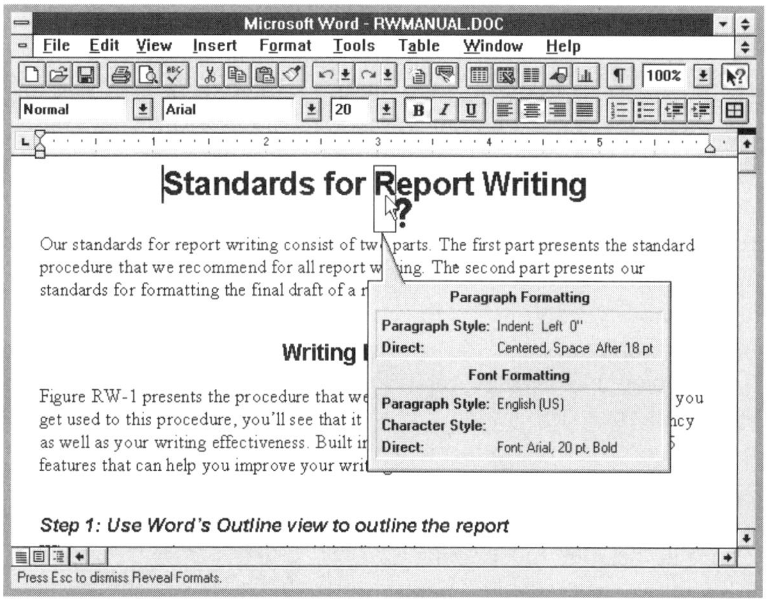

How styles and direct formatting affect each other

- When you apply a style to a paragraph, it overrides any direct formatting that has been applied to it.

- If you apply direct formatting to a paragraph after a style has been applied to it, the direct formatting overrides the style formatting.

- In the example above, direct formatting has been used to override the formatting that has been applied by the Normal style.

How use the Help button to display formatting information

- Click on the Help button in the Standard toolbar, then click on a paragraph.

- To remove the formatting information from the screen, click on the Help button again or press the Esc key.

The default formatting for the paragraph styles in the Normal template

Style	Character formatting	Paragraph formatting
Heading 1	Arial 14 point bold	Left aligned; single spaced 12 points before; 3 points after
Heading 2	Arial 12 point Bold italic	Left aligned; single spaced 12 points before; 3 points after
Heading 3	Times New Roman 12 point bold	Left aligned; single spaced 12 points before; 3 points after
Normal	Times New Roman 12 points	Left aligned; single spaced

Figure 4-2   How styles and direct formatting work together

How to modify a style

The trouble with the default styles is that you may not like the formatting they provide. For example, you may not like the italic character formatting that's provided by the default Heading 2 style. And you may not like the spacing before or after a paragraph when you use the Normal style. It's easy to modify a style, though, and figure 4-3 shows how.

After you apply the style you want to modify to a paragraph, you use direct formatting to format the paragraph the way you want it. Then, you include the direct formatting in the style by clicking in the Style box, pressing the Enter key to display the dialog box shown in figure 4-3, and pressing the Enter key again. This not only changes the style, but all the paragraphs in the document that have been formatted with that style.

The dialog box that asks whether you want to change a style

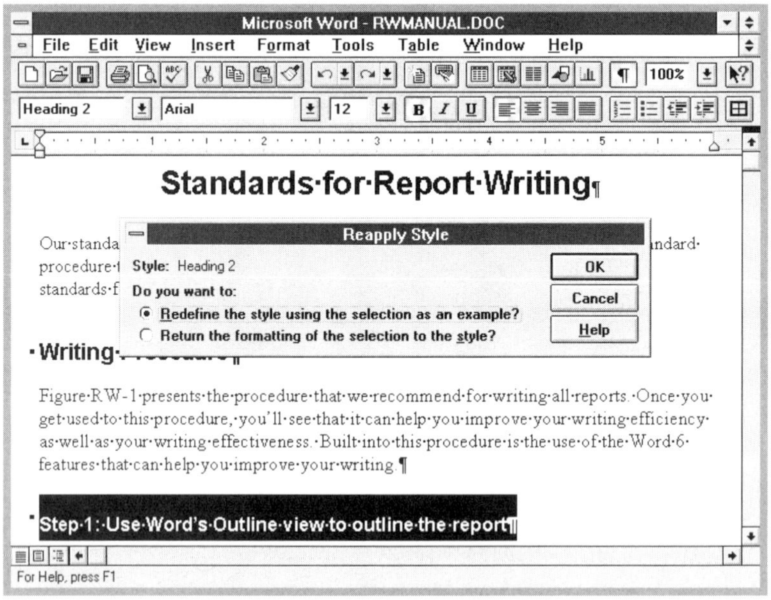

How to change the formatting in a paragraph style

1. If you want to change the character formatting for a style, select the entire paragraph that has the style applied to it including the paragraph mark as shown above. Otherwise, you can just move the insertion point into the paragraph.

2. Modify the formatting of the paragraph using the formatting techniques in chapter 3.

3. Click in the Style box to move the highlight there, and press the Enter key. The dialog box shown above is then displayed

4. Click on the OK button. Then, the style is changed and the new formatting is applied to all the paragraphs in the document that are formatted with that style.

Figure 4-3   The quickest way to modify a paragraph style

How to use Outline view with heading styles

One of the benefits that you get from using the default heading styles is the use of Outline view as summarized in figure 4-4. When you use Outline view, you can hide the text in a document and display just the headings as shown in this figure. Then, you can easily reorganize the document by moving the headings up and down. When you do, the text that follows the headings moves along with them. You can also use Outline view to raise or lower the level of a heading.

Figure 4-4 is intended only to introduce you to this powerful feature, which is commonly known as the *outline feature*. Then, if this sounds like a feature that you could benefit from, you can learn how to get the most from it in chapter 7. This feature is particularly useful for people who write reports because it lets you develop an outline for a report that later provides the headings that are used in the report.

The document in figure 4-3 in Outline view

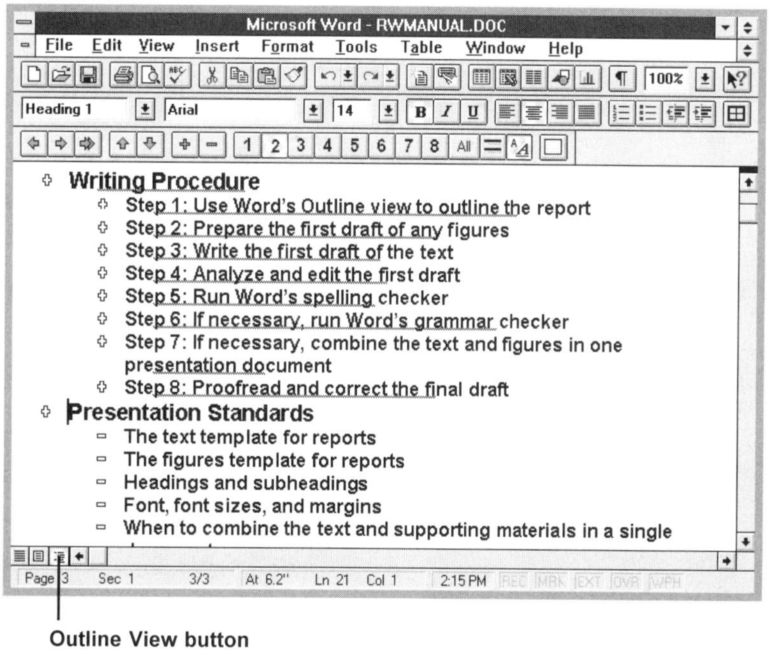

Outline View button

How to switch to Outline view

- Click on the Outline View button or choose the Outline command from the View menu.

How to display just the headings and subheadings

- Click on the button in the Outlining toolbar that indicates the number of heading levels that you've used. If, for example, you've used Heading 1 and Heading 2 styles, click on the 2 button. This hides the text below the headings and subheadings so the outline looks like the one above.

How to enter headings in Outline view

- When you press the Enter key at the end of a heading in Outline view, another heading at the same level is started. Then, you can type the heading.

- To raise or lower a heading to the next level, move the insertion point into it. Then, press Shift+Tab or click on the left arrow button in the Outlining toolbar to raise the heading. Or, press Tab or click on the right arrow button to lower the heading.

How to reorganize a document

- To move a heading and the hidden text below it up or down in the document, drag the plus or minus sign in front of a heading. Or, move the insertion point into the heading and click on the up or down arrow button in the Outlining toolbar.

Note

- This is just a brief introduction to this feature. In chapter 7, you can learn how to get the most from it.

Figure 4-4   How to use Outline view with heading styles

Exercise set 4-1

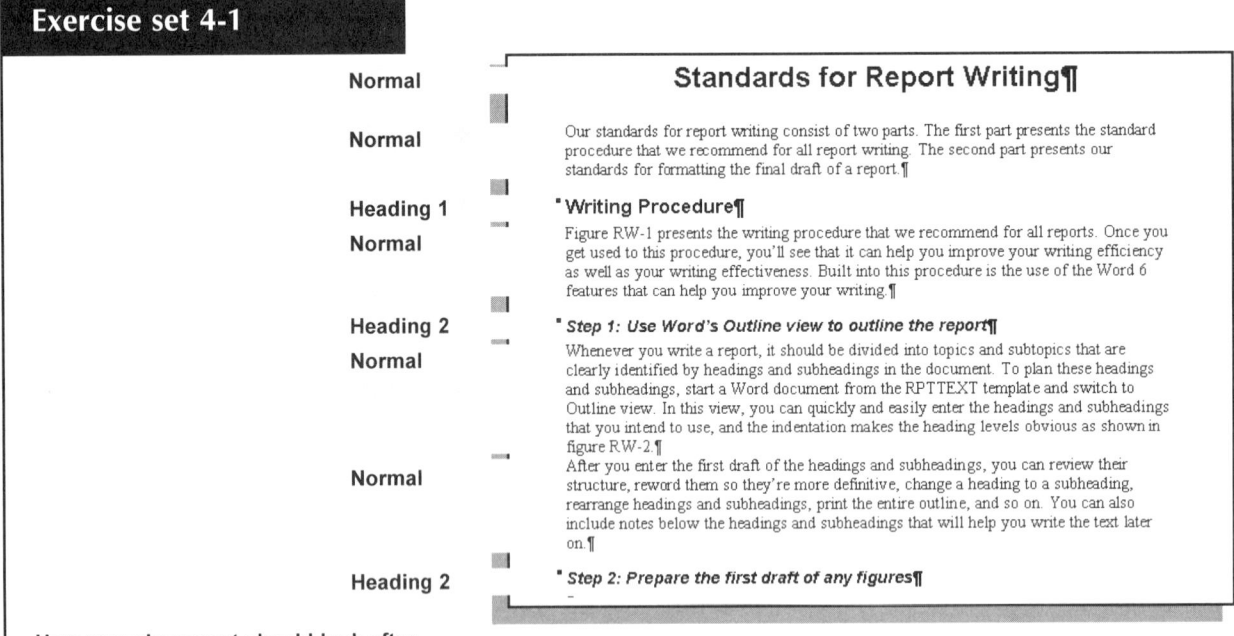

How your document should look after exercise 4

This exercise set is designed to show you how easy it is to format headings and subheadings when you use styles. In exercise 3, you'll create the document shown above and apply the indicated styles. Then, in exercises 4 through 7, you'll work with the styles to improve the formatting. You'll also be introduced to the use of Outline view.

1. Start a new document and type four paragraphs into it:

    Heading 1 paragraph
    Heading 2 paragraph
    Heading 3 paragraph
    Normal paragraph

    Next, apply the default heading styles to the first three paragraphs (the fourth should already have the Normal style). Use the mouse to apply the first two styles, and use the shortcut key to apply the third style. What character formatting and what paragraph formatting is applied by each of the four styles? To find out, click on the Help button in the Standard toolbar, then click on each of the four paragraphs.

2. Move the insertion point to the end of the Heading 1 paragraph and press the Enter key. What style is applied to the new paragraph? It should be the Normal style. Repeat this for each of the next three paragraphs. What style is applied to each new paragraph? Close the document without saving it.

3. Start a new document and type the title paragraph shown above. It will have the Normal style applied to it. Then, use direct formatting to change the font to Arial in 20 point bold and to change the paragraph formatting so the paragraph is centered with 18 points of spacing after it.

4. Type the next seven paragraphs of the report shown above. When you come to a heading or subheading paragraph, apply the Heading 1 or Heading 2 style to it. The remaining paragraphs should automatically be formatted with the Normal style. When you complete this exercise, your document should look like the one above (unless someone has changed the default formatting for the Heading or Normal styles).

5. Move the insertion point into the first paragraph (the title), and apply the Heading 1 style to it. Notice that the style formatting replaces the direct formatting. Then, press Ctrl+Z to remove the formatting applied by the Heading 1 style.

6. Use the procedure in figure 4-3 to change the formatting of the Heading 1 style so it is centered instead of left aligned. When you're through, move the insertion point to the end of the document; type a new paragraph that contains the words *Test Paragraph*; apply the Heading 1 style to it to make sure that this style provides for centering; then delete the test paragraph.

Standards for Report Writing

Our standards for report writing consist of two parts. The first part presents the standard procedure that we recommend for all report writing. The second part presents our standards for formatting the final draft of a report.

Writing Procedure

Figure RW-1 presents the writing procedure that we recommend for all reports. Once you get used to this procedure, you'll see that it can help you improve your writing efficiency as well as your writing effectiveness. Built into this procedure is the use of the Word 6 features that can help you improve your writing.

Step 1: Use Word's Outline view to outline the report

Whenever you write a report, it should be divided into topics and subtopics that are clearly identified by headings and subheadings in the document. To plan these headings and subheadings, start a Word document from the RPTTEXT template and switch to Outline view. In this view, you can quickly and easily enter the headings and subheadings that you intend to use, and the indentation makes the heading levels obvious as shown in figure RW-2.

After you enter the first draft of the headings and subheadings, you can review their structure, reword them so they're more definitive, change a heading to a subheading, rearrange headings and subheadings, print the entire outline, and so on. You can also include notes below the headings and subheadings that will help you write the text later on.

How your document should look after exercise 8

7. Use the procedure in figure 4-3 to change the character formatting for the Heading 2 style so it doesn't have italics. Because you're formatting characters, you need to select all the characters in the paragraph in step 1 of the procedure including the paragraph mark. When you're through, check to make sure that all the paragraphs with the Heading 2 style have been reformatted.

8. Use the procedure in figure 4-3 to change the Normal style so it provides 12 points of spacing after each paragraph. (Use the Paragraph command in the Format menu to change the Spacing After value.) Then, check the spelling and save the document with the name RWSTDS, but don't close it. At this point, your document should look like the one above.

9. Switch to Outline view using the technique shown in figure 4-4. Then, click on the 2 button in the Outlining toolbar so the text is hidden and only the headings are shown. Note that the Heading 2 paragraphs are indented but the Heading 1 paragraphs aren't.

10. Still in Outline view, move the insertion point to the end of the Step 2 heading and press the Enter key. What style is applied to the new paragraph? Next, enter the headings for steps 3 through 8 that are shown in figure 4-4, and enter the heading entitled "Presentation Standards." To raise that heading from level 2 to level 1, move the insertion point into the paragraph and press Shift+Tab or click on the left arrow button in the Outlining toolbar. Notice that the Heading 1 style is now applied to this paragraph.

11. Enter the next four level 2 headings shown in figure 4-4. To do that, enter the first heading; lower it from level 1 to level 2 by pressing the Tab key or clicking on the right arrow button in the Outlining toolbar; then enter the other headings. Now, switch back to Normal view, check the spelling, save and print the file, and close it.

How to use headers and footers

When you prepare a multi-page document, it usually makes sense to number the pages. To do that, you can use a *header* or a *footer*. Besides the page number, a header or footer can include the date, the file name of the document, and other identifying information.

Before you can work with the headers and footers in a document, you need to decide how you want to use them. Figure 4-5 gives you some ideas for that. In the simplest case, you can use the same header or footer on each page of a document. But you can also use a different header or footer on the first page of a document; you can use different headers and footers in each section of a document; and you can use different headers and footers on left and right hand pages. To specify the types of headers or footers you want, you use the Page Setup command.

A document that contains a footer in Page Layout view

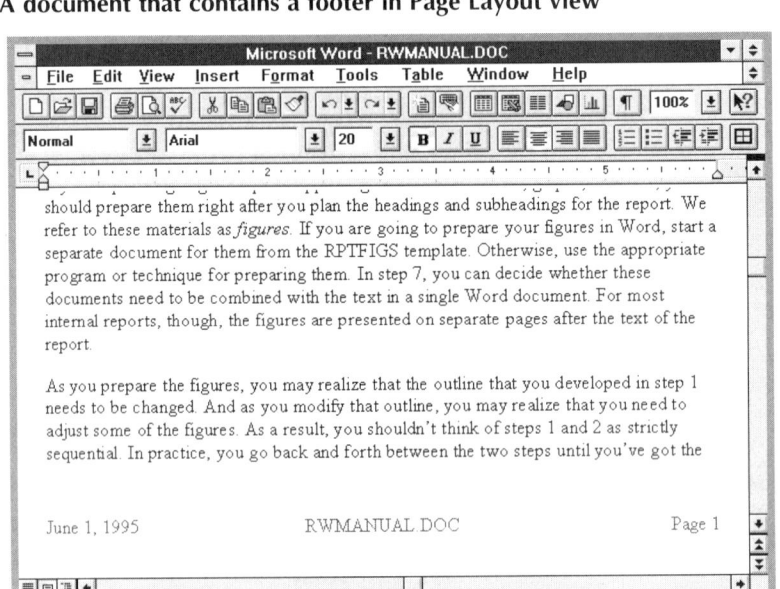

How headers or footers can be used in a one-section document

- The same header or footer can be used on every page.

- One header or footer can be used on the first page, and another one on all remaining pages. If necessary, the header or footer for the first page can be left blank.

How headers or footers can be used in a multi-section document

- By default, Word uses the same headers or footers for each section of a document.

- If necessary, you can use a different set of headers or footers for each section of a document. You can also use one header or footer for the first page within each section and another one for the remaining pages.

How headers or footers can be used in a document that's printed on both sides of the paper

- When you print a document on both sides of the paper, you can use different headers or footers on left and right hand pages.

Notes

- For most documents, you'll use either headers or footers, not both.

- Although you can see headers and footers in Page Layout view, you can't edit them directly.

Figure 4-5   How to use headers and footers

How to set the page layout options for headers and footers

Figure 4-6 shows how to use the options in the Page Setup dialog box that are related to headers and footers. In the Margins tab, you can specify the starting location of the headers and footers on the page. The default is one-half inch from the top of the page for a header and one-half inch from the bottom of the page for a footer. For most documents, these defaults are satisfactory so you won't have to change them.

In the Layout tab, you can specify whether you want more than one type of header or footer. If you want the same header or footer on all pages of the document, make sure that both Headers and Footers options are unchecked. This too is satisfactory for most documents. However, if the first page of a document is a cover page, you may want to check the Different First Page option so you can leave the header or footer on the first page blank.

The Margins tab of the Page Setup dialog box

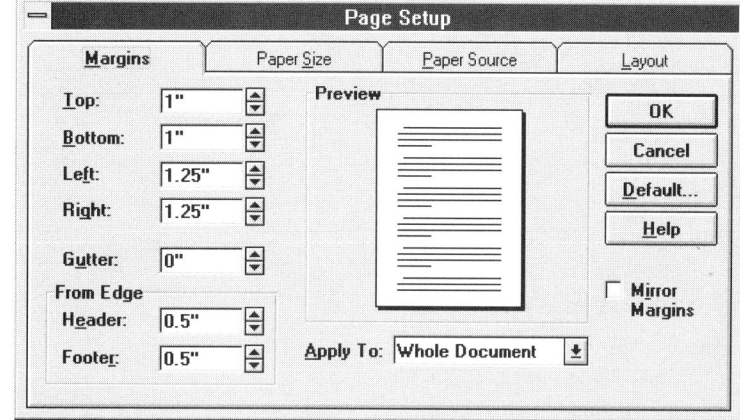

Operation

- To change the starting position of a header or footer, change the Header or Footer value in the From Edge group.

The Layout tab of the Page Setup dialog box

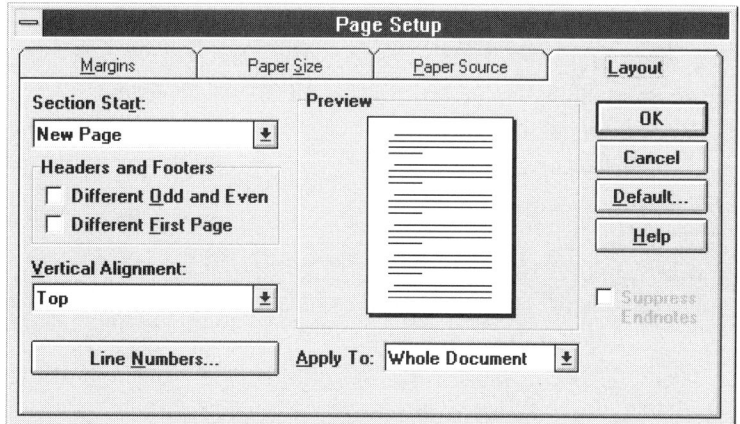

Operation

- If you don't want a header or footer on the first page of a document or if you want the header or footer on the first page to be different from the header or footer on the rest of the pages, check the Different First Page option.

- If the document is going to be printed on both sides of the paper and you want the headers or footers on the odd pages to be different from the headers or footers on the even pages, check the Different Odd and Even option.

Note

- If a document contains more than one section, the default is to apply the settings to the current section. To apply the settings to the entire document, choose the Whole Document option from the Apply To list.

Figure 4-6   How the Page Setup command affects headers and footers

How to work with headers and footers

Figure 4-7 shows how to work with the headers and footers in a document. When you access the Header or Footer command for the first time, the first header area in the current section of the document is displayed. You can tell which header is displayed by the description in the upper left corner of the header area. In the header shown at the top of figure 4-7, for example, you can see the word "Header." That indicates that this header is used on all pages of the document or, if you checked the Different First Page option, on all pages but the first one. You can see examples of two other header and footer descriptions at the bottom of the figure.

If a document contains more than one header, you can move from one header to another by using the Show Next and Show Previous buttons in the Header and Footer toolbar. To move to the footer area, you use the Switch Between Header and Footer button. The Header and Footer toolbar is displayed whenever you access a header or footer, and its buttons are summarized in figure 4-8.

To enter text into a header or footer, you simply type it into the header or footer area. Then, you can edit and format the text just as you can any other text in the document. You can also use three of the buttons in the Header and Footer toolbar to insert the page number, the current date, and the current time into a header or footer.

Access

| **Menu** | View ➡ Header and Footer |
| **Other** | Double-click on a header or footer in Page Layout view |

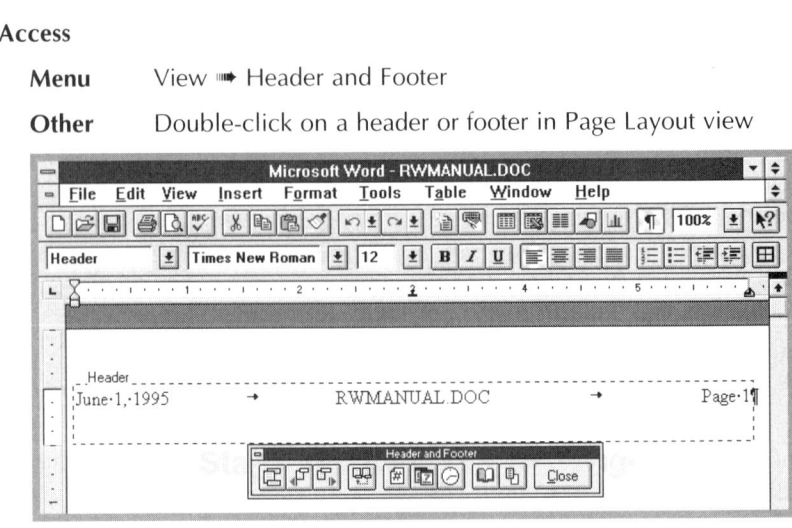

Operation

- When you access a header or footer, Word switches to Page Layout view if necessary, dims the document text, displays the area for editing the header or footer, and displays the Header and Footer toolbar.

- You can use the toolbar to switch to a different header or footer. See figure 4-8 for details.

- To change the header or footer for a single section, click on the Same as Previous button in the Header and Footer toolbar to turn that option off before you make the change (see figure 4-8). Otherwise, the change will be applied to all the sections in the document.

- Edit and format the header or footer just as you would any other text using the menus, toolbars, shortcut menus, and shortcut keys. You can also use the buttons in the Header and Footer toolbar to enter special fields. When you're done, click on the Close button or double-click in the document outside the header/footer area.

How to identify a header or footer

- When you access a header or footer, its description is displayed in the upper left corner of the header or footer area so you can tell which header or footer you're working with.

The header area for the first page of a document with a different first page header

First Page Header

The footer area for the second section of a document

Footer ·Section 2·   Same as Previous·

Figure 4-7   How to work with headers and footers

As you enter a header or footer, note that each area is formatted with a center and right tab stop as shown in the header at the top of figure 4-7. These tab stops are part of the default Header and Footer styles that are automatically applied to headers and footers. If you want to change the formatting, you can either change the style or override its formatting by applying direct formatting. In particular, because the tab stops are set up to work with the default margins, you'll want to change them if you change the document margins.

By default, Word assumes the headers and footers in all sections of a document are going to be the same. So if you change a header or footer in one section, it's changed in all the sections. This is indicated by the words *Same as Previous* in the upper right corner of the area. If want to change a header or footer in one section without affecting the headers or footers in the other sections, just click on the Same as Previous button in the toolbar and the Same as Previous message disappears.

Additional information

✓ If necessary, a header or footer can contain more than one line. If it's more than two lines or 24 points, though, you need to change the top and bottom margin settings for the document. Otherwise, there won't be enough space between the document and the header or footer.

✓ You can also number the pages in each section separately. To do that, choose the Page Numbers command from the Insert menu, click on the Format button in the resulting dialog box, and set the starting page number for the current section to the one you want.

Button	Name	Function
	Switch Between Header and Footer	Switches between the header and footer areas.
	Show Previous	Switches to the previous header or footer if two types are specified in the Page Setup dialog box.
	Show Next	Switches to the next header or footer.
	Same as Previous	If the document contains more than one section, tells Word whether the header or footer should be the same as the one in the previous section. The default is for the header or footer to be the same.
	Page Numbers	Inserts the page number as a field into the header or footer.
	Date	Inserts the current date as a field into the header or footer using the default date format or the format you last used. To insert a date with a different format, use the Date and Time command in the Insert menu.
	Time	Inserts the current time as a field into the header or footer.
	Page Setup	Displays the Page Setup dialog box so you can change the header or footer settings.
	Show/Hide Document Text	Shows or hides the document text while the header or footer area is displayed.
Close	Close	Closes the header or footer area and returns to the document.

Figure 4-8   The Header and Footer toolbar

How to insert the file name into a header or footer

The header at the top of figure 4-7 includes the file name. It's a good idea to include the file name in a header or footer so you can find the file more easily later on. Although you can type the file name directly into the header or footer, you can also insert it into the header or footer as a field as shown in figure 4-9. When you use this technique, you can be sure that the file name in the header or footer is always accurate.

Access

Menu   Insert ➡ Field

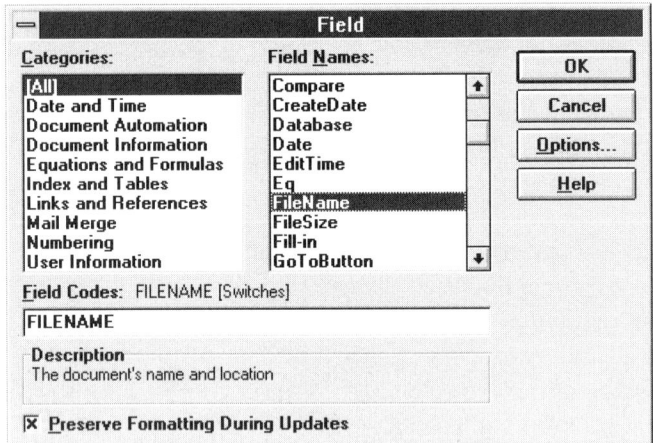

Operation

- Scroll the Field Names list to display the FileName option, then double-click on that option or highlight it and click on the OK button.

- Alternatively, you can click on the Document Information option in the Categories list, then double-click on the FileName option or highlight the option and click on the OK button.

Notes

- If you want the file name to include the entire path, you can click on the Options button, click on the Field Specific Switches tab, and add the \p switch to the field. You usually don't need the path, though.

- If the file name field is displayed as a field code, press Alt+F9 to display it as a file name.

- By default, fields are updated automatically when you print a document. If you print a document and the file name isn't updated, choose the Options command from the Tools menu, click on the Print tab, and check the Update Fields option. If you want to update the field before you print the document, you can move the insertion point into the field and press the F9 key.

Figure 4-9   How to insert the file name into a header or footer

Exercise set 4-2

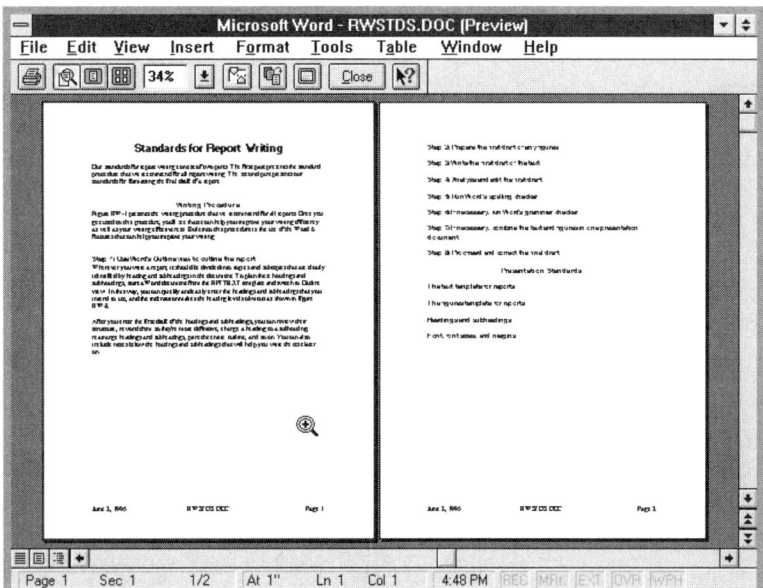

How the document should look in preview mode at the end of exercise 4

1. Open the RWSTDS file, access the Page Setup command, and make sure the header and footer settings are like those in figure 4-6. Because there are no check marks in the Headers and Footers group of the Layout tab, this provides for the same header and footer on all pages of the document.

2. Access the header area for the document as shown in figure 4-7 and notice the style that's applied to the paragraph in this area. Then, enter a header like the one in figure 4-7 that consists of the current date, the file name, and the page number preceded by the word *Page*. Use the buttons in the Header and Footer toolbar to insert the date and the page number, and use the procedure in figure 4-9 to insert the file name. When you're through entering the header, close the header area and print the first page of the document to see if the header prints the way you want it to.

3. Change the Page Setup options so they provide for two different headers: one for the first page; another for the remaining pages. This should remove the header from the first page. To see whether this is true, switch to Page Layout view and scroll to the top of the first page to see if it contains a header.

4. Access the header area for the first page, then switch to the header area for the other pages by clicking on the Show Next button in the Header and Footer toolbar. Next, click on the Page Setup button in the Header and Footer toolbar to access the Page Setup command, and turn off the option for a different first page header or footer. Last, use cut and paste techniques to delete the header and paste it into the footer area so it becomes a footer. To see whether this worked, preview the document. When you enter preview mode, notice that two pages of the document are displayed by default and the page that contains the insertion point is active. (The active page has a dark outline.) Click the magnifier pointer on the footer in the second page to magnify it and make sure it's right, then click again to return to the default preview display. Now, click on page one to activate it and click on the footer to magnify it. Click again to return to the default display, then click on the Close button to close the preview window. If the footer is correct, save and close the file with these additions. Otherwise, make the required adjustments before saving and closing the file.

Three more ways to move the insertion point

When you work with large documents, you should be aware that there are several ways to move the insertion point from one place to another in the document. Besides using the methods presented in the first three chapters, you can use the three that follow.

How to use the Go To command

Figure 4-10 shows how to use the Go To command. If you know what page number you want to move the insertion point to, you can get there with just a few clicks of the mouse or keystrokes. If you divide a document into sections, you can also use this command to move from the start of one section to another. And if you create bookmarks, you can use this command to go from one bookmark to another.

Additional information

✓ Another feature of Word that's related to the Go To command lets you move to the last three locations where you typed or edited text. To do that, press Shift+F5. This feature is most useful for returning to the last editing location when you first open a document.

Access

Menu   Edit ➧ Go To

Shortcut key   Ctrl+G

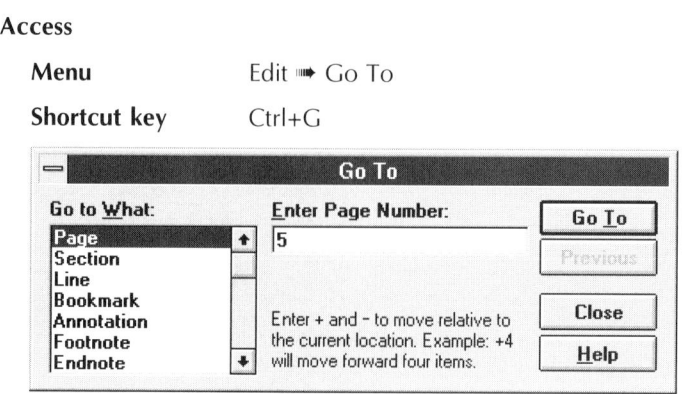

How to go to a specific page number

- Type the page number and click on the Go To button. This moves the cursor to the top of the page with that number, but the Go To dialog box remains on the screen. To remove it, click on the Close button or press the Esc key.

How to go to a specific section

- If a document is divided into sections, you can click on the Section option in the Go to What list. Then, you can either type a section number in the text box and click on the Go To button, or you can click on the Next or Previous button to move to the next or previous section.

How to go to a relative page number or section

- To move forward by pages or sections, enter a plus sign followed by the number of pages or sections you want to move by in the text box. To move backward by pages or sections, enter a minus sign followed by a number.

How to go to a bookmark

- If a document contains bookmarks (see figure 4-11), you can click on the Bookmark option in the Go to What list. Then, you can choose the bookmark that you want to go to from the list that drops down from the text box and click on the Go To button to go to that bookmark.

Note

- The Go To dialog box changes depending on the option you choose from the Go to What list. If you choose the Section option, for example, the name of the text box changes to Enter Section Number, and the Go To button changes to the Next button.

Figure 4-10   How to use the Go To command

How to use bookmarks

Figure 4-11 shows how to create and use *bookmarks*. If you have a large document and you frequently need to move from one place in it to another, the use of bookmarks can be useful. For most documents, though, it's quicker to use other techniques for moving the insertion point.

How to use Outline view

If you use the default heading styles, you can move from one heading to another using Outline view. To do that, switch to Outline view, hide all the text except for the headings by clicking on the appropriate button in the Outlining toolbar, and move the insertion point to the heading that you want to move to. When you return to Normal or Page Layout view, the document is scrolled so the heading you selected is displayed.

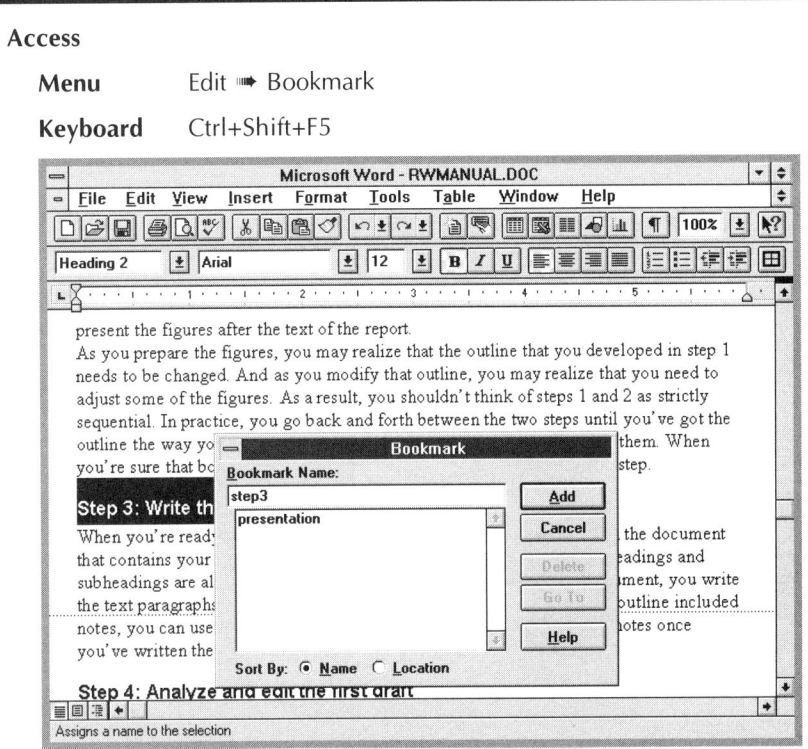

Access

Menu	Edit ➡ Bookmark
Keyboard	Ctrl+Shift+F5

How to add a bookmark to a document

1. Move the insertion point to the place in the document that you want to mark or select the text that you want to mark.

2. Access the Bookmark dialog box; type a bookmark name; and click on the Add button.

Two ways to move the insertion point to a bookmark

- Use the Go To command as described in figure 4-10.

- Access the Bookmark dialog box. Then, double-click on the bookmark name in the list box, or move the highlight to the bookmark name and click on the Go To button.

How to delete a bookmark from a document

- Access the Bookmark dialog box, move the highlight to the bookmark that you want to delete, and click on the Delete button.

Figure 4-11   How to use bookmarks

Exercise set 4-3

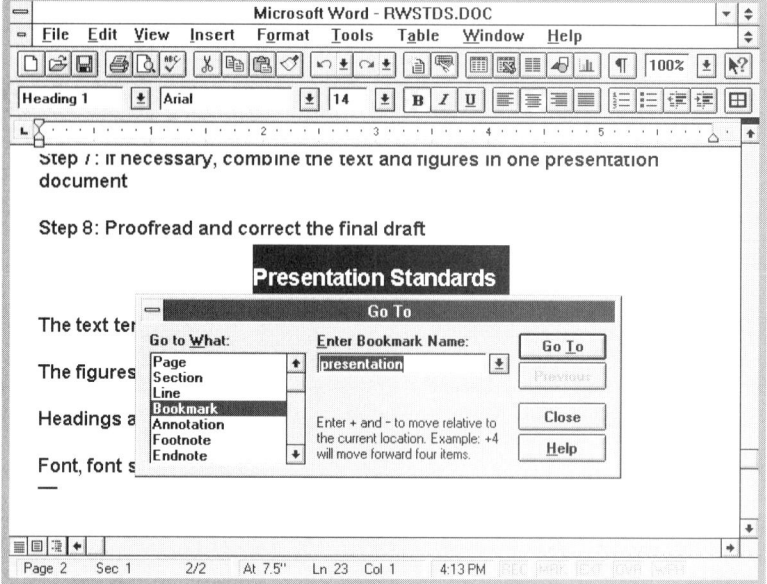

Step 7: If necessary, combine the text and figures in one presentation document

Step 8: Proofread and correct the final draft

Presentation Standards

The text te

The figures

Headings a

Font, font s

—

Go To

Go to What:
Page
Section
Line
Bookmark
Annotation
Footnote
Endnote

Enter Bookmark Name:
presentation

Go To

Previous

Enter + and − to move relative to the current location. Example: +4 will move forward four items.

Close

Help

How the document and the Go To
dialog box should look after you
move to the bookmark named
presentation in exercise 2

1. Open the RWSTDS file and insert page breaks before the Step 1, Step 2, and Step 3 heading paragraphs. This should make the document four pages in all. Then, press Ctrl+Home to move to the start of the document, and use the Go To command as shown in figure 4-10 to move to page 4. This is usually the fastest way to move four or more pages at a time. Now, use the Go To command to move back two pages in the document. To do that, enter -2 in the Enter Page Number box.

2. Use the procedure in figure 4-11 to create two bookmarks. The first should be named *procedure* and should mark the heading "Writing Procedure." The second should be named *presentation* and should mark the heading "Presentation Standards." Then, use the Go To command to move to the bookmark named *procedure*, and use the Bookmark command to go to the bookmark named *presentation*.

3. Switch to Outline view, move the insertion point to the heading "Writing Procedure," and switch back to Normal view. Where is the insertion point? Then, switch to Outline view, move the insertion point to the heading "Presentation Standards," and switch back to Normal view. Which is faster for switching from one heading to another: using bookmarks or using Outline view?

4. Close the document without saving the changes.

Editing and formatting skills for multi-page documents

When you edit and format a large document, you use the same skills that you use for editing and formatting a one-page document. In addition, though, you can use the Text Flow tab of the Paragraph command to apply some special formatting to paragraphs. You can use the Split command in the Window menu to display two portions of a document at the same time. And the Find and Replace commands become more important for large documents.

How to use the Text Flow tab of the Paragraph command

The Text Flow tab of the Paragraph command provides four options that affect the automatic page breaks in a multi-page document. These are summarized in figure 4-12. The first option is useful for all paragraphs, and the third one is useful for all heading paragraphs. The other two are occasionally useful for special purposes.

Like all paragraph formatting, the text flow options can be applied directly to a paragraph, or they can be applied to a style. Since the Widow/Orphan Control option is on in the default styles, though, you don't have to apply this option directly. Similarly, the Keep with Next option is on in the default heading styles.

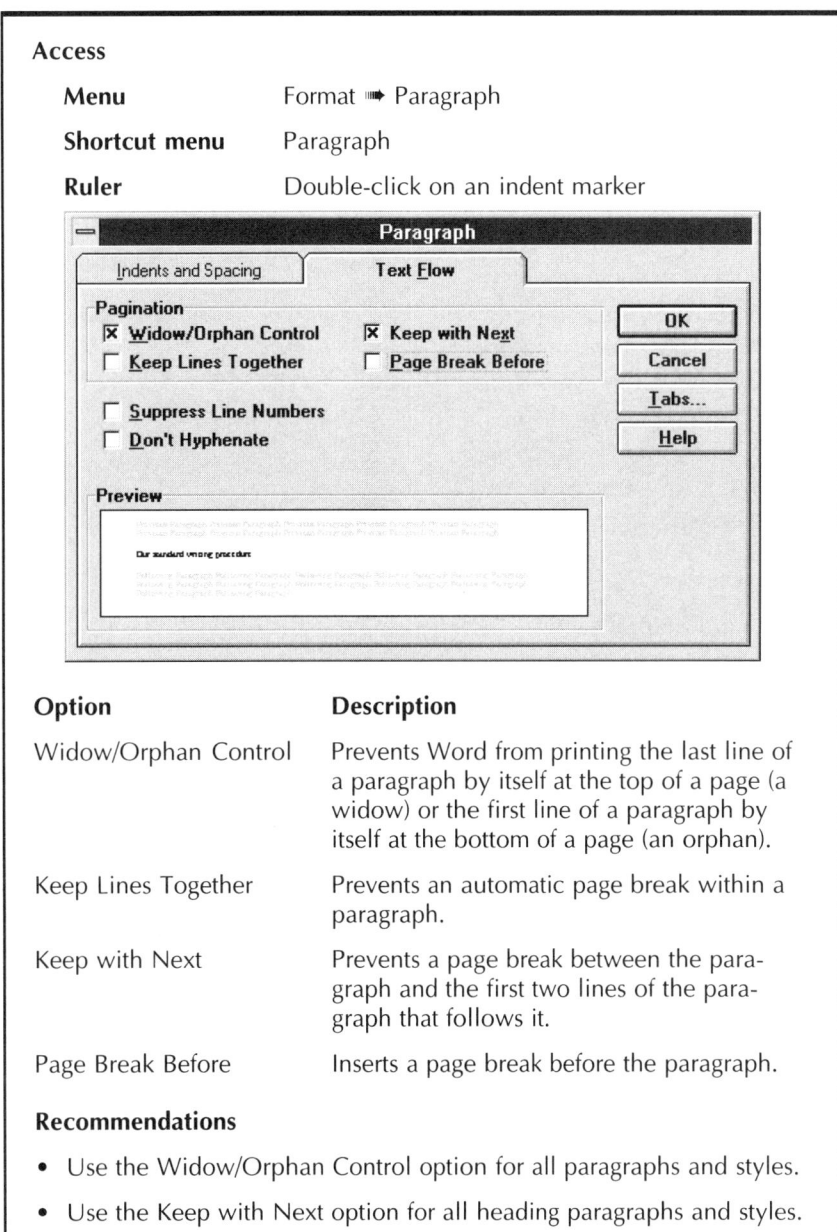

Access

Menu	Format ➡ Paragraph
Shortcut menu	Paragraph
Ruler	Double-click on an indent marker

Option	Description
Widow/Orphan Control	Prevents Word from printing the last line of a paragraph by itself at the top of a page (a widow) or the first line of a paragraph by itself at the bottom of a page (an orphan).
Keep Lines Together	Prevents an automatic page break within a paragraph.
Keep with Next	Prevents a page break between the paragraph and the first two lines of the paragraph that follows it.
Page Break Before	Inserts a page break before the paragraph.

Recommendations

- Use the Widow/Orphan Control option for all paragraphs and styles.
- Use the Keep with Next option for all heading paragraphs and styles.

Figure 4-12   How to use the Text Flow tab of the Paragraph command

How to display two portions of a document at the same time

When you work with a document that contains many pages, it's sometimes useful to display two different portions of the document at the same time. Then, you can copy or move text from one part of the document to another without having to scroll back and forth. Figure 4-13 shows how to work with a document this way. Notice that the two portions of the document are in two *panes* of the same window, not in two windows.

The easiest way to split a document window into two panes is to double-click on the *split box* that's identified in figure 4-13. Keep in mind as you work, though, that you're only working on one document, even though it's displayed in two panes. When you're through, the easiest way to undo the split is to double-click on the split box again.

The importance of the Find and Replace commands

The benefit that you can get from using the Find and Replace commands in a short document is often minimal. When you work with a document that contains many pages, though, the Find and Replace commands can be critical to your efficiency.

Remember that you can use these commands to find and replace formatted and unformatted words and phrases. You can use them to find and replace formatting like italics or centering and special characters like Tab characters and paragraph marks. You can also use them to find and replace styles.

A document that's displayed in two panes of a window

Split box

Two ways to split a document into two panes

- Double-click on the split box that appears at the top of the vertical scroll bar to split the window in half. Or, drag the split box to where you want to split the window.

- Choose the Split command in the Window menu. Then, drag the separator bar that appears to where you want to split the window, and click the left mouse button.

Two ways to return a split window to normal

- Double-click on the split box. Or, drag the split box to the top of the document window.

- Choose the Remove Split command from the Window menu.

How to switch from one pane to the other

- Click in the pane or press F6.

Notes

- Displaying a document in two panes can make it easier for you to move or copy text from one portion of a large document to another.

- The editing changes that you make in either window are applied to the same document.

- To display one document in two different windows (not panes), you can choose the New Window command from the Window menu. Then, if only those two windows are open, you can choose the Arrange All command to display both windows on the screen so they look similar to the panes shown above. This gives you a bit more flexibility than the use of panes does because you can move and size windows. Most of the time, though, it's quicker and easier to work with panes.

Figure 4-13   How to work with a document in two panes of a window

Exercise set 4-4

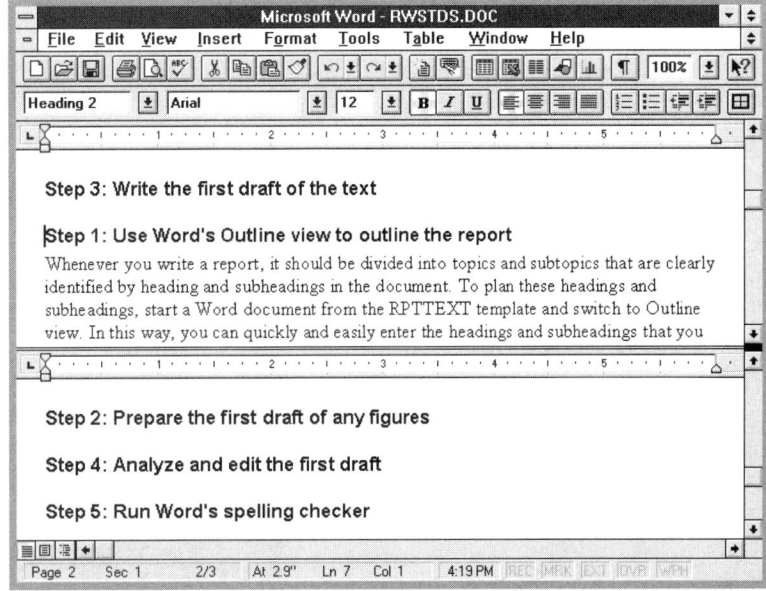

How the document window should look after you move the Step 3 heading in exercise 3

1. Open the RWSTDS file. Move the insertion point into the first Heading 1 paragraph, and use the Text Flow tab of the Paragraph command as shown in figure 4-12 to turn on the Page Break Before option. Also, if they're not already on, turn on the Widow/Orphan Control and Keep with Next options. When you return to the document, a page should be started right before the heading. This paragraph formatting overrides the formatting provided by the Heading 1 style, but just for the current paragraph.

2. Use the procedure in figure 4-3 to change the Heading 1 style so a page break is started before each paragraph that has that style applied to it. Then, check the second Heading 1 paragraph in the document to make sure that this worked properly.

3. Double-click on the split box to split the document into two panes. Next, scroll to the Step 1 heading in the top pane and to the Step 3 heading in the bottom pane. Then, cut the Step 3 paragraph from the bottom pane and paste it into the top pane ahead of the Step 1 heading. The document window should now look like the one above. Double-click on the split box to remove the split and note how the editing you did affects the document. Press Ctrl+Z twice to undo the cut and paste operation.

4. Use the Replace command to find all uses of the Heading 2 style and replace them with the Heading 3 style. To enter a find or replace value for a style, choose the Style option from the menu that's displayed when you click on the Format button in the Replace dialog box or use the style list in the Formatting toolbar. After you replace the Heading 2 styles with Heading 3 styles, use this command to find all Heading 1 styles and replace them with Heading 2 styles. When you're sure that this worked correctly, close the document but don't save it.

Printing skills for large documents

When you print large documents, three more printing skills come in handy. First, you need to know how to select the pages that you want to print. Second, you need to know how to set the printing options that apply to large documents. Third, it's nice to know how to cancel a print job.

How to select the pages for printing

Figure 4-14 presents the Print dialog box and shows how to select the pages you want to print. To print the current page, just click on the Current Page option. To print selected pages or a range of pages, enter the pages in the Pages box. To print just the odd or even pages in the range you specify, choose an option from the list that drops down from the Print box. These options are useful when you want to print both sides of the paper. After you print the odd pages on one side of the paper using the Odd Pages option, you can turn the paper over and print the even pages using the Even Pages option.

Access

Menu	File ➡ Print
Shortcut key	Ctrl+P

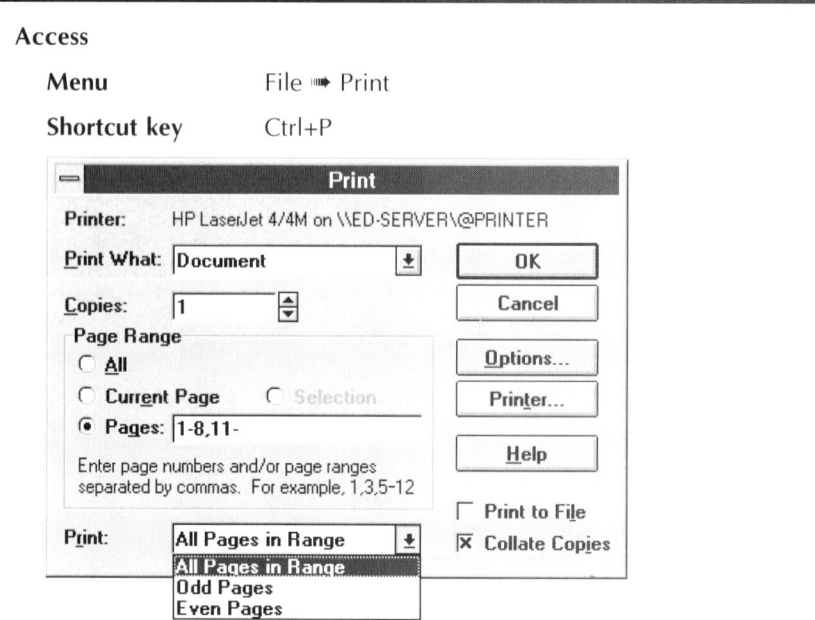

Operation

- To print the current page, click on the Current Page option.
- To print selected pages, identify the pages in the Pages text box as shown below.
- To print just the odd or even pages in the range you specify, choose an option from the Print list at the bottom of the dialog box.
- To print text that you select before you access the Print dialog box, click on the Selection option.

Typical entries in the Pages box

Entry	Meaning
4	Print page 4.
3,7	Print page 3 and page 7.
2-10	Print pages 2 through 10.
5-	Print pages 5 through the end of the document.
-6	Print pages 1 through 6.
3-5,7	Print pages 3 through 5 and page 7.
-4,6-8,10	Print pages 1 through 4, 6 through 8, and 10.

Figure 4-14 How to select pages for printing

How to set the options for printing

The Print tab of the Options dialog box shown in figure 4-15 lets you set some options related to printing. You can access this dialog box from the Tools menu or by clicking on the Options button in the Print dialog box.

If you include fields in your documents such as the current date or the file name, you'll want to be sure the Update Fields option is checked. Then, the fields are always updated before the document is printed. You'll usually want the Background Printing option checked too, so you can continue working while a document is being sent to the print queue.

Even if the Background Printing option is on, though, printing documents that contain graphic objects can cause long delays. Because of that, you may occasionally want to turn off the Drawing Objects option and print just the text. That can dramatically speed up printing.

You can also use the Print tab to choose the paper tray that you want the paper fed from when you print a document. This is useful when you want to print a document like a letter or a special report on preprinted paper that's in a secondary printer feed.

Access

Menu	Tools ➡ Options
Print dialog box	Options button

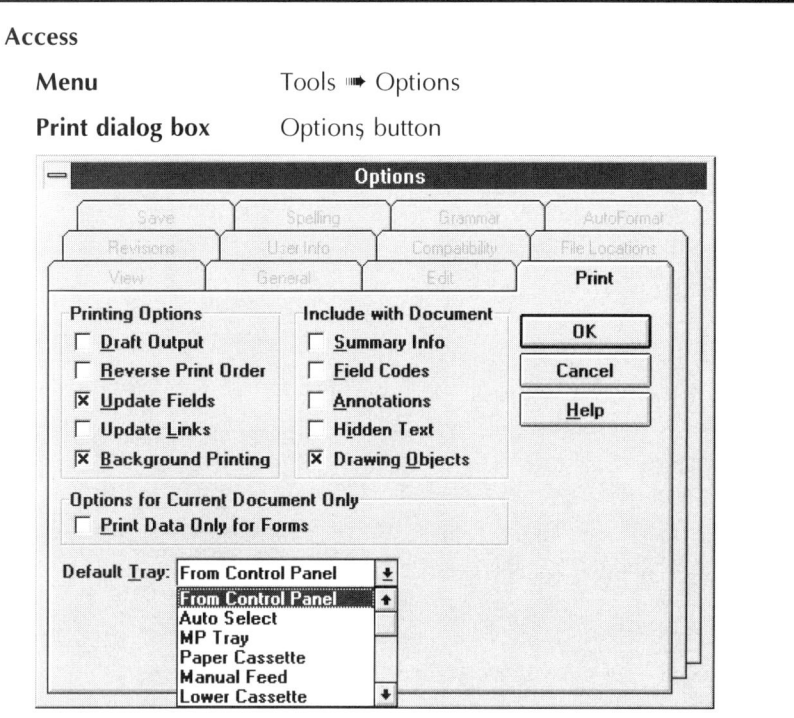

Printing Options group

The two options in this group you're most likely to use are Update Fields and Background Printing. If the Update Fields option is on, any fields in the document (like a date field) are updated before printing. If the Background Printing option is on, you can continue working while the document is being sent to the print queue. For jobs that contain graphic objects, though, the delays can still be frustrating.

Include with Document group

The options in this group let you select additional information to be printed with the document. If you check the Summary Info option, for example, the summary information for the document is printed along with the document. If you remove the check mark from the Drawing Objects option, only the text is printed. This can dramatically improve the printing speed for documents that contain pictures and other graphic objects.

How to print from a different paper tray

Choose an option from the Default Tray list. The default is to use the tray that's specified in the Windows Control Panel. If you want to set different paper sources for different portions of a document, use the Paper Source tab of the Page Setup command as described in figure 3-18.

Note

All of the options in the Print tab except the Print Data Only for Forms option apply to all the documents you print and remain in effect from one Word session to another.

Figure 4-15   How to set the printing options

How to cancel a print job

Suppose that you start the printing of a 20 page document and realize that you didn't check the spelling for it. To cancel the *print job*, you can use one of the three methods in figure 4-16.

If your PC is on a network, you need to distinguish between print jobs that are sent to a printer that's attached to your PC (a *local printer*) and those that are sent to a *network printer*. When you send a job to a local printer, Word sends it to the Windows Print Manager where it's put into a *print queue*. This is simply a list of the jobs that are waiting to be printed. Then, you can use Word to cancel a job before it reaches the Print Manager, and you can use the Print Manager to cancel a job once it's in the print queue.

When you send a job to a network printer, though, the job is usually sent directly to the net-work print queue without going through the Print Manager. Then, you can use Word to cancel a job before it reaches the network queue, but you may have no control over the job once it reaches the network.

To cancel a job that's in the print queue of the Print Manager, you can use the third procedure in figure 4-16. Because the Print Manager is a separate program that's started whenever you print a document, the first step is to switch to that pro-gram. One way to do that is to press Alt+Tab until you reach that pro-gram, but you can use any of the Windows techniques for switching programs. Once the Print Manager is displayed, you shouldn't have any trouble deleting the job that you want to cancel.

How to cancel a print job during background printing

• Double-click on the printer icon that replaces the time in the status bar:

Printer icon

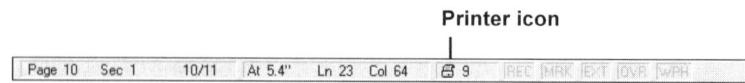

For text documents, you usually have to work quickly because it may take only a few seconds for a document to reach the Print Manager or network queue. Documents that contain graphics, though, usually take much longer than that.

How to cancel a job when the background printing option is off

• When the background printing option is off, this dialog box is displayed while the print job is being sent to the Print Manager or the network print queue:

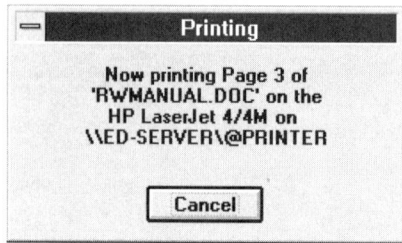

To cancel the job, click on the Cancel button or press the Esc key.

How to cancel a print job after it reaches the Print Manager

• Press Alt+Tab to switch from Word to the Print Manager.

• Highlight the job you want to cancel. Then, click on the Delete button (Windows 3.1) or press the Delete key (Windows 3.11).

Notes

• Windows is usually set up so it bypasses the Print manager when you send a job to a network printer. In that case, you can't use the Print Manager to cancel a print job.

• When a job is in a network print queue, you may not have any control over it. That depends upon the network you're using and how that network is set up.

Figure 4-16   How to cancel a print job

Exercise set 4-5

1. Open the RWSTDS file, and use the Print tab of the Options dialog box as summarized in figure 4-15 to turn off the Background Printing option and to turn on the Summary Info option. Then, print page 2 (not page 1) along with the summary information for the document.

2. With the Background Printing option still off, print the entire document, but cancel it as soon as the print job starts. Then, set the Summary Info and Background Printing options the way you want them, and close the RWSTDS file without saving it.

Perspective

Now that you've completed the first four chapters of this book, you have a starting set of the skills that are used by the best word processing users in business. All you need to do to become an accomplished professional is to use these skills for a few weeks. The more you use them, the more efficient you'll become. The more you experiment with them, the more you'll realize how easy it is to edit and format documents so they look just the way you want them to.

For some of you, in fact, the first four chapters may have presented all the skills you need. That's particularly true if you work with short documents that require limited formatting. Even then, however, it's worth reviewing the remaining chapters to see whether there are some additional Word functions that can help you work more effectively. At the least, you should review chapter 5 to learn how wizards and templates can help you and chapter 8 to see how tables can be used as an alternative to the use of tab stops.

If you want to become a master of Word 6, of course, you need to read all of the remaining chapters because each one presents skills that are useful in some situations. In chapters 6 and 7, for example, you can learn how to get the most from styles and the outline feature. In chapter 9, you can learn how to generate a table of contents from the heading styles that you've used. In chapter 10, you can learn how to format portions of a document in two or more columns. In chapter 11, you can learn how to use frames, pictures, and other graphic objects in a document. And in chapter 12, you can learn how to convert a file from another word processor to Word 6 format.

Summary

- Word comes with several default *styles* that you can use to format the paragraphs in a document. When you use styles, you can apply both character and paragraph formatting with one shortcut key or a few mouse clicks. The use of styles also makes it easy for you to reformat a document, and it lets you take advantage of the *outline feature* and the table of contents feature.

- Most multi-page documents should include either a *header* or a *footer* that contains the date and page number. It can also contain the file name of the document, which makes it easy for you to find the document on the PC later on.

- To move the insertion point in a large document, you can use the Go To command, bookmarks, and Outline view.

- The Text Flow tab of the Paragraph command lets you set options that control the automatic page breaks in a document. The Split command lets you divide a document into two *panes.* And the Find and Replace commands can be used to find and replace styles.

- From the Print dialog box, you can choose the pages you want to print. From the Print tab of the Options dialog box, you can choose options that affect how a document is printed. If you send a document to be printed, then realize it's not ready to be printed, you can cancel the *print job* before it reaches the *print queue.*

Section 2

The commands and features that help you work like a pro

Once you know how to create, edit, and format a Word document, you need to learn the other commands and features that the best professionals use. So chapter 5 shows you how to start documents from templates and wizards, and chapter 6 shows you how to get the most from the use of styles. These are closely-related features that every Word user can benefit from, so we suggest that you read these chapters next.

The rest of the chapters in this section present independent features that you can learn about in whatever sequence you prefer. If, for example, you need to prepare a table of contents, you can go from chapter 6 directly to chapter 9. If you want to prepare a table, you can go directly to chapter 8. If you want to format the text of your document in two or three columns, you can go to chapter 10. And when you want to learn more about the outline feature, you can go back to chapter 7. Eventually, though, you should make a point of reading all the chapters in this section because each one presents commands and features that you should at least be aware of.

Chapter 5

How to get the most from templates and wizards

One quick way to improve your productivity is to start all new documents from templates instead of starting them from scratch. Another alternative is to start new documents from wizards. In this chapter, you'll learn everything you need to know to get the most from these Word 6 features.

How to use templates and wizards

Word 6 comes with 27 templates and 10 wizards that you can start using right away. As you will see, they can help you create and format a new document with just a few keystrokes or mouse clicks. Once you become familiar with the templates and wizards that come with Word, you can learn to create templates of your own that will work just the way you want them to.

Template concepts

Figure 5-1 presents the concepts for working with templates. From a practical point of view, a *template* is just a document that is used for starting other documents. To distinguish it from other documents, though, its file name must have DOT as the extension.

When you start a new document in Word 6, it is always based on a template. If you choose the template that you want to start a document from, it's based on that template. Otherwise, it's based on the default template, which is named NORMAL.DOT. In the first four chapters, the assumption has been that all documents were started from the Normal template, but that's not the best way to work.

Additional information

✓ If you're upgrading to Word 6 from Word 2, you can continue to use your Word 2 templates. Word 6 automatically converts them to the correct format.

A memo started from the MEMO1 template that comes with Word

Basic template concepts

• All Word documents are started from a template. If you don't choose a specific template when you start a document, the document is based on the Normal template that comes with Word.

• For improved efficiency, you should start most (if not all) documents from a template that is designed for the type of document that you're going to create (not the Normal template).

• To help you get started right, Word 6 provides templates for 15 different types of documents. None of these, however, is likely to be exactly right for your purposes, so you'll want to modify them.

• When you start a document from a template other than the Normal template, the Normal template is still available to the document. However, the other template takes precedence over the Normal template whenever both templates provide the same item (like a style).

• A template can include starting text, page formatting, styles, shortcut key assignments, AutoText entries, custom toolbars, and macros. Most templates, though, include only starting text, page formatting, and styles. Template items like shortcut key assignments and AutoText entries are usually stored in the Normal template.

The benefits that you get from using templates

• With just a few keystrokes or mouse clicks, you can start a document like the one above including starting text, page formatting, headers, footers, styles, and more.

• Templates encourage consistent formatting for each type of document.

Figure 5-1   Template concepts

How to start a new document from a specific template

Figure 5-2 shows how to start a document from a template other than the Normal template. After you issue the New command from the File menu, you just choose the template that you want to base the new document on. In contrast, if you start a new document by using the shortcut key (Ctrl+N) or the New toolbar button, the New dialog box isn't displayed and the document is started from the Normal template.

In figure 5-1, you can see the document that's displayed when you choose the Memo1 template in the New dialog box. This template includes the text for the heading of the memo; it includes all the page formatting; and it includes a complete list of styles that you can use with a memo. To complete the memo, you just replace the bracketed entries with the correct information for the memo.

As you work with the Word 6 templates, you'll see that all paragraph formatting is based on the use of paragraph styles, which is presented in detail in the next chapter. You'll also see that some of the Word 6 templates use features like tables, columns, and frames, which are presented in subsequent chapters. When you complete those chapters, you should be able to use any of the templates with relative ease. But until then, you'll probably have trouble with the more complicated ones.

Access

Menu   File ➡ New

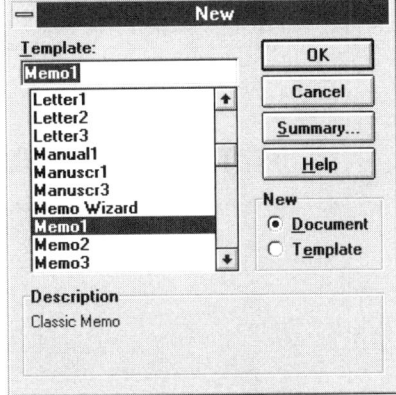

Operation

- Double-click on the template in the Template list box that you want to start the new document from. Or, highlight the template and click on the OK button to start the new document.

The templates and template names that come with Word 6

Fax cover sheet (Faxcovr1, 2)	Brochure (Brochur1)
Letter (Letter1, 2, 3)	Directory (Directr1)
Memo (Memo1, 2, 3)	Invoice (Invoice)
Presentation (Present1)	Manual (Manual1)
Press release (Presrel1, 2, 3)	Manuscript (Manuscr1, 3)
Report (Report1, 2, 3)	Purchase order (Purchord)
Resume (Resume1, 2, 4)	Thesis (Thesis1)
	Weekly time sheet (Weektime)

Guidelines for using templates

- Start with the simpler templates like those in the left column above. When you get used to working with those, you can try the more complicated templates.

- The numbers at the end of a template name indicate the type of formatting (Classic, Contemporary, Typewriter, or Elegant). The type is shown in the Description box of the New dialog box when you highlight a template. When in doubt, choose the Classic formatting.

- The paragraph formatting in all the templates is based on the use of styles, and the style information is stored in the paragraph marks. If you accidentally delete a paragraph mark and thus change the style and the formatting, use the Undo command (Ctrl+Z) to restore the formatting right away.

Note

- The templates listed in the New dialog box are those in the default template directory, which is usually C:\WINWORD\TEMPLATE (see figure 5-8).

Figure 5-2   How to start a new document from a specific template

How to start a new document from a wizard

If you need more help creating a new document, you might want to try one of the *wizards* that come with Word. When you use a wizard, it leads you step-by step through the create process. During that process, you choose options that determine how the document will be formatted and what information it will contain.

Figure 5-3 shows how to start a new document from a wizard. First, you choose the wizard you want to use from the New dialog box just as you do when you start a new document from a template. Then, you complete the dialog boxes that the wizard displays until it finishes and you are left with the start of a document. It's that easy.

If you compare the list of templates in figure 5-2 with the list of wizards in figure 5-3, you can see that four types of documents can be started from either a template or a wizard: fax cover sheets, letters, memos, and resumes. Which way is better? That depends on your preferences. In the next exercise set, you'll start a fax cover sheet in both ways so you can judge for yourself.

Two of the wizards that work the best are the Award and Calendar wizards. When you complete either of these wizards, the document is complete and ready for printing. So if you need an award certificate or a monthly calendar, be sure to try one of these wizards.

Procedure

1. Choose the New command from the File menu.

2. Double-click on the wizard for the kind of document you want to create, or highlight the wizard and click on the OK button to start the document. The first in a series of dialog boxes is then displayed. For instance, this dialog box is the first in the series for creating a letter from the Letter Wizard:

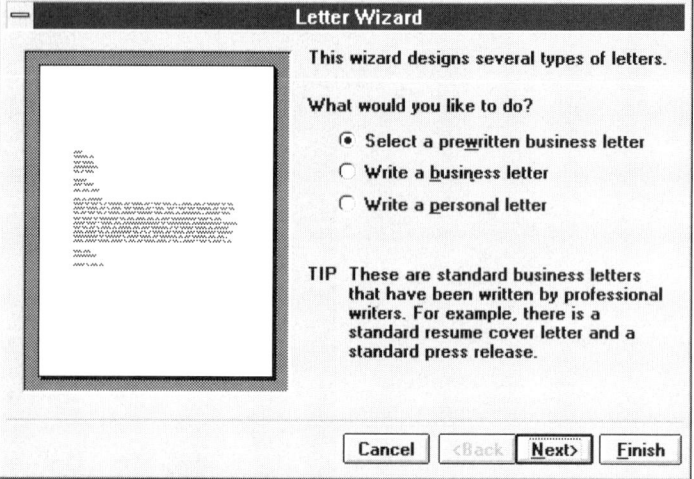

3. Complete each of the dialog boxes that are displayed. To preview an option, click on it. To go to the next dialog box, click on the Next button. To return to the previous dialog box, click on the Back button. In the last dialog box, click on the Finish button to complete the document.

The wizards that come with Word 6

Agenda Wizard	Memo Wizard
Award Wizard	Newsletter Wizard
Calendar Wizard	Pleading Wizard
Fax Wizard	Resume Wizard
Letter Wizard	Table Wizard

Notes

- When you use the Letter Wizard, you can start with one of the 31 prewritten business letters that come with Word 6. Each of these is a template that's stored in the C:\WINWORD\LETTERS directory.

- When you use a wizard, it remembers the choices that you make and the information that you supply and uses them as the defaults the next time you use that wizard.

Figure 5-3   How to start a new document from a wizard

How to preview a template

If you want to preview one of the Word 6 templates to see whether you'll want to use it, you can do that using one of the techniques in figure 5-4. When you use the Style Gallery command, you can see an example of a document that has been formatted by the template and its styles.

To learn more about a template, you can use the second procedure in figure 5-4. After you start a new document from the template, you can print it out to see what text, headers, and footers it contains. You can also print a list of its styles, AutoText entries, and shortcut key assignments by using the Print What list in the Print dialog box.

As you preview the templates, you're likely to find that none of them work just the way you want them to. Most templates, for example, have way too many styles for efficient use. The starting text usually doesn't contain all the information that you want. The formatting in many of the templates is of questionable quality. And some templates use advanced features in such complicated ways that they're difficult to work with. For these and other reasons, you usually want to modify the templates or create templates of your own. So that's what you'll learn right after this next exercise set.

How to use the Style Gallery command to preview a template

1. Issue the Style Gallery command from the Format menu so its dialog box is displayed:

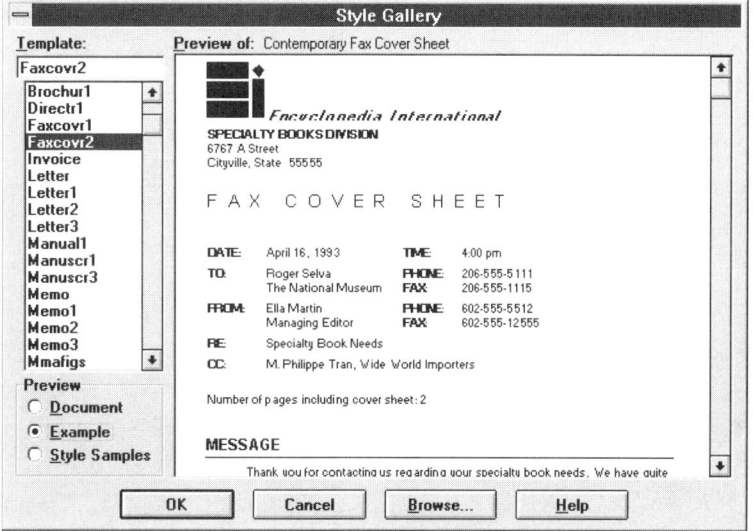

2. Click on the template that you want to preview, and click on the Example option in the Preview group to display an example of a document that's formatted by the selected template.

3. Click on the Cancel button to end the preview. Or, click on another template name to preview another template. Don't click on the OK button, though, because it tells Word to change the styles in the active document to those in the template.

How to print the starting text, styles, AutoText entries, and shortcut key assignments that are part of a template

1. Start a new document from a template that you want to preview.

2. If the new document contains text, use the Print command to print the text just as you would print any other document.

3. To print the styles, AutoText entries, or shortcut key assignments, start the Print command and choose the appropriate options from the Print What list before completing the command.

Typical shortcomings of the Word 6 templates

• Most of them contain too many styles for efficient use. For instance, the Letter1 template contains 86 styles.

• The font sizes, headers, footers, margins, and starting text are often inappropriate for business documents.

• The formatting in many of them requires the knowledge of advanced features, so the templates are relatively difficult to use.

Figure 5-4   How to preview one of the Word 6 templates

Mike Murach & Associates, Inc.
4697 West Jacquelyn
Fresno, CA 93722

Fax Cover Sheet

DATE:	May 10, 1995	TIME:	10:22 AM
TO:	Ken Wilson	PHONE:	916-555-1234
	IBM	FAX:	916-555-4321
FROM:	Mike Murach	PHONE:	209-275-3335
		FAX:	209-275-9035
RE:	Our purchase order		

Number of pages including cover sheet: 2

Message

Here's the purchase order for the equipment that we configured last Friday. If you have any questions, if I've omitted anything, or if there's any problem whatsoever, please get back to me right away.
—

How the fax cover sheet should look when you complete its entry in exercise 1

1. Use the New command as described in figure 5-2 to start a fax cover sheet from the Faxcovr1 template. Then, replace the bracketed information in the document with the text shown above (you can use your name and your company's name, address, and phone numbers if you prefer), and print the document. What formatting changes (if any) would you recommend for this template? Now, close the document without saving it.

2. Start another fax cover sheet from the Faxcovr1 template. Is any of the information that you entered in exercise 1 retained? This shows the need for modifying the template so it includes repeated information like your name and phone numbers. Now, close the document without saving it.

3. Use the procedure in figure 5-3 to start a fax cover sheet with the Fax Wizard. Choose the Portrait orientation and the Contemporary style, and enter the information that's requested. When you're returned to the new document, enter the remaining information shown in the cover sheet above. Did you have any trouble entering the information in the table and column format that this document uses? Next, print the document. What formatting changes (if any) would you recommend? Now, close the document without saving it.

4. Use the Fax Wizard to start another cover sheet. Does the wizard retain any of the information that you entered in exercise 3? (If you changed your address from the default, which is taken from the User Info tab of the Options dialog box, you'll notice that the new address was not saved.) Without entering any information into the starting document, close it without saving it.

5. Use the Style Gallery command that's summarized in figure 5-4 to preview the Letter1, Letter2, and Letter3 templates. Does this help you choose the template that you want to use for letters? Click on the Cancel button to close the Style Gallery dialog box.

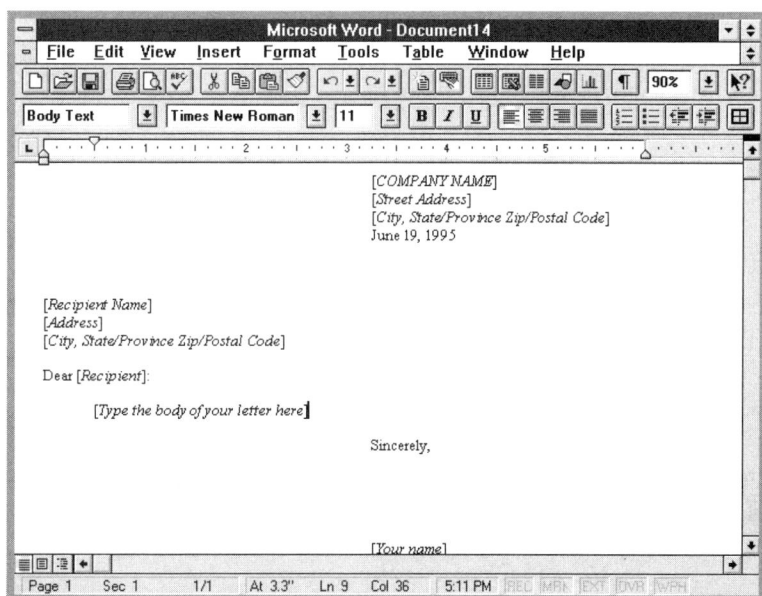

**How the letter started from the
Letter3 template looks in exercise 6**

6. Start a new document from the Letter3 template, but don't type anything into it. Pull down the Style list from the Formatting toolbar. Approximately how many styles are in this list? Watch the style name in the Style box of the toolbar as you move the insertion point from one paragraph to the next in the letter. What is the name of the style for the body paragraph in the letter? Delete the paragraph mark at the end of this body paragraph. What happens? Press Ctrl+Z to restore the style that was applied to this paragraph. Then, access the Print dialog box and display the Print What list to see that you can print a list of the styles that come with this template. Don't print them, though, because they require seven pages. Instead, close the Print dialog box, and close the document without saving it.

7. Use the Letter Wizard to prepare one of the 31 prewritten letters, but don't bother entering the recipient's name and address as you use the wizard. If none of the letters is of particular interest to you, try the "Thank you for applying" or the "Thank you for inquiring" letter. When the letter is displayed, review and evaluate its content. Is it a well written letter that meets your standards? Close the document without saving it.

How to create and modify templates

If you've done the first set of exercises, you should realize that most of the Word 6 templates will work better if you modify them. At the least, you should enter constant information like your name into each template you use. Beyond that, you may want to adjust the formatting so it's more readable or attractive, simplify some of the formatting so it's easier to use, delete some of the styles that you aren't going to use, and so on.

If you prefer not to modify the templates that come with Word 6, you can create your own templates from them. Or, you can create a template from a document that's formatted just the way you want it. If you start a document from a wizard, for example, you may want to save the resulting document as a template so you can use it again. Whether you create new templates or modify existing ones, your templates should work the way you want them to so you can get the most from them.

How to create a template from another template

Figure 5-5 shows how easy it is to create a template from an existing template. The key to this procedure is choosing the Template option in the New dialog box so a new template is started instead of a new document. Then, after you make the changes to the template, you can save the new template in the default template directory with a new template name.

Procedure

1. Issue the New command from the File menu to display this dialog box:

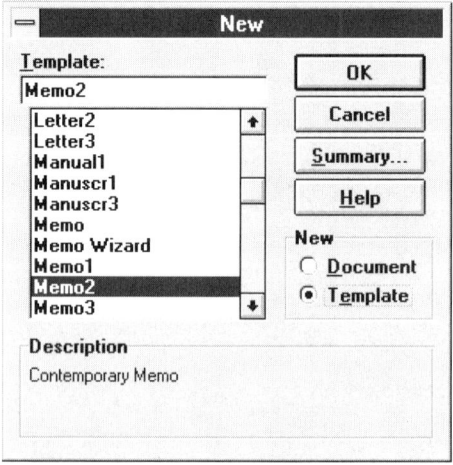

2. Choose the template that you want to base the new template on; check the Template option in the New group; and click on the OK button to open a template document:

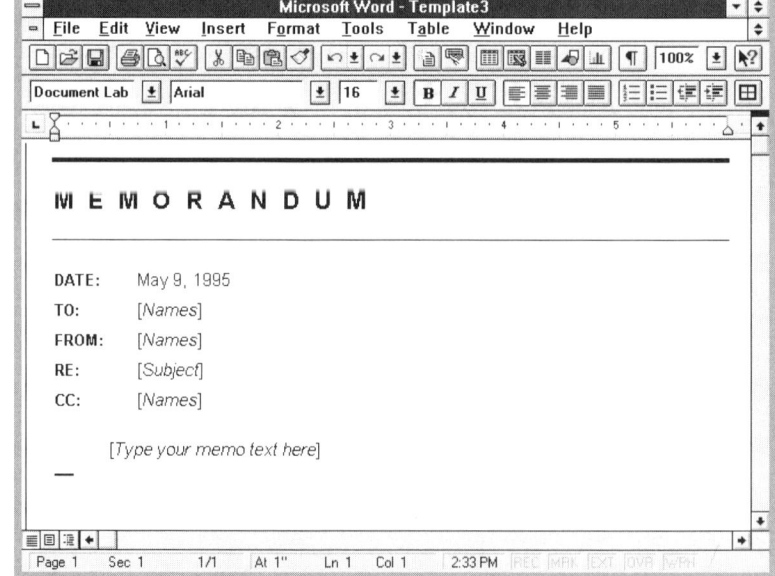

3. Make whatever changes you want to make to the template, just as if you were changing a document. For instance, you can replace the bracketed text with the actual text that you want to use. You can change the character formatting, paragraph formatting, and page formatting. And you can replace and modify styles as shown in chapter 6.

4. Use the Save command to save the template with a new name. The template is automatically saved in the default template directory with the DOT extension.

Figure 5-5   How to create a new template from another template

How to create a template from an existing document

Another way to create a new template is to create it from a document that works the way you want it to. If, for example, you've already created and formatted a memo, you can create a memo template from it. Figure 5-6 shows how. Just delete the text that you don't want in the template, and save the document in the template directory as a Document Template file.

This is usually the best way to create new templates because you're already familiar with the formatting, styles, and features that are used. As a result, you can use the templates efficiently right from the start. In contrast, when you create a new template from one of the Word templates, it takes extra time to figure out how the formatting works and how the styles should be used. For the more complicated templates, the extra time that's required can be extensive.

Procedure

1. Open the document that you want to start the template from. This document should have the starting text, formatting, and styles that you want to store in the new template.

2. Delete any text in the document that you don't want in the template, and make any other changes that you want for the template:

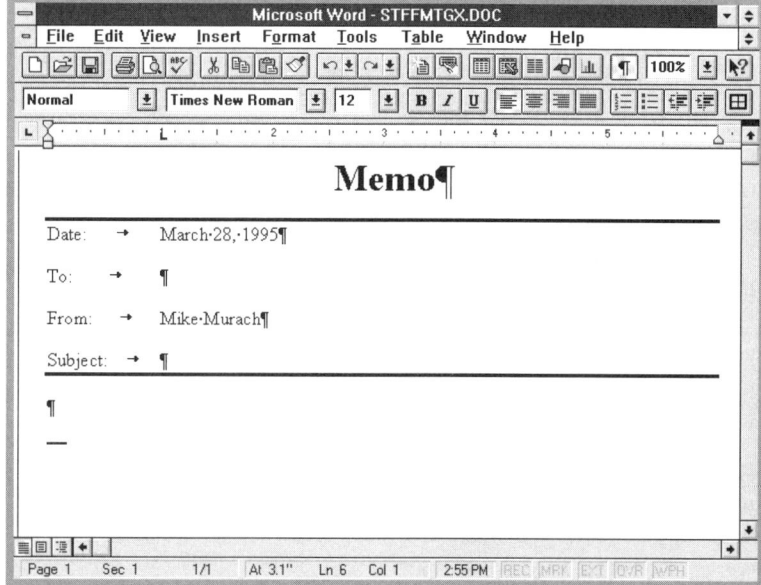

3. Issue the Save As command from the File menu to display this dialog box:

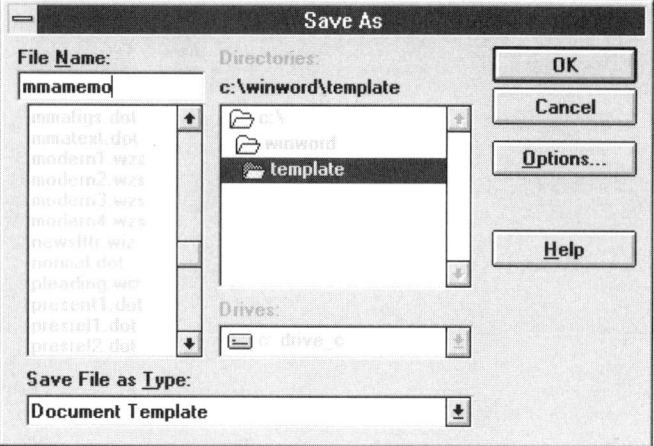

4. Choose the Document Template option from the Save File as Type list, and the drive and directory change so that the default directory for templates is identified. Then, enter the template name in the File Name box without an extension and click on the OK button to create the template.

Figure 5-6   How to create a new template from a document

Two ways to modify a template

If you want to use one of the Word 6 templates but the text or formatting isn't exactly what you need, you can modify it. You're also likely to want to make changes to the templates you create as you use them. Figure 5-7 shows two ways to make those changes.

The first way is to open the template as a document and modify it directly. To do that, you need to know where the template is stored. By default, the templates that you create are stored in the directory named C:\WINWORD\TEMPLATE, but you can store them in other directories if you want to.

The second way is to modify the template that's attached to a document as you modify the document. For a few simple changes like changing page margins or styles, that's often a practical way to modify a template. But if you're going to make many changes to a template, you're better off using the first method.

How to modify a template directly

1. Issue the Open command to display this dialog box:

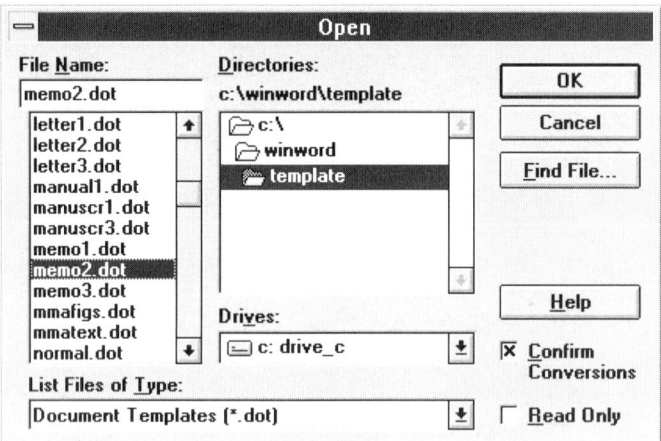

2. Use the Drives and Directories lists to identify the default directory for templates. Then, choose the Document Template option from the List Files of Type list and double-click on the template name in the File Name list to open the template.

3. Modify the template any way you like, then issue the Save command to save it.

How to modify a template from the document that it's attached to

As you edit and format a document, some of the dialog boxes that you work with give you a chance to update the attached template. Some examples follow:

- To change the font or page setup in a template, click on the Default button in the Font dialog box (figure 3-7) or the Page Setup dialog box (figure 3-16).

- To add an AutoText entry to a template, choose the template from the Make AutoText Entry Available To list in the AutoText dialog box (figure 2-11). Otherwise, the AutoText entry is added to the Normal template, which is available to all documents.

- To add or modify styles, check the Add to Template option in the New Style dialog box (figure 6-6) or Modify Style dialog box (figure 6-7).

- To add a shortcut key for a style to a template, choose the template name from the Save Changes In list in the Keyboard tab of the Customize dialog box (figure 6-8). Otherwise, the shortcut key is added to the Normal template, which is available to all documents.

When you update a template using one of these techniques, a message is displayed when you exit from the document that lets you confirm that you want to change the template.

Note

- You can also use the procedure in figure 5-5 to modify a template. To do that, save the template with its original name in step 4.

Figure 5-7   **Two ways to modify a template**

Exercise set 5-2

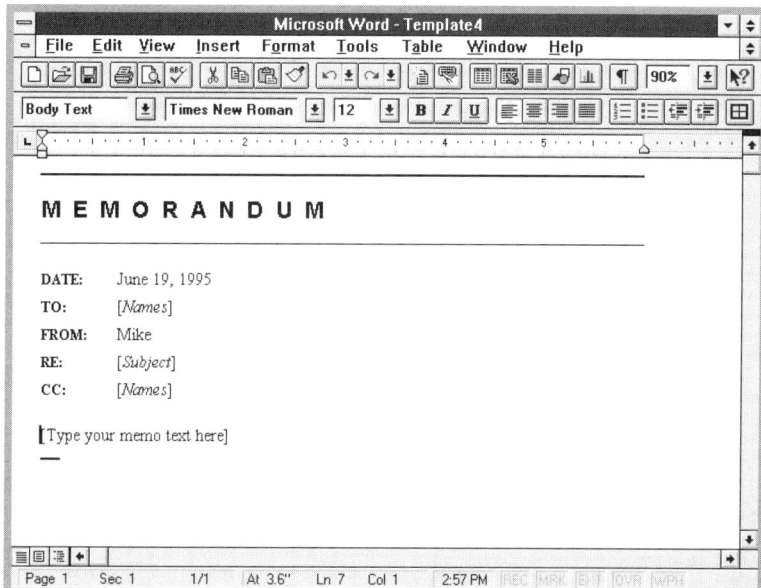

How the memo template should look before you save it in exercise 1

1. Use the procedure in figure 5-5 to start a new template from the Memo2 template. In step 3, enter your name into the From line, and change the formatting for the body text paragraph so it's not indented and so it uses 12 point Times New Roman that isn't italicized as shown above. If you remember how to change the style for a paragraph based on the changes you just made to the paragraph, change the style too. (If you change the style, you'll notice that the font used by other styles in the document changes too. That's because the other styles are based on the Body Text style. You'll see how this works in chapter 6.) Then, save the template as MYMEMO1, and close the file.

2. Start a new document from your MYMEMO1 template. Does the template reflect the changes you made to the Memo2 template in exercise 1? Close the document without saving it.

3. Use the procedure in figure 5-6 to create a new template from the STFFMEMO document that you created for chapter 3. In step 2, delete the entry in the To line, delete the entry in the Subject line, and delete the body text, but not the paragraph mark for the body text. Then, save the document as a template with the name MYMEMO2, and close the file.

4. Start a new document from your MYMEMO2 template. Does this work the way that you want it to? Close the document without saving it.

5. Open the MYMEMO2 template using the Open command as described in figure 5-7. Next, use the Page Setup command to change the top and bottom margins to 1.5 inches. Then, save the template and close it. This is one way to modify a template.

6. Start a new document from the new MYMEMO2 template. Then, use the Page Setup command to change the left and right margins to 1.5 inches. Instead of clicking on the OK button to complete the command, though, click on the Default button. When Word displays the dialog box that asks whether you want to save the changes in the MYMEMO2 template, click on the Yes button. This is one way that you can modify a template as you work on a document that's based on the template. Now, close the document without saving it, but click on the Yes button when Word asks again if you want to save the changes in the MYMEMO2 template.

Other skills for working with templates

You've already learned the skills that you need for getting the most from templates and wizards. Nevertheless, the two topics that follow present some additional information about the use of templates that can be useful in certain situations.

How to set up the directories for your templates

If you only require a few templates of your own, you can store them in the default template directory along with the Word 6 templates and wizards. That's the assumption that's been made to this point, and that works pretty well. The only trouble is that you have to search through the templates and wizards that you don't ever use each time you start a new document.

To avoid that inconvenience, you can use the Windows File Manager to copy all the templates and wizards that you use to a new directory. Then, you can use the File Locations tab of the Options dialog box as described in figure 5-8 to identify that directory. If you identify the new directory as the User Templates directory, the files in that directory are listed in the New dialog box instead of the files in the default template directory. In contrast, if you identify the new directory as the Workgroup Templates directory, the files in that directory are listed in the New dialog box along with the files in the User Templates directory.

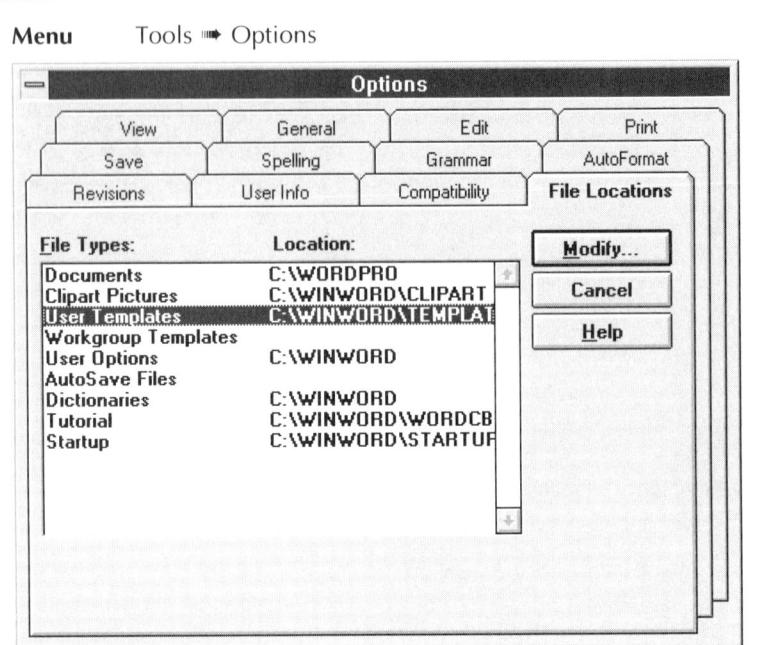

Access

Menu   Tools ➡ Options

Operation

- To change the User Templates or Workgroup Templates directory, move the highlight to it, click on the Modify button, and identify the directory in the dialog box that follows.

- If you need to create a new directory for templates, click on the New button when the Modify Locations dialog box is displayed.

Notes

- The starting default for the User Templates directory is C:\WINWORD\TEMPLATE. That's the directory that contains the templates and wizards that come with Word 6, but you can store other templates in it too. The templates in the User Templates directory are the ones that are listed in the New dialog box.

- The Workgroup Templates directory identifies a secondary directory where templates are stored. The templates in this directory are listed in the New dialog box along with the templates in the User Templates directory. When you install Word, this directory isn't specified, so it makes sense to use it for the templates that you create or for the templates that are shared by all the members in your workgroup.

Suggestion

- If you want just the templates and wizards that you use to show up in the list in the New dialog box, copy those templates and wizards to a new directory. Then, change the User Templates directory to the new directory.

Figure 5-8   How to set up the directories for your templates

When and how to use the Templates command

Figure 5-9 summarizes the three functions of the Templates command. Of the three, the Organizer function is the most useful, but you usually use it to organize styles. As a result, this function is presented in the next chapter.

If you start a document from one template and decide that you should have started it from another one, you can use the Templates command to attach a new template to the document. However, this doesn't always work the way you want it to because it doesn't change the page formatting. If you check the option for automatically updating styles, though, it does change the styles, which in turn changes the paragraph formatting.

The third function of the Templates command is an advanced function that most of us won't ever need. It makes other templates available to a document besides the one that's attached to it and the Normal template. Most of the time, that level of complexity causes more problems than it solves so it should be avoided.

Access

Menu   File ➡ Templates

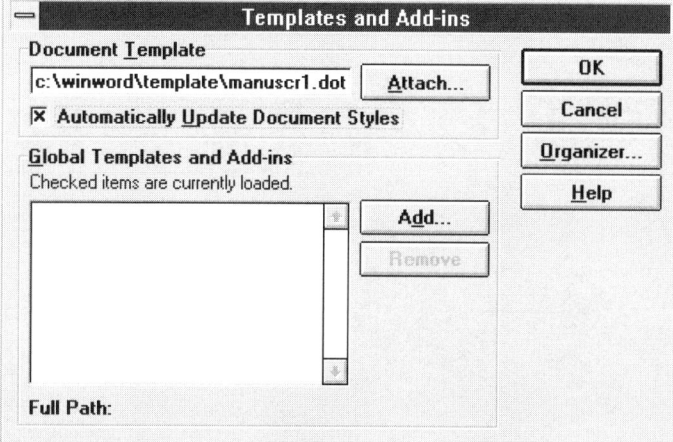

When and how to use the Organizer

- If you want to copy, rename, or delete any of the items in a template, you can click on the Organizer button and display its dialog box. This is most useful for working with styles, however, so it is presented in the next chapter.

When and how to attach another template to a document

- If you start a document from one template (like the Normal template) and decide that you would like to change to another template, you can use the Templates command to attach the new template. Then, the shortcut key assignments, AutoText entries, custom toolbars, and macros in the new template replace those in the original template. However, the page formatting isn't changed, and the styles aren't changed unless the Automatically Update Document Styles option is checked.

- To attach another template to a document, click on the Attach button and choose the template that you want to attach. Normally, you want the styles automatically updated when you attach the template, so you should check that option.

When and how to load a template for global use

- When you load a template for global use, the template's shortcut key assignments, AutoText entries, custom toolbars, and macros are available to any document during the current Word session. Since these items are normally stored in the Normal template, which is already available, you probably won't need this function.

- To load a template for global use, click on the Add button and choose the template that you want to add to the Global Templates and Add-ins list. Or, if the template is already in the list, check its box.

Figure 5-9   When and how to use the Templates command

Perspective

If you've done the exercises in this chapter, you should now see how easy it is to create, modify, and use templates. You should also realize that templates can help you work more efficiently by eliminating some of the routine work that you do whenever you start a new document. To get the most from templates, though, you also need to know how to get the most from styles. So before you create your own templates, you should read the next chapter.

After you read chapter 6, you should take the time to create one template for each type of document that you frequently create. If, for example, you've already prepared a memo, letter, and report that are formatted the way you want them, you can use those documents to create the templates you need for preparing new memos, letters, and reports. Another alternative is to create the templates you need from the Word 6 templates. Either way, it should take only a few minutes to create each template, and you'll get that time back many times over as you use the templates.

If you work in a department with others who prepare the same types of documents that you do, one person in the department can prepare the templates that everyone uses. That eliminates the duplication of effort throughout the department and helps standardize the documents that are prepared. Then, the department templates can be stored in the directory that's identified as the Workgroup Templates directory.

In some cases, of course, it makes sense to start a new document from an old document instead of from a template. If, for example, you frequently send faxes, memos, or letters to the same person, you can start new faxes, memos, or letters from the previous ones. This is the same principle that the use of templates is based on. Whenever possible, don't start a new document from scratch.

Summary

- A *template* is a document that is used for starting other documents. The file name for a template always has the extension DOT.
- To start a document from a template, use the New command in the File menu. You can also use this command to start a document from a *wizard*.
- To preview a template, you can use the Style Gallery command in the Format menu. You can also start a document from a template, print its starting text, and print a list of its styles, AutoText entries, and shortcut key assignments.
- You can create new templates from other templates or from documents that are formatted the way you want them. You can modify a template by working directly with the template or by working with a document that the template is attached to.
- The File Locations tab of the Options command in the Tools menu provides for two template directories. The templates in both directories are listed in the New dialog box.
- The Templates command in the File menu lets you attach a new template to a document that you've already started. That's one way to change the styles that are available to a document.

Chapter 6

How to create and use styles

In chapter 4, you learned how to use styles to format heading paragraphs. To get the most from the use of styles, however, you need to know how to use styles for all types of paragraphs. This also helps you get the most from your use of templates.

In fact, the effective use of styles is one of those skills that distinguishes the best professionals from other word processing users. Once you master the use of styles, you'll be able to quickly and consistently format your documents. You'll also work with more confidence when you use Word features that automatically apply styles.

Basic skills for using styles

In chapter 4, you were introduced to some of the basic skills for using styles. The topics that follow review and expand upon those skills.

Style concepts and terms

Figure 6-1 presents the concepts and terms that you need to know when you work with styles. To start, you should know that there are two types of styles. A *paragraph style* is applied to a paragraph. It controls paragraph formatting like indentation, line spacing, and tab settings as well as the character formatting for the text within a paragraph. The paragraph styles are the ones that provide the benefits listed in figure 6-1.

In contrast, *character styles* apply character formatting to text selections. If, for example, you want to italicize and boldface certain words in a document, you can apply a character style with that formatting. Often, though, you can format the characters in a selection just as quickly using shortcut keys or toolbar buttons. That's why character styles usually don't provide much benefit to the Word user. And that's why the emphasis in this chapter is on paragraph styles, not character styles.

To help you get started with styles, Word 6 provides a large starting set of *built-in styles*. These are predominately paragraph styles, but they also include a few character styles. In contrast, *user styles* are the additional styles that are available from the templates

A document formatted with styles

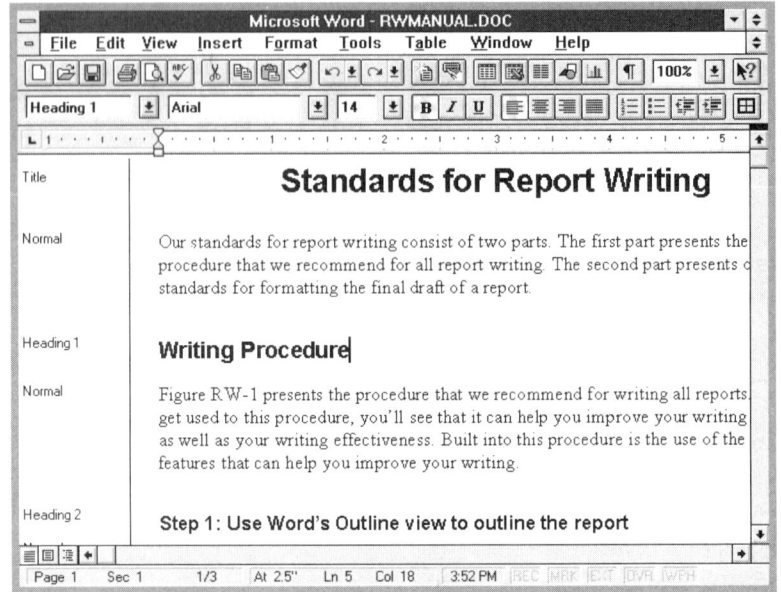

Concepts and terms for working with styles

- A *paragraph style* controls both the paragraph and character formatting of the paragraph that the style is applied to. A *character style* controls just the formatting of the characters that it is applied to.

- Word 6 comes with many *built-in styles* like the Heading 1 and Heading 2 styles for the headings and subheadings of a report and the Normal style for the text paragraphs within a report. *User styles* are the ones that are created for special purposes.

- When you start a new document, it is based on a template, and the styles from that template are copied into the document. Then, you can add, modify, and delete styles without affecting those in the template. If you don't choose a specific template when you start a new document, the Normal template is used.

The benefits that you get from using styles

- Styles help you work more efficiently because you can apply complex formatting to selected paragraphs with just a few mouse clicks or one shortcut key.

- Styles encourage consistent formatting within a single document and from one document to another.

- To change all the paragraphs in a document that are formatted with a specific style, you just have to change that style, not every paragraph that's formatted with the style.

- Knowing how to use styles makes it easier for you to use features like the outline feature and the table of contents feature.

Figure 6-1   Style concepts, terms, and benefits

plus the ones that you create. In the example in figure 6-1, the Heading 1, Heading 2, and Normal styles are built-in paragraph styles, but the Title style is a user style.

Whenever you use styles, you can think of it as *indirect formatting* because you don't apply the formatting directly to paragraphs or selected text. Instead, you apply a style, which supplies the formatting. In contrast, whenever you use shortcut keys, toolbar buttons, or menus to apply formatting, you can think of it as *direct formatting* because the formatting is applied directly to paragraphs and selected text.

How to open a style area in a document window

In figure 6-1, you can see a *style area* in the left side of the document window. In this area, you can see the names of the paragraph styles that have been applied to the paragraphs of the document. Another way to find out what style has been applied to a paragraph is to look in the Style box in the Formatting toolbar, but that only shows the style applied to the paragraph that the insertion point is in.

Figure 6-2 shows how to open a style area when you're using the Normal view. Note, however, that this option isn't available when you're using Page Layout view. The style area can be useful when you first start working with styles or when you're checking a document to make sure that the right styles have been applied to all paragraphs. Otherwise, you usually keep this area closed.

Access

Menu   Tools ➡ Options

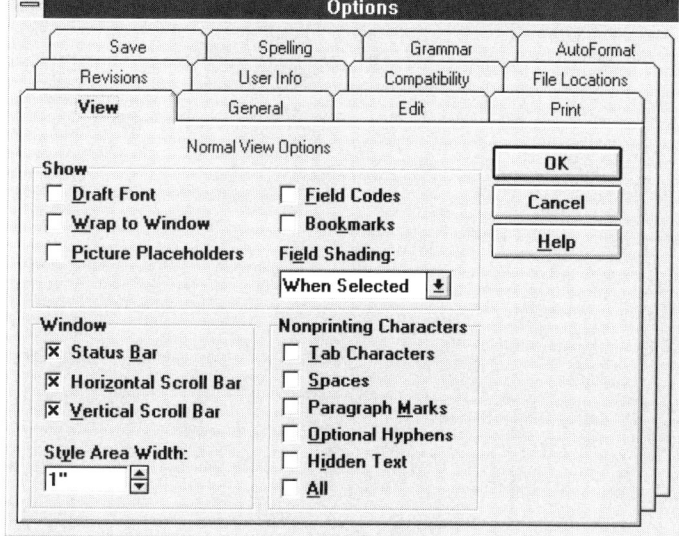

How to open the style area

1. If necessary, switch to Normal view.

2. Access the Options dialog box as shown above, then click on the View tab.

3. Set the Style Area Width option to a positive value. (One inch is about right.)

Two ways to change the size of the style area

• Drag the line between the style area and the document to the left or right.

• Reset the size of the style area in the View tab of the Options dialog box.

Two ways to close the style area

• Drag the line between the style area and the document off the screen to the left.

• Set the size of the style area to zero in the View tab of the Options dialog box.

Figure 6-2   How to open and close a style area

How to apply a style to a paragraph

The two best ways to apply a paragraph style are (1) to use the Style box in the Formatting toolbar or (2) to use a shortcut key. You can also use the Style command in the Format menu to apply a style, but that isn't as efficient.

Figure 6-3 shows you how to use the Style box in the Formatting toolbar to apply a paragraph style. To apply the style to one paragraph, just move the insertion point so it's anywhere in the paragraph. To apply the style to more than one paragraph, select a portion of each paragraph that you want to apply the style to; you don't have to select entire paragraphs. For a document that has a short list of styles (so scrolling isn't required), you can apply any style with just two mouse clicks using this technique.

Figure 6-3 also presents the shortcut keys that you can use for applying some of the built-in styles. When you're entering a document, these keys let you apply styles without lifting your hands from the keyboard so you can work more efficiently. Later, you'll learn how to assign a shortcut key to any style so you can apply all styles this way if you want to.

The Style list for a document that's started from a report template

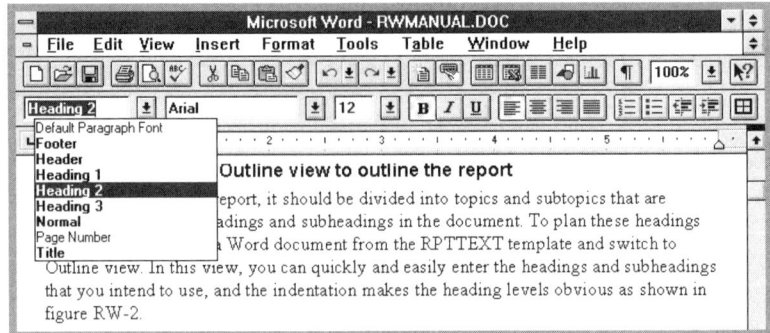

How to use the toolbar to apply a style to the selected paragraphs

1. Click on the arrow to the right of the Style box to display the Style list.

2. Click on the paragraph style you want to apply. The boldfaced style names are for paragraph styles; the others are for character styles.

The shortcut keys for applying styles

Key	Style or function
Ctrl+Shift+N	Normal style
Ctrl+Alt+1	Heading 1 style
Ctrl+Alt+2	Heading 2 style
Ctrl+Alt+3	Heading 3 style
Ctrl+Shift+L	List Bullet style
Ctrl+Shift+S	Highlights the style in the Style box. Then, you can press the Down-arrow key to display the Style list, the Up-arrow or Down-arrow key to move the highlight to other names in the Style list, and the Enter key to apply the highlighted style.

Notes

- The starting Style list for a document includes the most commonly used built-in styles like the Heading 1, Heading 2, and Heading 3 styles plus the styles in the template that the document is based on.

- To include all the available styles in the list, hold down the Shift key as you click on the arrow to the right of the Style box.

- If you type one or more letters in the Style box, Word scrolls to the first style that begins with those letters.

- When you apply a style to a paragraph, it overrides the direct formatting that has been applied to it. But if you apply direct formatting to a paragraph after a style has been applied to it, the direct formatting overrides the style formatting.

Figure 6-3   How to apply a style to a paragraph

How to use the Formatting toolbar to create or modify a paragraph style

Figure 6-4 shows how to use the Formatting toolbar to create or modify styles. This is often the quickest way to do these functions. As you'll see in the next topic, however, you have more control over how a style is defined when you use the Style command to create or modify the style.

To modify a style using the Formatting toolbar, you apply direct formatting to a paragraph that has the style you want to modify. Then, you use the toolbar to redefine the style so it includes the direct formatting.

To create a paragraph style using the Formatting toolbar, you use direct formatting to format a paragraph the way you want it for the new style. Then, you enter the name for the new style in the Style box and press the Enter key. When you do that, the new style is created and applied to the paragraph.

How to modify a paragraph style

1. If you want to change just the paragraph formatting for a style, move the insertion point into a paragraph that has that style. If you want to change the character formatting, select the entire paragraph including the paragraph mark. Then, format the paragraph the way you want it for the modified style.

2. Click in the Style box in the Formatting toolbar to highlight the name of the style that's applied to the selected paragraph. Then, press the Enter key so this dialog box appears:

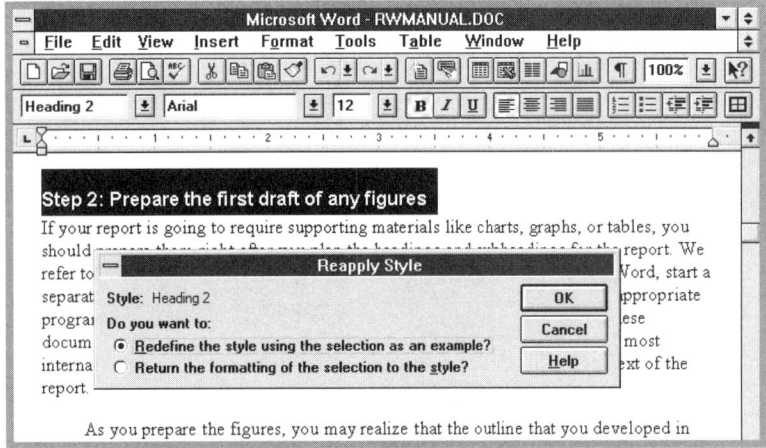

3. Click on the OK button to modify the style based on the formatting in the selected paragraph. That changes the formatting for all the paragraphs with that style. If you choose the second option in this dialog box, Word returns the formatting of the selected paragraph to the original formatting of the style.

How to create a new paragraph style

1. Move the insertion point into a paragraph with the style that you want to base the new style on. Then, format that paragraph the way you want it for the new style, and move the insertion point into a portion of the text that has the character formatting that you want for the style.

2. Click in the Style box in the Formatting toolbar and enter the name for the new style.

3. Press the Enter key to create the new style and apply it to the selected paragraph.

Figure 6-4   How to use the Formatting toolbar to create or modify a style

Exercise set 6-1

Title	**Standards for Report Writing**
Normal	Our standards for report writing consist of two parts. The first part presents the standard procedure that we recommend for all report writing. The second part presents our standards for formatting the final draft of a report.
Heading 1	
Normal	**Writing Procedure**
	Figure RW-1 presents the writing procedure that we recommend for all reports. Once you get used to this procedure, you'll see that it can help you improve your writing efficiency as well as your writing effectiveness. Built into this procedure is the use of the Word 6 features that can help you improve your writing.
Heading 2	**Step 1: Use Word's Outline view to outline the report**
Normal	Whenever you write a report, it should be divided into topics and subtopics that are clearly identified by heading and subheadings in the document. To plan these headings and subheadings, start a Word document from the RPTTEXT template and switch to Outline view. In this way, you can quickly and easily enter the headings and subheadings that you intend to use, and the indentation makes the heading levels obvious as shown in figure RW-2.
First Line Indent	After you enter the first draft of the headings and subheadings, you can review their structure, reword them so they're more definitive, change a heading to a subheading, rearrange headings and subheadings, print the entire outline, and so on. You can also include notes below the headings and subheadings that will help you write the text later on.

How the RWSTDS document should look after exercise 3

If you did the exercises for chapter 4, you created the start of a report like the one shown above. That's the document that you'll modify in the exercise sets for this chapter. If you didn't create this document, please do exercise sets 4-1 and 4-2 before you continue.

1. Open the RWSTDS file, and use the procedure in figure 6-2 to open a style area like the one shown above. Next, use the second procedure in figure 6-4 to create a new paragraph style named First Line Indent. To begin, move the insertion point into the second Normal paragraph after the Step 1 heading, the one starting with "After you enter." Then, indent the first line of the paragraph one-half inch, either by dragging the first-line indent marker in the ruler or by using the Paragraph command in the Format menu. Click in the Style box and enter the style name (First Line Indent), then press the Enter key.

2. Move the insertion point into the Normal paragraph above the one you just applied the new style to, and apply the new style to that paragraph using the Style list as described in figure 6-3. Is the first line of the paragraph indented? Reapply the Normal style to this paragraph by pressing Ctrl+Shift+N.

3. Move the insertion point into the first paragraph of the document (the title), and use the second procedure in figure 6-4 to create a new paragraph style named Title with the formatting in that first paragraph. Did the new style retain the 20 point Arial font and the spacing after the paragraph? On my PC it didn't, which I assume is a bug in Word 6. If you had that problem too, use the first procedure in figure 6-4 to modify the Title style so it has the proper formatting. When you do that, be sure to select the entire paragraph including the paragraph mark. Then, use the Font Size list to change the font size back to 20, use the Paragraph command in the Format menu to set the spacing before the paragraph to 0 and the spacing after the paragraph to 18 points, and use the Style box to redefine the style so it includes the new formatting. The document should now look like the one shown above.

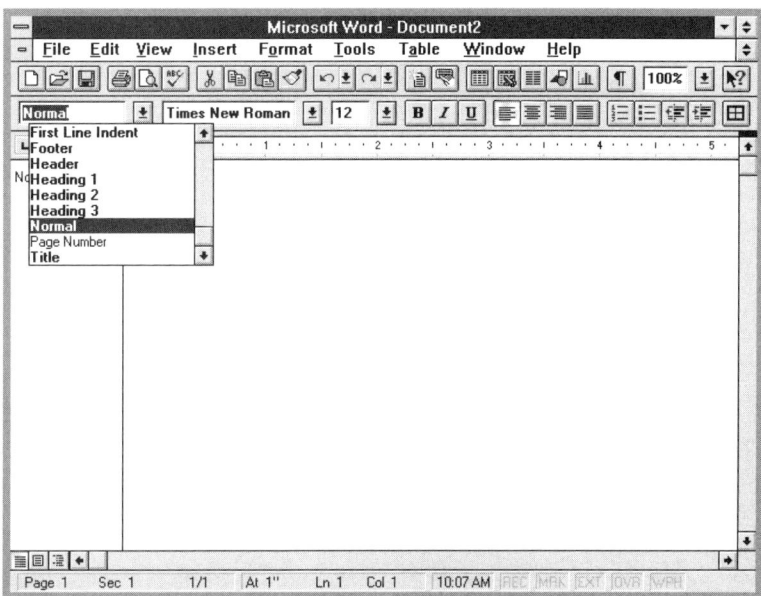

How the Style list should look in exercise 5

4. Now, this document has a complete set of styles for a simple report with two levels of headings. So save the document, but don't close it. Then, use the Save As command to start a template from the report by saving the file in the default template directory (C:\WINWORD\TEMPLATE) with the name MYREPORT.DOT. Next, delete all the text from the file (press Ctrl+A to select it and press the Delete key to delete it), and save the file again. When that's done, you've created a template that has the styles you've been using so you can close the file.

5. Use the New command in the File menu to start a new document from the MYREPORT template. Pull down the list of styles from the Formatting toolbar. Are the styles you created in this exercise set in the list as shown above? Use Page Layout view to see that this new document includes an appropriate footer that you originally created in exercise set 4-2. Then, close the document without saving it.

How to use the Style command to work with styles

The primary command for working with styles is the Style command in the Format menu. Its dialog box is presented in figure 6-5. The command buttons on the right side of this dialog box let you perform functions like applying, creating, and modifying a style. Since you can apply a style more easily by using the Formatting toolbar, you won't use this command for that purpose. Although you can also create and modify styles using the Formatting toolbar, you have more control over how the style is defined when you use the Style command. You can also use the Style command to delete styles from the document and to assign or change the shortcut keys that are assigned to the styles.

How to create a style

Figure 6-6 presents the information that you need for creating a style from the Style dialog box. Whenever you create a new style, it is based on an existing style called the *base style*. Then, the formatting for the new style is added to the base style.

By default, a new style is based on the style that's applied to the paragraph that the insertion point is in, but you can change that by choosing another style from the Based On list. Later, if you change the base style, any styles that are based on it are changed too. Most of the built-in styles are based on the Normal style, and the Normal style is usually the best base style for user styles too.

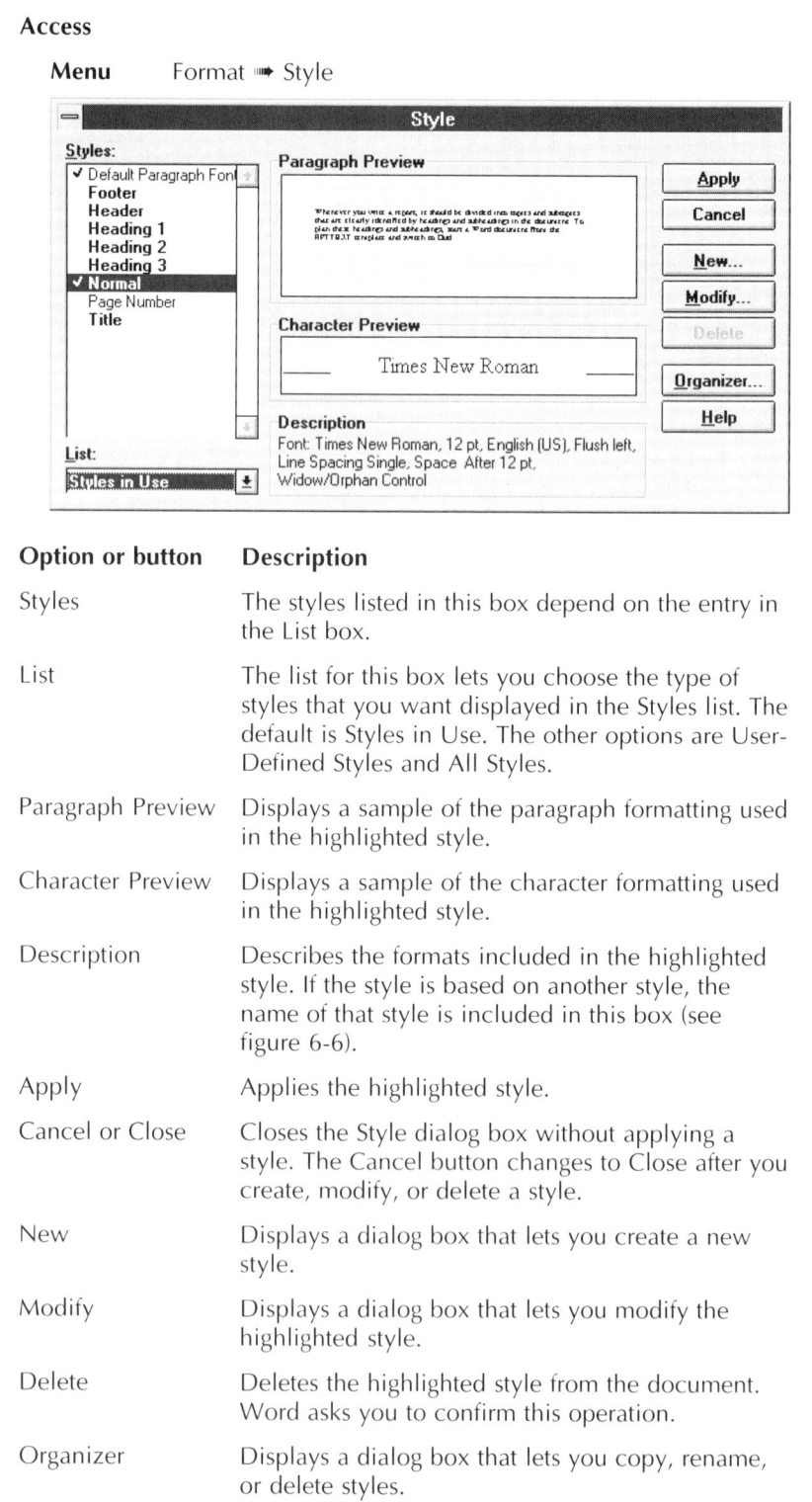

Access

Menu   Format ➡ Style

Option or button	Description
Styles	The styles listed in this box depend on the entry in the List box.
List	The list for this box lets you choose the type of styles that you want displayed in the Styles list. The default is Styles in Use. The other options are User-Defined Styles and All Styles.
Paragraph Preview	Displays a sample of the paragraph formatting used in the highlighted style.
Character Preview	Displays a sample of the character formatting used in the highlighted style.
Description	Describes the formats included in the highlighted style. If the style is based on another style, the name of that style is included in this box (see figure 6-6).
Apply	Applies the highlighted style.
Cancel or Close	Closes the Style dialog box without applying a style. The Cancel button changes to Close after you create, modify, or delete a style.
New	Displays a dialog box that lets you create a new style.
Modify	Displays a dialog box that lets you modify the highlighted style.
Delete	Deletes the highlighted style from the document. Word asks you to confirm this operation.
Organizer	Displays a dialog box that lets you copy, rename, or delete styles.

Figure 6-5   The Style dialog box

When you press the Enter key to end a paragraph that has a style applied to it, a new paragraph is created with the style specified in the Style for Following Paragraph box. For instance, you usually want a paragraph with the Normal style after a paragraph with a Heading 1 or Heading 2 style. By default, though, the style name in the Style for Following Paragraph box is the same as the name of the style you're creating. As a result, you will often want to change this entry when you create a new style.

If the paragraph that the insertion point is in includes any direct formatting, that formatting is automatically included in the style along with the formatting in the base style. If you want to change the formatting for the style, however, you can click on the Format button in the New Style dialog box. This drops down a menu of formatting options that include Font, Paragraph, and Tabs for a paragraph style. When you choose one of the menu options, the related dialog box is displayed so you can specify the formatting that you want applied to the style. You do that the same way that you specify direct formatting.

When you create a new style, it is always saved with the document that you're working on. If you also want to save the style in the template that the active document is based on, you can check the Add to Template option in the New Style dialog box. Then, when you click on the OK button to complete the function, the new style is added to both the active document and the template.

How to access the New Style dialog box

From the Style dialog box, click on the New button.

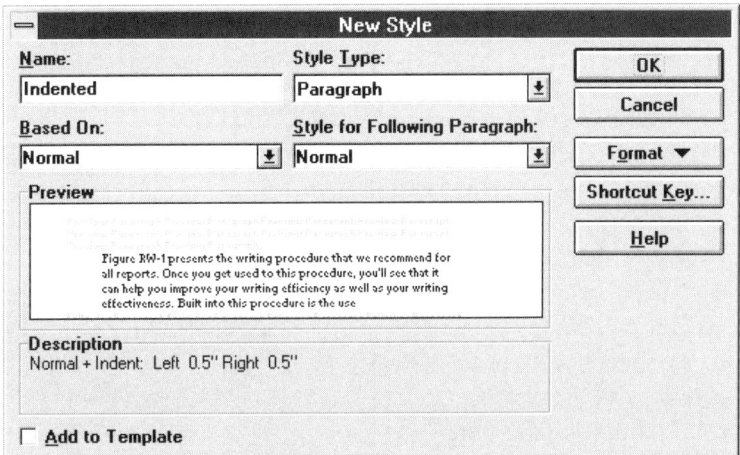

Option or button	How to use it
Name	Enter the name that you want to use for the new style. Note that style names are case sensitive, so *normal* is a different name than *Normal*.
Style Type	If necessary, choose a style type from the list. Since the default is Paragraph, you don't have to do this for a paragraph style. The other option is Character.
Based On	If necessary, choose the style you want to base the new style on. Normal works the best for most styles.
Style for Following Paragraph	If necessary, choose the style you want to use for the paragraph that follows a paragraph with the new style. For instance, you usually want the Normal paragraph style used after a paragraph that a heading style has been applied to.
Format	If necessary, click on the Format button to display a formatting menu (Font, Paragraph, Tabs, and so on). Then, choose an item from the menu, and use the dialog box that follows to set the formatting options. Repeat this until you have all the options set the way you want them.
Shortcut Key	Click on this button if you want to assign a shortcut key to the style (see figure 6-8).
Add to Template	Check this option if you want to add the new style to the template that the active document is based on.
OK	Click on this button to create the style and return to the Style dialog box.

Figure 6-6   How to use the Style command to create any style

How to modify a style

Figure 6-7 presents the information that you need for modifying a style. As you can see, the Modify Style dialog box is almost identical to the New Style dialog box. When you modify a style, you can change the name of the style, the style it's based on, or the style for the following paragraph. You can also change or enhance the formatting of a style using the Format button. When you complete the function, the modified style is always saved with the active document. But if you check the Add to Template option, the modified style is also saved with the template that the document is based on.

How to access the Modify Style dialog box

From the Style dialog box, highlight the style you want to modify in the Styles list, then click on the Modify button.

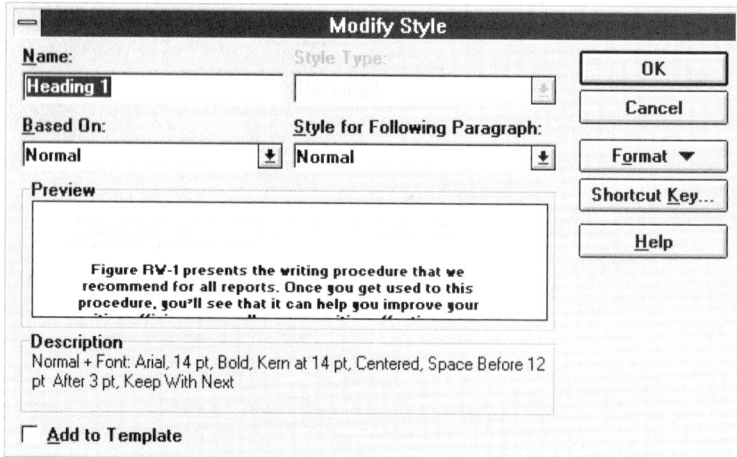

Option or button	How to use it
Name	If you want to rename the style, enter the name that you want to use. If you enter a new name for a built-in style, Word treats it as an alternate name because you can't rename the built-in styles. Then, you can use either name to apply the style.
Style Type	This is dimmed so you can't change it.
Based On	Choose a style from this list to change the style that the current style is based on.
Style for Following Paragraph	Choose a style from this list to change the style for the following paragraph.
Format	Click on the Format button to display a formatting menu (Font, Paragraph, Tabs, and so on). Then, choose an item from the menu, and use the dialog box that follows to set the formatting options. Repeat this until you have all the options set the way you want them.
Shortcut Key	Click on this button if you want to assign a shortcut key to the style or change the shortcut key that is currently assigned to the style (see figure 6-8).
Add to Template	Check this option if you want to add the modified style to the template that the active document is based on.
OK	Click on this button to modify the style and return to the Style dialog box.

Figure 6-7   How to use the Style command to modify any style

How to assign a shortcut key to a style

Figure 6-8 shows how to assign a shortcut key to a style. This assignment is saved in the template identified in the Save Changes In box. Usually, you'll want to save the shortcut keys in the Normal template even if your document is based on another template. That's because any item stored in the Normal template is available to all documents.

How to delete a style

You can also use the Style dialog box to delete styles from a document. To delete a style, highlight it in the Styles list and click on the Delete button. If the style you delete has been applied to any paragraphs in the document, those paragraphs are returned to the Normal style.

Although you can delete most of the styles that are available to a document, you can't delete a few of the built-in styles. In particular, you can't delete the Normal, Heading 1, Heading 2, and Heading 3 styles. If you highlight any of these styles, the Delete button is unavailable.

If you want to delete only a style or two, using the Style command is efficient. If you want to delete several styles, however, it's more efficient to use the Organizer that's shown in figure 6-11. You can also use the Organizer to delete styles from the template instead of from the document.

Procedure

1. Click on the Shortcut Key button in the New Style or Modify Style dialog box so this dialog box appears:

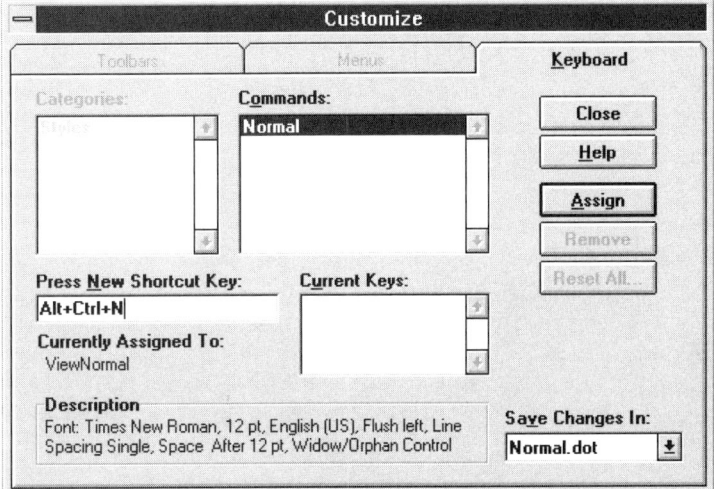

2. Click in the Press New Shortcut Key text box, then press the keys you want to assign to the style. This keystroke combination must include the Alt key, the Ctrl key, or both keys. This combination is then displayed in the text box.

3. Click on the Assign button, and the shortcut key is assigned to the style.

4. Click on the Close button, and Word returns you to the New Style or Modify Style dialog box.

Notes

• When you assign a shortcut key to a style, it's saved in the template specified in the Save Changes In box. The default is the Normal template. Then, when you close the active document later on, Word displays a dialog box that asks whether you want to save the changes that you've made in that template. If you don't save the changes, the shortcut key assignment will be canceled. (If you change the Normal template, this message isn't displayed until you exit from Word.)

• If a shortcut key is already assigned to a style, the keystroke combination appears in the Current Keys box. To remove a shortcut key assignment, highlight the keystroke combination and click on the Remove button.

• If the shortcut key you specify is already assigned to a Word feature, that feature is indicated below the Press New Shortcut Key box. For instance, the shortcut key in the dialog box above is assigned to the Normal command in the View menu. Then, if you assign that shortcut key to the style, it overrides the original assignment. If you later remove the shortcut key assignment from the style, the original assignment is restored.

Figure 6-8   How to assign a shortcut key to a style

Exercise set 6-2

Style name	Style after	Spacing before	Spacing after
Title	Normal	0	18
Heading 1	Normal	9	6
Heading 2	Normal	6	6
Normal	First Line Indent	0	6
First Line Indent	First Line Indent	0	6
Indented	Normal	0	6

The styles that you modify or create in the first 3 exercises

In this exercise set, you'll create one new style for the RWSTDS document, and you'll modify the other styles so they'll work better. Because all the styles are based on the Normal style, you should start by modifying that style.

1. Open the RWSTDS file and use the Style command to modify the Normal style as indicated by the table above. To do that, issue the Style command from the Format menu, click on the Normal style in the Styles list (if it's not already highlighted), and click on the Modify button. When the Modify Style dialog box is displayed, choose First Line Indent from the Style for Following Paragraph list. Then, click on the Format button to display its menu, click on Paragraph to display the Paragraph dialog box, change the Spacing After value to 6 points, and click on the OK button twice to return to the Style dialog box. At this point, the Normal style has been modified, and you can see its modified description in the dialog box. Because the First Line Indent style is based on the Normal style, this also changes the spacing after in that style.

2. Without leaving the Style dialog box, modify the Title, Heading 1, Heading 2, and First Line Indent styles so they have the spacing before and after shown in the table above and so each one starts a paragraph with the style shown above. When you're finished, click on the Close button to return to the document and see the changes in the spacing. Then, move the insertion point to the end of a Normal paragraph (right before the paragraph mark) and press the Enter key. Does the new paragraph have the First Line Indent style? If so, delete the new paragraph. Otherwise, modify the Normal style so this works right.

3. Use the Style command to create a new style named Indented with the characteristics shown in the table above. In addition, this style should be based on the Normal style and should be indented one-half inch from both margins. You can use a style like this for paragraphs that are taken directly from other sources (quotations).

4. Use the procedure in figure 6-8 to assign Ctrl+Alt+F as the shortcut key for the First Line Indent style. When you return to the document, move the insertion point into a paragraph with the Normal style and press the shortcut key to change the style to First Line Indent. Then, press Ctrl+Shift+N to return the paragraph to the Normal style.

5. At this point, you have an improved set of styles for preparing a report. After you use the Print command to print a list of these styles, save the document, but don't close it. Then, use the document to update the MYREPORT template. To start, use the Save As command to save the document as MYREPORT.DOT in the default template directory. This replaces the previous version of this template that you created in the last exercise set. Next, delete the text in the document, save the template again, and close the template.

6. Use the New command in the File menu to start a new document from the MYREPORT template. Apply the Title style to the first paragraph, type the word *Title*, and press the Enter key. What style does the new paragraph have? Type the words *Normal paragraph* and press the Enter key. What style does the new paragraph have? Type the words *First Line Indent paragraph* and press the Enter key. What style does the new paragraph have? Press the shortcut key for the Heading 1 style (Ctrl+Alt+1), type *Heading 1 paragraph*, and press the Enter key. The new paragraph should have the Normal style. If you set your styles up right, that's how easy it is to apply styles as you enter a document. Now, close the document without saving it.

Other skills for working with styles

At this point, you should know how to create, modify, and apply styles. Those are the skills that you'll use most of the time. To get the maximum benefit from styles, however, you occasionally need the skills that follow.

How to use the Style Gallery command to copy styles from another template into the active document

Once you take the time to set up the styles for one type of document, it makes sense to use them in other documents of the same type. If you get the styles right for one report, for example, you should use the same styles in all the reports you write. If you've read chapter 5, you know that the way to do that is to save the styles in a template. Then, when you start a new document from that template, the styles are copied into the new document.

Sometimes, though, you start a new document from one template, then decide that you want to use styles from another template. In that case, you can use the Style Gallery command to copy the styles from the other template into your document as shown in figure 6-9. When the styles are copied, they replace any styles in the active document with the same names. In effect, this reformats your document using the styles in the new template. To make sure that the new styles are going to work the way you want them to, you can preview the changes before you complete the command.

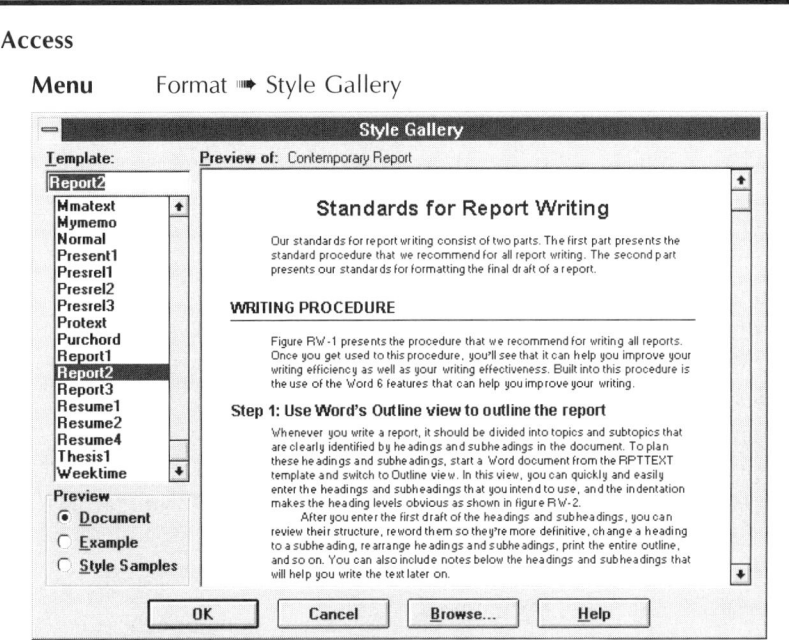

Access

Menu   Format ➡ Style Gallery

How to preview the styles in a template

- Highlight a template in the Template list. With the Document option on in the Preview group, the Preview Of window shows how the styles in that template will look when applied to the active document as shown above.

- If you're previewing the styles for one of the Word 6 templates, you can click on one of the other options in the Preview group. If you choose the Example option, a sample document is displayed with the styles applied. If you choose the Style Samples option, samples of the styles are displayed.

How to copy the styles from another template into the active document

- Double-click on the template in the Template list, or highlight the template and click on the OK button. This copies the styles from the highlighted template into the active document. If a style with the same name as a style in the template already exists in the document, the new style replaces the existing one. Then, the new formatting replaces the old formatting in all paragraphs that have that style.

Figure 6-9   How to use the Style Gallery command to copy styles from another template into the active document

How to use the Templates command to update the styles in a document

Figure 6-10 shows how you can change the styles in a document by attaching another template to the document. It also shows how you can turn on the Automatically Update Document Styles option so the styles in a document are automatically updated whenever the document is opened.

If you're working on a group project and everyone has to use the most recent version of the same template, the option for automatic updating is useful. Otherwise, you probably won't ever need this command. If you just want to change the styles in a document, you're better off using the Style Gallery command.

Access

Menu   File ➡ Templates

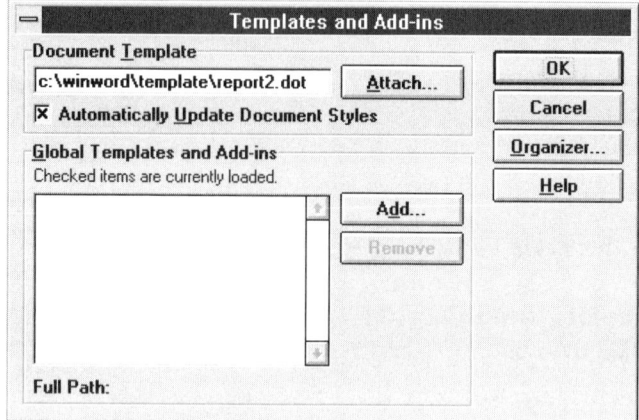

How to attach another template to a document and replace the styles in the document with those in the template

1. Access the Templates and Add-ins dialog box shown above.

2. Click on the Attach button, and choose the template that you want to attach to the document.

3. When you return to the Templates and Add-ins dialog box, check the Automatically Update Document Styles option.

4. Click on the OK button to attach the template and update the styles.

How to automatically update the styles in a document whenever the document is opened

• Access the Templates and Add-ins dialog box, check the Automatically Update Document Styles option, and click on the OK button. This doesn't update the styles right away, but it turns the option on so the document styles are automatically updated each time the document is opened.

Recommendations

• Use the Style Gallery command if you just want to copy styles from a template into a document. Don't use the Templates command to change the styles to those from another template unless you need to attach a different template to the document for other reasons (see figure 5-9).

• If you check the Automatically Update Document Styles option when you attach another template, be sure to turn this option off again after the template is attached unless you want the document styles updated each time you open the document.

• Don't turn the Automatically Update Document Styles option on unless you're sure that you are always going to want the document styles updated when you open the document. If this option is on and you don't want the styles updated, you can't open the document without updating the styles (or getting around this some other way).

Figure 6-10   **How to use the Templates command to update the styles in a document**

How to use the Organizer to work with styles

If you want to copy, rename, or delete styles in any document or template, you can click on the Organizer button in the Style or Templates and Add-ins dialog box. Word then displays the Organizer dialog box, which you can use in the variety of ways that are summarized in figure 6-11. For instance, you can use this dialog box to delete any of the styles in the active document; you can use it to copy styles from the active document to any template; and you can use it to copy styles from another document to the active document.

Sometimes, for example, you start a new document from a template, then decide that you would like to use one or more of the styles that you remember using in another document. If these styles aren't in a template, though, you can't use the Style Gallery command to copy them into the active document. But you can use the Organizer. To do that, you can close the Normal template on the right side of the dialog box and open the document that contains the styles you want to use. Then, you can copy some or all of the styles from that document into the active document.

How to access the Organizer dialog box

From the Style or Templates and Add-ins dialog box, click on the Organizer button.

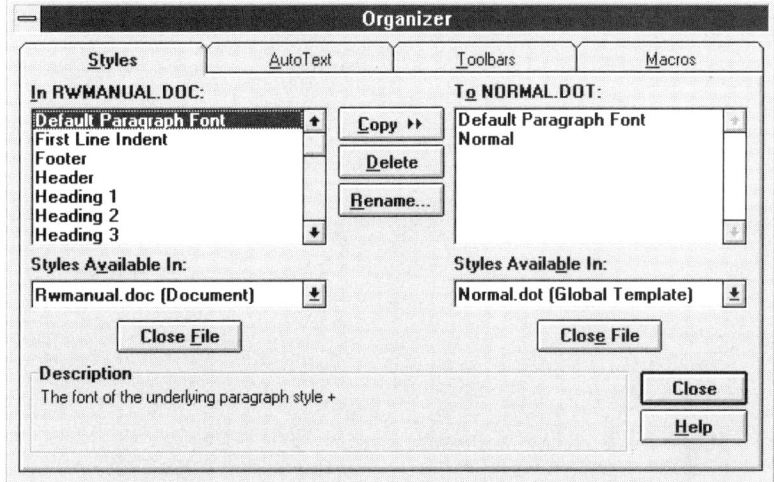

How to display the files or templates that you want to work with

- To close the style list on either the left or right side of the dialog box, click on the Close File button below the styles. This clears the list and changes the button to Open File. Then, click on the Open File button and identify another template or document in the Open dialog box to display the styles in that template or document.

How to copy, delete, or rename one or more styles

- To copy a style from one document or template to another, highlight the style and click on the Copy button (the arrowheads on the button change to indicate the proper copy direction). If you try to copy a style to a document or template that already contains a style with that name, Word asks if you want to overwrite the style.

- To delete a style, highlight the style and click on the Delete button. Word then displays a dialog box that asks you to confirm the operation.

- To rename a style, highlight the style and click on the Rename button. Word then displays a dialog box that lets you enter the new name for the style.

- To copy or delete more than one file at a time, you can highlight more than one style before you click on the Copy or Delete button.

Notes

- The other tabs in the Organizer dialog box can be used to copy, delete, or rename AutoText entries (see chapter 2), toolbars, and macros, but you usually don't need to do that.

- The Styles Available In lists include any global templates that are active, but there usually aren't any (see figure 5-9).

Figure 6-11   How to use the Organizer to copy, rename, and delete styles

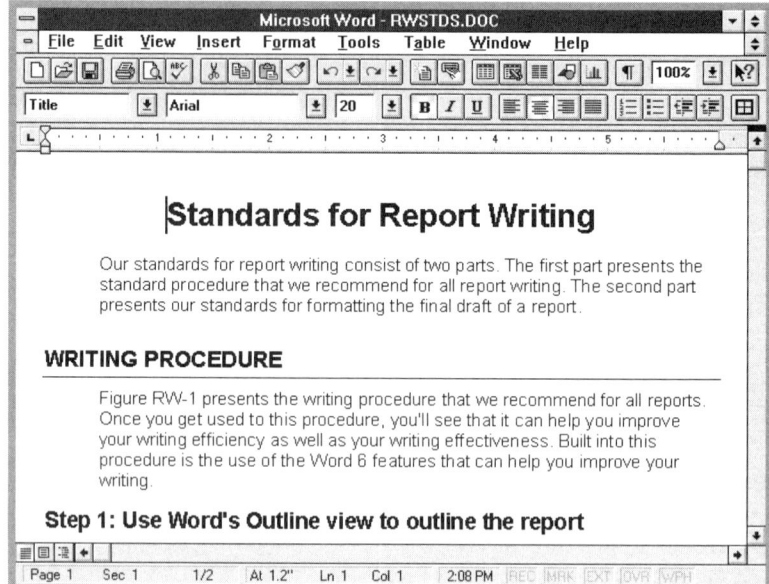

How the RWSTDS document should look after you copy the styles from the Report2 template in exercise 1

1. Open the RWSTDS file, and use the Style Gallery command shown in figure 6-9 to preview the way the Report1, Report2, and Report3 templates will change the formatting in the report. Then, apply the Report2 styles to the RWSTDS report. The document should now look like the one shown above. Print the first page of the document to see whether you like that formatting better, and close the file without saving it.

2. Open the RWSTDS file, and use the Templates command shown in figure 6-10 to attach the Report2 template to the document and update its styles. Is the result the same as in exercise 1? To make sure, print the first page of the document, and close the file without saving it.

3. Open the RWSTDS file, and access the Organizer from either the Style or the Templates dialog box. Note that the styles for the document are on the left, and the styles for the Normal template are on the right. Then, close the styles for NORMAL.DOT, open the styles for the MYMEMO2 template, and copy the Indented and First Line Indent styles from the document to the MYMEMO2 template. That's how easy it is to copy styles from one document or template to another.

4. With the Organizer dialog box still open, close the MYMEMO2 template, saving the changes, and open the Letter3 template that comes with Word. Scroll through the styles so you can see that there are far too many for efficient use. If you wanted to delete the styles that you don't intend to use, you could highlight them and click on the Delete button. Instead, close the Organizer and return to the RWSTDS document.

5. Move the insertion point into a Normal paragraph. Then, click on the Numbering toolbar button to number the paragraph, and use the Style box in the Formatting toolbar (see figure 6-4) to create a new style from the paragraph named Numbered List. Next, click on the Bullets toolbar button to bullet the paragraph that you had numbered, and use the Style box to create a new style from the paragraph named Bulleted List. These are two other styles that you may want to add to your templates for reports, memos, and letters. The alternative is to use the Numbering and Bullets buttons to directly format the Normal paragraph whenever you need numbered or bulleted paragraphs, but then you can't change the formatting for all numbered or bulleted paragraphs just by changing the appropriate style. Now, close the document without saving the changes.

How to get the maximum benefit from your use of styles

Figure 6-12 presents some recommendations that will help you get the maximum benefit from your use of styles. If you're working on your own, the most important recommendation is to take the time to develop a set of styles and a template for each type of document that you use frequently.

If you're new to styles, it's usually best to keep the styles in your first templates to a minimum and to use direct formatting for the requirements that your styles don't provide for. You shouldn't feel that you have to create a style for each formatting variation. Later, as the need for new styles becomes obvious, you can add them to your templates.

In contrast, it appears that the designers of the Word 6 templates have tried to create one style for every type of formatting that you might conceivably want to use. If you review the styles in the Report1 template, for example, you'll find 26 styles for lists alone. These provide for numbered lists, bulleted lists, and plain lists with varying indents and varying amounts of before and after spacing. That many styles, however, just make a template more difficult to use.

So if you want to create a new template that's based on one of the Word 6 templates, you can start by using the Organizer to delete the styles that you don't need. After the new template is created, you can use the Organizer to copy additional styles from the Word 6 template to your template, but only as you discover the need for them.

Minimum sets of styles for preparing reports, memos, and letters

Report	Memo	Letter
Title	Title	Date
Heading 1	Heading Item	Inside Address
Heading 2	Normal	Subject
Normal	First Line Indent	Greeting
First Line Indent	Indented	Normal
Indented		First Line Indent
		Indented
		Closing
		Signature
		PS

General recommendations

- Develop a set of styles for each type of document you frequently create, and save those styles in a template for that type of document. Then, start each new document from the appropriate template.

- Start with a minimum set of styles for each type of document, and use direct formatting to provide for occasional variations. Add styles to your templates only when the need for them becomes apparent.

- Don't try to develop a separate paragraph style for every formatting variation. To get the major benefits from styles, you just need to use styles for formatting the basic types of paragraphs in each document.

- To get a better idea of how styles can be set up and used, review the styles in the Word 6 templates. Keep in mind, however, that most of these templates have too many styles for efficient use.

Specific style recommendations

- Base most of your styles on the Normal style. This style should be left aligned (no indentation) with the font, font size, and spacing before and after that you want for most of the paragraphs in the document. Later, if you change the Normal style, all styles that are based on it are also changed.

- Set up all styles so the right style is applied to the next paragraph when you press the Enter key to end the current paragraph.

- If you like to use the keyboard to apply styles, assign shortcut keys to the styles that can't be started by the style for the previous paragraph.

- If you frequently use bulleted or numbered lists, you should develop styles for the paragraphs in those lists. Then, you can change the formatting in the lists by changing the styles. To start, you can develop one style for each type of list including the bullet or number, or you can develop one style for both types of lists and use the Bullets or Numbering button to apply the bullets or numbers.

Figure 6-12   How to get the maximum benefit from your use of styles

Perspective

Before you can use styles effectively, you need to modify some of the built-in styles, create a few styles of your own, and create or modify the templates that use the styles. Because that takes time and energy, it's easy to avoid doing it and to continue working the way you have been. I think that's the reason more people don't get the benefits that they ought to get from the use of templates and styles.

If you keep it simple, though, you should be able to set up the styles and templates you need in 30 minutes or less. That should help you save a few minutes each time you create and format a new document. Besides that, you'll format your documents more consistently, you'll be able to change their formatting with relative ease, and you'll free yourself to concentrate on the more important aspects of your job.

Summary

- Word 6 provides for both *paragraph styles* and *character styles*. Paragraph styles are the most useful, while character styles are of marginal benefit.

- The *built-in styles* are the ones that come with Word. To these, you can add *user styles*.

- When you start a Word document, it is always based on a template that can contain both built-in and user styles. Then, as the new document is created, the styles in the template are copied into the new document so they can be modified without affecting the styles in the template.

- To apply a style, you can use the Style box in the Formatting toolbar or a shortcut key. Word provides shortcut keys for four of the built-in styles, but you can assign a shortcut key to any style.

- You can modify or create a paragraph style using the Style box in the Formatting toolbar. However, you can't use this method to change the Based On style, to change the Style for Following Paragraph entry, to assign a shortcut key, or to save the new or modified style in the template for the active document. To do that, you have to use the Style command in the Format menu.

- To format a document with styles from another template, you can use the Style Gallery command. To update the styles in a document with styles from a template, you can use the Templates command. And to copy, rename, or delete styles in any document or template, you can use the Organizer that can be accessed by the Style or Templates command.

Chapter 7

How to get the most from the outline feature

In chapter 4, you learned how to use the Heading styles to format heading paragraphs. You were also introduced to the *outline feature* that depends on the use of those styles. This feature is valuable whenever you prepare documents that include headings and subheadings, and this chapter shows you how to get the most from it.

Basic skills for working with the outline feature

Figure 7-1 reviews the skills that you learned in chapter 4. Once you switch to Outline view, you can click on one of the number buttons in the Outlining toolbar to display just the headings of a document. These are the paragraphs that have been formatted by the Heading styles that come with Word. If, for example, you click on the 2 button, just the paragraphs that are formatted by the Heading 1 and Heading 2 styles are displayed. The body text paragraphs and lower level headings are hidden.

Figure 7-1 also presents the terms that you should know as you work with the outline feature. When you raise or lower the heading level of a paragraph, you *promote* or *demote* the paragraph. When you display or hide the subheadings or body text for a heading, you *expand* or *collapse* the heading.

An outline with two heading levels displayed and one heading expanded

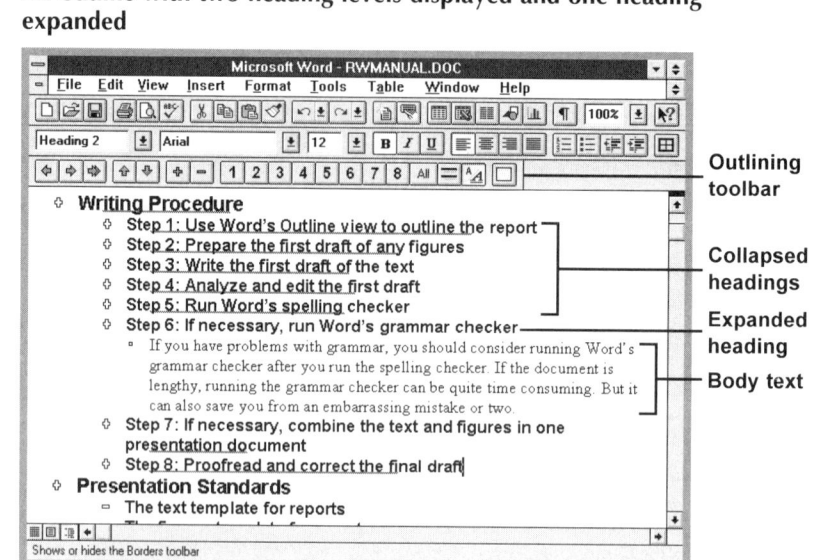

How to switch to Outline view

• Click on the Outline View button or choose the Outline command from the View menu.

How to display just the headings in a document

• Click on one of the number buttons in the Outlining toolbar to display that number of heading levels and no body text. In the example above, two levels of headings are shown.

Outlining terms

• To *collapse* a heading means to hide the subordinate headings or body text.

• To *expand* a heading means to show the subordinate headings or body text.

• To *promote* a heading means to raise it one level.

• To *demote* a heading means to lower it one level.

The symbols and notation used in Outline view

• A plus sign in front of a paragraph indicates a heading that has subordinate headings or body text.

• A minus sign in front of a paragraph indicates a heading that doesn't have subordinate headings or body text.

• A small square bullet in front of a paragraph indicates that the paragraph isn't formatted by a heading style so it's treated as body text.

• If a heading paragraph is underlined, some or all of the subordinate headings or body text is collapsed (hidden).

Figure 7-1   An introduction to the outline feature

How to enter an outline for a new document

Figure 7-2 presents the essential skills for entering the headings for a document in Outline view. When you're writing a document, this is an excellent way to plan the headings and subheadings that you're going to use in the document. Once you've got the headings and subheadings the way you want them, you can switch to Normal view and enter the body text for the document.

The last paragraphs in an outline for a new document

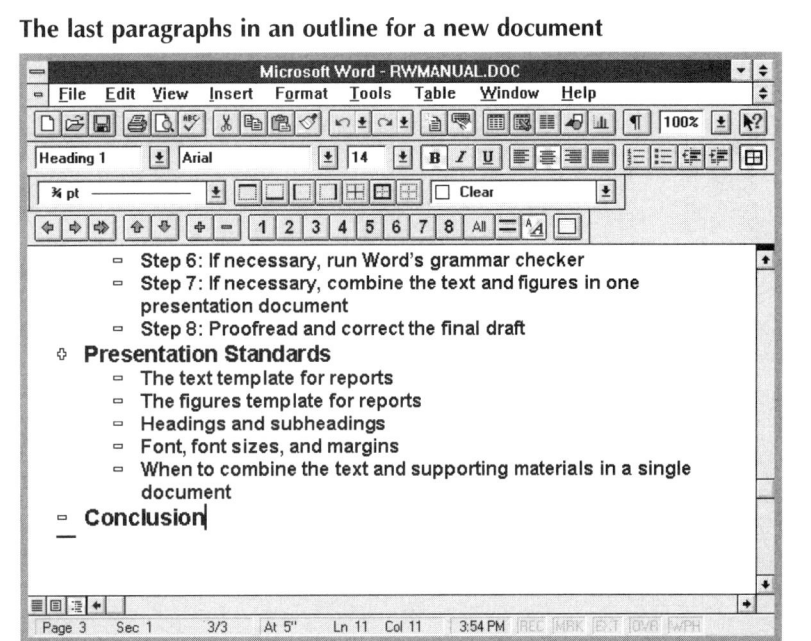

Operation

- Start a new document, switch to Outline view, and type the first paragraph. The Heading 1 style is automatically applied to it.

- When you press the Enter key to complete a heading paragraph, a new paragraph at the same heading level is started. If necessary, promote or demote the level of the new paragraph, type the text for the paragraph, and press the Enter key.

- To demote a heading paragraph, you can press the Tab key, press Alt+Shift+Right-arrow, or click on the right arrow button (Demote) in the Outlining toolbar.

- To promote a heading paragraph, you can press Shift+Tab, press Alt+Shift+Left-arrow, or click on the left arrow button (Promote) in the Outlining toolbar.

Note

- When you promote or demote a heading paragraph using the techniques described above, the appropriate heading style is automatically applied to the paragraph. You can also demote or promote a heading paragraph by directly applying the appropriate heading style.

Figure 7-2   How to enter an outline for a new document

How to use the mouse to reorganize an outline

Figure 7-3 shows how to use the mouse to reorganize an outline. This works whether or not you've entered the body text for a document. As a result, you can use these techniques when you're developing the outline for a new document or after the document is complete and you decide that it needs some reorganization.

If you experiment with these techniques, you'll quickly see that the outline feature helps you work more efficiently whenever you need to reorganize a document. To move a heading and its subheadings and body text, for example, you just drag the plus sign in front of the heading up or down. You don't have to select the headings, subheadings, and body text first. To promote or demote a heading and its subheadings, you just drag the plus sign in front of the heading to the left or right. When you do, the appropriate heading styles are automatically applied.

A heading and its subheadings as they're dragged to a new location

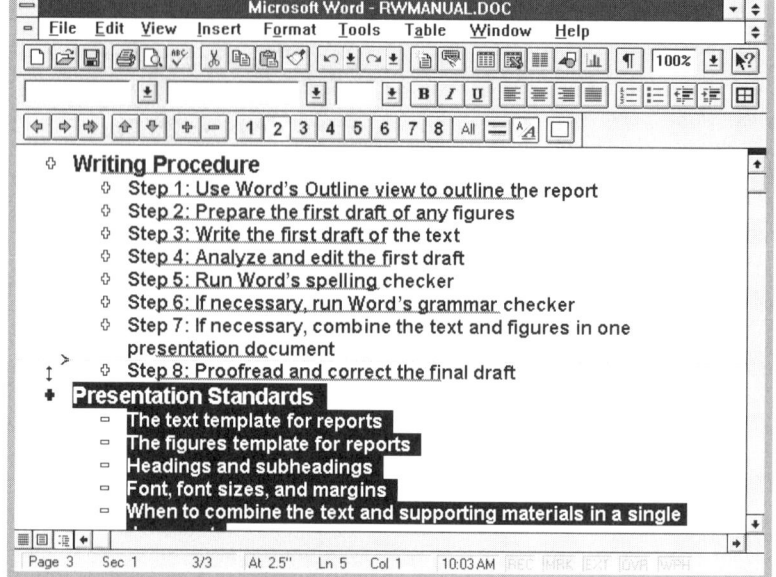

How to promote or demote headings and body text

- To promote or demote a heading and all of its subordinate headings, drag the plus sign in front of the heading to the left or right. Any body text that's subordinate to the headings moves along with the headings.

- To promote or demote just a heading paragraph or a paragraph of body text, drag the minus sign or body text symbol in front of the paragraph to the left or right.

How to move headings or body text up or down in an outline

- To move a heading and all of its subordinate headings and text up or down in an outline, drag the plus sign in front of the heading up or down.

- To move just a heading paragraph or a paragraph of body text up or down in an outline, drag the minus sign or body text symbol in front of the paragraph up or down.

How to expand or collapse headings and body text subordinate to a heading

- Double-click on the plus sign next to a heading.

Figure 7-3   How to use the mouse to reorganize an outline

How to use the shortcut keys and toolbar buttons for Outline view

Figure 7-4 presents the toolbar buttons and the shortcut keys that you can use with the outline feature. They provide other ways to move, promote, and demote headings. Notice that when you use these buttons and shortcut keys to work with expanded headings, you may have to select the subheadings and body text as described in the figure. To promote the subheadings along with an expanded heading, for example, you have to select the heading and subheadings. Otherwise, the subheadings aren't promoted.

The buttons and shortcut keys also provide other display options. For instance, you can click on the Show Formatting button to display an outline without any formatting, and you can click on the Show First Line Only button to display only the first line of the body text paragraphs. If you spend a few minutes experimenting with these buttons and shortcut keys, you'll see how easy they are to use.

How to print an outline

To print an outline, you use the Print command just as you do when you print a document. When you print from Outline view, though, the outline is printed just the way that it's displayed.

The buttons in the Outlining toolbar

Button	Name	Shortcut key
⇦	Promote	Alt+Shift+Left-arrow or Shift+Tab
⇨	Demote	Alt+Shift+Right-arrow or Tab
⇨⇨	Demote to Body Text	
⇧	Move Up	Alt+Shift+Up-arrow
⇩	Move Down	Alt+Shift+Down-arrow
⊕	Expand	Plus sign on numeric keypad
−	Collapse	Minus sign on numeric keypad
1 to 8	Show Heading 1-8	Alt+Shift+number on main keyboard
All	Show All	Alt+Shift+A
≡	Show First Line Only	Alt+Shift+L
ᴬA	Show Formatting	/ on numeric keypad

How to select headings or body text

- To select a heading paragraph or a paragraph of body text, click in the paragraph; click in the selection bar next to the paragraph; or click on the minus sign or body text symbol in front of a paragraph.

- To select a heading and its subordinate headings or text, click on its plus sign.

- To select more than one heading paragraph or paragraphs of body text, drag in the selection bar or drag over the text itself.

Notes

- Collapsed subheadings (hidden) are always promoted, demoted, or moved along with a heading. To move expanded subheadings along with their heading, select them using one of the techniques above.

- Body text always moves along with its heading when the heading is promoted or demoted whether it's collapsed or expanded. When a heading is moved, the body text moves with it only if it's collapsed. If it's expanded, you must select it using one of the techniques above if you want it to move with the heading.

- The last button in the Outlining toolbar is for use with the master document feature, which isn't covered in this book.

Figure 7-4   How to use the toolbar buttons and shortcut keys in Outline view

Exercise set 7-1

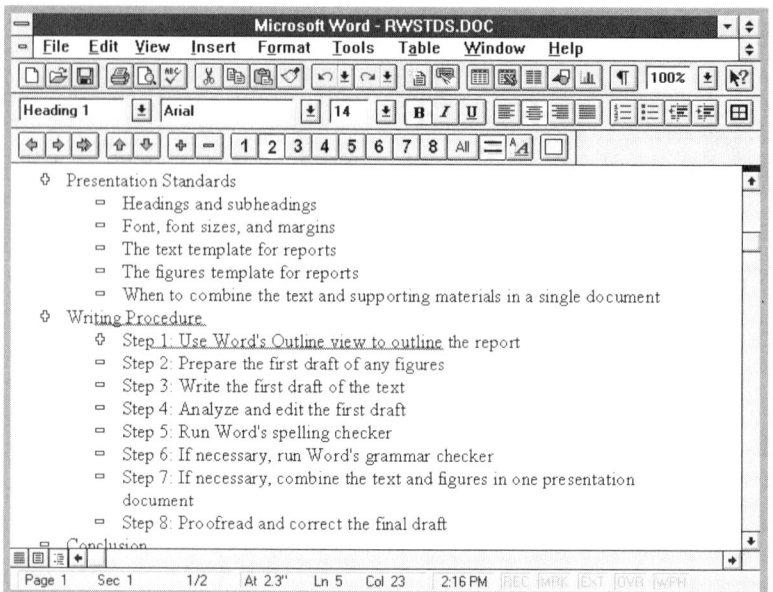

How your outline should look at the end of exercise 2

For this set of exercises, you'll use the document named RWSTDS that you created for chapter 4. If you did the exercises for chapter 6, you added styles to this document. If you haven't yet created this document, please do exercise set 4-1 before you continue (you don't need to add styles to it).

1. Open the RWSTDS file, switch to Outline view, and click on the 2 button in the Outlining toolbar to hide the body text. Next, move the insertion point to the end of the outline, and enter the last two headings shown in figure 7-2. Be sure to promote the Conclusion heading so it looks like the one in the figure. Then, save the document.

2. Click on the Show Formatting button to remove the formatting from the headings in the outline. Then, use the mouse to reorganize the outline so it looks like the one above. To do that, drag the plus sign in front of the Writing Procedure heading down so that it's just above the Conclusion heading. (Note how the mouse pointer changes when you move it over the plus sign.) Next, drag the minus signs for the first two subheadings after the Presentation Standards heading to their new locations. To make sure that the body text has been moved along with the headings, click on the All button and scroll through the outline, which now includes the body text. Click on the Show First Line Only button to display just the first line of each body text paragraph; click on the 1 button to display just the Heading 1 paragraphs; click on the 2 button so the outline looks like the one above again; and print the outline. That's how easy it is to reorganize a document when you use the mouse with the outline feature.

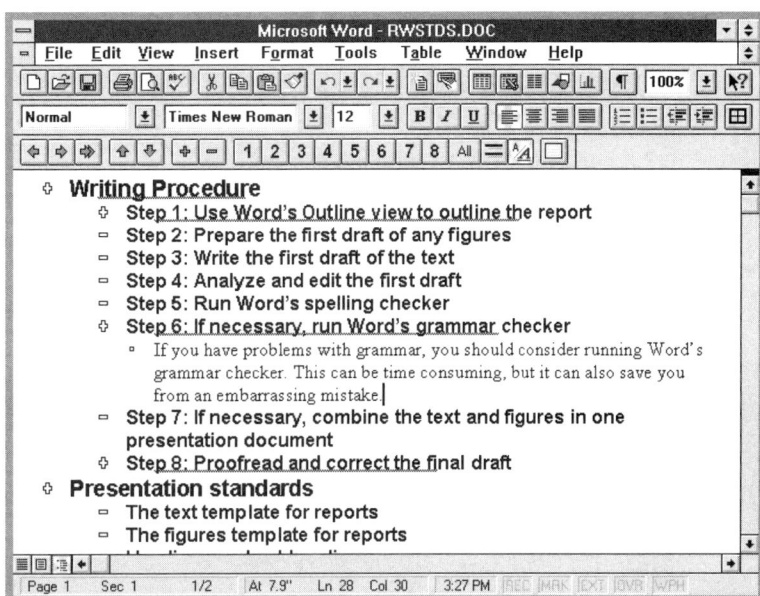

How your outline should look after you enter the body text in exercise 4

3. Now, use the keyboard to return the document to its original organization. To do that, move the insertion point into the Writing Procedure heading and press the minus sign on the numeric keypad to collapse its subheadings. Next, use Alt+Shift with the Up-arrow key to move the heading to the top of the outline, and press the plus key to expand its subheadings. Then, use the keyboard to select the first two subheadings below Presentation Standards, and use Alt+Shift with the Down-arrow key to move both headings to their original location. Press Alt+Shift+1 on the main keyboard to display just the level 1 headings; press Alt+Shift+A to display the body text; if only the first line of each body text paragraph is displayed, press Alt+Shift+L to display all the lines; press Alt+Shift+2 to return the outline to the way it was after exercise 1; and press the slash on the numeric keypad to show the formatting. This shows how easy the outline feature is to use from the keyboard.

4. To show that you can enter body text in Outline view, enter this paragraph after the Step 6 heading:

    If you have problems with grammar, you should consider running Word's grammar checker. This can be time consuming, but it can also save you from an embarrassing mistake.

    To do that, move the insertion point to the end of the heading and press the Enter key. Then, you can either apply the Normal style to the new paragraph or click on the Demote to Body Text button in the toolbar before you type the body text. When you're done, move the insertion point to the heading, hide the body text paragraph, save the file, and close it.

How to number the headings in an outline or document

You usually don't need to number the headings in an outline because the levels of indentation show the structure. You usually don't need to number the headings in a business document either. If you do prepare outlines or documents that require numbering, though, the topics that follow show how to number the headings with either predefined or custom number formats.

With predefined number formats

Figure 7-5 shows how to apply one of the predefined number formats to the headings and subheadings in a document. You can do that with just a few mouse clicks. Note, however, that you can't number just the outline. The numbers are also displayed when you switch to Normal or Page Layout view, and they're printed when you print the document.

Access

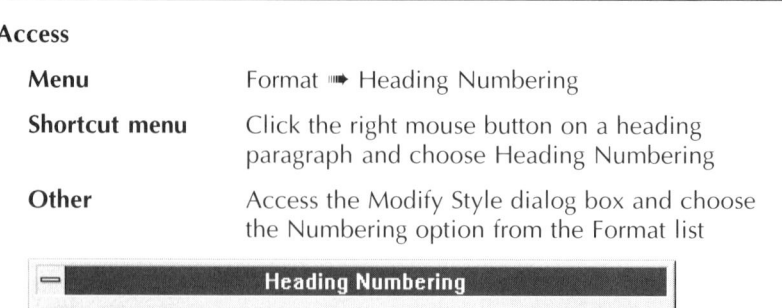

Menu	Format ➡ Heading Numbering
Shortcut menu	Click the right mouse button on a heading paragraph and choose Heading Numbering
Other	Access the Modify Style dialog box and choose the Numbering option from the Format list

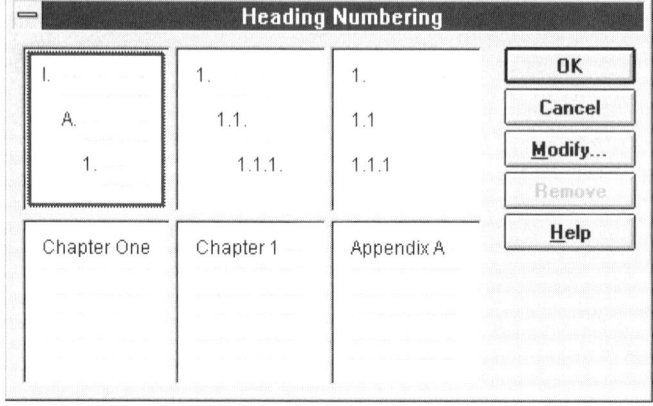

Operation

- To number the headings in a document, click on the numbering format that you want, and click on the OK button. Word then applies the heading numbers to the entire document.

- To remove the numbers from the headings in a document, click on the Remove button.

Notes

- The heading numbers are also displayed in Normal and Page Layout view. So if you want the numbers displayed and printed in Outline view but not in the other views, you have to remove the numbers when you work in the other views.

- You can't apply heading numbers to part of a document, even if you divide the document into sections.

Figure 7-5   How to number headings with predefined number formats

With custom number formats

Figure 7-6 shows how to apply custom numbers to the headings and subheadings in a document. If you experiment with the controls in this dialog box, you'll see that you can get the numbers exactly the way that you want them. Note, however, that you still can't number one portion of a document without numbering the entire document.

You can, however, number only selected heading levels. To remove the number from a heading level, choose the level from the Level list. Then, make sure that the Text Before and Text After boxes are empty, and choose the (none) option from the Bullet or Number list.

Access

Click on the Modify button in the Heading Numbering dialog box

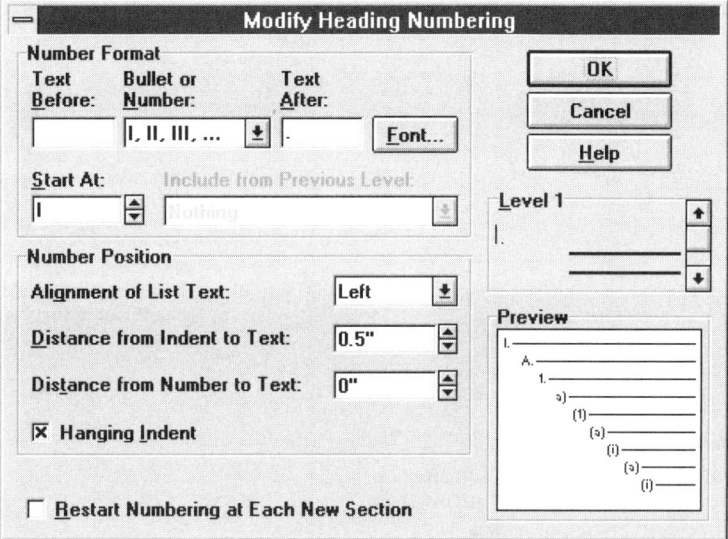

Operation

- To choose the heading level you want to modify, use the scroll bar in the Level list on the right side of the dialog box to scroll through the available options. Then, use the boxes in the Number Format and Number Position groups to format and position the numbers the way you want them.

- To remove numbering from a heading level, choose the (none) option from the Bullet or Number list and leave the Text Before and Text After boxes blank.

- Format as many levels as you want before clicking on the OK button to return to the Heading Numbering dialog box.

Notes

- Custom numbering can be useful when you want numbers at some heading levels, but not others.

- If you want to restart the heading numbering within a document, you can divide the document into sections and use the Restart Numbering option in the dialog box shown above.

Figure 7-6   How to number headings with custom number formats

Exercise set 7-2

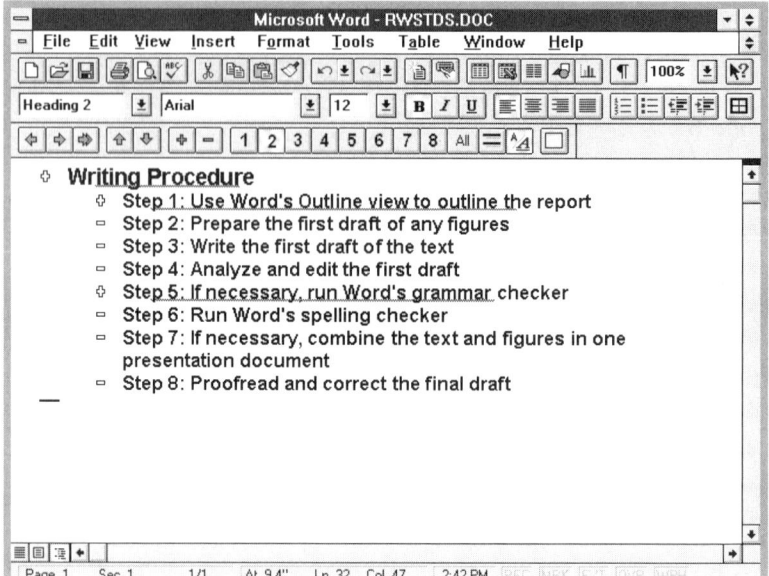

How the outline should look after you number the headings in exercise 3 and switch steps 5 and 6

1. Open the RWSTDS file. Since you left it in Outline view, it is opened in this view. Then, click on the 2 button to display only the first two heading levels of the document, click on the Show Formatting button to show the formatting for the headings, and number the headings with the first set of predefined numbers provided by the Heading Numbering command. Switch to Normal view to see that the headings are numbered and indented in that view too, and switch back to Outline view.

2. Number the headings with the third set of predefined numbers, and switch to Normal view to see how these numbers look in that view. Then, switch back to Outline view and remove the numbers.

3. This exercise has you modify the outline so it looks like the one above. Here, the numbers have been removed from the level 1 headings and the step numbers in the level 2 headings have been applied by the Heading Numbering command; they aren't part of the headings. To start, delete the headings from Presentation Standards to the end of the outline. Next, delete the word *Step*, the number, the colon (:), and the space after it that's in front of each of the Heading 2 paragraphs. Then, use the Heading Numbering command to remove the numbers from the level 1 headings and to apply a number format that consists of the word *Step*, a space, the number, a colon, and another space to the level 2 headings. When you complete the command, your outline should look almost like the one above. To complete this exercise, drag the Step 6 heading ahead of the Step 5 heading to show that the headings are automatically renumbered, and close the document without saving it.

Perspective

If you prepare documents like reports and proposals that require the use of headings and subheadings, the outline feature can help you work more efficiently. It can also help you organize your documents so they're more logical and effective. That's why the outline feature is one that should be used by most business professionals.

Summary

- When you switch to Outline view, the outline feature becomes available. This feature makes it easy for you to reorganize a document that uses the Heading styles for its headings and subheadings.

- In Outline view, you can use mouse techniques, shortcut keys, or buttons in the Outlining toolbar to *promote*, *demote*, *collapse*, *expand*, and move headings, subheadings, and body text.

- The Heading Numbering command in the Format menu lets you number the headings in an outline or document with predefined or custom number formats.

Chapter 8

How to create and use tables

The Word 6 table feature makes it easy to arrange information in tabular form without any of the difficulties that you encounter when you use tab stops and tab characters. This is a powerful feature that you can use for organizing many types of information. It's a feature that is remarkably easy to use. And it's a feature that every business professional should have one or more uses for.

Basic skills for creating and working with a table

With a little practice, you can create an empty table in just a few seconds. Then, you can enter the text into the table and adjust the column widths so they're appropriate for the text that they contain.

How to create an empty table

Figure 8-1 shows how to create an empty table using the Insert Table button or the Insert Table command. When you insert a table into a document, it consists of the number of *columns* and *rows* that you specify. If you don't know how many rows you want in the table, you can start with just a few because it's easy to add rows to the end of a table.

The intersection of each column and row in a table is called a *cell*. You enter the text of a table into the empty cells.

If you know a new table is going to be so wide that it will require horizontal orientation on the page, you can use the Page Setup command to choose Landscape orientation. Usually, it's more efficient to do that before you insert the table. Then, the table will automatically fill the space between the margins. If you change the orientation after you insert the table, you have to adjust the column widths so that the table uses all the available space.

How to use the Insert Table button to create a table

- Drag the mouse from the Insert Table button in the Standard toolbar to choose the number of columns and rows that you want in the table:

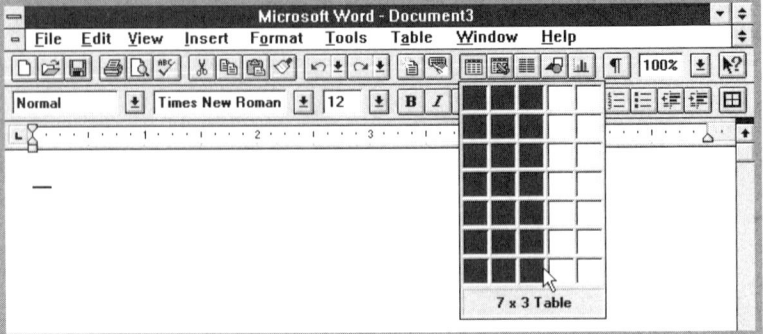

When you release the mouse button, an empty table is inserted into the document.

How to use the Insert Table command to create a table

- Choose the Insert Table command from the Table menu to display this dialog box:

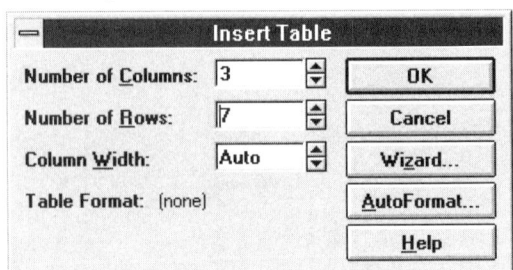

- Enter the number of columns and rows that you want in the table, and click on the OK button.

Notes

- When you create a table with the Insert Table button, the table fills the space between the left and right margins and the columns have equal widths. This is also true when you create a table with the Insert Table command and leave the Column Width setting at Auto. If you enter a specific size in the Column Width box, however, the new table has equal width columns of that size.

- If you click on the Wizard button in the Insert Table dialog box, the Table Wizard steps you through the creation of a formatted table. You can also access this wizard when you start a new document from the New command in the File menu. In general, though, using the wizard takes longer than creating and formatting a table using the other methods in this chapter.

Figure 8-1   How to create an empty table

How to enter and format the text of a table

Figure 8-2 shows how to enter text into an empty table. In general, you use the same techniques that you use outside a table, but you use some new keystrokes to move from one cell to the next.

You can also use the techniques that you're already familiar with to select and format the text within a cell. To select text, you can use either the mouse or the keyboard. To format the selected text, you can use shortcut keys, toolbar buttons, or menu commands.

You can also format the paragraphs within a cell using normal techniques. To center a paragraph, for instance, just place the insertion point in the paragraph and click on the Center button in the Formatting toolbar. To format more than one paragraph within a cell at the same time, select a portion of each one just as you do when you work with paragraphs outside a table.

Additional information

✓ By default, the gridlines for a new table should be displayed on your screen. Note, however, that these gridlines aren't printed when you print the table. To turn the gridlines on or off, choose the Gridlines command from the Table menu.

A 3 x 3 table after text has been entered into all three rows

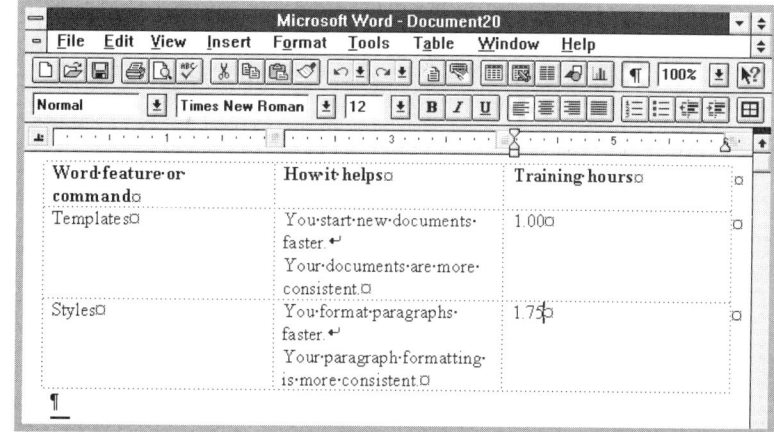

How to enter text into a table

• Use normal techniques for typing text into a cell. When an entry reaches the right side of a cell, the text is automatically wrapped to the next line and the height of the row is adjusted. To end a line before it wraps, press the Enter key to start a new paragraph or Shift+Enter to start a new line.

• To add another row to a table, press Tab when the insertion point is in the last cell of the last row in the table as shown above.

How to format the text in a table

• Use normal techniques for selecting and formatting the text in a cell. For instance, you can use Ctrl+B or the Bold toolbar button to bold selected text.

• Use normal techniques for selecting and formatting one or more paragraphs in a cell. For instance, you can use the alignment buttons in the Formatting toolbar to center or right align paragraphs within a cell. And you can use the indent markers on the ruler to indent paragraphs within a cell.

• To enter a tab character into a cell, press Ctrl+Tab.

The keys for moving the insertion point in a table

Key	Moves the insertion point
Tab	One cell to the right or from the last cell in a row to the first cell in the next row
Shift+Tab	One cell to the left or from the first cell in a row to the last cell in the previous row
Home	To the beginning of the active line in the active cell
End	To the end of the active line in the active cell
Alt+Home	To the first cell in the active row
Alt+End	To the last cell in the active row
Alt+Page-up	To the first cell in the active column
Alt+Page-down	To the last cell in the active column

Figure 8-2   How to enter and format the text in a table

How to change column widths

When you create a table, the starting column widths are all the same. But that's rarely what you want. Then, to adjust the column widths so they're appropriate for the cell entries, you can use the techniques in figure 8-3. Usually, you'll want to make these adjustments after you enter just a few rows of a table so you can see how the entries are going to look when the table is done.

The control keys presented in figure 8-3 can often make it easier to adjust column widths. These keys control what happens to the columns to the right of the one you're adjusting. If you don't use them, all the columns to the right of the one you're adjusting are adjusted too, which often leads to more adjustments.

A table as the first column boundary is dragged to the left

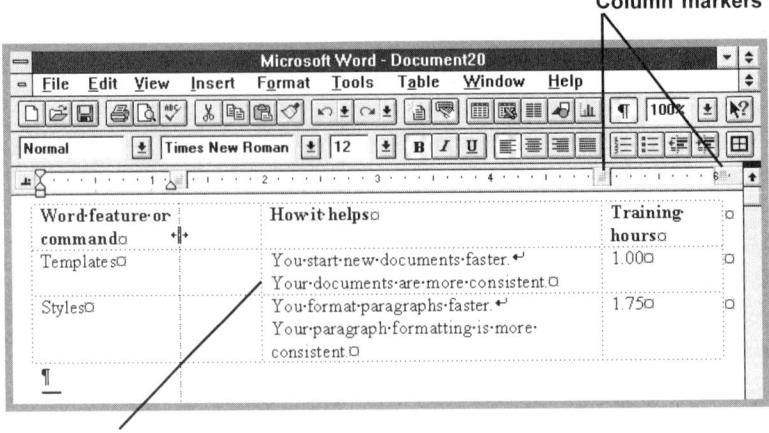

Column markers

Column boundary

How to use the mouse to change the width of a column

- To change the width of a column, drag its column marker or column boundary to the left or right.

- To change the width of a column to the width of its widest entry, double-click on its right column boundary. To change the widths of all columns to the widths of their widest entries, double-click on the left table boundary. If a column can't be adjusted to the width of its widest entry, nothing happens.

- When you change a column's width without holding down a control key, all the columns to the right are resized proportionately.

The control keys you can use as you change a column's width

Key	Function
Shift	Only the first column to the right is resized.
Ctrl	All the columns to the right become the same size.
Shift+Ctrl	The columns to the right do not change so the overall table width changes.
Alt	The width measurements are displayed in the ruler; you can use this key alone or in combination with the other control keys.

Figure 8-3   How to change column widths

Figure 8-4 shows how you can use the Cell Height and Width command to adjust column widths. This can be useful when you need more control over the column widths and the spaces between the columns. However, it takes more time to adjust the column widths with this command, and most people don't need this much precision.

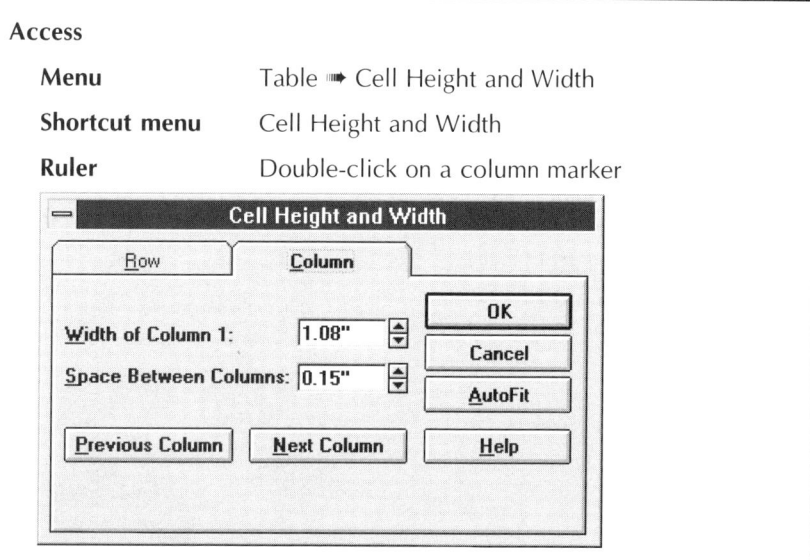

Access

Menu	Table ➡ Cell Height and Width
Shortcut menu	Cell Height and Width
Ruler	Double-click on a column marker

How to change column widths

- To change the width of a column, use the Next Column and Previous Column buttons to choose the column you want to change. Then, use the Width of Column spin box to change the column width.

- To change the width of a column to the width of its widest entry, choose the column, then click on the AutoFit button.

- To change the amount of space between the columns in the table, use the Space Between Columns spin box.

Figure 8-4   How to use the Cell Height and Width command to change column widths

How to align a table between the margins

Figure 8-5 shows how you can use the Cell Height and Width command to align a table between the margins. This is useful when you want to center a table between the margins or indent it from the left margin. You can also use this command to change row height, but you usually don't need to do that.

Access

Menu	Table ➡ Cell Height and Width
Shortcut menu	Cell Height and Width
Ruler	Double-click on a column marker

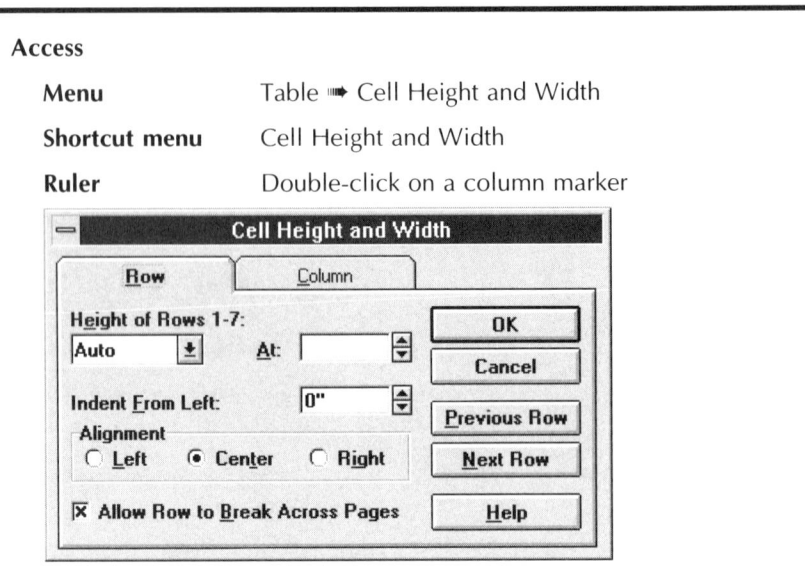

How to align a table between the margins

- If a table doesn't fill the space between the margins, you can choose an option from the Alignment group to left, center, or right align it. Or, you can enter a value in the Indent From Left box to indent the table from the left margin.

Notes

- The Allow Row to Break Across Pages option determines whether or not a row in the table can be split across two pages.

- You can also use the Row tab to change the height of one or more rows. You usually don't need to do this, though, because the row heights are automatically adjusted to the height of their contents.

Figure 8-5   How to use the Cell Height and Width command to align a table

Exercise set 8-1

Word feature or command	How it helps	Training hours
Templates	You start new documents faster. Your documents are more consistent.	1.00
Styles	You format paragraphs faster. Your paragraph formatting is more consistent.	1.75
Outliner	Helps you plan what you're going to write. Helps you reorganize a document.	0.50
Table of Contents	Generates a table of contents for a report or proposal from the heading styles.	0.25
Spelling Checker	Checks the spelling in a document.	0.25

The table that you create in this exercise set

In this exercise set, you'll create the table shown above. The exercises that follow guide you through its creation.

1. Start a new document, and use the procedure in figure 8-1 to create a 3 x 3 table. If the gridlines aren't displayed when you return to the document, choose the Gridlines command from the Table menu.

2. Enter the text shown above into the first three rows of the table, using Shift+Enter to start each new line within a cell. Then, select the text in all three cells of the first row and apply bold formatting to it.

3. Click anywhere in the table to remove the selection from the first row, then drag the column marker to the left of the Training hours column so the width of that column is about one inch. Next, hold down the Shift key and drag the column boundary to the right of the Word feature column so that column is about 1.5 inches. The columns should now have the approximate proportions of the columns shown above.

4. Move the insertion point into the last cell in the last row. Then, press the Tab key to start a new row, and enter the data for the last three rows shown above.

5. Move the insertion point into the last column of the first row. Next, hold down the Shift key and press the down arrow until all the cells in that column are highlighted. Then, click on the Align Right button in the toolbar to align the selected text and numbers on the right side of their cells.

6. At this point, your table should like just about like the one above. So check it now and make whatever adjustments are necessary. Then, print the table, save the document as WORDTBL, and close the file.

How to edit and format a table

When you work with a table, you need to learn some new selection techniques. Once you master these, it's easy to edit and format a table as the following topics illustrate.

How to select cells, rows, columns, or an entire table

Figure 8-6 presents the essential mouse and keyboard techniques for selecting portions of a table. As you select, you need to be aware of the *end-of-cell* and *end-of-row marks*. If you select the text in a cell without selecting the end-of-cell mark, a subsequent command may not work the way you expect. Similarly, if you select the cells in a row without selecting the end-of-row mark, a command that's supposed to work with rows won't be available or won't work the way you expect.

A table with one row selected and the mouse pointer in the column selection area

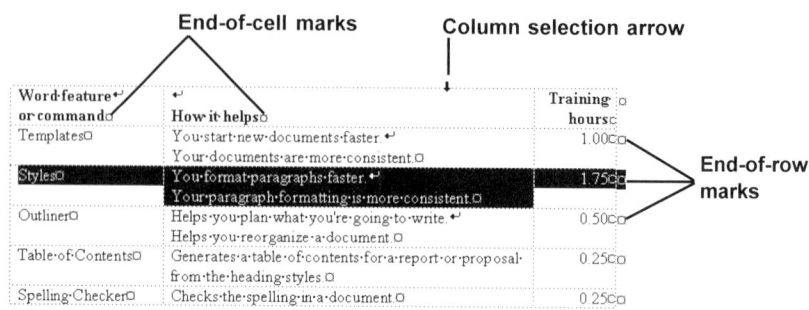

How to use the mouse to select portions of a table

- To select one row, click in the selection area to the left of the row outside the table. To select more than one row, drag in this area.

- To select one column, move the mouse pointer near the top gridline of the table until it turns into a down arrow like the one shown above and then click. To select more than one column, drag when the mouse pointer is a down arrow.

- To select a cell, click in the selection area to the left of the text in the cell. The mouse pointer will tilt to the right when it's in the right position. To select more then one cell, drag the mouse over the cells.

- You can also select a row by double-clicking in the selection area to the left of the text in any cell in the row.

The keys for selecting portions of a table

Key	Selects
Tab	The contents of the next cell
Shift+Tab	The contents of the previous cell
Shift+Arrow	Whole cells once the arrow key leaves the boundary of the active cell

Commands in the Table menu for selecting portions of a table

Command	Selects
Select Row	The row that the insertion point is in or the rows that the selected cells are in
Select Column	The column that the insertion point is in or the columns that the selected cells are in
Select Table	The table that the insertion point is in

Figure 8-6   How to select cells, rows, columns, or an entire table

Additional information

✓ To display the end-of-cell and end-of-row marks, click on the Show/Hide button in the Standard toolbar.

How to insert or delete rows, columns, or cells

Figure 8-7 shows how to insert or delete rows or columns. At the top of the figure, you can see that the Table menu changes depending on what's selected in the table when you access it. In this case, the first two commands are Insert Rows and Delete Rows because two rows are selected. If columns were selected, the commands would change to Insert Columns and Delete Columns.

The Insert Table button in the Standard toolbar also changes depending on what's selected. If rows are selected, the button changes to Insert Rows. And if Columns are selected, it changes to Insert Columns. That makes it particularly easy to insert columns or rows.

You can also insert and delete cells using the Table menu or toolbar button. However, you're not likely to need to do that often.

The commands in the Table menu when rows are selected

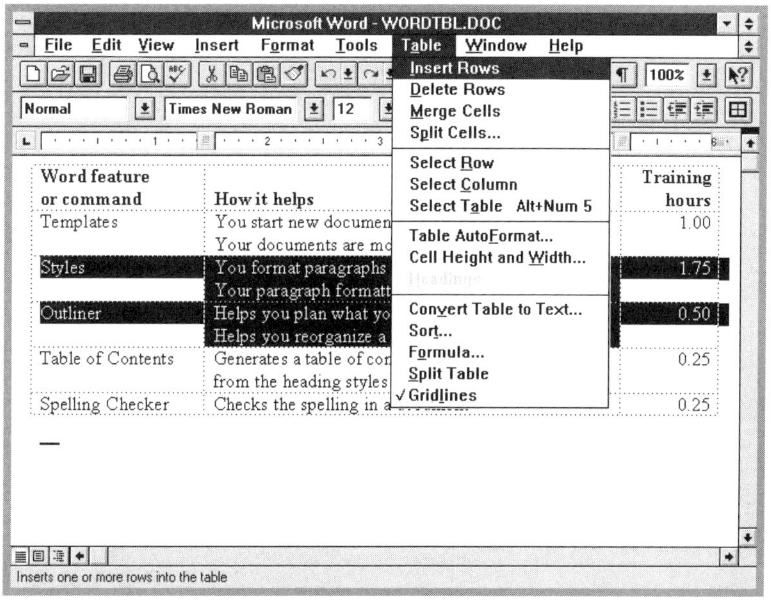

How to insert rows into a table

- Select one or more rows. Then, choose the Insert Rows command from the Table or shortcut menu, or click on the Insert Rows button in the Standard toolbar. This inserts the number of selected rows above the selection.

How to insert columns into a table

- Select one or more columns. Then, choose the Insert Columns command from the Table or shortcut menu, or click on the Insert Columns button in the Standard toolbar. This inserts the number of selected columns to the left of the selection.

How to delete rows or columns

- Select the rows or columns. Then, choose the Delete Rows or Delete Columns command from the Table or shortcut menu, choose the Cut command from the Edit or shortcut menu, or click on the Cut button in the Standard toolbar.

Notes

- When you select one or more rows, the Insert Table toolbar button becomes the Insert Rows button. When you select one or more columns, it becomes the Insert Columns button.

- If you press the Delete key when rows, columns, or cells are selected, the contents of the cells are deleted, but the rows, columns, and cells remain.

- You can also insert or delete cells by selecting the cells and choosing the Insert Cells or Delete Cells command from the Table or shortcut menu. In its dialog box, you tell Word which way the cells around the inserted or deleted cells should be moved to accommodate them. Note, however, that you should rarely, if ever, need this command.

Figure 8-7   How to insert or delete rows or columns

How to copy or move cells, rows, columns, or tables

Figure 8-8 shows how to copy or move portions of a table or an entire table using either drag-and-drop or cut, copy, and paste techniques. When you copy or move rows or columns, complete rows or columns are moved including the cell contents. When you copy or move cells, however, only the contents are copied or moved.

The table in figure 8-7 after the Templates row has been moved down

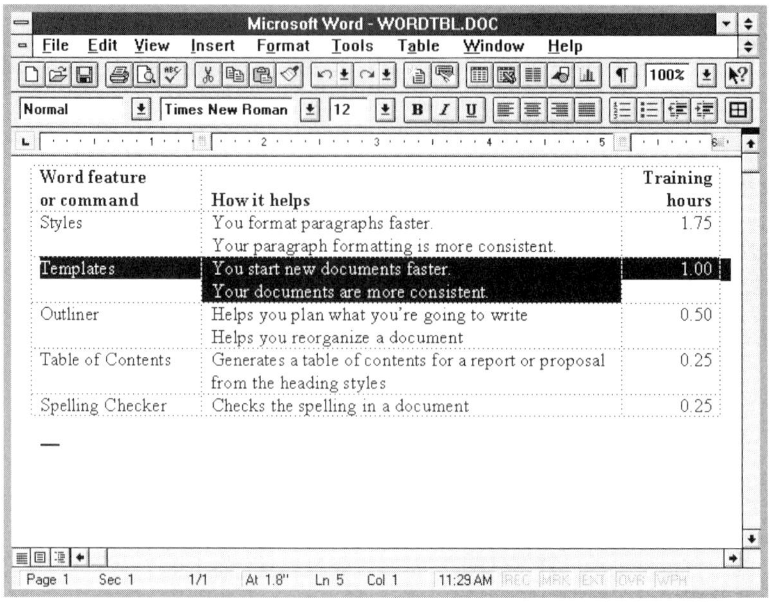

Word feature or command	How it helps	Training hours
Styles	You format paragraphs faster. Your paragraph formatting is more consistent.	1.75
Templates	You start new documents faster. Your documents are more consistent.	1.00
Outliner	Helps you plan what you're going to write Helps you reorganize a document	0.50
Table of Contents	Generates a table of contents for a report or proposal from the heading styles	0.25
Spelling Checker	Checks the spelling in a document	0.25

How to use drag-and-drop techniques to move or copy a selection

• To move a selection, drag the selected cells, rows, columns, or table to a new location and release the mouse button.

• To copy a selection, hold down the Ctrl key as you drag the selected cells, rows, columns, or table to a new location.

How to use cut, copy, and paste techniques to move or copy a selection

• Use the Cut or Copy command to cut or copy the selected cells, rows, columns, or table to the clipboard. Then, move the insertion point to a new location and use the Paste command to paste the contents of the clipboard.

• You can use shortcut keys, the Standard toolbar, the shortcut menu, or the Edit menu to access the Cut, Copy, and Paste functions.

Notes

• If you select rows or columns, the rows or columns are moved or copied along with their contents. If you select cells, just the contents of the cells are moved or copied.

• If you select the text in a cell without selecting the end-of-cell mark, the text is added to any text in the destination cell and it takes on the formatting of the destination cell. If you select the end-of-cell mark along with the text, the text and its formatting replace any text and formatting in the destination cell.

Figure 8-8 How to copy or move cells, rows, columns, or tables

How to merge or split cells or tables

Sometimes, it makes sense to merge two or more cells in a row or column to form one cell. In figure 8-9, for example, the cells in the top row of the table were merged so a table heading could be entered into the row and centered.

Sometimes, it also makes sense to split one or more cells into more cells, to split one table into two, or to combine two tables. All of these functions are easy to do if you ever need them, and they're summarized in figure 8-9.

A table after three cells in the top row have been merged and a table heading has been centered in the merged cell

Word features and commands for improved writing		
Word feature or command	**How it helps**	**Training hours**
Styles	You format paragraphs faster. Your paragraph formatting is more consistent.	1.75
Templates	You start new documents faster. Your documents are more consistent.	1.00
Outliner	Helps you plan what you're going to write Helps you reorganize a document	0.50
Table of Contents	Generates a table of contents for a report or proposal from the heading styles	0.25
Spelling Checker	Checks the spelling in a document	0.25

How to merge two or more cells

- Select the cells you want to merge, and choose the Merge Cells command from the Table menu.

How to split one or more cells

1. Move the insertion point into the cell you want to split, or select the cells you want to split.

2. Choose the Split Cells command from the Table menu so this dialog box is displayed:

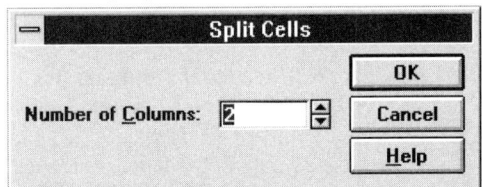

3. Enter the number of cells you want to split each cell into, and click on the OK button.

How to split a table

- Move the insertion point into the row that you want as the first row in the new table. Then, choose the Split Table command from the Table menu.

How to merge two tables

- Move the tables together so there are no paragraph marks between them.

Figure 8-9   How to merge or split cells or tables

How to apply borders or shading to a table

Do you remember using the Borders toolbar in chapter 3 to apply borders and shading to paragraphs? If you do, you won't have any trouble using this toolbar to apply borders and shading to tables. Just select the portion of the table that you want to work with and use the toolbar as summarized in figure 8-10. You can also use the Borders and Shading command to apply borders and shading, but that's usually not necessary.

A table with borders and shading

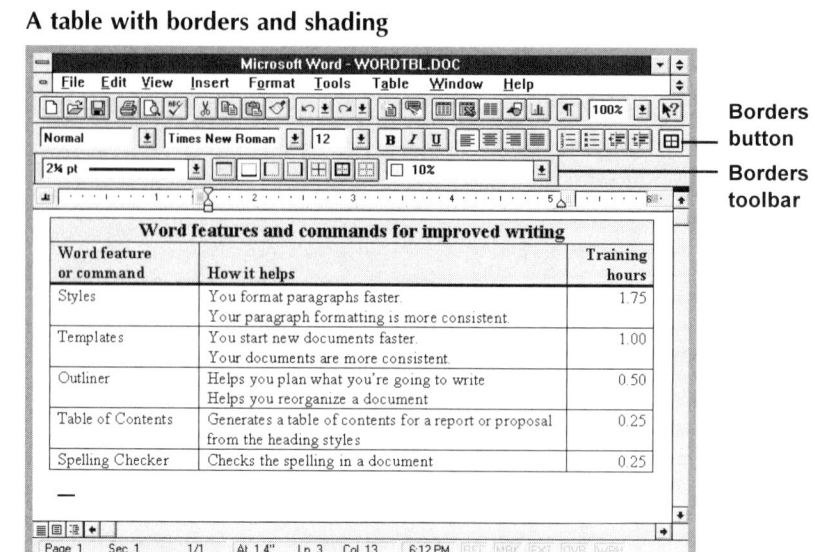

How to display the Borders toolbar

- Click on the Borders button in the Formatting toolbar.

How to use the Borders toolbar to apply borders or shading to selected cells

- Click on the buttons that apply the borders that you want. If necessary, choose a line style from the Line Style list before you apply a border.

- Choose the shading style that you want from the Shading list.

How to use the Borders toolbar to remove borders

- Select the cells that have the borders you want to remove. Then, click on the Top, Bottom, Left, Right, Inside, or Outside Border button that applied the border. Or, click on the No Border button.

How to use the Borders toolbar to remove shading

- Select the cells that have the shading you want to remove. Then, choose the Clear option from the Shading list.

How to use the Borders and Shading command to apply borders and shading to selected cells

- Choose the Borders and Shading command from the Format menu. Then, use the Borders and Shading tabs to apply the borders and shading that you want. This gives you more control than working with the Borders toolbar, but you usually don't need that and it's less efficient.

Figure 8-10   How to apply borders and shading to a table

How to use the Table AutoFormat command

Another way to format a table is to use the Table AutoFormat command that's presented in figure 8-11. This command lets you apply any one of 34 predefined *autoformats* to a table. Some are simple, and some are fancy, but you should be able to find one that you like for just about any table.

If you have a good idea of how you want to format a table, it's probably quicker to apply the formatting yourself rather than searching through the autoformats for one that you like. On the other hand, if you don't really know how you want to format a table, the autoformats can give you some good ideas. And, if you find an autoformat you like, you may be able to use it for other tables you create.

Access

Menu	Table ➡ Table AutoFormat
Shortcut menu	Table AutoFormat

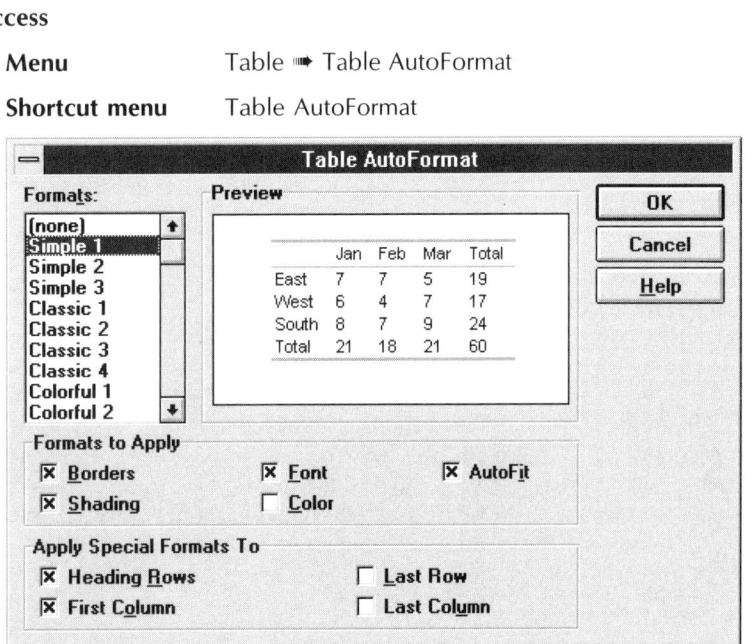

Operation

- Click on an autoformat in the Formats list to display the format in the Preview box.

- Click on the options in the Formats to Apply group to apply or remove specific formatting. If you choose the AutoFit option, the column widths are adjusted to the contents of the columns.

- Click on the options in the Apply Special Formats To group to apply or remove formatting from specific areas of the table.

- When the formatting in the Preview box looks the way you want it, click on the OK button to apply the formatting to the table that the insertion point is in.

How to remove the formatting from a table

- Choose the (none) option from the Formats list. This removes both autoformatting and any other formatting that's been applied to the table.

Figure 8-11   How to use the Table AutoFormat command to format a table

Exercise set 8-2

Word features and commands for improved writing		
Word feature or command	How it helps	Training hours
Styles	You format paragraphs faster. Your paragraph formatting is more consistent.	1.75
Templates	You start new documents faster. Your documents are more consistent.	1.00
Outliner	Helps you plan what you're going to write. Helps you reorganize a document.	1.50
Table of Contents	Generates a table of contents for a report or proposal from the heading styles.	0.25
Spelling Checker	Checks the spelling in a document.	0.25

How the Word feature table should look after exercise 5

1. Open the WORDTBL file, and use the mouse techniques in figure 8-6 to select in succession: the second row; the third column; the third and fourth rows; and the second and third columns. Then, use the keyboard techniques to make the same selections.

2. Select the second and third rows of the table, and use the mouse to find the Insert Row button in the Standard toolbar, but don't click on it. Instead, use the shortcut menu for the selected rows to insert two rows into the table. Then, select the third column and use the Insert Column button in the toolbar to insert a column into the table. Last, delete the new rows and column.

3. Select the Templates row of the table and use the drag-and-drop technique to move the row so it's after the Styles row. Next, select the third column of the table and use copy and paste techniques to copy it so it becomes both the second and fourth column. Then, delete the second column.

4. Add a new row to the top of the table, merge its three cells into one, and enter the heading shown above into the single cell. Notice that the text you enter is boldfaced and right aligned like the text in the last cell of the second row (the row you inserted the new row in front of). Then, increase the font size of the text to 14 points and center it.

5. Use the Borders toolbar to add the borders and shading shown in the table above. To start, select the entire table and click on the Inside Border and Outside Border buttons. Then, select the first two rows of the table, choose the 2-1/4 pt line style, click on the Bottom Border button, and choose 10% in the Shading list. Your table should now look like the one above. If it doesn't, make the necessary adjustments. Then, print the table and save it, but don't close it.

6. Use the Table AutoFormat command to apply the Simple 2 format to the table. Did this work the way you wanted it to? If not, click on the Undo button to reverse the formatting. Then, delete the first row of the table (the one with merged cells) and apply the Simple 2 format again. Did it work the way you wanted it to this time? Try one or more of the other autoformats. Is this more efficient than formatting the table yourself? When you're done experimenting, use the AutoFormat command to remove all formatting from the table to see what happens. Then, close the document without saving the changes.

Other skills for working with a table

Now, you know everything you need to know for creating tables that present information in an effective format. But there's more you can do with tables. Although you may never need the table functions that follow, you should at least be aware that they're available.

How to total the numbers in a column or row

When you create tables that contain numbers, you often want to present column or row totals. With Word 6, you can do that with the Formula command as shown in figure 8-12.

What makes this easy is that Word assumes you want to total either a row or column when you issue the command. As a result, the Formula dialog box often contains the function that you need when the dialog box is displayed. If, for example, you issue the Formula command when the insertion point is at the bottom of a column of numbers, the function that's displayed is this:

=SUM(ABOVE)

Then, if that's the right function, you can click on the OK button to return to the table with the column total displayed. Otherwise, you can replace the word in the parentheses with LEFT, RIGHT, or BELOW to tell Word where the cells are that you want summed.

A SUM function is used to add the numbers in the right column

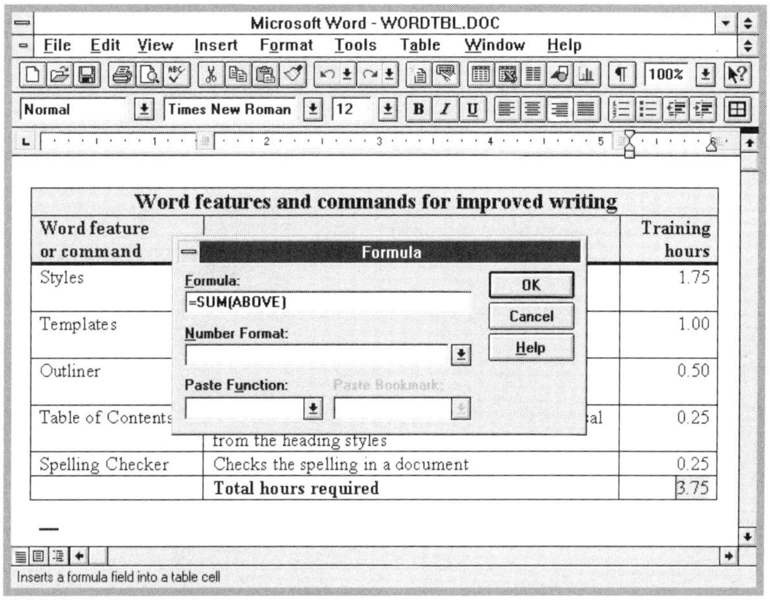

How to enter a SUM function

1. Move the insertion point into the cell that is going to contain the sum of the numbers in the row or column.

2. Choose the Formula command from the Table menu to display the dialog box shown above.

3. The function that's usually displayed in the Formula dialog box is the one shown above. It adds the numbers in the cells above the active cell. If the displayed function isn't what you want, you can replace the word in parentheses with Left, Right, Above, or Below.

4. Click on the OK button. Word then inserts a field into the active cell that displays the result of the calculation. (If the field code is displayed instead of the field results, press Alt+F9.)

Three ways to update a formula field

• Move the insertion point into the field and press F9.

• Move the insertion point into the field, display the shortcut menu, and choose the Update Field command.

• Print the document. (If this doesn't work, check the Update Fields option in the Print tab of the Options dialog box.)

Notes

• If you want to specify a precise range of cells in the parentheses for a function, you can enter a range reference like C3:C7. This means to add the numbers in rows 3 through 7 of the third column (C).

• You can use the Number Format list to change the format of the resulting value.

• Word 6 also provides functions like AVERAGE and COUNT. To paste one into the Formula box, use the Paste Function list.

Figure 8-12   How to total the numbers in a column or row

How to use formulas to perform calculations

You can also use the Formula command to perform arithmetic operations on the numbers in a table as shown in figure 8-13. If you have experience with Excel or some other spreadsheet program, you shouldn't have any trouble with this. But if your math background is limited and this gives you trouble, you can easily get by without it. (Don't be afraid to use SUM functions, though.)

If you experiment with formulas in Word, you'll see that this feature is extremely limited, especially when compared with a spreadsheet program. One problem is that there's no easy way to enter formulas into the cells or to copy them to other cells. Another problem is that the formulas aren't automatically recalculated when the numbers in the table are changed. Instead, you have to use one of the techniques described in figure 8-12 to update the fields. Because of these limitations, you should use Excel or some other spreadsheet program whenever you need to do serious mathematical work.

Additional information

✓ To update all the fields in a document, press Ctrl+A to select the entire document and then press F9.

A table and the Formula dialog box for cell D6

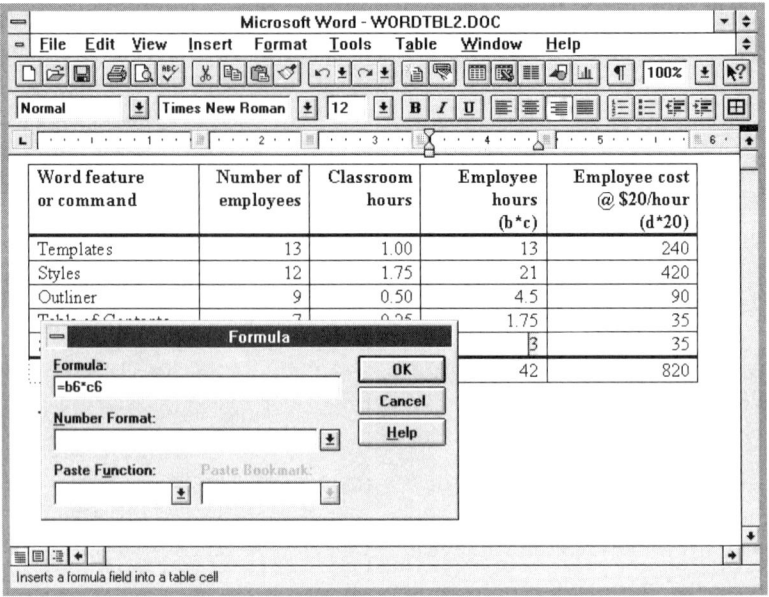

How to enter a formula into a cell

1. Move the insertion point into the cell, and choose the Formula command from the Table menu to display the dialog box shown above.

2. Replace the function that's displayed in the Formula box with the formula you want. A formula starts with an equals sign and is followed by a cell reference or numeric value, an arithmetic operator, another cell reference or numeric value, and so on.

3. Click on the OK button. Word then inserts a field into the active cell that displays the result of the calculation. (If the field code is displayed instead of the field results, press Alt+F9.)

How to determine a cell reference

- A cell reference consists of a column letter and row number. So the cell reference A1 refers to the cell in the first column and first row of a table, and E3 refers to the cell in the fifth column and third row:

	A	B	C	D	E
1	A1				
2					
3					E3

The arithmetic operators that you can use in formulas

+   Addition

-   Subtraction

*   Multiplication

/   Division

Figure 8-13   How to use formulas to perform calculations

How to convert text to a table

Sometimes, you start entering tabular information into a document with tab stops and tab characters and realize that you would be better off using a table. Other times, you start by setting up the headings for a table using tab stops so you know how many columns you'll need in the table. In either case, you can then convert the text that you've entered into a table as shown in figure 8-14.

When you use this procedure to convert text that's separated by tabs, each tab character starts a new column in the resulting table. As a result, each line in the text should have the same number of tab characters. If they don't, the columns in the resulting table probably won't come out the way you want them. That's why you usually want to check the formatting of the text before you convert it to a table.

How to convert a table to text

Figure 8-14 also shows how to convert a table to text. This can be useful when you need to export the data in a table to a program that doesn't provide for the conversion of tables.

How to convert text to a table

1. Select the text that you want to convert to a table. Then, choose the Convert Text to Table command from the Table menu so this dialog box is displayed:

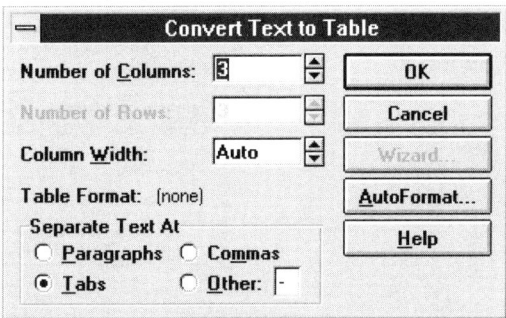

2. Choose an option from the Separate Text At group. The default depends on the selected text and is usually what you want. Then, click on the OK button.

How to convert a table to text

1. Select the rows that you want to convert. Then, choose the Convert Table to Text command from the Table menu so this dialog box is displayed:

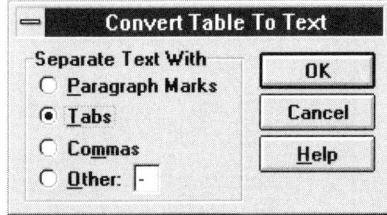

2. Choose an option from the Separate Text With group. Then, click on the OK button.

Notes

- You can also change the column width or apply an autoformat to the table in the Convert Text to Table dialog box.

- You can also use the Insert Table button in the Standard toolbar to convert selected text to a table. Then, the dialog box isn't displayed, and Word determines the separator character based on the selected text.

Figure 8-14   How to convert text to a table or vice versa

How to repeat headings on each page of a multi-page table

Figure 8-15 shows how you can repeat heading rows on each page of a table that requires more than one page. In the table at the top of the figure, for example, the first row of the table will be repeated on each page. That way, you can tell at a glance what the contents of each column is. Note that this feature does not work if the table is split by a manual page break. In that case, you can repeat the heading rows by copying them to each page.

Access

Menu   Table ➡ Headings

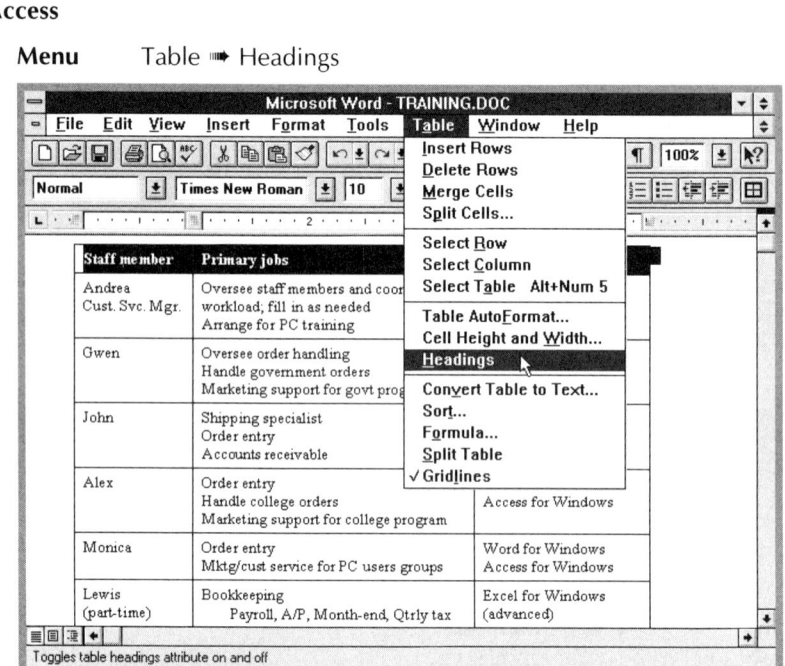

Operation

• Select the row or rows you want repeated on each page. Then, choose the Headings command from the Table menu.

• The table headings are only repeated if the table is split by a soft page break, not a manual page break.

• The repeated headings aren't displayed in Normal view, but they are displayed in Page Layout view and Print Preview mode, and they're always printed.

Figure 8-15   How to repeat table headings for multi-page tables

How to sort the rows in a table

Figure 8-16 shows how to sort the rows in a table based on the data in one or more columns. Notice that if the table you're sorting has a heading row like the one in figure 8-13, Word identifies the columns in the table by the text in the heading row. If the table doesn't have a heading row, the columns are identified by number.

If you want to sort a table that has two or more heading rows, you can't just place the insertion point in the table and sort it. If you do, the second heading row is treated as the first row of data, which isn't what you want. Instead, you have to select the rows you want to sort before you issue the Sort command. Note that you can still include a heading row in the selected rows, but if you do, you have to choose the Header Row option in the Sort dialog box because the default will be No Header Row.

You may also need to select the rows in a table that you want to sort if the table includes a total row. Then, you can omit the total row from the selection so it's not sorted with the other rows.

Access

Menu   Table ➡ Sort

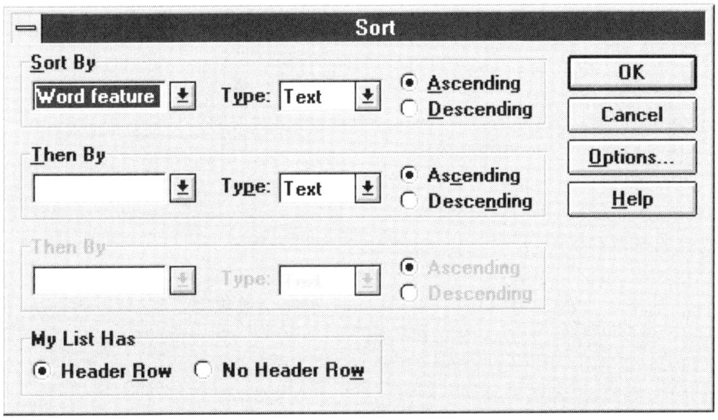

Procedure

1. Move the insertion point into the table and access the Sort dialog box.

2. If the table has one heading row, the Header Row option should be on. Then, the Sort By list identifies the columns by the text in the heading row. If a table has no heading row, the No Header Row option should be on. Then, the Sort By list identifies the columns by number.

3. Choose the column you want to sort by from the Sort By list, choose a type from the Type list, and choose the Ascending or Descending option. Then, click on the OK button to sort the rows below the heading row.

Notes

- If you use the procedure above to sort a table that has more than one heading row, Word treats the second heading row as the first row of data. To avoid this, select the rows you want to sort before you access the Sort dialog box. You can include one heading row in the selection.

- You should also select the rows you want to sort if the table contains a total row. If you don't, Word will treat the total row as a row of data and sort it with the other data rows.

- If necessary, you can use the Then By groups in the Sort dialog box to sort the rows by more than one column.

- When you sort by a column that contains numeric data, choose Number from the Type list. When you sort by a column that contains dates, choose Date from the Type list. Otherwise, the sort may not work correctly.

Figure 8-16   How to sort the rows in a table

Exercise set 8-3

Word feature or command	Number of employees	Classroom hours	Employee hours	Employee cost @ $20/hour
Templates	13	1.00	13	260
Styles	12	1.75	21	420
Outliner	9	0.50	4.5	90
Table of Contents	7	0.25	1.75	35
Spelling Checker	12	0.25	3	60
		Totals	43.25	865

The table that you create in exercises 3 and 4

1. Open the WORDTBL file, add the row shown in figure 8-12 to the end of the table, and enter and format the text in the second column of the new row. Then, move the insertion point into the last cell of the table and use the Formula command to sum the numbers above it. When the Formula dialog box is displayed, the correct formula should be in the Formula box so all you have to do is click on the OK button. That's often how easy it is to add the numbers in a column or row.

2. Change the number of training hours in the Outliner row so it is 1.50 instead of .50. Note that the total at the bottom of this column doesn't change so it's incorrect. To recalculate it, move the insertion point into the cell and press the F9 key. Now, save the document, but don't close it.

3. Start a new page in the document. Then, use tabs to separate these headings as you type them across the top of the page:

    Word feature
    Employees
    Classroom hours
    Employee hours
    Employee cost

    Use only one tab between each heading even if it looks funny, and end the line by pressing the Enter key. Then, select the paragraph and use the Convert Text to Table command to start a table with five columns.

4. Enter the rest of the text shown above in the heading row and enter the first three columns of the last six rows in the table. Then, add the borders to the table. When you add the thick border between the first two rows, be sure to add it to the bottom of the first row. And when you add the border between the last two rows, be sure to add it to the top of the last row. (Otherwise, the borders will move when you sort the table in the exercise 6.) Also, don't merge the cells in the first three columns of the last row, just remove the border between these columns (otherwise, the sum functions won't work right in the next exercise).

5. Use the Formula command to calculate the numbers in rows 2 through 6 of columns D and E and to sum the numbers in these columns. This exercise shows that entering formulas into a table can be quite time consuming. In fact, you can probably work faster by doing the calculations yourself and typing the results into the table. Now, save the document, which contains two tables, as WORDTBLS, but don't close the file.

6. In this exercise, you'll sort the rows in the table you just created. Since the table includes a total row, however, you can't just place the insertion point in the table as described in the procedure in figure 8-16. Instead, select all of the rows except for the total row, then choose the Sort command from the Table menu. When the Sort dialog box appears, click on the Header Row option, then sort by the Employee cost column in descending sequence. Did the sort work the way you wanted it to? If not, undo the sort, make the necessary adjustments, and sort the table again. When the table is sorted properly, close the file without saving it.

Perspective

If you've done the exercises for this chapter, you should now realize that the Word 6 table feature is both powerful and easy to use. At its best, it provides one more tool that can help you organize your activities and information. That's why most business professionals should take the time to master it.

Summary

- A table consists of *columns* and *rows*, and the intersection of each column and row is called a *cell*.

- You can create an empty table in just a few seconds using the Insert Table button in the Standard toolbar or the Insert Table command in the Table menu. Then, you can enter the text into the table using some special keystrokes for working with tables.

- The easiest way to adjust a column width is to drag a *column marker* in the ruler or a *column boundary* in the table. You can also use the Cell Height and Width command to adjust column widths. You can also use this command to adjust the space between columns and to align a table between the margins.

- When you select rows or columns, the Insert Table toolbar button, the Table menu, and the shortcut menu adjust to the selection. This makes it easy for you to insert or delete rows or columns.

- To move or copy cells, you can use drag-and-drop or cut, copy, and paste techniques.

- When necessary, you can merge cells or tables and split cells or tables.

- To apply borders and shading to portions of a table, you can use the Borders toolbar or the Borders and Shading command in the Format menu. You can also format a table using the Table AutoFormat command in the Table menu.

- To add the numbers in a column or row, you can use the Formula command in the Table menu. You can also use this command to perform arithmetic operations on the numbers in a table.

- If necessary, you can convert text in a document to a table and vice versa. You can also repeat the table headings on each page of a table, and you can sort the rows in the table.

Chapter 9

How to prepare a table of contents, lists, footnotes, and endnotes

Word provides three features that are useful when you prepare documents like reports, proposals, or research papers. These features let you compile a table of contents or a list with just a few mouse clicks, and they take the drudgery out of using footnotes and endnotes.

How to prepare a table of contents

When you use Heading styles to format the headings and subheadings in a document, you can create a table of contents for it in less than a minute. Later, if you change the headings or subheadings, you can recompile the table of contents in seconds.

How to define and compile a table of contents

Figure 9-1 shows how to define and compile a table of contents. When you complete the procedure, the table of contents is inserted into the document as a field. Then, you can update this field whenever the text in one of the headings or subheadings is changed. You'll learn how to do that in a moment.

The procedure in figure 9-1 assumes that you want to create the table of contents from the Heading styles that you've applied to the headings in a document. Although there's another way to identify the headings that you want to include in a table of contents, the use of Heading styles is far more efficient so the other method isn't presented in this book.

If you don't want to include all heading levels in a table of contents, you can use the Show Levels spin box to limit the number of levels that are included. If, for example, you use the Heading 1, 2, and 3 styles in a document, you can enter 2 in the Show Levels box to compile a table of contents that uses only the Heading 1 and 2 styles.

The start of a table of contents with the Classic format that's compiled from the Heading 1 and Heading 2 styles in a report

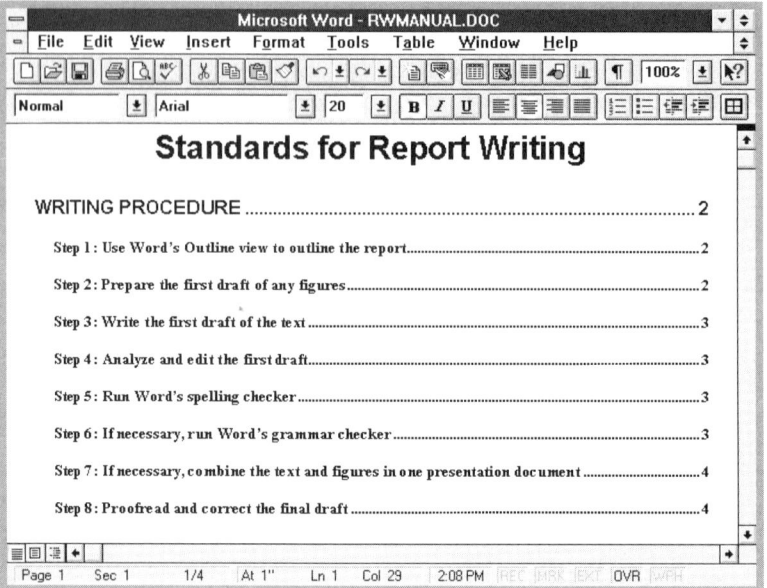

Procedure

1. Move the insertion point to where you want the table of contents inserted into the document. Then, choose the Index and Tables command from the Insert menu, and click on the Table of Contents tab to display this dialog box:

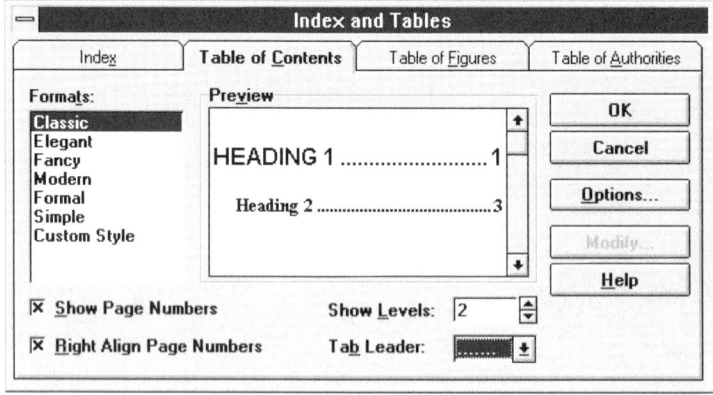

2. Choose the format that you want from the Formats list, and review it in the Preview box.

3. If necessary, use the two check boxes, the Show Levels spin box, and the Tab Leader list to modify the format you've chosen. You can also modify the styles used for the table of contents by clicking on the Modify button (see figure 9-2).

4. Click on the OK button to compile the table of contents and insert the results into the document as a field. (If the field code is displayed instead of the field results, press Alt+F9.)

Figure 9-1   How to define and compile a table of contents

How to modify the styles for a table of contents

When you compile a table of contents from the Heading styles in a document, Word automatically applies the TOC styles to the paragraphs in the table. The TOC 1 style is applied to the paragraphs derived from the Heading 1 style, the TOC 2 style is applied to the paragraphs derived from the Heading 2 style, and so on. Then, if you don't like the formatting that is applied by the TOC styles, you can modify the styles.

Figure 9-2 shows how to modify one or more of the TOC styles. If you have already read chapter 6 and know how to modify styles, you shouldn't have any trouble with this. Otherwise, you should read chapter 6 and do its exercises before you try to modify the TOC styles.

Procedure

1. From the Table of Contents tab of the Index and Tables dialog box shown in figure 9-1, highlight the Custom Style format in the Formats list and click on the Modify button to display this dialog box:

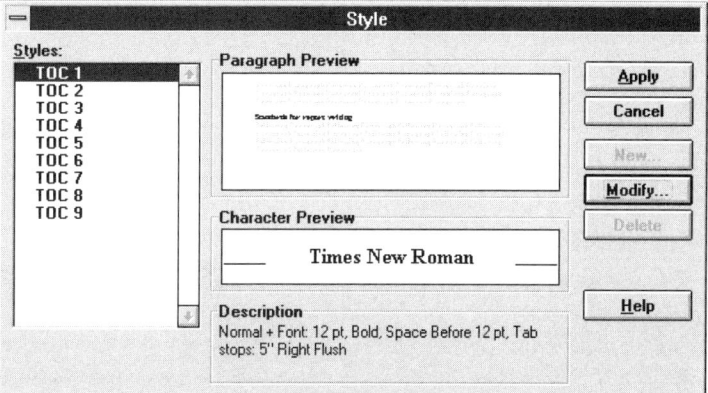

2. Click on the style you want to modify in the Styles list, and click on the Modify button. Then, modify the style using the techniques of chapter 6. Repeat this until all the styles are the way you want them.

3. Click on the Close button in the Style dialog box (the Cancel button changes to Close after you modify a style), and click on the OK button in the Index and Tables dialog box to compile the table of contents.

Notes

- The built-in TOC styles are automatically applied to a table of contents when it's compiled. This is true for all of the table of contents formats, but you can only modify the TOC styles when you choose the Custom Style format.

- You can also modify the TOC styles after you compile a table of contents by choosing the Style command from the Format menu.

Figure 9-2   How to modify the styles for a table of contents

Other skills for working with a table of contents

Figure 9-3 presents some other skills that you may need as you work with a table of contents. If you need to recompile a table of contents, for example, you can print the page that it's on or move the insertion point into it and press F9. If you want to modify the formatting in a table of contents, you can move the insertion point into it and repeat the procedure in figure 9-1.

If you want to have two tables of contents in a single document, you can do that too. In a large document, for example, one table of contents can show just the first heading level, and another can show two or more levels.

Additional information

✓ By default, a field like a table of contents is shaded when you move the insertion point into it. If it isn't, access the View tab of the Options dialog box and choose the When Selected option from the Field Shading list.

Three ways to recompile a table of contents

- Print any portion of the document. (If this doesn't work, check the Update Fields option in the Print tab of the Options dialog box.)

- Move the insertion point into the table, and press F9.

- Click the right mouse button in the table to display the shortcut menu, and choose the Update Field command.

How to choose what's updated when you recompile a table of contents that has page numbers

- If the table of contents you're recompiling has page numbers, this dialog box is displayed:

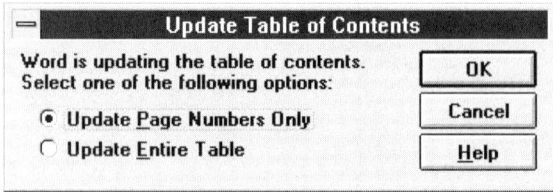

- Choose the Update Page Numbers Only option if the headings haven't changed, but the page numbers have. Choose the Update Entire Table option if both page numbers and headings have changed.

- Click on the Cancel button if you don't want to update the table.

How to change the format of a table of contents

1. Move the insertion point into the table of contents, and use the procedure in figure 9-1 to define a new one. Then, when you click on the OK button, this dialog box is displayed:

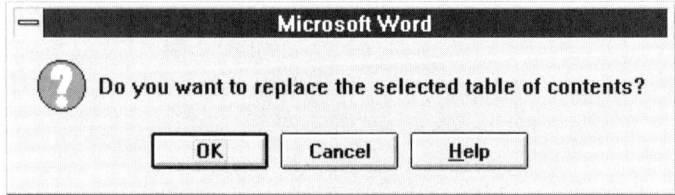

2. Click on the OK button to replace the existing table.

How to insert a second table of contents into a document

1. Use the procedure in figure 9-1 to define the second table. When you click on the OK button to compile the new table, Word selects the existing table and displays this dialog box:

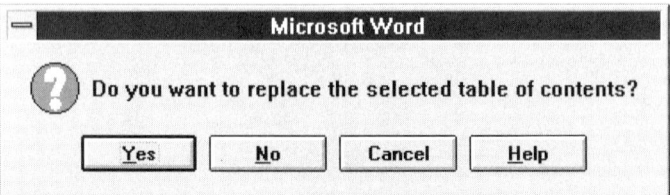

2. Click on the No button to insert another table instead of replacing the existing one.

Figure 9-3   Other skills for working with a table of contents

Exercise set 9-1

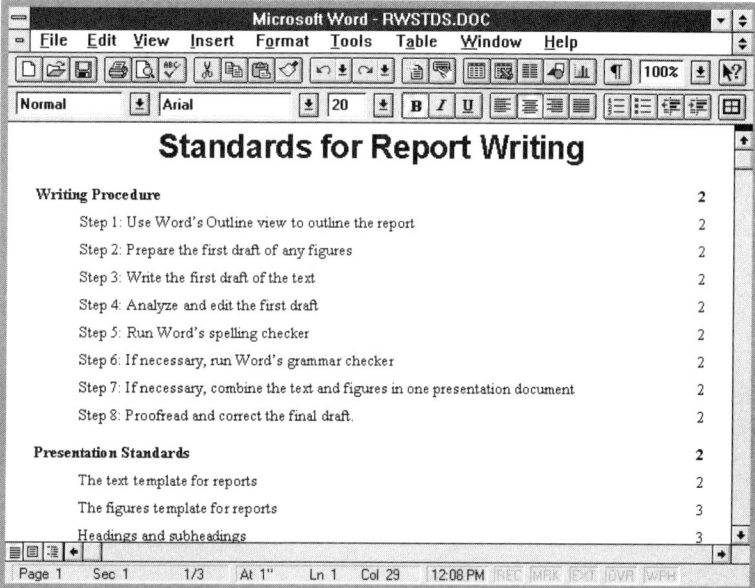

The table of contents that you compile for exercise 4

1. Open the RWSTDS file that you created for chapter 4 and may have updated in later chapters, and switch to Normal view (if necessary). Then, move the insertion point in front of the first paragraph after the report title, and insert a manual page break. Next, insert a table of contents before the page break so that only the report title and the table of contents are on the first page. (If you insert the page break after you insert the table of contents, the page numbers in the table of contents will be incorrect.) The table should be defined with the Elegant style, page numbers, and the dot tab leader. (Although the document contains only two heading levels, you can leave the Show Levels option at its default of 3.) Use Print Preview to review the table of contents to see whether you like its formatting.

2. Exit from preview mode, and move the insertion point into the table of contents. Then, redefine the table of contents with the Simple format. Do you like this formatting better?

3. Change the first heading in the document (not in the table of contents) from Writing Procedure to Our Writing Procedure. Next, move the insertion point into the table of contents, and press the F9 key to update the table. When the Update Table of Contents dialog box appears, choose the Update Entire Table option. Check the first heading in the table to make sure this worked correctly. Then, change the first heading back the way it was, and display the shortcut menu for the table of contents so you can see the Update Field command, but don't use it. Instead, print the first page of the document to make sure that the table of contents gets updated that way too.

4. Develop a custom format for the table of contents so it looks like the one above. To do that, move the insertion point into the table of contents, access the Index and Tables dialog box, and use the procedure in figure 9-2 to modify the styles. The TOC 1 style should have 12 points of spacing before it and zero points after it, and the TOC 2 style should have the Regular font style (not italic) and a .4 inch indent. When you've got the formatting right, save the file with a new name, RWTOC, and close it.

How to prepare a list

If you prepare documents with tables or other types of figures in them, you may want to include a list of the tables, figures, or both with the document. To do that, you can compile a list from paragraphs that have a particular style applied to them. Or, you can compile a list from Word captions that have been inserted into the document.

From styles that you've applied

One way to identify a table or figure is to type the identifying text in a paragraph above or below it and apply a special style to the paragraph. For instance, you could apply a style called Table Caption to the paragraphs that identify tables and a style called Figure Caption to the paragraphs that identify figures. When you use this method, you usually include numbering in the identifying text, like Table 2 or Figure 5-1.

After you identify the tables or figures, you can use the procedure in figure 9-4 to compile a list of the paragraphs that have one of the special styles applied to them. This procedure is similar to the procedure that you use for compiling a table of contents. When you're done, the list is inserted into the document as a field, and you can update it or redefine its format using the same techniques that you use for a table of contents. Note that Word refers to a list like this as a *table of figures*.

A list of the figures in this chapter compiled from paragraphs with the Figure legend style

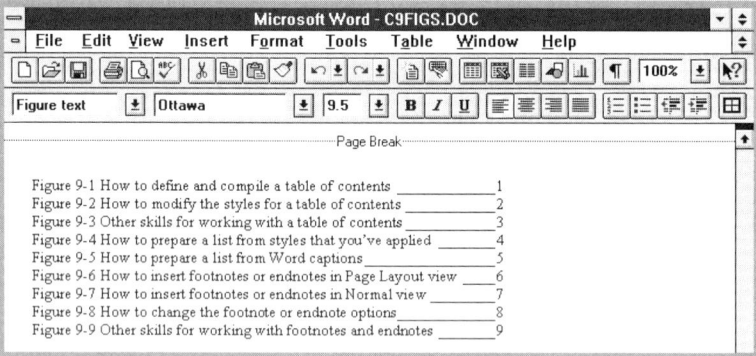

Procedure

1. Move the insertion point to where you want the list inserted. Then, choose the Index and Tables command from the Insert menu, and click on the Table of Figures tab to display this dialog box:

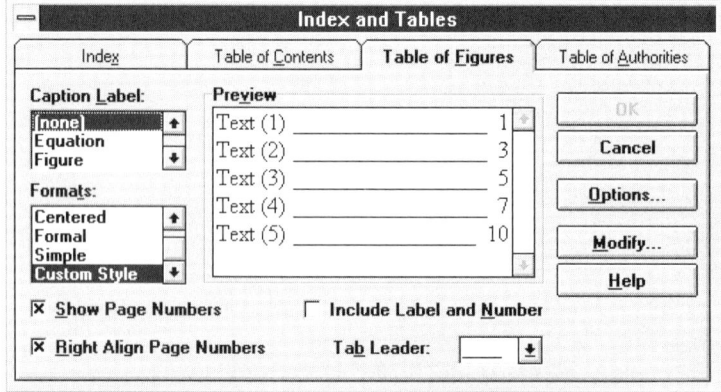

2. Click on the Options button to display this dialog box:

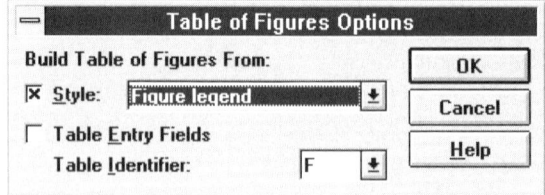

3. Choose the style from the Style list that you want to compile the list from. Then, click on the OK button to return to the Index and Tables dialog box.

4. In the Index and Tables dialog box, choose the format that you want from the Formats list. If necessary, use the two check boxes and the Tab Leader list to further modify the format you've chosen.

5. Click on the OK button to compile the table of contents and insert the results into the document as a field. (If the field code is displayed instead of the field results, press Alt+F9.)

Figure 9-4   How to prepare a list from styles that you've applied

From Word captions

Figure 9-5 shows another way to identify tables or figures and to compile lists. With this method, you insert Word *captions* into a document to identify the tables or figures. These captions include the labels and sequence numbers for the tables or figures in the document so you don't have to enter them. Also, because the numbers in the captions are fields, they can be updated when the sequence of the tables or figures is changed.

If you're going to insert items into your documents like those listed in the AutoCaption dialog box, it makes sense to use this automatic feature. For those items that aren't automatically captioned, you can still use the first procedure in figure 9-5 to insert their captions.

Once the captions are inserted into the document, you can compile one list for each type of caption using a procedure like the one in figure 9-4. Note that you don't need to choose the style you want to compile the list from because Word automatically uses the Caption style. However, you do have to choose a label type so that only the captions with that type of label are included in the list.

Additional information

✓ You can use the New Label button in the Caption or AutoCaption dialog box to enter the name for another type of caption.

✓ You can use the Numbering button to customize the number format for a caption type.

✓ The options you choose in the AutoCaption dialog box affect all Word documents.

How to apply a Word caption to a table or figure

1. Select the item you want to add a caption to, and choose the Caption command from the Insert menu to display this dialog box:

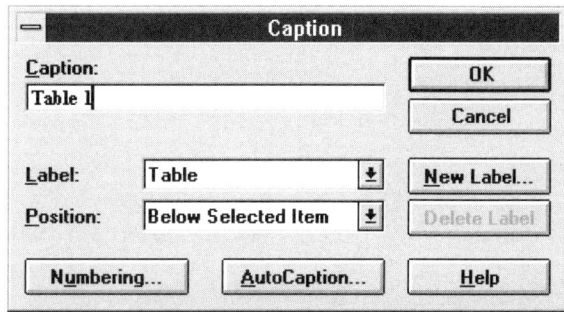

2. Choose a label type from the Label list (Table, Figure, or Equation), choose a position from the Position list (Above or Below Selected Item), and enter the identifying text in the Caption box following the caption label and number. (You can also enter the text directly into the document after you insert the caption.)

3. Click on the OK button. Word inserts a caption of the selected type and the next available number above or below the selected item.

How to automatically apply Word captions to tables or figures

1. Click on the AutoCaption button in the Caption dialog box shown above to display this dialog box:

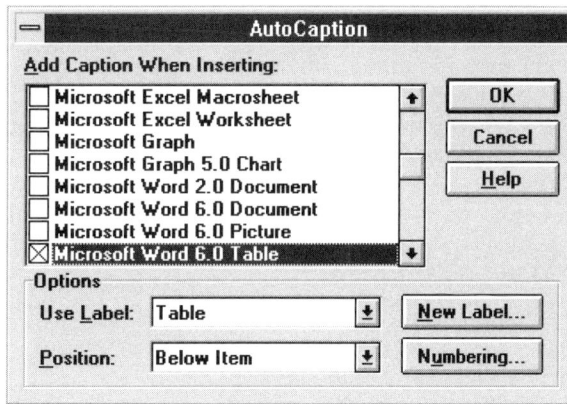

2. Check an item in the Add Caption When Inserting list, choose a label type from the Use Label list, and choose a position from the Position list.

3. Click on the OK button. After that, Word automatically adds a caption label and number when you insert an item of the type you indicated into the document. Then, you can add text after the caption label and number to identify the item.

How to compile a list from Word captions

• Access the Table of Figures tab as shown in figure 9-4. Then, choose a label type from the Caption Label list, choose any other formatting options that you want, and click on the OK button to compile the list.

Figure 9-5   How to prepare a list from Word captions

Exercise set 9-2

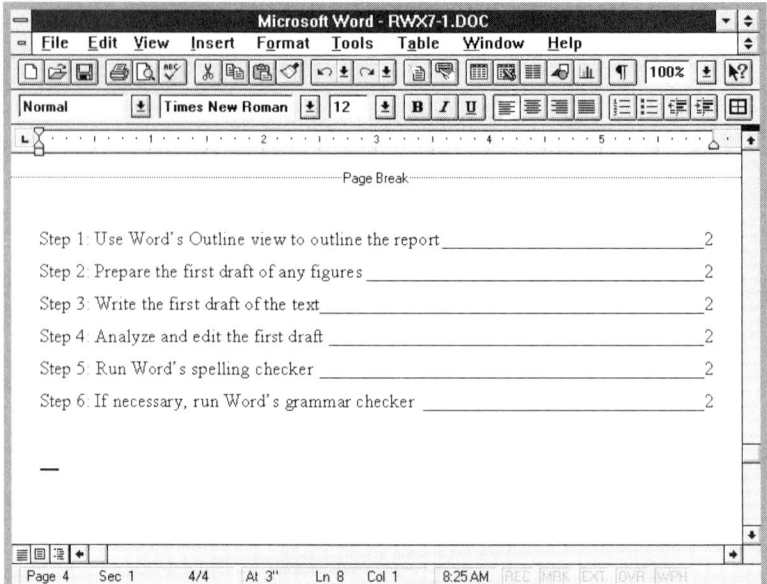

The list that you compile for exercise 3

Although the exercises that follow are unrealistic, they show how easy it is to compile a list from styles that you apply to the paragraphs that identify the tables or figures in a document.

1. Open the RWTOC file that you created for exercise set 9-1, move the insertion point into the first Heading 2 paragraph (Step 1), and create a new style from it named Step List. The easiest way to do that is to click in the Style box in the Formatting toolbar, type Step List, and press the Enter key. Then, apply this style to the next five Heading 2 paragraphs (Step 2 through Step 6).

2. Move the insertion point to the end of the document, start a new page, and insert a list on the new page that is compiled from the Step List styles. This list should have the Simple format, page numbers, and a line tab leader. When you click on the OK button to compile the list, Word displays a message that asks whether you want to replace the current table of figures. Since the document doesn't contain a table of figures yet, that doesn't make much sense (this is a confusion in the program that occurs when the document contains a table of contents). To continue, respond No, and the list is inserted into the document.

3. Redefine the list you just inserted into the document so it has the formatting shown in the list above. To do that, choose Custom Style as the format, click on the Modify button, and modify the Table of Figures style so the font is regular in 12 point size and the paragraph has 6 points of spacing after it.

4. Apply the Step List style to the paragraph with the Step 7 heading. Then, update the list and the table of contents at the same time. To do that, press Ctrl+A to select the entire document, press F9 to update all the fields in the selected text, and respond to the messages that follow. When you're done, review the list and the table of contents to make sure that the updating has taken place. Then, close the document without saving it.

Exercise set 9-3

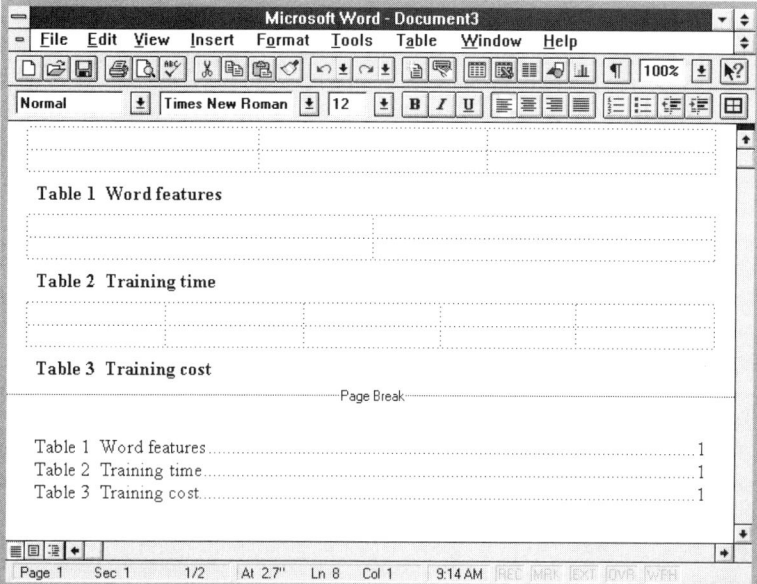

The tables and list of tables that you create for exercise 1

These exercises show how you can use Word captions to identify tables and figures and how you can compile lists from them. All of the exercises assume that you know how to create and use tables, and the last exercise assumes that you've done the exercises for chapter 8.

1. Open a new document, choose the Caption command from the Insert menu, and click on the AutoCaption button. Check the Microsoft Word 6.0 Tables option in the resulting dialog box, choose the Table and Below Item options, and click on the OK button to return to the document. Captions will now be inserted into the document automatically whenever you insert a table. Next, insert three two-row tables like those shown above and note the captions that are inserted below the tables. Then, add the text shown above after the table numbers. Last, start a new page and compile a list from the captions using the Custom Style format and the default options. Your document should now look like the one above.

2. Select the second table and the full paragraph that its caption is in, and move it after the third table. Note that the table numbers don't change, and the list doesn't change either. Select the second caption and press the F9 key to update its number. You can repeat this procedure to update the number in the third caption and the list, but select the entire document instead and press the F9 key to update all the fields at once. After you review the changes, close the document without saving it.

3. Open the WORDTBLS file that you created for chapter 8. It should contain two tables. Next, use the first procedure in figure 9-5 to insert a caption above each table like the first two captions shown above. Note that you have to select the entire table to add a caption to it. When you add the caption to the first table, it will be centered because the text in the first row of the table is centered. To left align the caption, click on the Align left button in the Formatting toolbar. This shows how you can add Word captions to existing tables. Now, compile a list from these captions. Then, save the document and close it.

How to use footnotes and endnotes

If you prepare documents that require footnotes or endnotes, Word 6 makes it easy. You just enter the required notes, and Word takes care of the numbering and formatting.

How to insert footnotes or endnotes into a document

Figure 9-6 shows how to enter footnotes or endnotes in Page Layout view. For efficiency, you can use the shortcut key to insert the *reference mark* for each note. Then, you only need to use the Footnote and Endnote dialog box when you want to change the formatting options.

Access

Menu   Insert ➠ Footnote

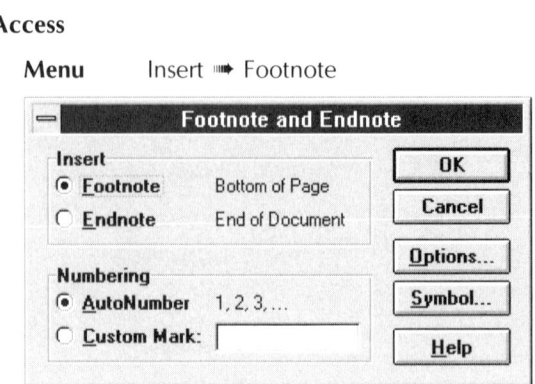

How to insert a footnote or endnote

1. Move the insertion point to where you want to insert the reference mark for the footnote or endnote, and access the Footnote and Endnote dialog box.

2. Choose the Footnote or Endnote option from the Insert group and click on the OK button. Word inserts the reference mark and moves the insertion point to the footnote or endnote area:

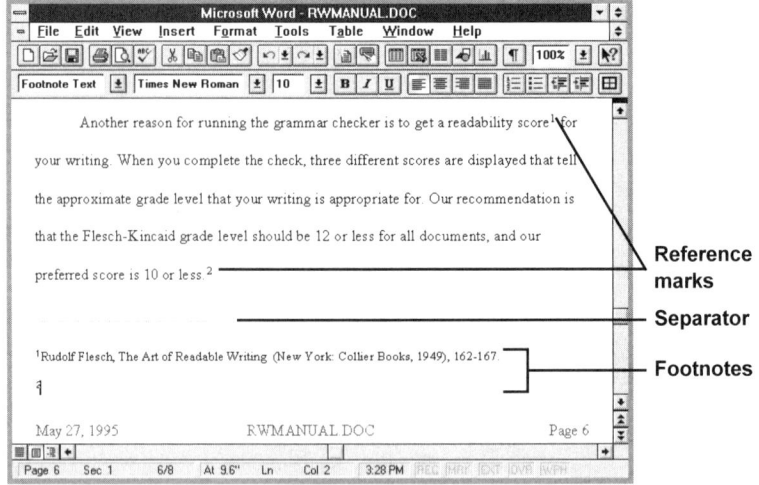

3. Enter the text of the note in the footnote or endnote area. Then, continue working with the document.

Shortcut keys for inserting the reference mark and moving to the footnote or endnote area (no dialog box is displayed)

Key	Type
Ctrl+Alt+F	Footnote
Ctrl+Alt+E	Endnote

Figure 9-6   How to insert footnotes or endnotes in Page Layout view

Figure 9-7 shows how to enter footnotes or endnotes in Normal view. In this view, the *note pane* is opened when you issue the Footnote command from the Insert menu or use the footnote or endnote shortcut keys. The benefit of using this pane is that you can always see the text that the reference mark is applied to and the related note at the same time. If you like, you can keep the note pane open as you enter or edit a document.

A document with an open note pane

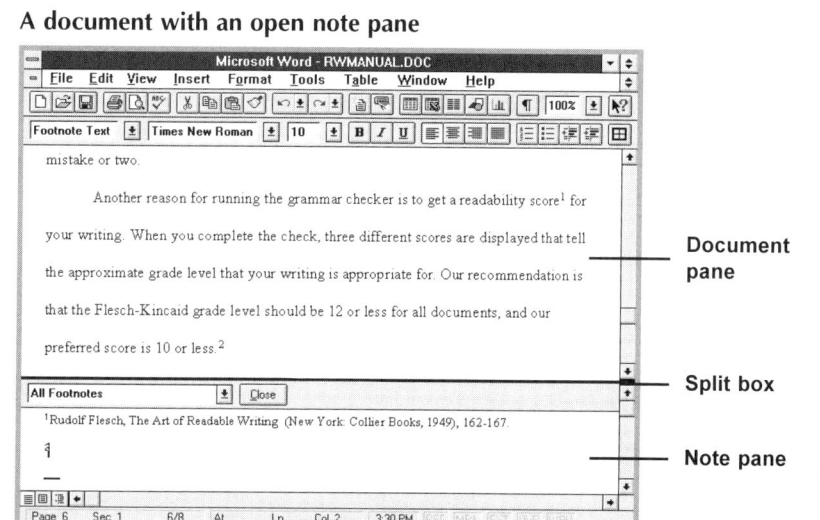

Document pane

Split box

Note pane

How to insert a footnote or an endnote

1. Move the insertion point to where you want to insert the reference mark.

2. Issue the Footnote command to display the dialog box shown in figure 9-6 or use one of the shortcut keys to bypass the dialog box.

3. If the dialog box is displayed, choose the Footnote or Endnote option from the Insert group. Then, click on the OK button so Word inserts the reference mark and opens a note pane like the one above. If you use a shortcut key, the reference mark is inserted and the note pane is opened with no intervening dialog box.

4. Enter the text of the footnote or endnote in the note pane. Then, click on the Close button at the top of the note pane to close the pane, or switch to the document pane and continue working on the document with the note pane open.

Notes

* You can change the size of the note pane by dragging the split box in the vertical scroll bar.

* The document pane and note pane scroll together so the reference marks in the document and the associated notes in the note pane are displayed at the same time.

* To switch to and from the note pane, press the F6 key or click in the other pane.

* You can open the note pane without inserting a reference mark in the document by choosing the Footnote command from the View menu.

Figure 9-7   How to insert footnotes or endnotes in Normal view

How to change the footnote or endnote options

If you want to change the default options that are used with footnotes or endnotes, you can use the dialog box shown in figure 9-8. The option you're most likely to change is the numbering format for endnotes because the default is lowercase Roman numerals. Otherwise, the default options are usually satisfactory.

Access

Access the Footnote and Endnote dialog box as shown in figure 9-6, and click on the Options button.

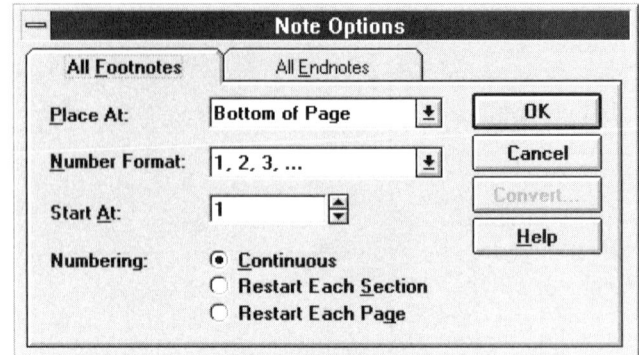

Option or button	Description
Place At	Determines where the footnotes and endnotes are placed. For footnotes, the options are Bottom of Page and Beneath Text. For endnotes, the options are End of Document and End of Section.
Number Format	Determines the format that's used for the note numbers (some aren't numbers). The default for footnotes is Arabic numerals (1, 2, 3, ...). The default for endnotes is lowercase Roman numerals (i, ii, iii, ...).
Start At	Lets you choose the number to be used as the first reference mark. The default is the first number shown in the Number Format box.
Numbering	Lets you restart the numbering of footnotes at the beginning of each section or page, or restart the numbering of endnotes at the beginning of each section. The default is to number footnotes and endnotes continuously throughout the document.
Convert	Lets you convert all the footnotes in a document to endnotes, all the endnotes to footnotes, or both.

Note

When you click on the OK button, you're returned to the Footnote and Endnote dialog box. Then, you can click on the OK button to insert a footnote or endnote using the new options. Or, you can click on the Close button to close the dialog box without inserting a footnote or endnote.

Figure 9-8   How to change the footnote or endnote options

Other skills for working with footnotes and endnotes

Figure 9-9 presents several other functions that you may need when working with footnotes or endnotes. To delete a footnote or endnote, for example, you just delete its reference mark. To change the format of a reference mark, footnote, or endnote, you just change the related style. And to move from one reference mark to another in a large document, you can use the Go To or Find command. With the note pane open, both the reference mark and the note are displayed as you move from one mark to another.

Incidentally, you can use both footnotes and endnotes in the same document. I mention this not because you're likely to require both but because you may accidentally enter both types in the same document. Then, you can change the footnotes to endnotes or vice versa by using one of the last two procedures in figure 9-9.

How to move a note's reference mark

- Select the reference mark and use drag-and-drop or cut and paste techniques to move it. If necessary, the footnotes or endnotes are automatically renumbered.

How to delete footnotes or endnotes

- To delete a single footnote or endnote, select the note's reference mark and press the Backspace or Delete key. The footnotes or endnotes are automatically renumbered.

- To delete all footnotes or endnotes, use the Replace command in the Edit menu. In the Find What text box, enter the Footnote Mark or Endnote Mark option from the Special list, and leave the Replace With text box blank.

Two ways to move the insertion point from one reference mark to the next

- Use the Go To command in the Edit menu. Choose the Footnote or Endnote option from the Go to What list. (If the note pane is open, make sure that the insertion point is in the document pane before you issue this command. Otherwise, Word will search only the note pane.)

- Use the Find command in the Edit menu. In the Find What text box, enter the Footnote Mark or Endnote Mark option from the Special list. If you choose All from the Search list, Word will search both the document pane and the note pane if it's open. If you choose the Up or Down option, Word will search only the active pane.

How to change the format of the reference marks, notes, or separators

- To change the format of the reference marks, change the related style: Footnote Reference or Endnote Reference.

- To change the format of the note, change the related style: Footnote Text or Endnote Text.

- To change the format of the note separators and continuation notices, choose the appropriate option from the list at the top of the note pane to display the item you want to change, and change it.

How to convert footnotes to endnotes or vice versa

- To convert all footnotes to endnotes or all endnotes to footnotes or to swap endnotes and footnotes, access the Footnote and Endnote dialog box and click on the Options button. Click on the Convert button in the next dialog box, and choose the appropriate option from the next dialog box. Click on the OK button to return to the Footnote and Endnote dialog box, and click on the Close button.

- To convert some notes to the other form, select the notes you want to convert in the note pane. Then, click the right mouse button on the selected notes to display the note shortcut menu, and choose the Convert To Footnote or Convert To Endnote command.

Figure 9-9   Other skills for working with footnotes and endnotes

Exercise set 9-4

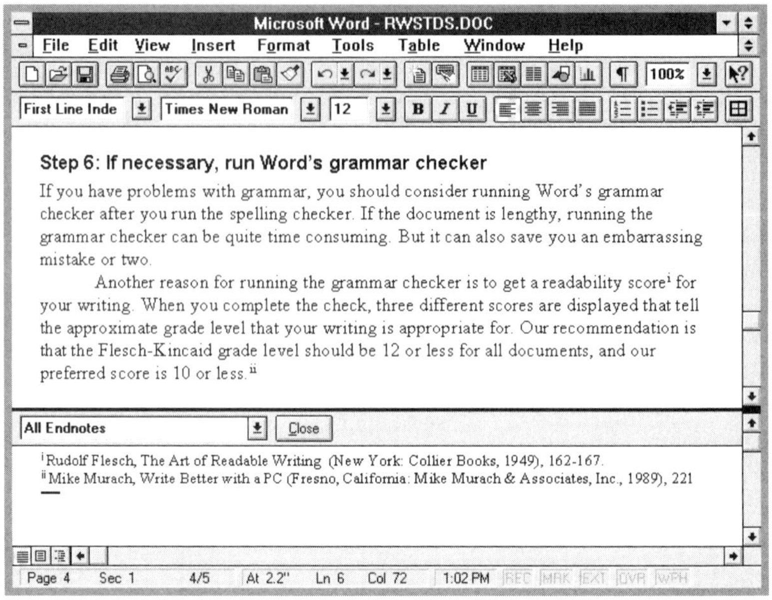
Microsoft Word - RWSTDS.DOC
File Edit View Insert Format Tools Table Window Help
First Line Inde
Times New Roman
12
100%
Step 6: If necessary, run Word's grammar checker
If you have problems with grammar, you should consider running Word's grammar checker after you run the spelling checker. If the document is lengthy, running the grammar checker can be quite time consuming. But it can also save you an embarrassing mistake or two.
Another reason for running the grammar checker is to get a readability score[i] for your writing. When you complete the check, three different scores are displayed that tell the approximate grade level that your writing is appropriate for. Our recommendation is that the Flesch-Kincaid grade level should be 12 or less for all documents, and our preferred score is 10 or less.[ii]
All Endnotes
Close
[i] Rudolf Flesch, The Art of Readable Writing (New York: Collier Books, 1949), 162-167.
[ii] Mike Murach, Write Better with a PC (Fresno, California: Mike Murach & Associates, Inc., 1989), 221
Page 4 Sec 1 4/5 At 2.2" Ln 6 Col 72 1:02 PM

The two endnotes that you create for exercise 1

1. Open the RWSTDS file, switch to Normal view (if necessary), scroll to the Step 6 heading, and enter the second body paragraph shown above into the document along with the two endnotes. (Don't worry if your first body paragraph is different from the one shown above.) Then, close the note pane, and move to the end of the document to see that the endnotes aren't displayed. To display them, switch to Page Layout view.
2. Use the dialog box shown in figure 9-8 to change the numbering for the endnotes to Arabic (1, 2, 3). Then, return to the endnotes in Page Layout view to observe this change.
3. Switch to Normal view, and use the View menu to open the note pane. Then, click in the document pane to make it active, and use the Go To command to move between the two endnote reference marks. Last, use the Find command to move from one reference mark to the next.
4. Use one of the procedures in figure 9-9 to convert all the endnotes in the document to footnotes. Then, switch to Page Layout view and review the footnotes.
5. Delete the reference mark for the first footnote. Is the footnote removed from the page too? Is the second footnote renumbered? Close the document without saving it.

Perspective

The features presented in this chapter make it easy to prepare tables of contents, lists, footnotes, and endnotes. In fact, it's hard to imagine how these features could be any easier to use. So if you prepare documents that require tables of contents, lists, footnotes, or endnotes, you'd be remiss not to use the Word features to create them.

Summary

- To define and compile a table of contents from the Heading styles in a document, you use the Index and Tables command in the Insert menu.

- You can prepare a list (or *table of figures*) from styles that you've applied to paragraphs or from Word *captions*. You can use the Caption command in the Insert menu to insert one caption at a time or to set Word up so captions are inserted automatically whenever you create an item like a table.

- When you insert a footnote or endnote into a document in Normal view, Word adds a *reference mark* to the document and lets you enter the footnote or endnote in the *note pane*. In Page Layout view, you enter the footnote or endnote at the bottom of the page or the end of the document.

Chapter 10

How to use columns, graphic objects, and frames

The first nine chapters of this book present the skills that you need for entering, editing, and formatting the text of typical business documents like letters, memos, and reports. If you need to prepare documents like newsletters, though, you need to know how to format a document with two or more columns across the page. If you use graphic objects, you need to know how to insert them into your documents. And if you have to combine figures and graphic objects with text in an effective presentation format, you need to know how to use frames. Those are the skills you'll learn in this chapter.

How to use columns

After you finish entering and editing a document, you can quickly format all or part of the text into two or more columns. Then, you can adjust the column formatting so that the text fits the way you want it to. Alternatively, you can apply the column formatting before you enter the text so you can see how the text will lay out as you enter it.

How to use the Columns toolbar button to format a section with columns

Figure 10-1 shows the quickest way to apply column formatting to a document. If text is selected when you use the Columns button, the selection becomes a new section in the document; the text before it becomes another section; and the text after it becomes a third section. You'll want to use this technique if only part of the document will be formatted with two or more columns. Otherwise, you can simply place the insertion point anywhere in the document or section you want to format before you use the Columns button.

If you're working in Normal view when you apply column formatting, you'll notice that the text is still displayed in a single column. To see how the text will actually lay out on the page, you can switch to Page Layout view. In general, it's more efficient to enter the text in Normal view, and it's more efficient to adjust the column formatting in Page Layout view.

How to apply column formats to selected text

1. Select the text that you want to format.

2. Click on the Columns button in the Standard toolbar, and drag the pointer to the number of columns you want:

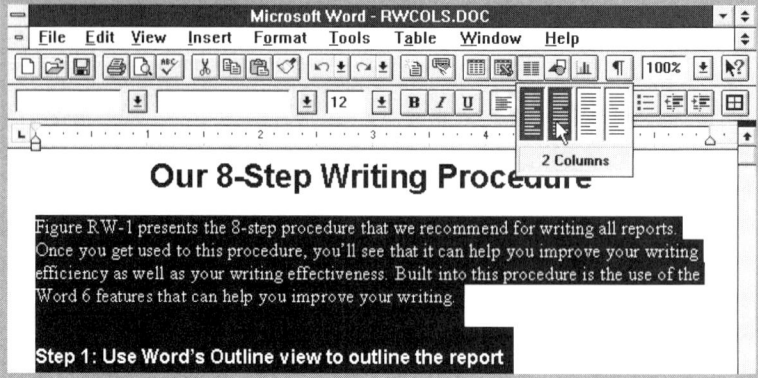

3. When you release the mouse button, Word places the text in a new section and formats it with equal-width columns:

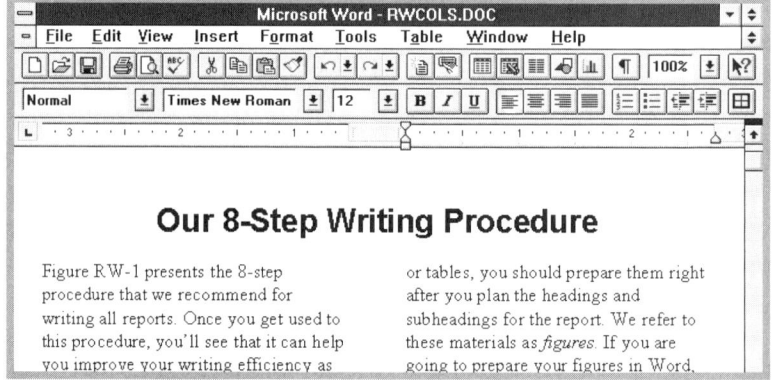

How to apply column formats to a selected section

• Move the insertion point into the section that you want to format, and use the Columns button to choose the number of columns. When you release the mouse button, Word formats the section with equal-width columns.

Notes

• To see the layout of the columns, you have to work in Page Layout View. In Normal view, you can see the column and section breaks, but the text is displayed in a single column.

• Before you format text with columns, you may want to decrease the left and right page margins so more text fits across the page. You may also want to decrease the font size in the body text so more characters fit on each line.

Figure 10-1   How to use the Columns button to apply column formats

How to use the Columns command to apply or adjust column formatting

You can also use the Columns command shown in figure 10-2 to apply column formatting to a section or selection. When you use this command, you can create columns of unequal widths, change the size of the spacing between the columns, and insert a vertical line between the columns. If you choose the This Point Forward option from the Apply To list, you can also start a new section that the formatting is applied to.

To adjust the column formatting for a section after you apply it, you move the insertion point into the section and issue the Columns command. If, for example, you use the Columns toolbar button to format a section with two equal-width columns, you can use the Columns command to change the formatting so it provides for unequal column widths.

Access

Menu	Format ➡ Columns
Ruler	Double-click on a column marker

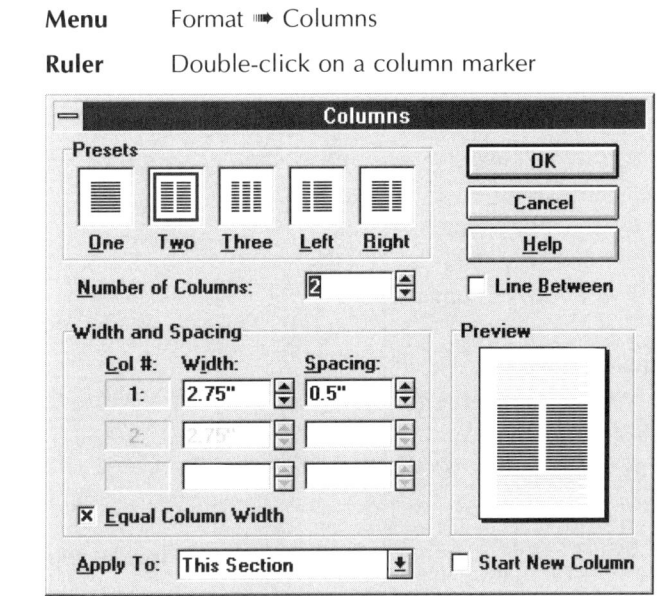

Group or option	Description
Presets	Five predefined column formats.
Number of Columns	The number of columns you want.
Line Between	Inserts a vertical line between the columns.
Width and Spacing	Lets you specify column widths and the spacing between columns.
Equal Column Width	If this option is checked, you can only define equal column widths for the section.
Apply To	Lets you choose the part of the document you want to apply the column formatting to: Whole Document, This Section, This Point Forward, or Selected Text.
Start New Column	If this option is checked, a column break is inserted into the document at the insertion point.

Operation

- To apply column formatting to existing text or a section, select the text or move the insertion point into the section before issuing this command.

- To change the column formatting in a section, move the insertion point into it before issuing this command.

Figure 10-2   How to use the Columns command to apply or change column formats

How to use the ruler to change column widths

Figure 10-3 shows how you can use the ruler to adjust the column widths. In Page Layout view, you can change the column widths, the spacing between columns, and the page margins for the section. In Normal view, you can still change the column widths, but you can't change the space between columns or the margins.

The ruler makes it easy to experiment with the columns in a document when you're not sure how you want them to lay out. If you need precise page layout, however, you should use the Page Setup and Columns commands to set page margins, column widths, and the spacing between columns. But before you use these commands, you need to start by designing the page layout so you know what the margin and column widths should be.

How to use the ruler to change column widths in Page Layout View

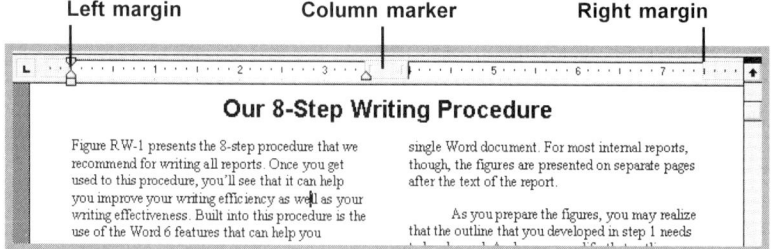

- To change just the column widths, drag the column marker. However, you can't change the widths if the Equal Column Width option is on.

- To change the space between columns (and thus change the column widths), drag the left or right edge of the column marker.

- To change the left or right page margin for the entire section (and thus change the column widths), drag the left or right margin.

How to use the ruler to adjust column widths in Normal view

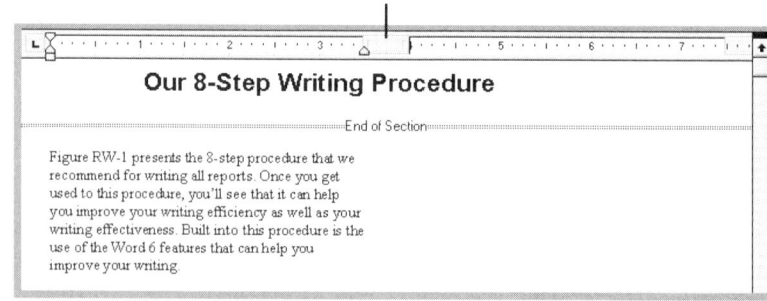

- In Normal view, you can only drag the column marker to change column widths. This works the same as it does in Page Layout view.

Figure 10-3   How to use the ruler to change column widths

Other skills for working with columns

Figure 10-4 presents three other skills for working with columns. If you want to end a column and move the text that follows to the next column, you insert a *column break* into the text. To balance the column endings at the end of a document, you can use the Break command to insert a section break into the document. And to return to single column formatting, you can use any of the three techniques presented in the figure.

Access

Menu   Insert ➡ Break

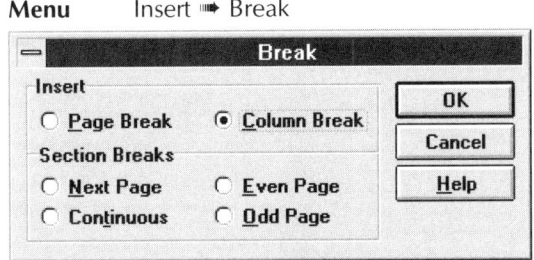

Two ways to insert a column break into a document so the text that follows moves to the top of the next column

• Press Ctrl+Shift+Enter.

• Access the Break dialog box and choose the Column Break option.

How to insert a section break into a document so the columns in a section are balanced

• Move the cursor to the end of the text that you want to balance. Then, access the Break dialog box and choose the Continuous option in the Section Breaks group. This starts a new section on the same page with the same column formatting. This is especially useful for newsletters because it lets you place two or more articles on the same page with one article below another.

Three ways to return to single column formatting

• Select the text that you want to return to single column formatting. Then, use the Columns toolbar button shown in figure 10-1 to start a new section with that formatting.

• Use the Columns command shown in figure 10-2 to start a new section with single column formatting by choosing the This Point Forward option from the Apply To list.

• Use the Break command shown above to start a new section. (Choose the Next Page option instead of the Continuous option if you want the new section to start on the next page.) Then, use the Columns toolbar button or the Columns command to format this section with a single column.

Figure 10-4   Other skills for working with columns

Exercise set 10-1

Writing Procedure

Figure RW-1 presents the writing procedure that we recommend for all reports. Once you get used to this procedure, you'll see that it can help you improve your writing efficiency as well as your writing effectiveness. Built into this procedure is the use of the Word 6 features that can help you improve your writing.

Step 1: Use Word's Outline view to outline the report

Whenever you write a report, it should be divided into topics and subtopics that are clearly identified by heading and subheadings in the document. To plan these headings and subheadings, start a Word document from the RPTTEXT template and switch to Outline view. In this way, you can quickly and easily enter the headings and subheadings that you intend to use, and the indentation makes the heading levels obvious as shown in figure RW-2.

After you enter the first draft of the headings and subheadings, you can review their structure, reword them so they're more definitive, change a heading to a subheading, rearrange headings and subheadings, print the

entire outline, and so on. You can also include notes below the headings and subheadings that will help you write the text later on.

Step 2: Prepare the first draft of any figures

Step 3: Write the first draft of the text

Step 4: Analyze and edit the first draft

Step 5: Run Word's spelling checker

Step 6: If necessary, run Word's grammar checker

If you have any problems with grammar, you should consider running Word's grammar checker. This can be time consuming, but it can also save you from an embarrassing mistake.

Step 7: If necessary, combine the text and figures in one presentation document

Step 8: Proofread and correct the final draft

How your document should look after exercise 2

1. Open the RWSTDS file that you created for chapter 4 and may have updated for subsequent chapters. Next, use the Page Setup command to set the left and right margins for the document to .8 inch. Then, select the text from the first paragraph after the Writing Procedure heading through the last paragraph before the Presentation Standards heading, and use the Columns toolbar button to format the selection with two columns.

2. Scroll through the document in Normal view. How many sections does it contain? Switch to Page Layout view and scroll through the document again. Notice that although the document consists of three sections, the first two sections are on the same page. To place the section with two-column formatting and the heading that goes with it on a separate page, insert a page break before the Writing Procedure paragraph. Then, change the heading so its font size is 20 and it has no spacing before it and 12 points of spacing after it. Now, scroll down to the Presentation Standards heading and insert a page break before it so it starts on a new page. The second section of your document should now look like the one above.

3. Click on the Show/Hide button in the Standard toolbar and scroll through the document again to see how this changes the way the page breaks and section breaks are displayed. Click on this button again to hide the nonprinting characters.

4. Scroll to the end of the second page to see that the column endings are balanced. Insert a column break (Ctrl+Shift+Enter) before the Step 2 heading. This moves that heading to the top of the second column and unbalances the column bottoms as well as the column tops. To balance the column tops, remove the spacing before the Step 2 paragraph. You often need to make this type of adjustment to balance the column tops. In fact, this two-column layout will work better if you remove the spacing before all the Heading 2 styles. So change the style so it works that way now.

Writing Procedure

Figure RW-1 presents the writing procedure that we recommend for all reports. Once you get used to this procedure, you'll see that it can help you improve your writing efficiency as well as your writing effectiveness. Built into this procedure is the use of the Word 6 features that can help you improve your writing.

Step 1: Use Word's Outline view to outline the report

Whenever you write a report, it should be divided into topics and subtopics that are clearly identified by heading and subheadings in the document. To plan these headings and subheadings, start a Word document from the RPTTEXT template and switch to Outline view. In this way, you can quickly and easily enter the headings and subheadings that you intend to use, and the indentation makes the heading levels obvious as shown in figure RW-2.

After you enter the first draft of the headings and subheadings, you can review their structure, reword them so they're more definitive, change a heading to a subheading, rearrange headings and subheadings, print the entire outline, and so on. You can also include notes below the headings and subheadings that will help you write the text later on.

Step 2: Prepare the first draft of any figures

Step 3: Write the first draft of the text

Step 4: Analyze and edit the first draft

Step 5: Run Word's spelling checker

Step 6: If necessary, run Word's grammar checker

If you have any problems with grammar, you should consider running Word's grammar checker. This can be time consuming, but it can also save you from an embarrassing mistake.

Step 7: If necessary, combine the text and figures in one presentation document

Step 8: Proofread and correct the final draft

How your document should look after exercise 5

5. Use the Columns command shown in figure 10-2 to add a line between the columns. Now, the second section of your document should look like the one above, although it may include some additional text in the second column. At this point, save the document with the name RWCOLS, but don't close it.

6. Switch to Normal view so you can see the section break at the end of section 2 (End of Section), and delete the section break. Because the section break contains the formatting information for a section, the second section takes on the formatting of what was section 3, which returns it to a one column format. Now, delete the text from the Presentation Standards heading to the end of the document, delete the column break before the Step 2 heading, and format the second section with two columns again. Switch back to Page Layout view, and note that the column endings aren't balanced. To balance them, use a section break as shown in figure 10-4.

7. Use the Columns command to change the widths of the columns so the left column is 2.5 inches, the space between is .3 inch, and the right column is whatever's left over. When you return to the document, check to see whether the column endings are still balanced. Next, use the ruler in Page Layout view to change the column widths any way you want. Then, change the width between the columns and change the section margins. Close the file without saving it.

How to use graphic objects

If you want to use *graphic objects*, or just *graphics*, from other programs in a Word document, you can do that. If, for example, you use *Paintbrush* to create a file that contains a drawing, you can insert the drawing into a document. And if you use *Excel* to create a chart, you can paste it into a document.

How to insert a graphic object into a document

Figure 10-5 shows how to use the Picture command to insert a graphic object into a Word document. Here, each file contains one object. In this example, the files are stored in the Clipart directory that comes with Word 6 so you should have it on your PC. When you complete the command, the graphic is inserted into your document at the insertion point.

To save disk space, you can turn the Link to File option on and the Save Picture in Document option off. Otherwise, the graphic object is stored in both the Word document and the graphic file. If disk space isn't a problem, though, you won't need this capability.

Additional information

✓ You can use the File Locations tab of the Options command to set the default directory for Clipart Pictures. This is the directory that's displayed when you issue the Picture command.

Access

Menu   Insert ➡ Picture

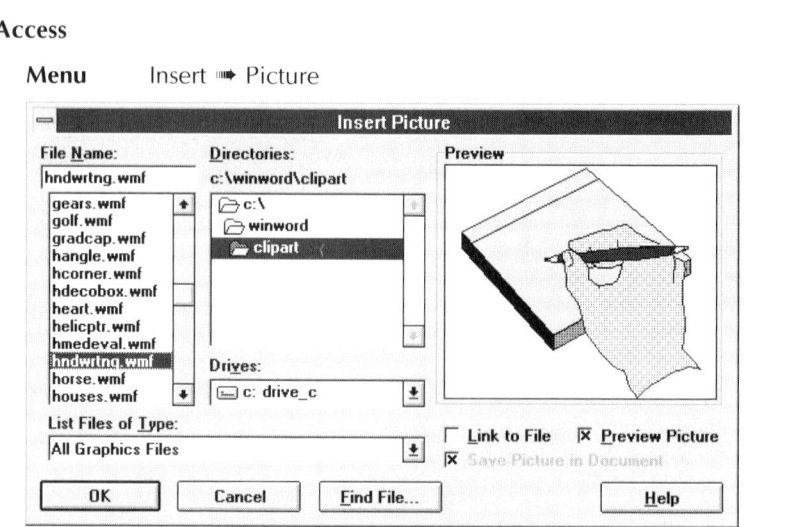

Operation

- To display just the names of a specific type of graphic file in the File Name list, choose a type from the List Files of Type list.

- To preview a picture as shown above, check the Preview Picture option and highlight the file you want to preview.

- To insert a picture into a document, double-click on its name or click on the OK button when its file name is highlighted.

The types of graphic files that Word can insert

Extension	Type	Extension	Type
DXF	AutoCAD Format 2-D	PCT	Macintosh PICT
PLT	AutoCAD Plot File	DRW	Micrografx Designer/Draw
CGM	Computer Graphics Metafile	PCX	PC Paintbrush
WPG	DrawPerfect	TIF	Tagged Image Format
EPS	Encapsulated Postscript	BMP	Windows Bitmap
HGL	HP Graphic Language	WMF	Windows Metafile
PIC	Lotus 1-2-3 Graphic		

Note

- If you check the Link to File option and remove the check from the Save Picture in Document option, the graphic isn't actually inserted into your file. Instead, the document contains a pointer to the graphic file. This can save disk space.

Figure 10-5   **How to insert a graphic object into a document**

How to paste a graphic object from another program

If you create a graphic object in another Windows program like *1-2-3* or Excel, you can use the procedure in figure 10-6 to copy it to the clipboard and paste it into your document. Normally, the regular Paste command is all you need for this purpose. But you can also use the Paste Special command.

When you issue the Paste Special command, a dialog box is displayed that provides two options: Paste and Paste Link. If you choose the Paste option, the result is the same as if you used the Paste command: the graphic is embedded in the document. But if you choose the Paste Link option, Word inserts a link that identifies the file that contains the graphic object. Then, if the graphic object is changed, Word can automatically update the graphic when the document that it's in is opened.

If you've heard the term *Object Linking and Embedding (OLE)*, you now know how it's implemented. If you experiment with it, though, you'll see that it requires extra machine time so it slows down your PC's performance. And if you're only going to use a graphic object for one printing of a document, you simply don't need this capability.

Additional information

✓ In most cases, a linked object appears in the document the same way as an embedded object. However, if you display the field codes for the objects, you'll see that they're different.

A Word document after an Excel chart has been pasted into it

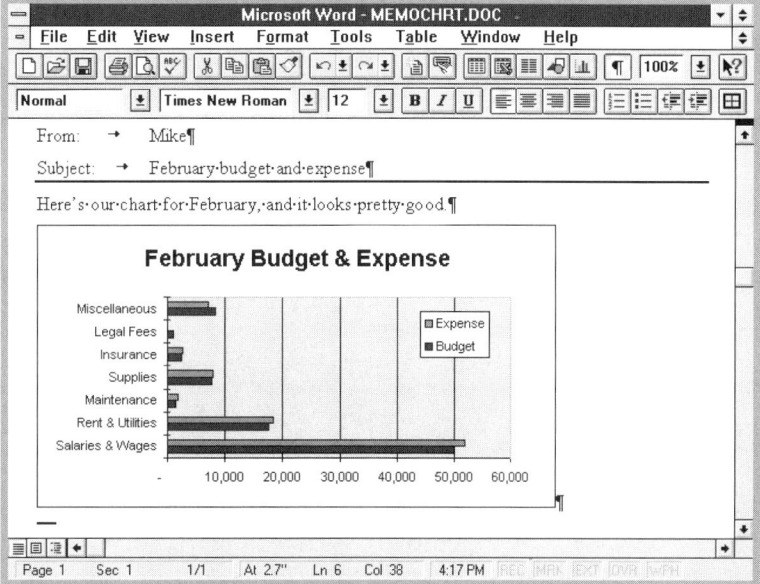

How to use the Paste command

1. Start the other program and open the file that contains the graphic object.

2. Use the Copy command to copy the object to the clipboard.

3. Switch from the other program to Word.

4. Use the Paste command to copy the graphic object from the clipboard into the Word document. As always, you can use the shortcut key (Ctrl+V), the toolbar button, the shortcut menu, or the Edit menu to access this command.

How to use the Paste Special command

• In step 4 of the above procedure, you can also choose the Paste Special command from the shortcut or Edit menu to paste the graphic object from the clipboard into a document.

• If you use the Paste option in the Paste Special dialog box, the result is the same as using the Paste command.

• If you use the Paste Link option in the Paste Special dialog box, the object isn't copied into the Word document but is linked to the document using Object Linking and Embedding. Then, if the object is modified by someone using the other program, the object is modified in Word too.

Figure 10-6   How to paste a graphic object from another program into a document

How to select, size, move, copy, and delete a graphic object

Figure 10-7 presents the skills you need for working with graphic objects. For simple requirements, these may be all that you need. For more precise layout work, though, you need to use frames.

When you link or embed a graphic object in a Word document, you can edit the graphic by double-clicking on it. Although you're not likely to need to do that, you may double-click on a graphic accidentally as you work with it. If you do, the results depend on the application that was used to create the graphic. In some cases, you can return to the normal Word window by clicking on the Close button that's displayed or by clicking outside the graphic object. But if the application that was used to create the graphic is started, you have to use the Exit command in the program's File menu to exit from the program and return to Word.

How to apply borders or add captions to graphic objects

If you want to apply a border to a selected object, you can use the Borders toolbar button or the Borders and Shading command. Note, however, that you can't shade a graphic object this way.

You can also add Word captions to graphic objects using the Caption command in the Insert menu. If you've read chapter 9, you know that you can set this up so the captions are applied automatically whenever an object is inserted into the document. Or, you can insert one caption at a time.

A Word document after a Word picture has been inserted into it

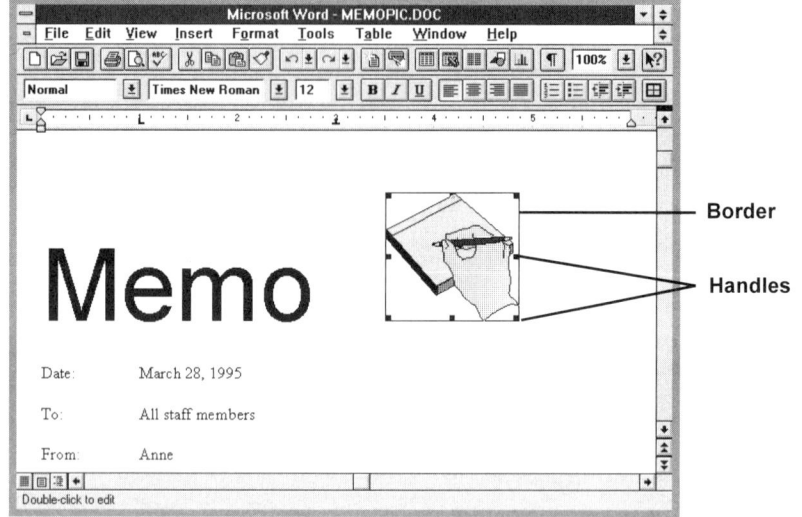

How to select a graphic object

• Click on it to display its border and handles.

How to move or copy a selected object

• To move an object, place the mouse pointer inside the border so it turns into an arrow and drag. To copy, hold down the Ctrl key as you drag. You can also use normal cut, copy, and paste techniques to move or copy an object.

How to size or crop a selected object

• To size the object, place the mouse pointer over a handle so it turns into a double-headed arrow and drag the handle. As you drag, Word displays the size of the object as a percent of its original size in the left side of the status bar.

• If you want to crop the object, hold down the Shift key as you drag a side, top, or bottom handle. As you drag, Word displays the amount that the object has been cropped in the left side of the status bar.

• You can also use the Picture command in the Format menu to size or crop a graphic object.

How to delete a selected object

• Press the Delete key.

Note

• If you double-click on a graphic object, Word lets you edit it. Depending on the program that was used to create the object and whether the object is embedded in or linked to the document, the Word screen is modified so that the editing tools are available or the program used to create the object is started.

Figure 10-7   How to select, size, move, copy, or delete a graphic object

Exercise set 10-2

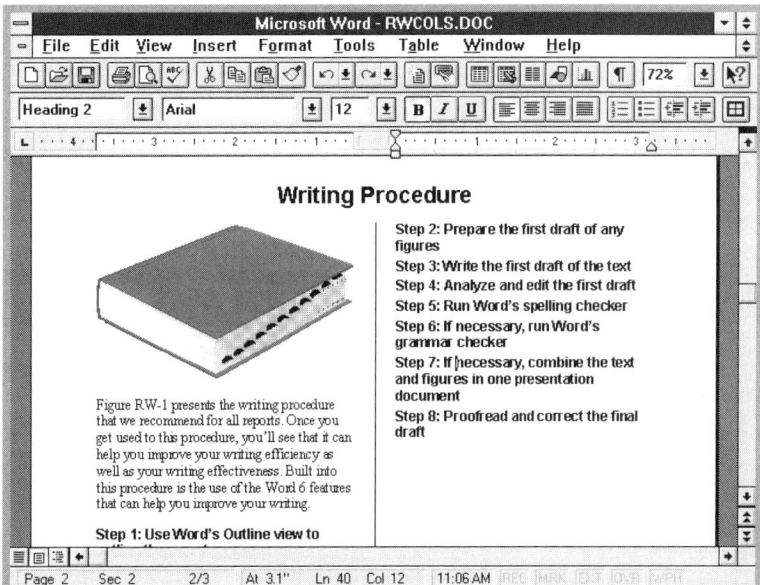

How your document should look after exercise 3

1. Open the RWCOLS file that you created in exercise set 10-1. Next, start a new paragraph after the Step 5 heading, and use the command in figure 10-5 to insert the dictionary clip art (the file named DICTNARY) into the paragraph. Then, enlarge the graphic object to 150% of its original size by dragging a corner handle. (Look in the status bar to determine the size of the object as you drag.)

2. Drag a side handle so the dictionary is only about one inch wide. What happens? Delete the paragraph mark of the paragraph that the dictionary is in. What happens? Move the dictionary so it's at the top of the left hand column. What happens? Size the dictionary so it's about an inch wider than one column. What happens?

3. Size the dictionary so it's the width of one column. Next, hold down the Shift key as you drag the top handle down to about the middle of the graphic. What happens? This is known as cropping a graphic object. Use the same technique to return the object to the way it was. (Use the status bar to tell when the object is no longer cropped.) Then, hold down the Shift key and drag the bottom handle down to add about one line of space between the dictionary and the text below it. The second section of your document should now look like the one above.

4. Double-click on the dictionary. This starts Word's drawing feature and displays its toolbars in the Word window. You could then use these toolbars to modify the graphic object. To return to the normal Word window, click on the Close Picture button in the floating Picture toolbar.

5. Use the Borders toolbar to apply a 1-1/2 point border to the dictionary. This doesn't look good, however, because the border is too close to the dictionary. Now, delete the graphic object and its border, and close the file without saving it.

How to use frames

When you use Word *frames* to store text or graphics, you get three benefits. First, you can place the frame wherever you want it in the document. Second, you can easily move or size the frame whenever you need to. And third, you can wrap text around the frame in an attractive page layout.

How to insert a frame into a document and insert text or a graphic object into the frame

The first procedure in figure 10-8 shows how to insert an empty frame into a document. Note that this frame is placed to the right of three paragraphs without using column formatting. This placement ease is one of the benefits that you get from the use of frames.

Once you create the frame, you can insert text or a graphic into it from another file. Or, you can paste text or a graphic into it from the clipboard. You can also enter text into an empty frame as you'll see in a moment.

Another way to get text or a graphic into a frame is to select the text or graphic before issuing the Frame command. Then, the frame is placed around the selection, and the frame is sized accordingly.

How to insert a frame into a document

1. Issue the Frame command from the Insert menu. If the document is in Normal view, Word will ask if you want to switch to Page Layout view. If you respond Yes, the command continues. Otherwise it's canceled.

2. Move the mouse pointer to where you want to start the frame. Then, click and drag until the frame is the desired size:

3. Release the mouse button so the frame is inserted into the document with the insertion point inside it:

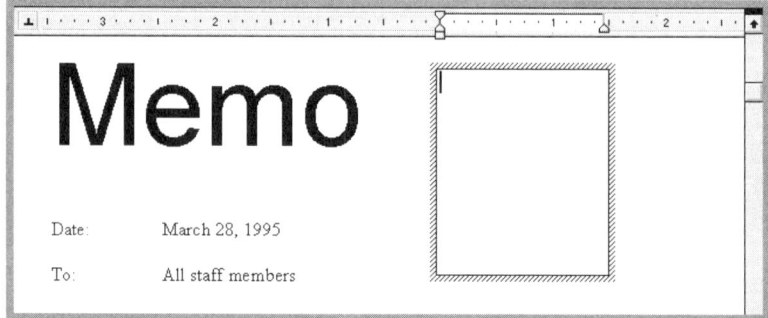

How to insert a graphic object or text into a frame

- To insert a graphic object, use the Picture command in the Insert menu. Or, paste the object from the clipboard. The height of the frame is adjusted automatically so that the object maintains its correct proportions.

- To insert text, use the File command in the Insert menu to insert an entire file. Or, paste the text from the clipboard. The height of the frame is adjusted automatically so that the text fits.

How to add a frame to a graphic object or text

- Select the text or graphic object before you issue the Frame command, and the frame is inserted around it.

Note

- Before you can insert text or a graphic object into a frame, the insertion point must be inside it as shown above, or the frame must be selected (see figure 10-10).

Figure 10-8   How to insert a frame into a document and insert a graphic object or text into the frame

How to enter, edit, and format the text in a frame

Figure 10-9 shows that you can use normal Word techniques to enter, edit, and format the text in a frame. By default, Word automatically adjusts the height of the frame to accommodate the text that you enter. It also adjusts the frame height when you change the height of the text by editing or formatting it.

If you apply a style to a paragraph inside a frame, you may be surprised by the result. In most cases, the paragraph is placed outside the frame because the style isn't defined with a frame. Even if the style is defined with a frame, however, this won't work the way you want it to. To avoid this problem, you can enter the text and apply the styles outside of a frame. Then, you can select the formatted text and add the frame to it as described in figure 10-8.

A frame as text is entered into it

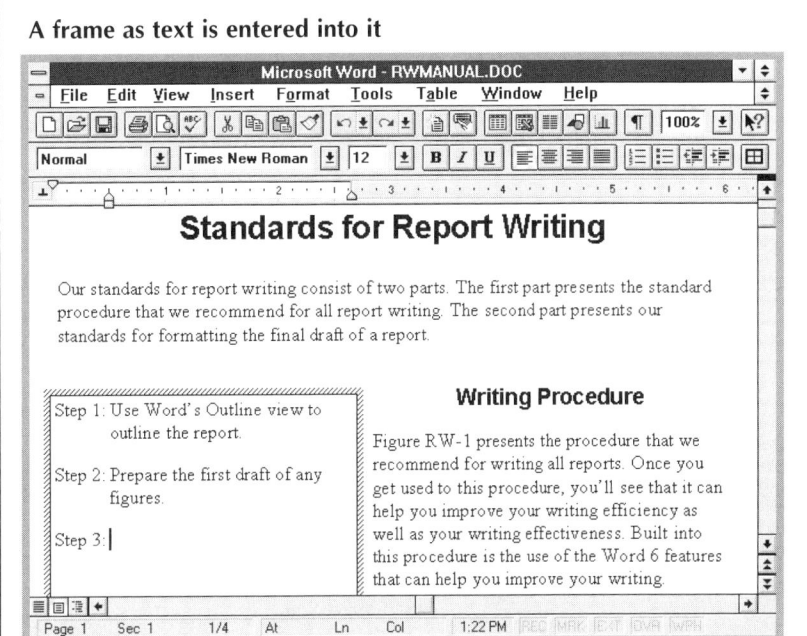

How to enter text into a frame

- Click inside the frame so Word places the insertion point there. Then, enter the text using standard Word techniques.

- By default, Word increases the height of the frame to provide for the text that you enter into it.

How to edit and format the text in a frame

- Use normal editing and direct formatting techniques. If this changes the height of the text, the frame height is automatically adjusted unless the default has been changed (see figure 10-11).

- In most cases, applying styles to the paragraphs in a frame doesn't work the way you want. If you need to use styles, apply the styles to the text, then insert the frame around the formatted text.

Figure 10-9   How to enter, edit, and format text in a frame

How to select, size, move, copy, and delete a frame

Figure 10-10 shows how you can work with a frame and its contents. To select a frame, just click on its border when the mouse pointer changes to the positioning pointer. If the frame contains a graphic object, you can also click inside the frame border to select the frame. Then, you can size, move, or copy the frame.

When you size a frame, the result depends on its contents. If the frame contains a graphic, the frame and the graphic are sized at the same time. If the frame contains text, the text size doesn't change as the frame is sized, but the text layout is adjusted to the new width of the frame. If all the text can't fit vertically in the frame, some of it may be hidden. By default, though, you can't reduce the height of a frame so it's less than what's required for the display of all the text in the frame.

A selected frame that contains a graphic object

How to select a frame

• Click on the frame's border. When the pointer is in the correct position, it changes to the positioning shape shown above.

• If the frame contains a graphic object, you can click inside the frame to select it. If you click inside a frame that is empty or contains text, the insertion point appears but the frame is not selected.

How to move or copy a selected frame

• To move a frame, drag when the mouse pointer is in the shape shown above. To copy, hold down the Ctrl key as you drag. You can also use cut, copy, and paste techniques to move or copy a frame.

How to size a selected frame that contains text

• Place the mouse pointer over a handle so it turns into a double-headed arrow and drag the handle. Or drag the frame margins in the horizontal or vertical ruler. If you decrease or increase the width of a frame, the text lines within it are adjusted to the new width.

• To maintain the proportion of height to width as you drag a corner handle, hold down the Shift key. To maintain centering that you've applied from the Frame dialog box, hold down the Ctrl key as you drag. To maintain both, hold down both keys.

How to size or crop a selected frame that contains a graphic object

• Place the mouse pointer over a handle so it turns into a double-headed arrow and drag the handle. If you want to crop the object, hold down the Shift key as you drag.

• You can also size and crop a graphic object in a frame by using the Picture command in the Format menu.

How to delete a selected frame and its contents

• Press the Delete key.

Figure 10-10 How to select, size, move, copy, or delete a frame

How to format a frame

To format a frame, you select it and issue the Frame command that's summarized in figure 10-11. This command lets you give precise settings for the size and location of a frame. Although you can use the mouse to establish the approximate size and location for a frame, you'll often want to use the Frame command to establish the final size and location. You may also find that it's easier to use the Frame command to set some locations for a frame than it is to use the mouse.

The Frame command also lets you do some things that you can't do with the mouse. In particular, it lets you choose whether or not text is wrapped around the frame. And it lets you specify how much space is left between the frame and the text outside the frame.

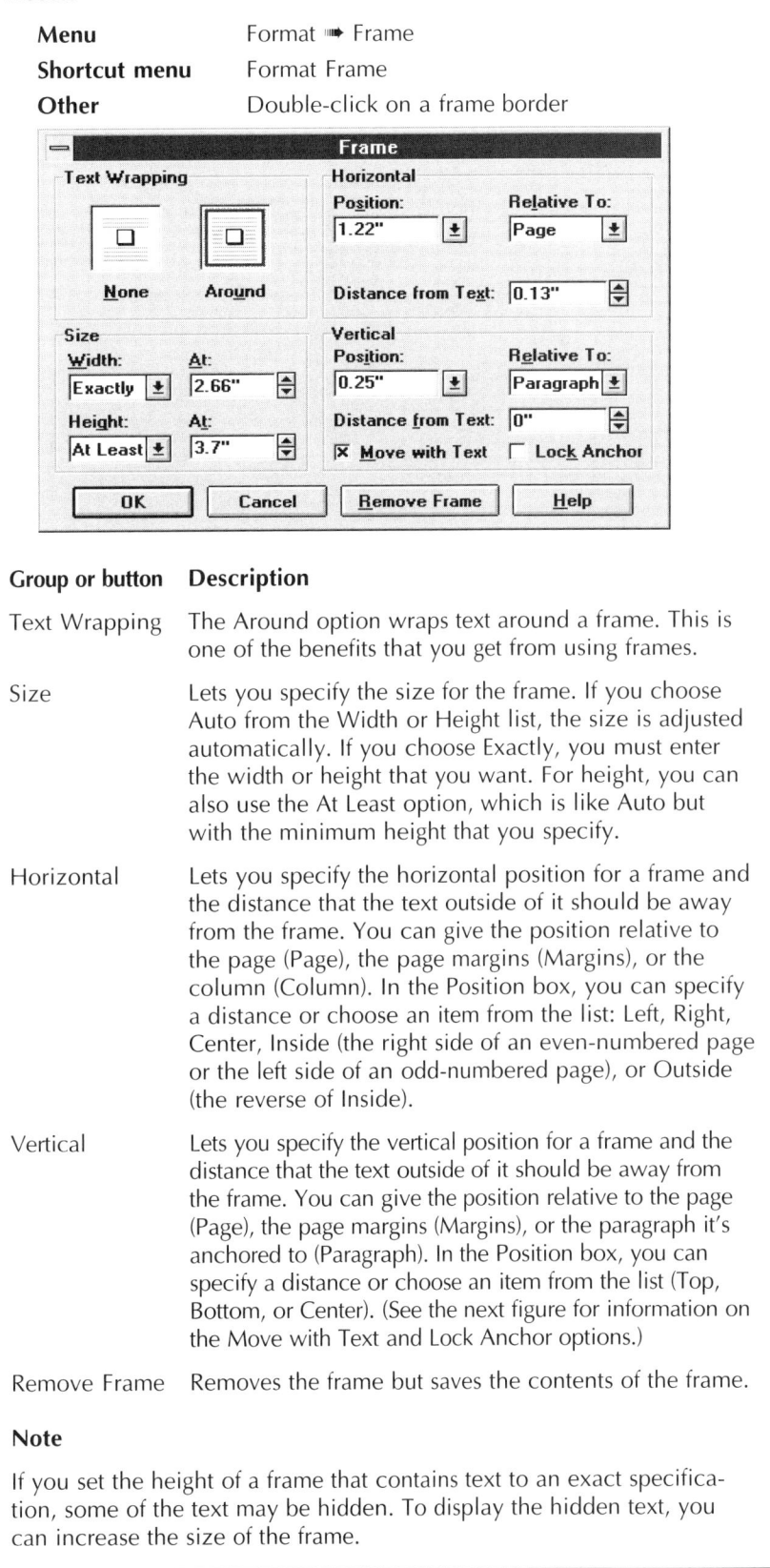

Access

Menu	Format ➡ Frame
Shortcut menu	Format Frame
Other	Double-click on a frame border

Group or button	Description
Text Wrapping	The Around option wraps text around a frame. This is one of the benefits that you get from using frames.
Size	Lets you specify the size for the frame. If you choose Auto from the Width or Height list, the size is adjusted automatically. If you choose Exactly, you must enter the width or height that you want. For height, you can also use the At Least option, which is like Auto but with the minimum height that you specify.
Horizontal	Lets you specify the horizontal position for a frame and the distance that the text outside of it should be away from the frame. You can give the position relative to the page (Page), the page margins (Margins), or the column (Column). In the Position box, you can specify a distance or choose an item from the list: Left, Right, Center, Inside (the right side of an even-numbered page or the left side of an odd-numbered page), or Outside (the reverse of Inside).
Vertical	Lets you specify the vertical position for a frame and the distance that the text outside of it should be away from the frame. You can give the position relative to the page (Page), the page margins (Margins), or the paragraph it's anchored to (Paragraph). In the Position box, you can specify a distance or choose an item from the list (Top, Bottom, or Center). (See the next figure for information on the Move with Text and Lock Anchor options.)
Remove Frame	Removes the frame but saves the contents of the frame.

Note

If you set the height of a frame that contains text to an exact specification, some of the text may be hidden. To display the hidden text, you can increase the size of the frame.

Figure 10-11   How to format a frame

How to work with anchors

As you edit a document, you may be surprised to see frames move in ways that appear to be unpredictable. The mystery may be solved, though, when you learn how *anchors* work in conjunction with frames. Figure 10-12 explains.

The basic notions are: (1) that a frame is always anchored to a paragraph, and (2) that a frame is always moved to the same page as the paragraph it's anchored to. So if a paragraph is moved to a new page due to editing, the frame that's anchored to it is also moved to that page.

To find out which paragraph a frame is anchored to, you can select the frame and display the nonprinting characters. Then, the anchor for the frame is displayed next to the paragraph that the frame is attached to. If you want the frame anchored to a different paragraph, you can drag the anchor to that paragraph. And if you want to be able to move the frame without changing the paragraph that it's anchored to, you can use the Frame command to lock the anchor to the paragraph.

A document with a locked anchor for the selected frame

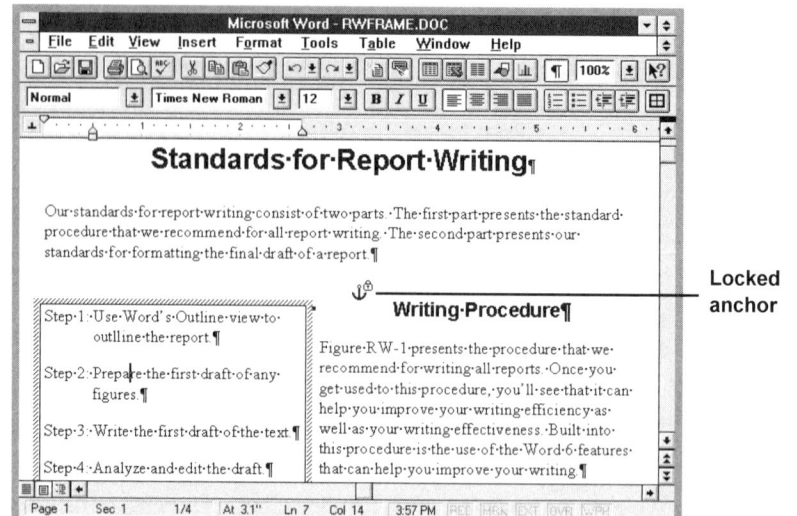

How the anchor determines frame movement

- When you create or move a frame, Word anchors it to the closest paragraph. After that, the frame maintains a relationship with that paragraph. If the document is edited and the paragraph moves to another page, the frame that's anchored to it moves too.

- To keep a frame and the first paragraph that refers to it on the same page, you can move the anchor to the appropriate paragraph.

- To keep a frame anchored to a paragraph when you move the frame, you can lock the anchor to a paragraph.

How to display the anchor for a selected frame

- Click on the Show/Hide button in the Standard toolbar. If you can't see the anchor, choose the Page Width option from the Zoom Control list in the Standard toolbar because the anchor may be in the margin.

How to move an anchor to another paragraph

- Drag the anchor symbol to another paragraph. Note, however, that you can't move an anchor when it's locked.

How to lock an anchor to a paragraph

- Check the Lock Anchor option in the Frame dialog box. When you return to the document, a padlock is added to the anchor symbol as shown above.

How to stop the movement of a frame whenever its paragraph moves

- Remove the check from the Move with Text option. However, the frame still moves when the paragraph is moved to another page.

Figure 10-12   How to work with anchors

Other skills for working with frames

Figure 10-13 presents two related skills for working with frames. First, you can use the techniques you learned in chapter 9 to add captions within frames. Second, you can use the Borders toolbar button or the Borders and Shading command to apply borders or shading to frames.

A document with a framed table that includes a caption

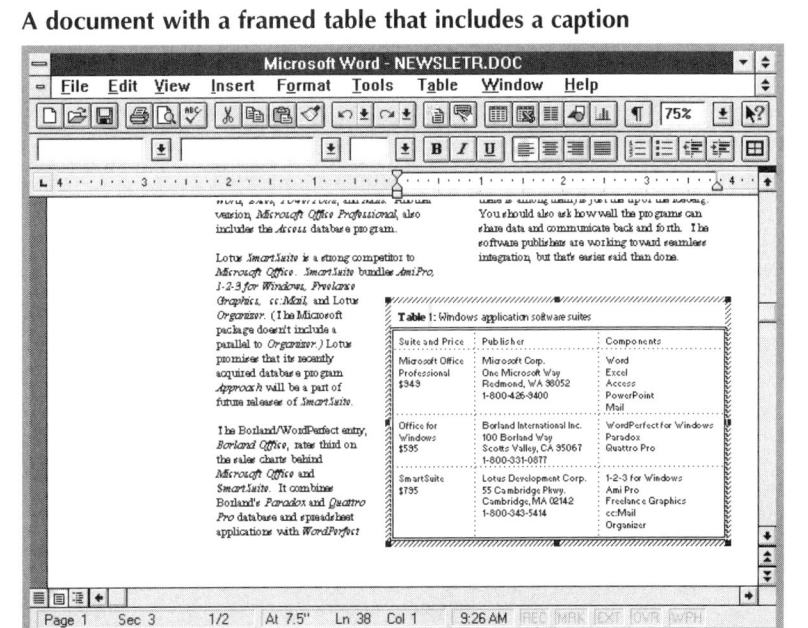

How to insert a Word caption into a frame

- Select the frame, and use the Caption command in the Insert menu to insert a caption as explained in chapter 9.

- The caption for a frame is inserted inside the frame as shown above. That way, the caption always moves with the frame.

How to apply borders or shading to a selected frame

- Use the Borders toolbar or the Borders and Shading command in the Format menu to apply the borders and shading just as you apply them to paragraphs.

- If you use a caption inside a frame, you usually don't want to apply a border or shading to the frame. Instead, you apply it to selected text or the graphic object within the frame.

- If you use the Picture command in the Insert menu to insert a graphic object into a frame, the object can't be shaded.

Note

- By default, an empty frame or a frame that contains text is outlined with a thin border. If you insert a graphic object into a frame, the border disappears.

Figure 10-13 Other skills for working with frames

Exercise set 10-3

How your document should look after exercise 1

Standards for Report Writing

Our standards for report writing consist of two parts. The first part presents the standard procedure that we recommend for all report writing. The second part presents our standards for formatting the final draft of a report.

1. Use Outline view to outline the report.
2. Prepare the final draft of any figures.
3. Write the first draft of the text.
4. Analyze and edit the first draft.
5. Run the spelling checker.
6. If necessary, run the grammar checker.
7. If necessary, combine text and figures into one document.
8. Proofread and correct the final draft.

Figure 1 Our 8-step writing procedure

Writing Procedure

Figure RW-1 presents the writing procedure that we recommend for all reports. Once you get used to this procedure, you'll see that it can help you improve your writing efficiency as well as your writing effectiveness. Built into this procedure is the use of the Word 6 features that can help you improve your writing.

Step 1: Use Word's Outline view to outline the report

Whenever you write a report, it should be divided into topics and subtopics that are clearly identified by heading and subheadings in the document. To plan these headings and subheadings, start a Word document from the RPTTEXT template and switch to Outline view. In this way, you can quickly and easily enter the headings and subheadings that you intend to use, and the indentation makes the heading levels obvious as shown in figure RW-2.

After you enter the first draft of the headings and subheadings, you can review their structure, reword them so they're more definitive, change a heading to a subheading, rearrange headings and subheadings, print the entire outline, and so on. You can also include notes below the headings and subheadings that will help you write the text later on.

The exercises that follow are designed to give you an idea of how frames can be used to lay out the pages of a document in an attractive and effective presentation format. They are just a start, however. If you need to do this type of work, please continue to experiment on your own.

1. Open the RWSTDS file that you created for chapter 4 and may have updated in subsequent chapters. Enter the numbered list shown above into the document above the Writing Procedure heading. (If you did the exercises for chapter 6, the Normal style is set up so that when you press the Enter key, a paragraph with the First Line Indent style is started. Since that's not what you want, you can change the Normal style, or you can create a new style for the numbered list.) Select the text you just entered and add a frame around it. Next, size the frame so it's about three inches wide and move it so that the top of the frame is even with the top of the Writing Procedure paragraph. Then, if you've already read chapter 9, select the text in the frame and use the Caption command in the Insert menu to insert a Figure caption below the selection with the text shown above. Now, use the Borders toolbar to apply 10% shading to the list, and your document should look like the one above.

2. Increase the width of the frame to about 4 inches to see what happens. Then, decrease the width to 2 inches. Next, move the frame so it's on the right margin instead of the left. This shows how easy it is to lay out pages when you work with frames.

3. Use the Frame command in the Format menu to size the frame so it's 2.5 inches wide with automatic adjustment for height and to center the frame both horizontally and vertically relative to the margins. This doesn't look good, but it shows what's possible.

4. Use the Show/Hide toolbar button to display the anchor for the frame. If necessary, drag the anchor to the Writing Procedure paragraph. Then, click on the Show/Hide button again to hide the nonprinting characters. Next, use the Frame command to align the frame at the right margin and zero inches from the top of the paragraph that it's anchored to.

How your document should look after exercise 6

Standards for Report Writing

Our standards for report writing consist of two parts. The first part presents the standard procedure that we recommend for all report writing. The second part presents our standards for formatting the final draft of a report.

Writing Procedure

Figure RW-1 presents the writing procedure that we recommend for all reports. Once you get used to this procedure, you'll see that it can help you improve your writing efficiency as well as your writing effectiveness. Built into this procedure is the use of the Word 6 features that can help you improve your writing.

Step 1: Use Word's Outline view to outline the report

Whenever you write a report, it should be divided into topics and subtopics that are clearly identified by heading and subheadings in the document. To plan these headings and subheadings, start a Word document from the RPTTEXT template and switch to Outline view. In this way, you can quickly and easily enter the headings and subheadings that you intend to use, and the indentation makes the heading levels obvious as shown in figure RW-2.

1. Use Outline view to outline the report.
2. Prepare the final draft of any figures.
3. Write the first draft of the text.
4. Analyze and edit the first draft.
5. Run the spelling checker.
6. If necessary, run the grammar checker.
7. If necessary, combine text and figures into one document.
8. Proofread and correct the final draft.

Figure 1 Our 8-step writing procedure

Step 2: Prepare the first draft of any figures

Step 3: Write the first draft of the text

Step 4: Analyze and edit the first draft

Step 5: Run Word's spelling checker

Step 6: If necessary, run Word's

---

5. Click outside the frame, then change the left and right page margins of the document to .8 inch. Format the document in two columns from the Writing Procedure heading to the end of the document. Then, make whatever adjustments are necessary so the top of the framed list is even with the top of the Writing Procedure heading and so the frame is the width of the column.

6. Move the insertion point to the start of the first paragraph after the Step 1 heading, and use the Picture command in the Insert menu to insert the monitor in the Word Clipart directory into the document. Next, select the picture, and use the Frame command in the Insert menu to put a frame around it. Then, use the mouse to size the frame so it's about one inch square and align it at the right side of the column and at the top of the paragraph it's anchored to. Since this doesn't look too good, use the Frame command in the Format menu to align the frame at the left margin again and move it so that it's .8 inch below the top of the paragraph it's anchored to. (It should be positioned about four lines down in the paragraph as shown above.) When you've adjusted it so it looks the way you want it, print the first page of the document, save the document with the name RWFRAME, and close it.

7. Use the New command in the File menu to start a newsletter by using the Newsletter Wizard defaults. When the wizard ends and the document is displayed, scroll through the document to see what formatting features it uses. These include columns, frames, and tables. Once you've read the first ten chapters in this book, you're familiar with all the features that are used by the Word templates and wizards so you can take full advantage of them. Now, close the document without saving it.

Perspective

If you just need to format the text in a document with columns, you should be able to do so with little extra time. You should also be able to use a few graphic objects and frames effectively in short documents without much trouble. That's why every Word user in business should at least be familiar with the use of columns, graphic objects, and frames.

When you start to use columns, graphic objects, and frames on most of the pages in a large document, though, you are clearly going beyond word processing into the area of graphic arts or desktop publishing. If you've done the exercises for this chapter, you may already realize how time consuming just the page layout can be. To do it right also requires graphic design skills that most business people don't have. For these reasons, it's usually best to assign this type of work to a graphics or desktop publishing specialist.

When it comes to extensive desktop publishing work, however, Word may not be the best program for your applications. In that case, you can export your documents to a desktop publishing program like *PageMaker*. A program like this can make it easier to do some kinds of page layout. It may also be more dependable when working with extremely large documents.

Summary

- The easiest way to apply column formatting to text is to select the text and use the Columns toolbar button. This creates columns of equal widths.

- To apply or change column formatting, you can use the Columns command in the Format menu. To change column widths, you can also use the ruler.

- To end the text in one column and skip to the top of the next column, insert a *column break* into the text. To balance the column endings on a page, insert a section break.

- To insert a graphic object into a document, use the Picture command in the Insert menu. To paste a graphic object into a document from the clipboard, use the Paste command.

- To move, copy, or size a graphic object, select the object and use the mouse to drag the border or handles.

- To insert a frame into a document, use the Frame command in the Insert menu. To format a frame, use the Frame command in the Format menu.

- To move, copy, or size a frame, select the object and use the mouse to drag the border or handles.

- Each frame is *anchored* to a paragraph and moves from page to page with that paragraph. To make sure this relationship works the way you want it to, you can move a frame's anchor to another paragraph, and you can lock the anchor so it can't be moved.

Chapter 11

How to set defaults, convert files, and get on-line help

This chapter presents three more Word features. First, it shows you how to change the way Word looks and operates by setting default options. Second, it shows you how to convert a file that was created by another program to Word 6 format, and vice versa. Third, it shows you how to use the Help feature to get on-line information about Word. Although you may not need all three features, you should read about them anyway so you can decide for yourself when they might be useful.

How to set defaults

When you install Word 6, the installation program sets up several values and codes that affect the way Word works. These are called *default options*, *default settings*, or just *defaults*. Although you can use Word without ever changing the starting defaults, you'll probably want to change some of them so Word will work the way you want it to.

To change the Word defaults, you use the Options command in the Tools menu. The dialog box that's displayed when you choose this command contains 12 tabs. Some of the options in these tabs have been referred to in other chapters of this book because they affect the way some features work. Now, you'll learn about four of these tabs in more detail.

The View options

Figure 11-1 shows the View tab of the Options dialog box. Note that this tab is slightly different when you access it from Normal view than it is when you access it from Page Layout view. If you experiment with these options, you can quickly see how they change the view of either the document window or the Word window. These options stay in effect until you change them again.

Access

Menu   Tools ➡ Options

Normal view options

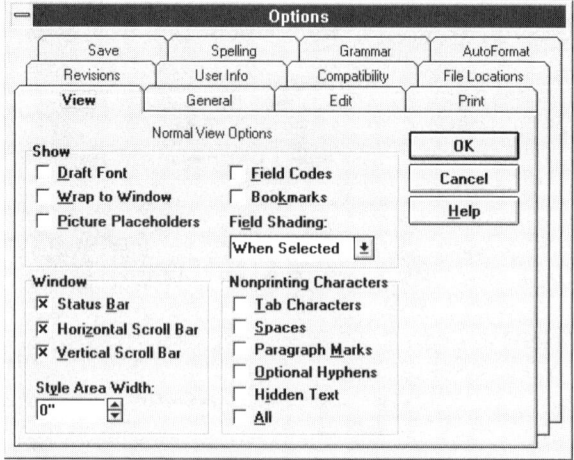

Page Layout view options

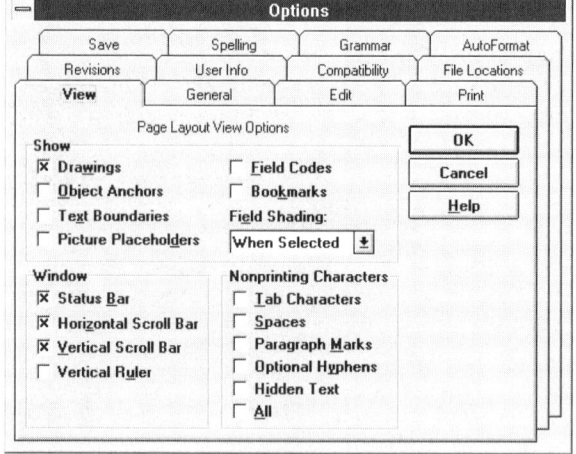

Show group

These options let you choose the way some components of a document are displayed. If you choose the Picture Placeholders option, for example, graphic objects are displayed as empty borders, which can speed up scrolling. If you choose the Always option from the Field Shading list, Word fields are always shaded, not just when they're selected.

Window group

These options let you hide or display window components.

Nonprinting Characters group

These options identify the nonprinting characters that you want displayed all the time.

Figure 11-1   How to set the View options

The Edit options

Figure 11-2 shows the Edit tab of the Options dialog box and summarizes its primary options. The options that are checked are the ones that are on by default when you install Word. Sometimes, however, new Word users don't like the way one or more of the first three options work so they turn them off.

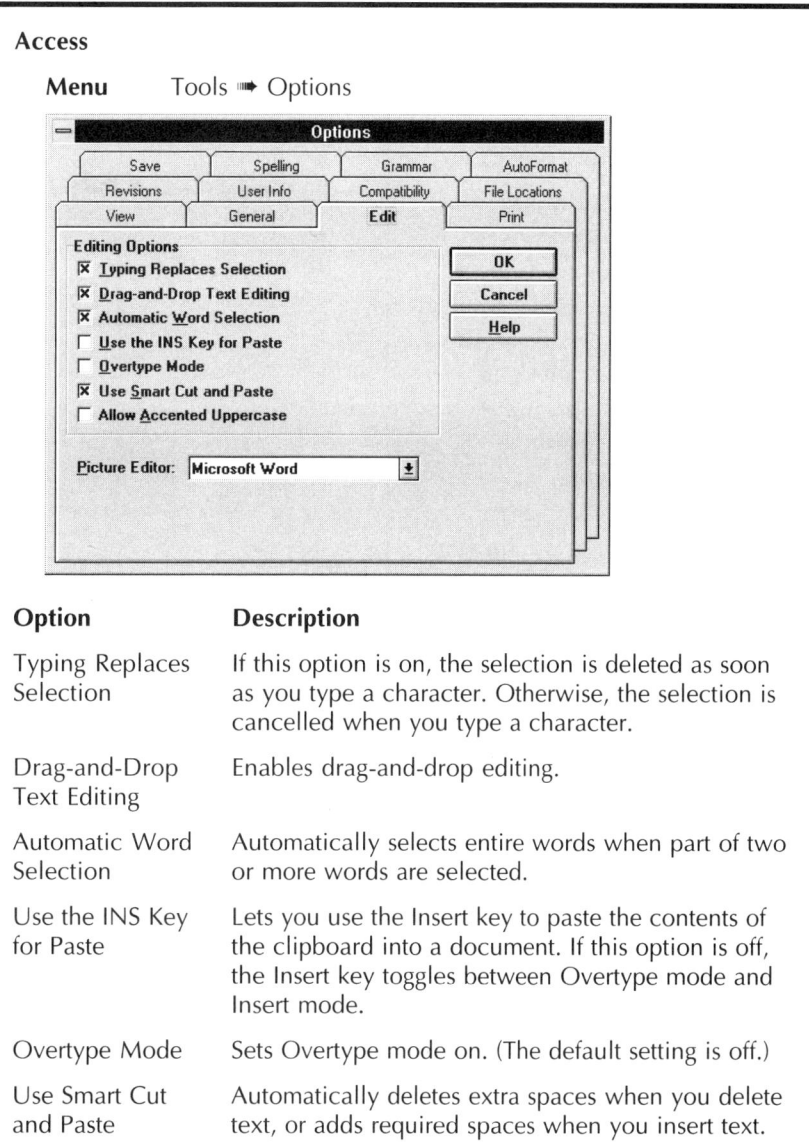

Access

Menu   Tools ➡ Options

Option	Description
Typing Replaces Selection	If this option is on, the selection is deleted as soon as you type a character. Otherwise, the selection is cancelled when you type a character.
Drag-and-Drop Text Editing	Enables drag-and-drop editing.
Automatic Word Selection	Automatically selects entire words when part of two or more words are selected.
Use the INS Key for Paste	Lets you use the Insert key to paste the contents of the clipboard into a document. If this option is off, the Insert key toggles between Overtype mode and Insert mode.
Overtype Mode	Sets Overtype mode on. (The default setting is off.)
Use Smart Cut and Paste	Automatically deletes extra spaces when you delete text, or adds required spaces when you insert text.

Figure 11-2   How to set the Edit options

The Save options

Figure 11-3 shows the Save tab of the Options dialog box and summarizes its primary options. The most important one is the Automatic Save option, which turns on the *AutoSave feature*. When this feature is on, all open documents are automatically saved at fixed time intervals. Then, if your PC fails so you aren't able to save the latest versions of the open files and exit from Word the normal way, the documents are automatically recovered when you restart Word. That way, you never lose more work than what you can do in one time interval.

If you experience frequent power failures in your area or if your PC seems to be having problems, you may want to reduce the time interval for autosaves from the installation default of 10 minutes. On the other hand, if you're working with a large document that contains so many graphic objects that the autosaves are time consuming, you may want to temporarily increase the time interval. But you should always keep this option on.

The Always Create Backup Copy option provides another form of backup. It keeps two versions of each file that you save: the latest version and the version before that, which is saved with the BAK extension. Then, if you accidentally delete or corrupt the latest version, you still have the backup version. Although you may find this additional level of protection comforting when you're new to Word, you'll probably want to drop it later on because it doubles the number of files that you create.

Access

Menu	Tools ➡ Options
Other	Click on the Options button in the Save As dialog box

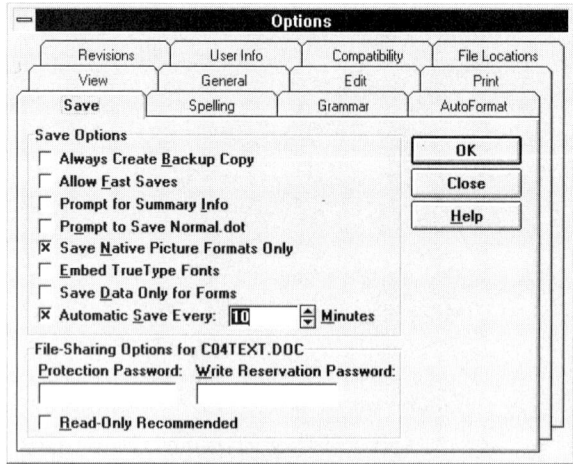

Option	Description
Always Create Backup Copy	Changes the extension of the last disk version of the active document to BAK whenever you save the document, and saves the new version with its regular name. That way, there are always two copies of each document on disk.
Prompt for Summary Info	Displays the Summary Info dialog box whenever you save a new document.
Prompt to Save Normal.dot	Displays a dialog box that asks if you want to save changes made to the Normal template. Otherwise, changes made to this template are saved automatically.
Automatic Save	By default, this option saves open documents automatically every ten minutes so you can recover them in case of a PC failure.

How the AutoSave feature works

- If your PC fails while you're using Word, you can recover the documents you were working on from the autosave files. To do that, just start Word again. As it starts, Word automatically recovers the documents from the autosave files and opens one document window for each file. In the title bar of each window, the word "Recovered" is displayed.

- If you exit from Word normally, the autosave files are deleted because they aren't needed for document recovery.

Figure 11-3   How to set the Save options

The File Locations options

Figure 11-4 shows the File Locations tab of the Options dialog box. If you've read the other chapters in this book, you should already be familiar with the five types of files in the summary.

If you use one directory for most of your Word files, you should specify that directory as the Documents location. You may also want to change the directories for graphic objects (Clipart Pictures), user templates, or workgroup templates.

If you use the AutoSave feature, you may also want to specify the directory where you want the autosave files stored. By default, these files are stored in a directory that's specified in your AUTOEXEC.BAT file. Since recovery takes place automatically, you usually don't need to know what that directory is. For unusual recovery problems, though, the autosave files will be easier to find if an autosave directory is specified in the File Locations tab. Occasionally, these files can help you recover lost text that can't be recovered through other methods.

Access

Menu   Tools ➡ Options

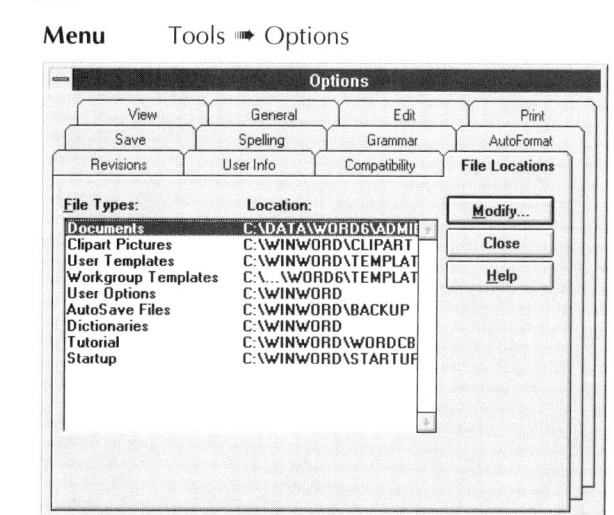

File type	Description
Documents	This is the directory that's displayed the first time you use the Open command in each Word session.
Clipart Pictures	This is the directory that's displayed the first time you use the Picture command in the Insert menu in each Word session.
User Templates	By default, Word templates and wizards are stored in the directory shown above, but you can change this. The templates in the directory you specify are displayed when you use the New command in the File menu to start a new document.
Workgroup Templates	You can use this directory for your own templates or workgroup templates. The templates in this directory are displayed along with the ones in the User Templates directory when you use the New command to start a new document.
AutoSave Files	By default, no directory is specified, and Word saves its autosave files in the TEMP directory specified in the AUTOEXEC.BAT file. If you enter a directory here, though, the autosave files are stored in that directory. Then, you can find the files more easily if you have an unusual recovery problem.

Operation

- To change the location for a file type, move the highlight to it, then click on the Modify button and choose the directory in the dialog box that follows.

- If you need to create a new directory for a file type, click on the New button when the Modify Location dialog box is displayed.

Figure 11-4   How to set the File Locations options

Exercise set 11-1

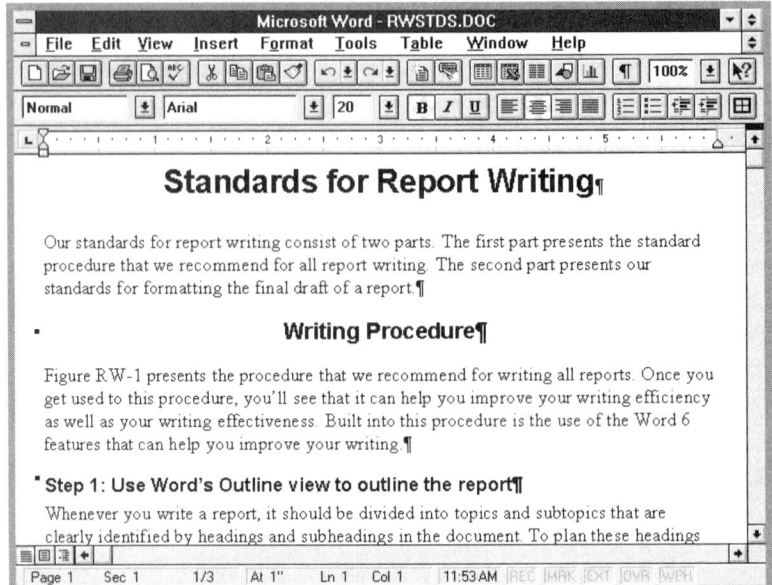

How your document should look after exercise 1 even though the nonprinting characters aren't displayed

1. Open the RWSTDS document that you created for chapter 4. Then, access the View tab of the Options dialog box, turn on the Paragraph Marks option in the Nonprinting Characters group, and return to the document. Click on the Show/Hide button in the Standard toolbar to see that the paragraph marks are displayed as shown above whether or not the other nonprinting characters are displayed. If you like working with the paragraph marks displayed, keep this option on. Otherwise, return to the View tab and turn it off.

2. Access the Save tab of the Options dialog box. Is the Automatic Save option on? If not, turn it on. What is the time interval for this option? If you want your files saved more or less frequently, change this interval now. Next, access the File Locations tab. What directory if any is given for AutoSave Files? What directory is given for Documents? If you want to change these directories, do so now.

3. With the Options dialog box still open, this is a good time to review the other options that have been mentioned in this book. Does the User Info tab contain the correct information? Does the General tab provide for at least the last four file names at the bottom of the File menu? Does the Print tab provide for the updating of fields (like a table of contents field) whenever a document is printed? This is a useful option that should be on by default. Now, click on the OK button to save any changes you made and close the Options dialog box.

4. Access the Save As dialog box and click on the Options button. This is another way to get to the Save options. Similarly, you can access the Print options from the Print dialog box, the Spelling options from the Spelling dialog box, and so on. Now, close the dialog box, and close the file without saving it.

How to convert files to and from Word 6 format

If you're converting to Word 6 from an earlier release of Word or from another word processing program, you'll probably want to convert your existing files to Word 6 format. Occasionally, you may also want to convert some of your Word 6 files to the format of some other program. When you use Word 6, both types of conversion are easy to do.

How to open a file created by another program

Figure 11-5 shows how to use the Open command to open a file created by another program and convert it to Word 6 format. Usually, you can just choose the All Files option from the List Files of Type list, then highlight the file you want to open and click on the OK button. Word does the rest automatically.

If Word doesn't recognize the format of the file you're trying to convert, you can usually solve the problem by using the program that created the file to convert the file to an intermediate format that Word does recognize. To convert a WordPerfect 6 file to Word 6, for example, you can first use WordPerfect 6 to save the file in WordPerfect 5.1 format. Then, Word can convert the WordPerfect 5.1 file to Word 6.

When Word converts a file, the characters are usually transferred to the new format without any problems. The conversion of the formatting, though, is likely to be something less than perfect. For a large document, this may mean that you have to do a considerable amount of formatting to get the

Access

Menu	File ➡ Open
Shortcut key	Ctrl+O
Standard toolbar	

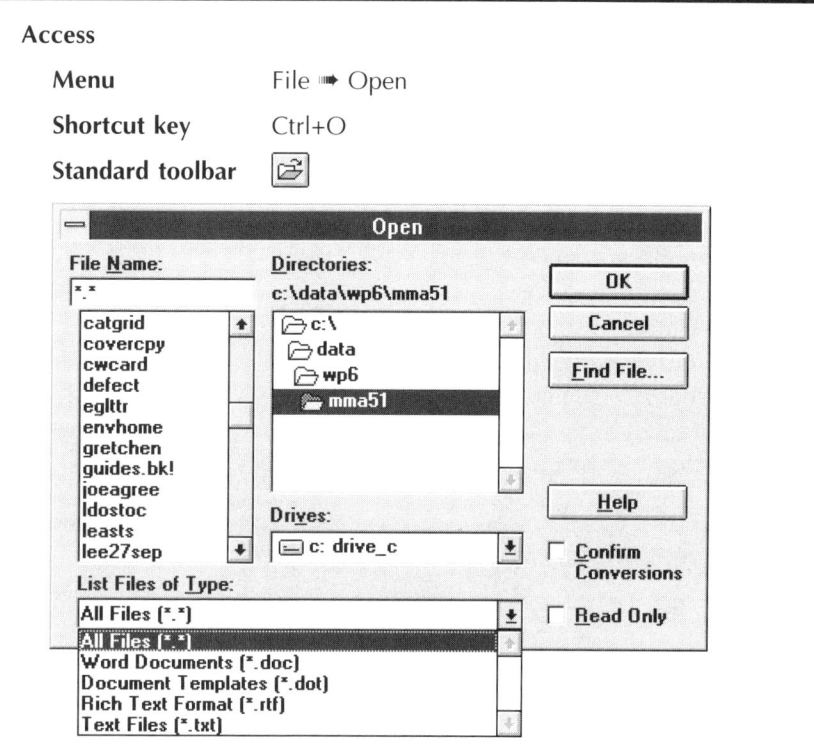

Operation

- Choose the All Files option from the List Files of Type list so all the file names are displayed, not just those with the DOC extension.

- Identify the drive and directory that contains the file, highlight the name of the file you want to convert, and click on the OK button. For most file formats, that's all it takes.

- If you open a file that was created by a spreadsheet or database program, the data is converted to a Word table. For a spreadsheet file, Word displays a dialog box that lets you choose a worksheet, a named range, or the entire spreadsheet for conversion.

The dialog box that's displayed when the Confirm Conversions option is checked or when Word doesn't recognize the file format

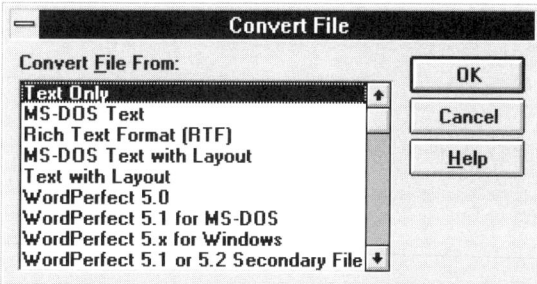

- Click on the OK button to confirm that Word has correctly identified the file format. Or, choose another format if you don't think the highlighted one is correct.

Figure 11-5   How to open a file created by another program

document the way you want it. Even if the formatting is converted properly, you'll probably want to make some changes to take advantage of the Word 6 features.

Keep in mind, then, that you can use shortcut keys with styles to quickly format paragraphs. And you can use the Replace command to find and replace various types of formatting including styles. With these features and the other skills that you've learned in this book, you should be able to quickly and easily format a converted document the way you want it.

How to save a file created by another program as a Word 6 file

Figure 11-6 shows two methods for saving a file created by another program as a Word 6 file. The first method is usually better because it lets you choose a new directory for the file and change the file name. With the second method, a dialog box is displayed that forces you to decide what format you want to save the file in. This protects you from saving the file in the original format by accident and then closing the file. The limitation of this method is that it doesn't let you change the directory and file name.

Additional information

✓ You can use the File command in the Insert menu to convert and insert a file into a document.

✓ You can use the Database command in the Insert menu to convert and insert a database file into a document as a table.

Access

   Menu   File ➧ Save As

   Shortcut key   F12

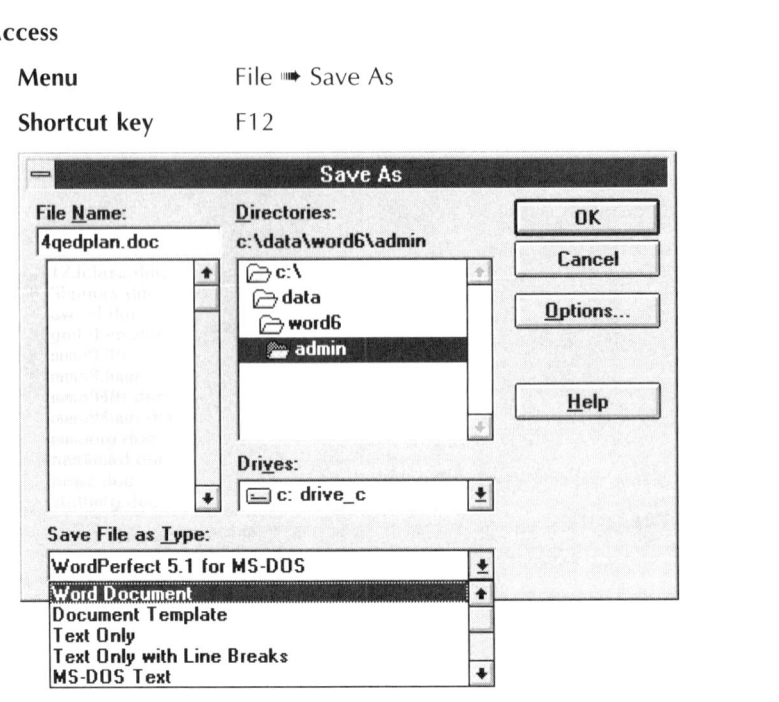

Method 1

- Access the Save As dialog box, and choose the Word Document option from the Save File as Type list. The extension for the file name in the File Name box then changes to DOC.

- If necessary, identify the drive and directory where you want to save the file using the Drives and Directories boxes. You can also change the file name if you need to. Then, click on the OK button to save the file in Word 6 format.

Method 2

1. Issue the Save command instead of the Save As command, and Word displays this dialog box:

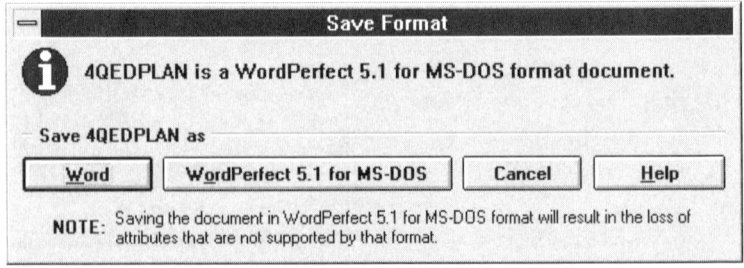

2. Click on the Word button to save the file as a Word document. Note, however, that you can't change the file name or directory this way.

Figure 11-6   **How to save a file created by another program as a Word 6 file**

How to save a Word 6 file in another program's format

If you work with people who haven't yet converted to Word 6, you may have to convert Word 6 files to their formats from time to time. Figure 11-7 shows how. Just choose the type of file from the Save File as Type list and complete the dialog box.

If Word doesn't provide for the program that you want to transfer the file to, you can probably solve the problem with an intermediate file format. If, for example, you save the file in WordPerfect 5.1 format, most other programs will be able to convert it to their formats.

Access

Menu	File ➥ Save As
Shortcut key	F12

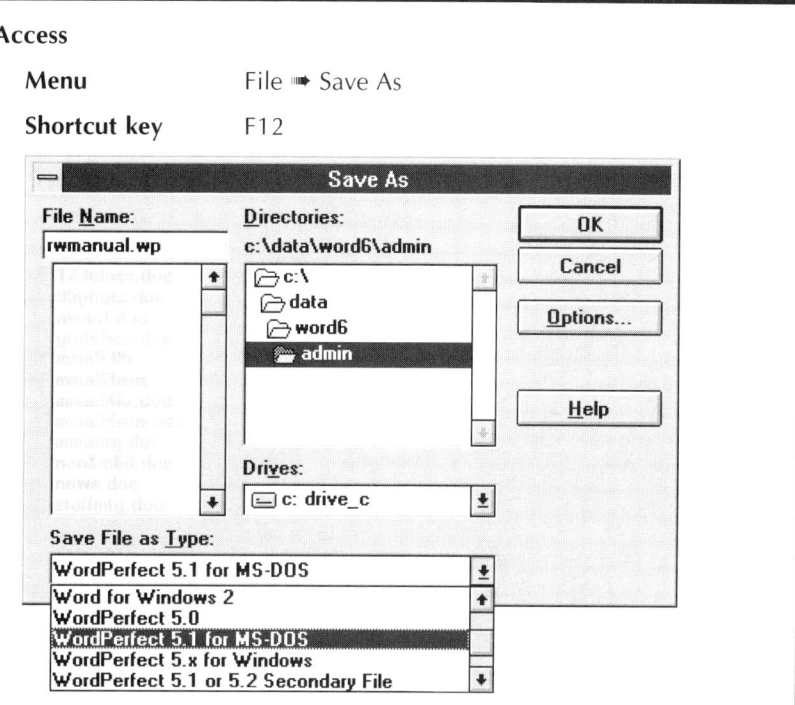

Operation

- Choose the file format that you want to save the Word document in from the Save File as Type list.

- Change the file name in the File Name box or at least change the extension so you'll be able to identify the format of the new file.

Notes

- If you can't save the file in the format of the program that you want to transfer the file to, the WordPerfect 5.1 for MS-DOS format will usually work as an intermediate format because most programs can convert a file from that format.

- If all else fails, you can save the Word document as a text file, which has a generic format that can be used to transfer text from one program to another. All programs should be able to convert files from that format, but you lose all character and paragraph formatting.

- When you save a file that you've converted to another format, Word displays the Save Format dialog box shown in figure 11-6. This dialog box lets you save the document as a Word file or in the format it was converted to.

Figure 11-7   How to save a Word 6 file in another program's format

Exercise set 11-2

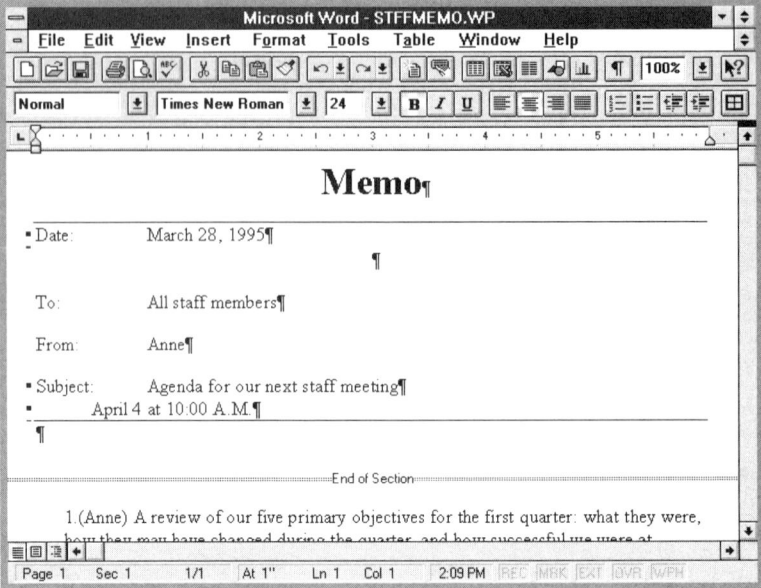

How the STFFMEMO document looks after you save it in WordPerfect 5.1 format and open it again

1. Open the STFFMEMO file that you created for chapter 3. Then, save it in WordPerfect 5.1 for MS-DOS format as STFFMEMO.WP (be sure to change the extension), and close the file. When Word asks if you want to save the changes to the file, click on the No button since no changes were made.

2. Access the Open dialog box, check the Confirm Conversions option, and open the STFFMEMO.WP file. Did any of the formatting change? If so, it just shows that file conversion is an imperfect process.

3. Use the Save command as described in the second method in figure 11-6 to save the file in Word 6 format, but keep the extension as WP. Then, close the file.

When and how to use the Help feature

If you experiment with the Help feature of Word, you'll see that it provides a wide variety of information. In general, this information is most useful when you already know how to use a function or feature, but you just can't remember some detail.

In contrast, the Help information is least useful when you're trying to learn the basics of Word or how to use a new feature or function. In those cases, the Help information is likely to frustrate you. For those purposes, you need a book like this one that presents only the information you need in a logical presentation sequence.

An introduction to the commands in the Help menu

Figure 11-8 shows the Help menu and summarizes its commands. When you issue one of these commands, a window opens for the Help information. This window is actually an application window for a separate program that provides the Help information. As a result, you can minimize, maximize, restore, move, and size the window using standard techniques.

The Help menu

Help
Contents
Search for Help on...
Index
Quick Preview
Examples and Demos
Tip of the Day...
WordPerfect Help...
Technical Support
About Microsoft Word...

Command	Function
Contents	Displays the table of contents for the Help information.
Search for Help on	Searches for Help information on a particular topic.
Index	Displays an alphabetical list of the Help topics.
Quick Preview	Presents three tutorials on how to work with Word 6.
Examples and Demos	Presents examples and demos for Word features and functions.
Tip of the Day	Displays tips about working with Word 6. Also lets you turn this feature on so a tip is displayed each time you start Word.
WordPerfect Help	Displays the Word equivalents for WordPerfect operations. You can also access this command by double-clicking on the WPH indicator in the status bar.
Technical Support	Gives answers to common technical questions and describes how to get technical support from Microsoft.
About Microsoft Word	Displays copyright information about Word. Also lets you access the System Info dialog box for technical information about your PC's configuration.

Figure 11-8   The commands of the Help menu

How to get context-sensitive Help information

Although you can use the Help menu to get the information that you need, using one of the techniques in figure 11-9 is usually quicker. When you use these techniques, you get *context-sensitive* information. In other words, you get information about the function you're trying to perform without having to search for it.

In the first screen in figure 11-9, you can see the context-sensitive Help information for the Save As command. This illustrates both the strength and weakness of the Help information that you get with Word. The strength is that the Help window offers a large amount of information. The weakness is that the information introduces complexities (like document protection and macros) that are likely to confuse and distract you rather than help you.

You can also get context-sensitive Help about a document component like a paragraph, picture, or frame. To do that, you use the Help button in the Standard toolbar. In the second screen in figure 11-9, for example, you can see the formatting information for a frame.

Three ways to get context-sensitive Help information

- Press the F1 key after you've started an operation.

- Click on the Help button in a dialog box.

- Click on the Help button in the Standard toolbar. Then, click on the menu command, toolbar button, or component that you want to get information about.

The context-sensitive Help information for the Save As command

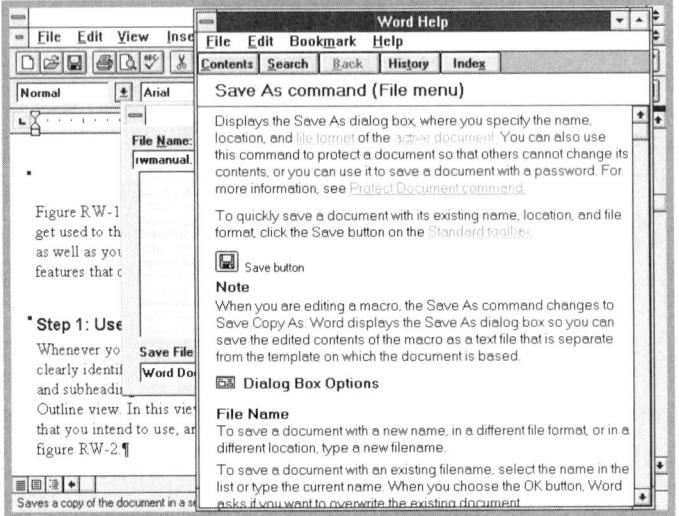

The formatting information box that's displayed when you click the Help pointer on a document component like a paragraph or frame

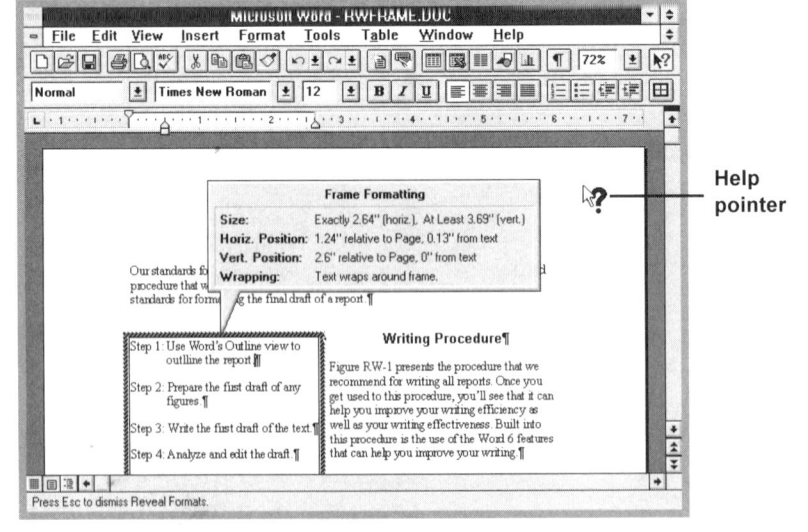

Help pointer

Figure 11-9   How to get context-sensitive Help information

How to navigate through the Help information

Figure 11-10 shows the opening window for the Contents command of the Help menu. As you can see, this command displays the table of contents for Word's Help information. To choose an entry from the table of contents, you just click on it. Then, Word displays a list of topics for that entry so you can choose from them.

You can also use the buttons in the Help window to navigate through the Help information. The button you're most likely to use is the Search button, which you'll learn more about in a moment. In addition, you can use the Back button to return to the previous Help screen. You can use the History button to display a list of the topics you've used and to return to any of those topics. And you can use the Index button to display the index for the Help information.

Access

Menu	Help ➡ Contents
Shortcut key	F1 (when no operation is in progress)

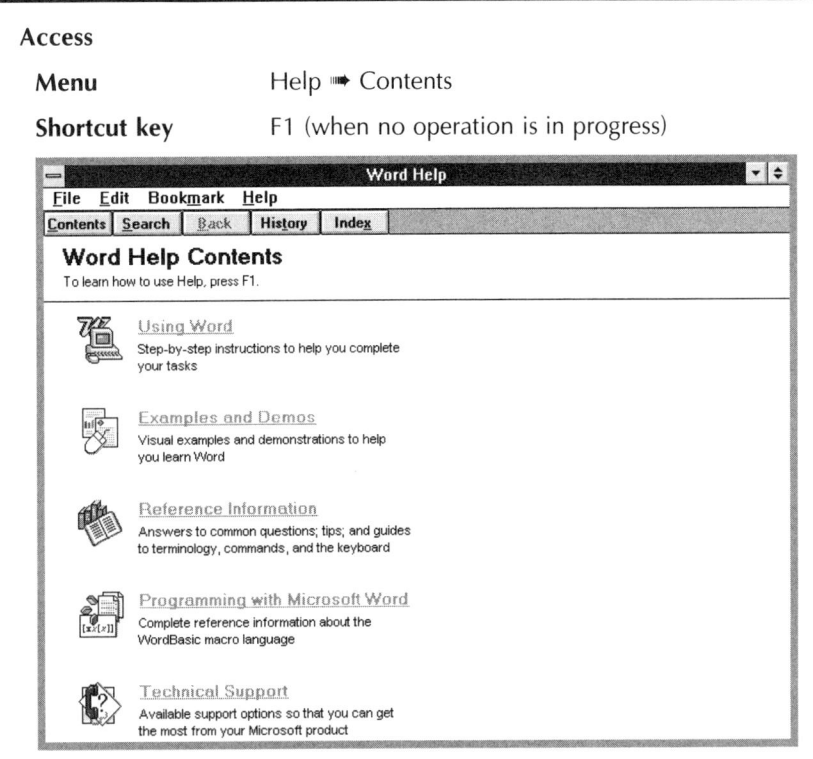

Operation

- To choose an entry from the table of contents, click on the icon or the underlined title. Then, Word displays a list of the topics or demos that are available for that entry. To continue, click on a topic title or demo button.

- To return to the first table of contents screen shown above, click on the Contents button.

- To display the Search dialog box, click on the Search button.

- To return to the previous screen, click on the Back button.

- To display a list of the topics you've used in the current Help session, click on the History button. Then, you can return to a topic by double-clicking on it.

- To display the Help index, click on the Index button.

Figure 11-10   How to use the Contents command

When you click on the Search button, a dialog box like the one in figure 11-11 is displayed. However, you can also access this dialog box without going through the table of contents by using the other access methods shown in this figure. The easiest way is to double-click on the Help button in the Standard toolbar.

In the Search dialog box, you enter text that identifies the operation or feature you want information on. Then, Help displays a list that's based on the text you enter. When you choose an item from the list, Help displays another list that contains the topics that are available for that item. Then, you can choose a topic to display its Help information.

How to print Help information

If you want to keep a permanent copy of the information that you find through the Help feature, you have a couple of options. First, you can print a copy of the current topic by issuing the Print Topic command from the File menu of the Help application window. Second, you can copy a topic or a portion of a topic to the clipboard by issuing the Copy command from the Edit menu of the Help application window. Then, you can paste the information into a Word document and print that document.

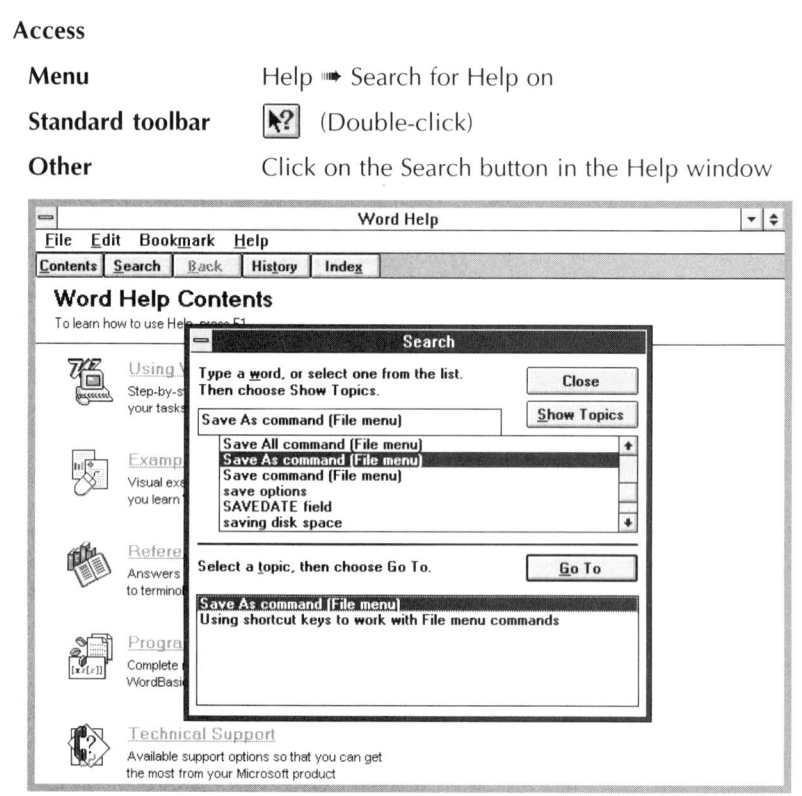

Access

Menu	Help ➡ Search for Help on
Standard toolbar	[?] (Double-click)
Other	Click on the Search button in the Help window

Procedure

1. Access the Search dialog box, then enter text in the text box near the top of the dialog box to scroll the list below the text box.

2. Double-click on an item in the list or highlight an item and click on the Show Topics button. The topics for that item are displayed in the list at the bottom of the dialog box.

3. Double-click on a topic in the list or highlight a topic and click on the Go To button to display the information for that topic.

Figure 11-11   How to use the Search for Help on command

Exercise set 11-3

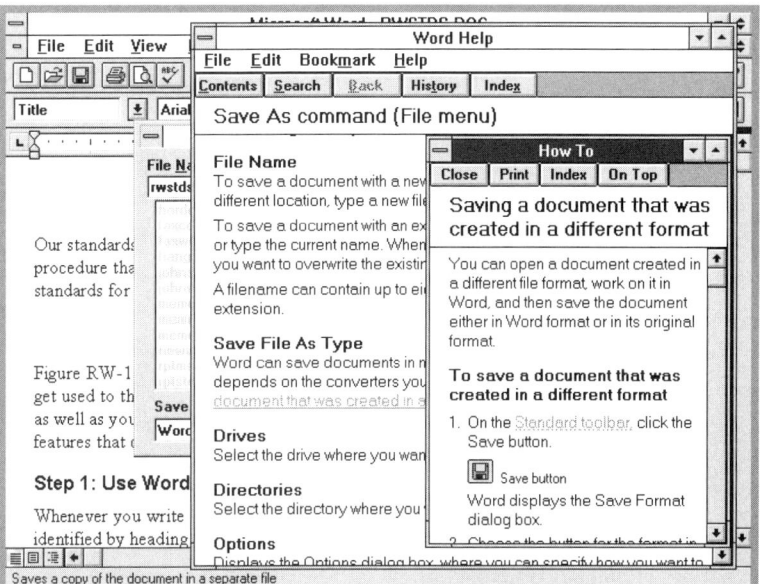

The Help information that you display in exercise 1

1. Open the RWSTDS file, and choose the Save As command from the File menu. When the dialog box appears, click on the Help button or press F1 to display context-sensitive Help information. Drag the sides of the Help window to show that you can change its size, and drag the title bar to shown that you can move the window. Then, look for a reference in the Help text about saving a document that was created in another format. Click on that reference to access the How To window for that topic as shown above. Is the information useful and easy to understand?

2. Click on the Close button to close the How To window, and click on the Contents button to display the Help table of contents. Click on the Reference Information entry to display its subentries, and click on the Menu Commands subentry. Can you display information about a specific command like the Save As command this way? No, you can't, and that obviously limits the value of this navigation path.

3. Click on the Search button and enter the letter *s* in the Search dialog box. Then, highlight "Save As command (File menu)," click on the Show Topics button, and double-click on the "Save As command (File menu)" topic. Is this the same information that was displayed when you first accessed Help from the Save As dialog box? Click on the Search button to return to the Search dialog box, click on the Show Topics button for the Save As command again, and double-click on the "Using shortcut keys" topic to find out what the shortcut key is for this command.

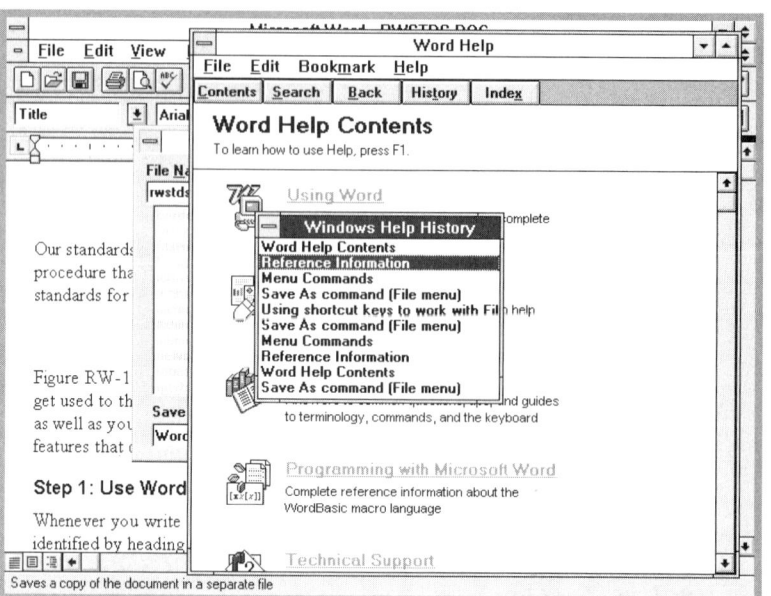

**The Help window after you click on
the History button in exercise 4**

4. Click on the Close button in the How To window, and click on the Back button three times to return to the table of contents. Then, click on the History button to display a list of the Help topics you've accessed. Double-click on the first entry for the Save As command to display that Help information again. Then, double-click on the control-menu box for the Help window to close that window and return to the Save As dialog box. Click on the Cancel button to cancel the operation.

5. Click on the Help button in the Standard toolbar, pull down the File menu, and click on the Save As command. This is another way to access Help information for a command or toolbar button. Now, pull down the File menu in the Help window. If you choose the Print Topic command, the Help information is printed. Instead, choose the Exit command to close the Help window and return to the document.

6. Click on the Help toolbar button again, then click on the first heading paragraph to display its formatting information, click on the first text paragraph to display its formatting information, and click on the status bar to display its Help information. Double-click on the control-menu box of the Help window to close this window.

7. Close the RWSTDS document without saving it.

Perspective

This chapter presents the last of the commands and features that you need to know to use Word efficiently and professionally. Although Word provides many other commands and features, most of them are either so limited that you can easily get by without them or so advanced that most Word users in business don't need them. For a summary of the features that aren't presented in this book, please review the appendix that follows.

Summary

- The Options command in the Tools menu lets you access 12 tabs that you can use to change the Word *defaults*.

- You can use the Open command to open a file that was created by another program and convert it to Word 6 format. And you can use the Save As command to save a file in another program's format.

- As you perform an operation, you can get *context-sensitive* Help information by pressing F1 or clicking on the Help button in a dialog box. You can also use the Help button in the Standard toolbar and the commands in the Help menu to get Help information.

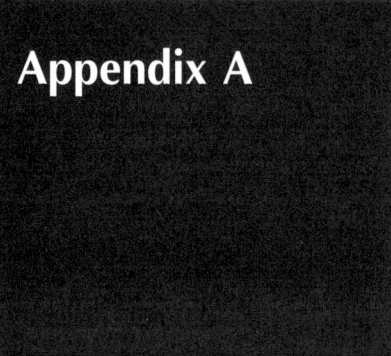

Appendix A

The Word features and commands that aren't presented in this book

If you master the features and commands that are presented in this book, you're going to be a thoroughly competent Word user. And yet, you may be wondering what you've missed. Are there useful features and commands that you aren't aware of? Are there features and commands that could help you work even better?

To help you answer those questions, this appendix summarizes the features and commands that aren't presented in this book. Its purpose is to save you the time that it takes to search through menus, Help information, books, and manuals as you try to find out what each feature and command does. Then, if you find a feature or command in this summary that you think you need for the type of work that you do, you can learn more about it.

If you're a Word user in business, one of the features that you're likely to need is the Mail Merge feature. This feature makes it easy to prepare form letters, envelopes, labels, and lists for the records in a data file. This feature also lets you create and maintain data files. Or, if you prefer, you can use the Mail Merge feature with data files that are created and maintained by other programs. This feature is so useful, in fact, that we created a mini-book about it called *How to use the Mail Merge feature.* You can think of this mini-book as a final section in this book, because it uses the same presentation methods including practice exercises.

If you decide that you need some of the other features or commands and you have trouble learning how to use them on your own, we also offer a reference book called *The Essential Guide to Word 6.* In case you have it, the summary includes references to its chapters and figures. As you can see, this book covers almost all of the Word features and commands.

Now that you've read this book, though, you should be able to master many of the minor features and commands without any manuals or books. If, for example, you want Word to check the grammar in a document, try using the Grammar command in the Tools menu. If you want to add notes to a document that can be viewed but aren't printed, try using the Annotation command in the Insert menu and then the Annotations command in the View menu. Or if you want to find a misplaced file, try using the Find File command in the File menu. As long as you know what the feature or command is supposed to do, you will often be able to get the results you want after a few minutes of experimentation.

As you gain confidence, you'll find that experimentation is often the quickest and best way to learn new commands and to refresh your memory about how to use other commands. Just access a command, study its dialog box, maybe click on the Help button for more information, try some options, and learn by doing. All good professionals do that for the commands that they use infrequently because no one can remember how all the commands and options work.

Major features

Feature	Description	Reference
Mail Merge	This feature lets you prepare form letters, envelopes, labels, and lists for the records in a data file. It also makes it easy for you to create and maintain a data file or to use a data file that's maintained by another program.	How to use the Mail Merge feature or Essential Guide: Chapter 24
Microsoft Graph	This is a separate program that comes with Word 6, but it's so tightly integrated with Word 6 that it appears to be part of the same program. With Microsoft Graph, you can create charts from the data in tables in much the same way that you create charts from the data in a worksheet when you use a spreadsheet program.	Essential Guide: Chapter 20

Minor features

Feature	Description	Essential Guide reference
Drawing	This feature lets you create object-oriented drawings in your documents by using the tools in the Drawing toolbar.	Chapter 19
Grammar checking	Word analyzes your documents for grammar and style errors, reports problems, suggests corrections, and calculates readability scores.	Figures 10-7 to 10-10
Workgroup tools	These tools help you work more productively in a group by providing for document protection, annotations, and revision marking.	Chapter 25
Indexing	The Index tab in the Index and Tables dialog box lets you mark the entries for an index and prepare the index from the marked entries. You can also use a concordance file to identify the entries for an index.	Figures 22-8 to 22-10
Master Document	This feature lets you treat several files as a single document so you can more easily reorganize the document, number the pages, prepare a table of contents, and so on.	Figure 27-5 (introduction only)
Legal documents	The Pleading Wizard helps you prepare a legal pleading paper. The Table of Authorities tab in the Index and Tables dialog box helps you prepare that kind of table.	Figure 27-9 (introduction only)
Equation program	The Equation program that comes with Word 6 helps you prepare scientific and mathematical equations.	Figure 27-8 (introduction only)
WordArt	The WordArt program that comes with Word 6 lets you apply artistic effects to text that go well beyond the basic formatting features of Word.	Figure 27-7 (introduction only)
Customization	Word 6 lets you customize the toolbars, menus, and keyboard layout.	Figures 21-4 to 21-7 (toolbars only)
Forms	With this feature, you can create forms that can be filled in on-line. The fields that can be filled in are called *form fields*, and the rest of the document is protected from changes.	Figure 27-3 (introduction only)
Recording macros	This feature lets you record the use of commands and keystrokes in a *macro*. Then, you can play the macro whenever you want to repeat the recorded commands and keystrokes.	Figure 27-1 (introduction only)
WordBasic	WordBasic is the macro language that comes with Word 6. It can be used to create powerful macros. However, it is a language for programmers, not business people.	Figure 27-2 (introduction only)
Object Linking & Embedding	This is actually a Windows feature that's supported by Word 6. It lets you embed or link an object from another program in a Word document and maintain a relationship with the object so it is always up-to-date in the document.	Chapter 26

Miscellaneous commands

Command	Function	Essential Guide reference
File ➡ Find File	Lets you find files with the name or extension that you specify on the disk drive that you specify. It also lets you copy, print, and delete any of the files that are found. For most file management, though, we recommend the use of the Windows File Manager.	Figures 12-9 to 12-15
View ➡ Full Screen	Switches to or from Full Screen view. In this view, the title bar, toolbars, and ruler are hidden so the document occupies the full screen.	Figure 3-5
View ➡ Annotations	Opens the annotations pane so you can see any annotations that have been inserted into the document.	Figure 22-6
Insert ➡ Page Numbers	Inserts headers or footers into a document that consist of page numbers only.	Figure 8-8
Insert ➡ Annotation	Lets you enter an annotation into a document.	Figure 22-5
Insert ➡ Field	Lets you insert a Word *field* like the date field or the file name field into a document. In all, Word provides for more than 70 fields.	Figure 27-4 (introduction only)
Insert ➡ Form Field	Lets you insert *form fields* into a document as part of the Forms feature.	Figure 27-3 (introduction only)
Insert ➡ Cross-reference	Lets you insert a field that refers to a document component like a heading, table, or figure. This field can be automatically updated when the component or page numbering changes.	Figure 27-6
Insert ➡ File	Lets you insert a file into the active document.	Figures 12-6, 17-20
Insert ➡ Object	Lets you insert an embedded object into the active document as part of the Object Linking and Embedding feature.	Figures 26-1, 26-2
Insert ➡ Database	Lets you insert a database file into the active document as a table.	Figure 24-23
Format ➡ Drop Cap	Lets you format the first few characters in a paragraph as dropped capital letters.	Figure 5-12
Format ➡ AutoFormat	Automatically formats a document based on the options that you choose.	Figure 7-7
Tools ➡ Hyphenation	Lets you start automatic hyphenation.	Figures 7-8, 7-9
Tools ➡ Language	Lets you specify the language that you want to use for selected text.	Figure 27-10
Tools ➡ Word Count	Displays statistics for the current document including the number of pages, words, characters, paragraphs, and lines.	Figure 7-15
Tools ➡ Envelopes and Labels	Lets you prepare envelopes and labels.	Chapter 23
Tools ➡ Protect Document	Lets you set protection options and a password for the active document.	Figure 25-2
Tools ➡ Revisions	Lets you specify revision options for the active document.	Figures 25-3 to 25-6

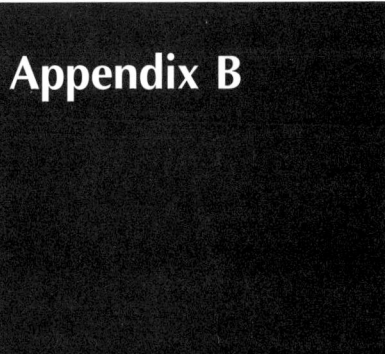

Shortcut keys for working with Word 6

This appendix summarizes the keys for working with the functions that are presented in this book. These keys are most useful when you're entering text into a document. That way, you can issue commands and apply formatting without using the mouse so your hands never leave the keyboard.

Keys that issue menu commands

Key	Command
Ctrl+N	New
Ctrl+O or Ctrl+F12	Open
Ctrl+S or Shift+F12	Save
F12	Save As
Ctrl+P or Ctrl+Shift+F12	Print
Ctrl+Z	Undo
Ctrl+Y or F4	Repeat
Ctrl+X	Cut
Ctrl+C or Shift+F2	Copy
Ctrl+V	Paste
Ctrl+A	Select All
Ctrl+F	Find
Ctrl+H	Replace
Ctrl+G or F5	Go To
Ctrl+Shift+F5	Bookmark
Ctrl+K	AutoFormat
F7	Spelling
Shift+F7	Thesaurus

Keys that move the insertion point in a document

Key	Moves the insertion point
Ctrl+Left-arrow	Left one word
Ctrl+Right-arrow	Right one word
Ctrl+Up-arrow	Up one paragraph
Ctrl+Down-arrow	Down one paragraph
Home	To the beginning of the line
End	To the end of the line
Ctrl+Home	To the beginning of the document
Ctrl+End	To the end of the document
Page-up	Up one screen
Page-down	Down one screen
Ctrl+Page-up	To the top of the current screen
Ctrl+Page-down	To the bottom of the current screen
Ctrl+Alt+Page-up	Up one page
Ctrl+Alt+Page-down	Down one page
Shift+F5	To the previous editing location (Word remembers your last three editing locations)

Keys that move the insertion point in a table

Key	Moves the insertion point
Tab	One cell to the right or from the last cell in a row to the first cell in the next row
Shift+Tab	One cell to the left or from the first cell in a row to the last cell in the previous row
Home	To the beginning of the active line in the active cell
End	To the end of the active line in the active cell
Alt+Home	To the first cell in the active row
Alt+End	To the last cell in the active row
Alt+Page-up	To the first cell in the active column
Alt+Page-down	To the last cell in the active column

Keys that delete text

Key	Deletes
Delete	The character to the right of the insertion point or the selected text
Ctrl+Delete	The word to the right of the insertion point or the first word in the selected text
Backspace	The character to the left of the insertion point or the selected text
Ctrl+Backspace	The word to the left of the insertion point or selected text

Keys for formatting characters

Key	Format
Ctrl+B	Bold
Ctrl+I	Italics
Ctrl+U	Underline
Ctrl+Shift+W	Word underline
Ctrl+Shift+D	Double underline
Ctrl+Shift+=	Superscript
Ctrl+=	Subscript
Ctrl+Shift+K	Small Caps
Ctrl+Shift+A	All Caps
Ctrl+Shift+>	Increase font to next largest font size
Ctrl+Shift+<	Decrease font to next smallest font size
Ctrl+]	Increase font size by one point
Ctrl+[	Decrease font size by one point
Ctrl+Spacebar or Ctrl+Shift+Z	Remove character formatting

Keys for formatting paragraphs

Key	Format
Ctrl+L	Left align
Ctrl+E	Center
Ctrl+R	Right align
Ctrl+J	Justify
Ctrl+M	Move left indent to the next tab stop
Ctrl+Shift+M	Move left indent to the previous tab stop
Ctrl+T	Hanging indent; increase the indent to next tab stop for a paragraph already formatted with a hanging indent
Ctrl+Shift+T	Decrease the indent of a paragraph formatted with a hanging indent to the previous tab stop
Ctrl+1	Single spacing
Ctrl+2	Double spacing
Ctrl+5	Spacing of 1.5 lines
Ctrl+0 (zero)	Add or remove one line of white space before the paragraph
Ctrl+Q	Remove paragraph formatting

Keys for applying styles

Key	Style or action
Ctrl+Shift+N	Normal
Ctrl+Alt+1	Heading 1
Ctrl+Alt+2	Heading 2
Ctrl+Alt+3	Heading 3
Ctrl+Shift+L	List Bullet
Ctrl+Shift+S	Highlights the Style box in the Formatting toolbar

Keys for working with the outline feature

Key	Function
Shift+Tab or Alt+Shift+Left-arrow	Promote paragraph
Tab or Alt+Shift+Right-arrow	Demote paragraph
Alt+Shift+Up-arrow	Move up in outline
Alt+Shift+Down-arrow	Move down in outline
+ on numeric keypad	Expand heading
- on numeric keypad	Collapse heading
Alt+Shift+number on main keyboard	Show headings from 1 through the number
Alt+Shift+A	Show all paragraphs
Alt+Shift+L	Show first line only in text paragraphs
/ on numeric keypad	Show or hide the formatting of the paragraphs

Keys for working with two or more panes or document windows

Key	Function
Ctrl+Alt+S	Split a window into two panes or return a split window to a normal window
F6	Switch to the next pane
Shift+F6	Switch to the previous pane
Ctrl+F6	Switch to the next window
Ctrl+Shift+F6	Switch to the previous window

Keys for inserting line, page, and column breaks

Key	Function
Shift+Enter	Insert a new line character
Ctrl+Enter	Insert a manual page break
Ctrl+Shift+Enter	Insert a column break

Keys for inserting text, hyphens, and notes

Key	Function
F3	Insert the text for an AutoText abbreviation
Ctrl+Hyphen	Insert an optional hyphen that will only appear if a break is required at the end of a line
Ctrl+Shift+Hyphen	Insert a nonbreaking hyphen so it won't be split at the end of a line
Ctrl+Alt+F	Insert a footnote
Ctrl+Alt+E	Insert an endnote

Keys for working with fields

Key	Function
Alt+Shift+D	Insert a Date field into the document
Alt+Shift+T	Insert a Time field into the document
Alt+Shift+P	Insert a Page field into the document
Ctrl+Shift+F9	Convert the selected field result to text
F9	Update the selected fields
Alt+F9	Change all fields from results to codes or vice versa
F11	Move the insertion point to the next field
Shift+F11	Move the insertion point to the previous field

Keys for working with dialog boxes

Key	Function
Tab	Move the focus to the next control in a dialog box
Shift+Tab	Move the focus to the previous control in a dialog box
Ctrl+Tab	Switch to the next tab in a dialog box
Ctrl+Shift+Tab	Switch to the previous tab in a dialog box

Other keys for working with Word

Key	Function
F1	Access on-line Help
Shift+F4	Repeat the last Find or Go To command
Shift+F10	Display a shortcut menu
Ctrl+Tab	Insert a tab character into a cell within a table

Keys for working with Windows

Key	Function
Alt+Tab	Display a panel that names the next application that can be switched to
Alt+Esc	Switch to the next application
Ctrl+Esc	Display the task list

Index

5 chapters, 71 pages (60 have illustrations or practice exercises), **$9.95**

ISBN 0-911625-88-7

Word 6 for Windows:
How to use the Mail Merge feature

You're all ready to do a mail merge in Word 6 for Windows. You have your form letter set up, and you've got the names and addresses in a data file. Now all you have to do is sort the addresses into zip-code sequence. So you click on the sort button in the mail merge, and...oops. The records aren't sorted correctly.

As the Appendix in this *Pro* book points out, the Word feature that many business users need to know next is the Mail Merge feature. Unfortunately, even though the Mail Merge is easier to use in Word 6 than in earlier versions of Word, you can still run into plenty of problems. So this short book is designed to help you over the trouble spots...whether you're a new or experienced mail merge user.

In fact, in just half an hour, you'll be doing your first mail merge. Then, you can learn more whenever you need to. This book will teach you: how to use the specific features Word provides for merging envelopes, labels, and lists...how to handle common problems, like dealing efficiently with the sorting bugs that are in releases 6.0 through 6.0c...how to merge Word documents with information in external data files (like *Access, Oracle,* or *dBase* databases)...how to use Word fields to control complicated merges...plus everything else you need to know to get the most out of the Mail Merge feature. And all the information is presented just as it is in this *Pro* book, with plenty of examples and practice exercises.

So keep building on your Word skills. To handle mail merges like a pro, get this book TODAY.

Contents

- An introduction to the Mail Merge feature
- How to create and maintain a Word data file
- How to create a main document
- How to merge a data file with a main document
- How to work with external data files

27 chapters, 575 pages,
326 illustrations, **$25.00**

ISBN 0-911625-80-1

The Essential Guide:
Word 6 for Windows

by Steve Eckols

Do you want to know how to use some of the other Word features listed in the Appendix, besides the Mail Merge feature? If so, this *Essential Guide* is the quick, comprehensive reference you need.

The *Essential Guide* covers every feature of Word from beginning to advanced in the same practical, job-oriented way that this *Pro* book does. To make it an efficient reference, author Steve Eckols has divided the content into 27 task-oriented chapters in 5 sections, with subheads that make it easy to quickly find what you're looking for. He's also illustrated every feature, putting all the information you need in the figures. That means you can often start using a new feature without even reading the text. And you can look up forgotten details about any feature in just a moment or two.

As one customer put it: "This book has made my 'computer life' much easier. There were several problems I had while working in Word 6.0 that I never could figure out and couldn't find any reference to in the Microsoft manuals. I had given up and gone on to other areas when I received your book. Lo and behold, I easily found answers to all the problems in this text!" And another said, "At 575 pages, *The Essential Guide* is a fat book, and a fat reference book, well indexed, is what I want when I need to do something a little out of the ordinary with Word 6 for Windows. So I'll be keeping this book close at hand." If you're ready for an extensive Word reference book that will provide you with answers on demand, *The Essential Guide: Word 6 for Windows* is for YOU.

**You'll find advanced features like these
(see Appendix A in this *Pro* book for more details):**
- Preparing envelopes and labels
- Grammar checking
- Drawing
- Charting using Microsoft Graph
- Customizing toolbars
- Workgroup features
- OLE (Object Linking & Embedding)
- The basics of Mail Merge
- Indexing

Work Like a Pro with Excel 5 for Windows

by Anne Prince

In 10 minutes or less, any Excel user in business ought to be able to do any of these tasks:

- Enter all of the required formulas and functions for a one-page worksheet
- Format the worksheet data so it's easy to read and understand
- Format the printed output with headers, footers, and repeated column titles
- Combine the worksheets from several files into one easy-to-use workbook
- Create a chart that presents selected data in a convincing format

Yet many, if not most, Excel users don't work this efficiently. In fact, many work at a pretty elementary level, even if they've been using Excel for years.

For example, they don't know the fastest way to do things (in Windows programs, you often have 3 or more choices). They don't remember how to do even the functions that they use regularly (they have to hunt through the menus each time). They aren't aware of the software features that would help them the most (they just use Excel as a glorified calculator). And they get mired in formatting their work, the part that should be a snap.

If that sounds uncomfortably familiar, take heart. Whether you're a beginner or an experienced Excel user, *Work Like a Pro with Excel 5 for Windows* will teach you how to use Excel as the time-saving business tool it was designed to be...just as this *Pro* book has taught you to use Word 6.

As you might expect, the *Pro/Excel* book is set up just like this *Pro* book, with plenty of examples, practice exercises, and real-world perspective. And it's organized the same way, too: Section 1 gets you started right with Excel; Section 2 expands on the basics to help you work more professionally each day. As a result, you'll be using Excel more efficiently within minutes of opening the book.

So don't wait to start using Excel the way it was meant to be used. Get your copy of *Work Like a Pro with Excel 5 for Windows* today.

Pull data from corporate or departmental databases into Excel where you can analyze it more easily using Excel's features

EXCEL 5

HOW TO WORK WITH
**Lists
Pivot tables &
External databases**

For Windows

Anne Prince

• Create and filter
  simple databases

• Sort and
  summarize data

• Create pivot tables

• Work with data from
  external databases

4 chapters, 60 pages (49 have illustrations or practice exercises),
$11.95

ISBN 0-911625-87-9

Excel 5 for Windows:
How to work with lists, pivot tables, and external databases

by Anne Prince

Every Monday, John enters the previous week's sales at his PC so he can work with the figures using Excel. He could save half an hour by downloading the numbers instead (his PC is networked to the corporate Oracle database where the sales are kept). But he doesn't know how.

Did you know you can use Excel to work with data in an external database, like an Oracle, Access, or dBase IV database? To start, you use Microsoft Query, a program that comes with Excel, to import data from the database into an Excel *list*. Then, you can use Excel features to analyze and summarize the data.

For example, in Excel, you can sort and automatically subtotal the data. You can use filters to limit which data you want to work with. You can create pivot tables to summarize selected list data with just a few clicks of the mouse (you can use pivot tables to work with external databases directly, too). And of course, you can also create Excel lists from scratch and then use the same features to sort, filter, and summarize them.

If you try to master these features on your own, we bet it will take you at least 12 hours, and probably twice that long...even if you have the 5 best-selling Excel books and the Excel manual at your side. The trouble is, the material in those books is incomplete, and sometimes inaccurate. So you'll be forced to do extensive, time-consuming experimentation.

But now, Anne Prince has done the hard work for you. Everything you need to know is in this 60-page book. And it's presented in the same way as the information in this *Pro* book, to make learning quicker and easier than ever before. Try the *Excel Lists* book TODAY and see for yourself.

Contents

• How to set up a list and use filters and forms

• How to sort and summarize the data in a list

• How to use pivot tables

• How to use Microsoft Query to import data from an external database

The *Essential Guides*
are exhaustive reference books that let you convert to a new program in half a day... then teach you new skills whenever you need them

The books in our *Essential Guide* series differ from our *Work Like a Pro* books in a couple of ways. First, they're comprehensive reference books that present *all* the useful features of a program. Second, they assume that you're converting or upgrading to a new software release and that you already have some word processing or spreadsheet experience.

But like the *Pro* books, the *Essential Guides* are chock-full of illustrations that show you at a glance how each feature works. And the short, specific chapters tell you all you need to know to use a feature...you don't have to flip back and forth between chapters (consulting the index in between), trying to put all the pieces together yourself. All you have to do is decide what you want to learn next:

- **Section 1** (the first 3 chapters) in each *Guide* gets you started fast with a new release ("It's like having your own personal tutor," is how one customer put it). In just 3 to 5 hours, you'll be using the new program with confidence...and you'll be using all the best new features of the program.

- **Section 2** covers all the features that every word processing or spreadsheet user *should* be using every day. Never had time to master these skills before? You'll be delighted at how quickly you can pick them up just by using these books.

- The chapters in the **remaining sections** focus on specific features and are independent of each other. That means you can read them in whatever sequence you prefer and learn new features right when you need them. After you do this for a few months, you'll be an outstanding user of the program.

But don't take my word for it. First, read the opinions of people who have used one of the *Guides* (see the facing page). Then, find out just how satisfying it can be to make use of all the power your software puts at your fingertips...try one of the *Essential Guides* for yourself, right away!

Essential Guide	Pages	Illus.	ISBN	Price
Word 6.0 for Windows	560	326	0-911625-80-1	$25.00
Excel 5.0 for Windows	497	295	0-911625-79-8	$25.00
1-2-3 for Windows, Release 4	477	310	0-911625-75-5	$20.00
WordPerfect 6.0 for Windows	600	334	0-911625-83-6	$25.00
WordPerfect 6.0 for DOS	498	274	0-911625-81-X	$25.00

What people are saying about the *Essential Guides*

"The innovative method of presentation used in the figures is superb. Each figure is complete in itself. I found that I could use them to perform operations without reading the text in the accompanying chapters."

—Ed Laskowski, Sierra Vista (Arizona) IBM PC Users Group

"When I am working with a software package and need information fast, I need a book that can tell me what I need to know right away. This book meets those 'speediness' requirements. After the first section, the book is organized so that you can turn to the subject you're interested in, and get started right away."

—Jim English, Hagerstown (Pennsylvania) PC Users Group

"Thorough and comprehensive—covers the basics step-by-step and gets into plenty of juicy stuff for the real gurus."

—Bruce Morris, *National Computer Tectonics*

"Compared to the Que publication *Using 1-2-3 Release 4 for Windows*, the Murach book reads like a novel in that it holds your interest and delivers what it promises.... This book solved some of the perplexing problems I have found in the several versions of Lotus 1-2-3 that I have used in the past 6 years."

—Syd Calish, Napa Valley (California) PC Users Group

"The Font chapter is my personal favorite. I went from having no knowledge of the special fonts to complete mastery in less than a half hour."

—Steven J. Lavitan, New Jersey PC Users Group

"Some of the most experienced and dedicated users of WordPerfect 5.* for DOS report that the maze of new features in WordPerfect 6.0 can be confusing and intimidating. Although I found the user's manuals to be largely up to WordPerfect's high standards, they still left me with many unanswered questions and a bit of confusion about where to find answers to specific problems. On the other hand, I found *The Essential Guide* to be so intuitively organized that finding a particular subject was natural and easy."

—*CompuServe* Magazine

"As an experienced Word for Windows user, I found this book to be so good that I have deleted my WINWORD.HLP file to save almost 2MB of hard disk space."

—Mark Stotzer, Monterey Bay (California) PC Users Group

"Designed to steer you through an upgrade or conversion to Excel 5.0 for Windows as quickly, as easily, and as thoroughly as possible, this book includes features its competition never thought of. Using an organization of 5 separate sections and 24 chapters, the book lets you skip the material you already understand and points you toward the information you seek."

—Jerry Haberkost, PC Users Group of South Jersey

"This neat book is written in down-to-earth plain English. You won't get lost in it...and you learn faster because of its concentration on the things that most people need immediately."

—Delta DOS Users Group, Michigan

"Each chapter is devoted to a particular subject. No need to refer to many parts to obtain an understanding of your topic. Since it is all fully explained in one place, you don't feel that you are being bounced around to obtain an answer. And each chapter's loaded with illustrations."

—Jack Stahl, Harrisburg (Pennsylvania) PC Users Group

"Is it worth spending $25 for a 600-page reference book for a program which can be bought as a competitive upgrade for under $90 and which comes with its own 968-page reference? Definitely. This book contains readable features and diagrams which will get you up and running in no time flat."

—Peter J. LaRose, Rockland (New York) PC Users Group

"Kick the learning curve habit, buy an *Essential Guide* today!"

—John Skinner, President, Charlotte County (Florida) PC Users Group

The least you need to know about *Windows 3.1*

A short course that takes you from DOS to *Windows* in 6 hours or less

Plus a unique reference to other *Windows* essentials

Steve Eckols

12 chapters, 337 pages, 160 illustrations, **$20.00**

ISBN 0-911625-74-7

The Least You Need to Know about *Windows 3.1*

by Steve Eckols

- **A short course that turns you into a confident Windows user in 6 hours or less**
- **Plus a unique reference to other everyday Windows skills**

Do you know how to use Windows like a pro? If not, let *The Least You Need to Know about Windows 3.1* take you from ignorance to Windows competence in less than a day:

- **At the end of 2 hours**, you'll be moving around in Windows with ease, running more than one program at a time and switching between them quickly (no matter whether they're DOS or Windows programs).

- **At the end of 3-4 hours**, you'll be able to use the basic features of *any* Windows application program and transfer data easily between programs. If you've been working in DOS, that means you can convert from your DOS programs to their Windows counterparts in a minimum of time.

- **At the end of 4-6 hours**, you'll be using the Windows File Manager to manage your files and directories more easily than you ever could with a shell program or with DOS.

Then, you can use the rest of the book (chapters 6-12) to learn new skills in just 10-15 minutes each. And you can read these chapters in any order, whenever you need them.

Comment Form

Your opinions count

If you have any comments, criticisms, or suggestions for us, I'm eager to get them. Your opinions today will affect our products of tomorrow. And if you find any errors in this book, typographical or otherwise, please point them out so we can correct them in the next printing. Thanks for your help. *Mike Murach*

Book title: *Work Like a Pro with Word 6 for Windows*

Dear Mike:

_____
_____
_____
_____
_____
_____
_____
_____
_____
_____
_____
_____

Order Form

To order more quickly,

Call toll-free 1-800-221-5528
(Weekdays, 8 to 5 Pacific Time)
Fax: 1-209-275-9035

Mike Murach & Associates, Inc.
4697 West Jacquelyn Avenue
Fresno, California 93722-6427
(209) 275-3335

Name (& Title, if any) _____

Company (if company address) _____

Street address _____

City, State, Zip _____

Phone number (including area code) _____

Fax number (if you fax your order to us) _____

Qty	Product code and title		*Price
____	LWIN	**The Least You Need to Know about Windows 3.1**	$20.00
____	PRMW	**Work Like a Pro with Word 6 for Windows**	20.00
____	MWMM	**Word 6: How to use the Mail Merge feature**	9.95
____	MWW6	**The Essential Guide: Word 6 for Windows**	25.00
____	PREX	**Work Like a Pro with Excel 5 for Windows**	20.00
____	EXLS	**Excel 5: How to work with lists, pivot tables, & external databases**	11.95
____	EEX5	**The Essential Guide: Excel 5 for Windows**	25.00
____	ELW4	**The Essential Guide: 1-2-3 for Windows Release 4**	20.00
____	WPW6	**The Essential Guide: WordPerfect 6 for Windows**	25.00
____	EWP6	**The Essential Guide: WordPerfect 6 for DOS**	25.00

☐ Bill me for the books plus UPS shipping and handling (and sales tax within CA).

☐ Bill my company. P.O.# _____

☐ I want to **SAVE 10%** by paying in advance.
   Charge to my ____Visa ____MasterCard ____American Express:

   Card number _____

   Valid thru (mo/yr) _____

   Cardowner's signature _____

☐ I want to **SAVE 10% plus shipping and handling**. Here's my check for the books minus 10% ($_____). California residents, please add sales tax to your total. (Offer valid in U.S.)

*Prices are subject to change. Please call for current prices.

NO POSTAGE
NECESSARY
IF MAILED
IN THE
UNITED STATES

BUSINESS REPLY MAIL

FIRST-CLASS MAIL   PERMIT NO. 3063   FRESNO, CA

POSTAGE WILL BE PAID BY ADDRESSEE

Mike Murach & Associates, Inc.

4697 W JACQUELYN AVE
FRESNO CA 93722-9888